CHINESE CUBANS

ENVISIONING CUBA

Louis A. Pérez Jr., editor

KATHLEEN LÓPEZ

CHINESE CUBANS

A Transnational History

THE UNIVERSITY OF NORTH CAROLINA PRESS
Chapel Hill

The paper in this book meets the guidelines for permanence
and durability of the Committee on Production Guidelines for
Book Longevity of the Council on Library Resources.

The University of North Carolina Press has been
a member of the Green Press Initiative since 2003.

Library of Congress Cataloging-in-Publication Data
López, Kathleen.
Chinese Cubans : a transnational history / Kathleen López.
pages cm. — (Envisioning Cuba)
Includes bibliographical references and index.
ISBN 978-1-4696-0712-2 (cloth : alk. paper) —
ISBN 978-1-4696-0713-9 (pbk. : alk. paper)
1. Chinese—Cuba—History. 2. Chinese—Cuba—Ethnic identity 3. Contract
labor—Cuba—History—19th century. 4. Community development—Cuba—
History. 5. Cuba—Emigration and immigration—History—19th century.
6. Cuba—Ethnic relations. I. Title.
F1789.C53L67 2013
972.91′004951—dc23
2012049086

Parts of this book are based on previous publications:
"'One Brings Another': The Formation of Early-Twentieth-Century
Chinese Migrant Communities in Cuba," in *The Chinese in the Caribbean*,
edited by Andrew R. Wilson (Princeton, N.J.: Markus Wiener Publishers, 2004),
93–127; "Afro-Asian Alliances: Marriage, Godparentage, and Social Status in
Late-Nineteenth-Century Cuba," *Afro-Hispanic Review* 27.1 (2008): 59–72;
"The Revitalization of Havana's Chinatown: Invoking Chinese Cuban History,"
Journal of Chinese Overseas 5.1 (2009): 177–200. Used with permission.

Contents

Illustrations, Maps, and Tables

Note on Names and Terminology

To the extent possible, names of local people, places, and institutions are rendered as they appear in the relevant sources of the era. Most Chinese migrants in Cuba had at least two names, a Chinese name and a Western or hybrid name (e.g., Tung Kun Sen and Pastor Pelayo), and used both in daily interactions, depending on the context. I generally use both names, when known, upon first mention.

For proper Chinese names, I use the standardized pinyin transliteration system adopted by the People's Republic of China (e.g., Taishan). However, in several instances I retain nonstandard spelling (e.g., Chee Kung Tong, *Kwong Wah Po*) to reflect the form of the name adopted by the migrants themselves in their local setting. For the names of well-known Chinese figures such as Sun Yat-sen and Chiang Kai-shek, I retain the more common transliterations. For the names of Chinese people in general, the last name comes first (e.g., Chen Lanbin). A glossary lists Chinese characters for the significant terms in this study.

I use the term "Chinese Cuban" throughout the book in a broad sense, referring to Chinese migrants in Cuba, ethnic Chinese born in Cuba, and at times, mixed descendants.

When quoting from primary documents, I retain the original spelling, punctuation, and word usage.

CHINESE CUBANS

A Transnational History

Two Lives

In 1859, the fifteen-year-old Tung Kun Sen (Dong Gongcheng), a native of Dongguan County in Guangdong Province, China, was kidnapped and taken to the Spanish Caribbean colony of Cuba as part of the infamous coolie trade. He signed a contract of indenture that obligated him to work for eight years on a sugar estate in Cárdenas, Matanzas Province. There he was baptized and given the name Pastor Pelayo, after Cuban planter Ramón Pelayo. After completing his term of service, he was forced to recontract for another eight years.

When Pastor Pelayo finished his indenture, he was in his thirties and had no hope of returning to China. He migrated eastward to the sugar districts of central Cuba. There he moved from estate to estate, earning wages as part of a *cuadrilla*, or work gang, and eventually became a labor contractor. Recently out of bondage, the former indentured laborer came into daily contact with enslaved African men and women on the cusp of emancipation. Through earnings from his work gangs, he managed to accumulate enough money to purchase freedom for a domestic slave named Wenceslaa Sarría and her brothers. Pastor Pelayo and Wenceslaa Sarría entered into a common law union and had nine children together, who they raised among a network of people of Chinese and African descent in the town of Cienfuegos.

Pelayo emerged as a leader among the local Chinese, establishing an immigrant association and a theater. Both Pelayo and his first Cuban-born son, Blas, supported the War for Independence from Spain in 1895 and registered as eligible voters after the establishment of the new Cuban republic. In 1913 Pastor Pelayo died, insolvent due to a penchant for gambling. He is buried in a plot at La Reina Cemetery in Cienfuegos, much of which today is inundated with water and overgrown with weeds.

Just a few years later, when the Cuban government permitted the wartime importation of contract labor, a second major wave of Chinese laborers crossed the Pacific. Among them was Lui Fan (Lü Fan), who in 1918 at age eighteen emigrated from his village in Xinhui County, Guangdong Province. Lui Fan initially worked on a plantation to fulfill Cuba's need to increase

Lui Fan (far right) with Lui villagers in Havana, Cuba, 1929. (Courtesy of Violeta Luis)

sugar production during World War I. He soon abandoned the estate and began peddling vegetables in the town of Cienfuegos. Carrying two baskets on a bamboo pole balanced on his shoulders, Lui Fan became a familiar sight in his Cuban neighborhood, where he was known as Francisco Luis.

A decade passed before Lui Fan made his first trip to his home village in China. He built a new house and married, with all of the villagers celebrating at an extravagant banquet. After his second return visit in 1930, his daughter Baoqing was born, but he was unable to see her until another return visit in 1932. His second daughter was born later that year, after he had departed for Cuba. From overseas, he named her Mali, after the Western name María or Mary.

Lui Fan never again returned to China, leaving his two daughters to grow up in the village without their father. Both married and had families of their own, but they maintained their father's ancestral home in Lui Village, near the market town Daze. Lui Fan dutifully sent home remittances once or twice a year, and for special occasions such as the birth of a grandchild, he sent home more money than usual.

Back in Cuba, Francisco Luis developed a relationship with a Cuban woman, with whom he also had two daughters, Lourdes and Violeta, each of which he also gave a Chinese name, Guiguí and Guipó. The domestic ar-

Francisco Luis (Lui Fan) with his Cuban daughters, Lourdes and Violeta Luis, in Cienfuegos, Cuba, 1952. (Courtesy of Violeta Luis)

rangement deteriorated, however, when their mother abandoned the family after three years. Luis raised his two Cuban daughters on his own, while continuing to support his Chinese family. He encouraged a relationship between his Cuban daughters and his Chinese daughters by sending photos and writing letters on their behalf. His Cuban daughters believed that they were corresponding with Chinese cousins. From the beginning, however, his Chinese daughters knew that they had half-sisters in Cuba and referred to them as "Third Sister" (*sanmei*) and "Fourth Sister" (*simei*).

In addition to maintaining a transpacific family, Francisco Luis belonged to the fraternal organization Chee Kung Tong and an occupational guild, read Chinese newspapers, donated to China's resistance against the Japanese occupation in World War II, and attended Cantonese opera performances. He raised his Cuban daughters in a strict Catholic environment but taught them complementary points in the philosophies of Confucius and Laozi. After Francisco Luis died in Cuba in 1975, his Cuban daughters were unable to transfer his remains back to China for burial. Across the ocean, fellow villagers emphasized that the Lui women needed to depend on themselves, and communication between the four sisters ceased for over a quarter of a century.

The Chinese in Cuba

Different layers of migrations produced the multifaceted Chinese Cuban community over the course of a century. The expansion of Western economies and European imperialism in Asia, Africa, and the Americas pulled multitudes of men like Tung Kun Sen into an orbit of international labor migration. Between 1848 and 1888 more than two million Chinese, the majority from southeastern Guangdong and Fujian Provinces, boarded ships bound for plantations, railroads, and mines in the Americas, Australia, and Southeast Asia.[1] In one stream of this migration known as the coolie trade, approximately 142,000 Chinese signed contracts of indenture to work in Cuba (and another 100,000 in Peru), providing a crucial segment of the labor force prior to and during the period of gradual abolition of African slavery, which did not end in Cuba until 1886. Beginning in the 1860s and 1870s, several thousand free Chinese arrived as merchants and craftsmen, many of whom had spent time in California. Nineteenth-century Chinese migration to Cuba coincided with a nationalist uprising, bookmarked by the unsuccessful Ten Years' War (1868–78) and a U.S. intervention and Spanish surrender in 1898.

Despite an official ban on the entry of Chinese laborers imposed by the United States in 1899, they continued to migrate to Cuba throughout the republican period (1902–59). A second major wave of Chinese migrants entered Cuba after 1917, when restrictions on labor immigration were lifted to promote sugar production during World War I. The global depression of 1929 and nativist policies in Cuba led to a decrease in the Chinese migrant population. Chinese continued to enter on a smaller scale until the Cuban Revolution of 1959, when the Communist government took power.

This book examines the transnational history of these migrants and their multiple identities as Chinese and Cuban. Whether indentured or free, most migrants ultimately aimed to accumulate resources and return to China, rather than settle permanently in Cuba. The coerced nature of the coolie system, however, left little possibility for return. Free Chinese migrants in the republican period worked to maintain transnational ties to China, but many of them came to identify themselves as Cuban.

The Chinese in Cuba did not experience institutionalized discrimination to the same extent as their counterparts in the United States, which maintained a policy of exclusion from 1882 to 1943, or Mexico, where anti-Chinese campaigns led to their violent expulsion from the northern state of Sonora in 1931. Nor were they victims of sustained anti-Chinese riots, as in Peru and Jamaica. Rather, Chinese participation in the Cuban wars for independence spanning 1868 to 1898, their successful formation of cross-racial alliances, and the professed dedication of the Cuban republic to an ideal of a racial democracy, created the conditions for their incorporation into the national citizenry. At the same time, however, a negative view of Chinese developed in the Cuban press, in government and police reports, and in popular attitudes. As elsewhere in the Americas, they were described as clannish, corrupt, diseased, and unassimilable and were accused of competing unfairly with native Cuban workers. Such attitudes call into question the inclusive nature of Cuban national and cultural identity.

Historical scholarship on the Chinese in Cuba has traditionally focused on the period of the coolie trade from 1847 to 1874, leaving unexplored the transition of Chinese from indentured to free laborers in the late nineteenth century and the formation of transnational communities in the early twentieth century. Spanning the two major migrations, this book examines how racist ideologies in a multiethnic society, class stratification, gender imbalance, kinship and business networks, and generational differences converged to shape Chinese identities in Cuba. Situated between the Spanish and Qing empires, or the Cuban and Chinese republics, the Chinese in Cuba did not conform to political and legal definitions of national identity and citizenship. Chinese migrants themselves altered both official and popular conceptions of what it meant to be Chinese or Cuban in different contexts.

The constant presence of Asians in debates on the ideal composition of a nation demonstrates their centrality for the region. The story of the Chinese in Cuba lends insight into broader issues of labor and society in the postemancipation era, the relationship between race and citizenship, and the interconnectedness of national and transnational identifications.

Africans and Asians in the Americas

The nineteenth-century system of Asian indentured labor must be examined within the context of slavery and colonial empires in the Americas. As the shackles of African slavery came undone, from 1791 in French Saint Domingue (Haiti) to 1888 in Brazil, the demand for labor in the European colonies and newly independent republics of Latin America and the Caribbean remained high. The recruitment of Asians under contract offered a potential solution to the approaching end of slave labor. African slaves and Asian coolies therefore became historically linked through a global network of international labor migration, "kinsmen and kinswomen in that world created by European masters."[2]

In the context of the nineteenth-century Caribbean, "coolies" referred to Chinese and East Indians bound by labor contracts, generally five years in the British colonies and eight years in Spanish Cuba and independent Peru. In Cuba, Chinese were primarily inserted into the sugar, railroad, mining, and construction industries, while in Peru they worked on coastal sugar plantations and guano pits. The contract between worker and employer detailed the obligations of both parties. The laborer was to receive a minimal monthly wage combined with food, clothing, lodging, and medical attention and was to be released from all obligations upon termination of the contract period.

In practice, though, the coolie system approximated a "new system of slavery," incorporating mechanisms of oppression and control inherited from over three centuries of African bonded labor. The coolie traffic to Cuba and Peru so closely resembled Atlantic slavery that it became known as the "trata amarilla" (yellow trade). Chinese laborers suffered abominable conditions and treatment until an international investigation in 1874 resulted in the ending of the trade. A number of scholars have highlighted the significance of Asian indentured laborers as a supplement to or replacement for slavery and their insertion into multiracial Latin American and Caribbean societies.[3]

This book expands current scholarship by moving beyond the period of indentured labor to demonstrate the mechanisms by which Chinese in Cuba made the transition to free wage earners and entrepreneurs.[4] Like African slaves, Chinese coolies protested the labor regime through forms of resistance and rebellion, engagement with the legal system, marriage and godparenthood, interracial alliances, and participation in ethnic associations. I probe the historical connectivity among diasporic Asians and Africans in the Americas, in particular through the relationships Chinese built across racial and ethnic lines (and the limitations of these alliances in a hierarchical society).

After the end of slavery, Chinese continued to circulate throughout Latin America and the Caribbean with the advent of new export economies in the late nineteenth century. Histories of immigrant workers in this period emphasize ethnic tensions. Thomas Holloway, for example, finds that national and regional distinctions among coffee laborers in São Paulo, Brazil, limited working-class alliances. Due to high turnover of the rural labor force, geographical isolation of plantations, rudimentary development of noneconomic institutions, and planter control, a common status as coffee worker proved inadequate for breaking down distinctions between Italians,

Spaniards, Portuguese, Japanese, Syrio-Lebanese, and Eastern Europeans.[5] Walton Look Lai also finds a lack of labor solidarity between Chinese, Indians, and blacks in the British West Indies.[6] Planters and industrialists used racial, ethnic, linguistic, and cultural divisions among their work force to their advantage. Depicted as clannish and passive, Chinese were thought to be unlikely to mix with native workers or to resist poor labor conditions.

Those in power did play upon ethnic divisions in factory and field, but behind the headlines about anti-Chinese riots and labor strikes, another story emerges, which can be traced only in marriage and baptismal records, the deeds to houses, and other archival records. In the day-to-day interactions of nonwhite peoples, Chinese migrants were forming alliances. My work follows recent scholarship in labor history and ethnic studies that, instead of focusing on a single ethnic group, investigates how those identified as minorities "of color" have interacted with each other or have been racialized in comparison with each other. I examine interracial interactions and alliances that although often small-scale, cumulatively had a great impact on the development of the Chinese community and the process of incorporation into the Cuban nation.

Immigration and National Identity in Latin America and the Caribbean

The relationship between Asia and Latin America extends back 250 years to the Manila Galleon trade, a global exchange system between Europe, Asia, and the Americas. Goods from China were transported through the Spanish colonial port cities of Acapulco in Mexico and Manila in the Philippines, bringing the first Asian settlers to the region. The massive influx of Asian laborers beginning in the mid-nineteenth century altered the economic and cultural development of Latin America and the Caribbean; yet, as Evelyn Hu-DeHart reminds us, the Asian presence has received relatively little attention from historians.[8] Scholarship on immigration in the region has been concerned principally with the transition to wage labor, development of export economies, and assimilation of ethnic groups into mainstream society.[9] Studies of ethnic minorities and nation building, meanwhile, have focused primarily on the struggles of African and indigenous peoples to play a political role in the emerging nation states, usually in the shadow of elite discourses of mestizaje (racial or cultural mixing) that often sought to incorporate marginal groups while disempowering them.[10]

Recently, however, scholars have embarked on a project to expand research on Asians throughout the Americas, including Mexico, Central America, South America, and the Caribbean islands. In her books and articles on the Chinese in Mexico, Peru, and Cuba, Evelyn Hu-DeHart has pioneered this effort to integrate Asians into the scholarship on Latin America and the Chinese diaspora. This book on the Chinese in Cuba aims to add a comparative dimension to the existing knowledge about ethnic minorities and nation building in Latin America and the Caribbean.[11] What can the Asian presence tell us about constructions of national identity in Latin America and the Caribbean? In the case of Cuba, with its dominant theories of racial harmony and transculturation, what accounts for the continued surfacing of anti-Chinese sentiment?

Transnational and Hemispheric Migrations

Until recently, the history of Asians in the Americas has been fragmented by national boundaries. Scholarship has focused on the success or failure of Asians to incorporate into host societies, their role in developing agriculture, and their struggles for full civil and legal rights, providing in-depth portraits of particular communities.[12] Yet Asians were migrating between empires and nations, so this approach excludes from analysis important dimensions of their experience, such as the lives they lived before they left Asia, the relationships they maintained with families, businesses, institutions, and governments back home, and the diasporic ties they forged to Asian migrants in other countries. This study therefore takes a transnational and hemispheric perspective. With a geographical focus on Cuba, a historical emphasis, and qualitative investigation of both home and host countries, I probe the nature, intensity, and significance of transnational migration for everyday lives. I cast a wide net to document the ways individuals, families, and organizations have maintained social, economic, political, and cultural relations across national borders.[13]

My work builds on and is in dialogue with the scholarship on the Chinese diaspora, which initially focused on Southeast Asia and the Philippines.[14] The first studies of Chinese migration to Latin America and the Caribbean focused on the coolie trade to Cuba and Peru and its implications for the Chinese government and society during the Qing dynasty. In their respective monographs, Robert L. Irick and Yen Ching-hwang investigate the intricacies of the trade in indentured labor and the change in the stance of the Qing government from prohibiting emigration to defending Chinese subjects abroad. They demonstrate that beginning in the 1860s the protection of overseas Chinese became an important component of Chinese foreign policy, linked by progressive Chinese officials to the forging of a modern nation-state.[15]

Other scholars using transnational approaches have begun to bridge a long-standing gap between the fields of Asian and Asian American studies in the United States. Madeline Hsu, for example, uncovers strategies Taishanese migrants in the United States developed to form an "elastic community" encompassing both migrants and their dependents at home. She finds that despite the distance and time spent abroad, migrants made intense efforts to maintain ties to their villages beginning in the late nineteenth century and in the process transformed the South China landscape. Adam McKeown examines Chinese overseas communities in the early twentieth century from a transnational perspective that considers the global circulation of people, goods, money, and information. Whether petty merchants in Chicago, cosmopolitan businessmen in Peru, or immigrant pioneers in Hawaii, Chinese, he shows, fostered connections to common international networks.[16]

A long-standing question in the study of Asians in the Americas is how to explain the low numbers of women who emigrated during the pre–World War II period. Chinese migration to Cuba was almost exclusively male, even after the end of the coolie period.[17] Standard explanations for the gender imbalance in U.S. immigration history focus on legal exclusion—especially of the Chinese—high costs of transport, preferences of labor recruiters for males, and patriarchal norms that prohibited Asian women from traveling.[18] Using a global and comparative methodology, Sucheta Mazumdar offers a fresh perspective on the low numbers of Cantonese and Punjabi women who emigrated to the United States in the nineteenth century, finding that they were needed as laborers in their home villages, which had been affected by recent European capitalist incursions. Like Hsu, Mazumdar suggests that those who remained behind also be considered as part of transnational migration history.[19]

This study of the Chinese in Cuba pays careful attention to their concerns as *huaqiao*, or "overseas Chinese." I examine how Chinese migration to Cuba shaped Cantonese family and village life. Here, I engage with an expanding field of scholarship known as *qiaoxiang* (overseas Chinese home area) studies, which focuses on how kinship groups and local communities in China adapt to the large-scale emigration of Chinese men. Since the late 1980s, survey research has yielded detailed portraits of family life, education, employment, and investment in South China emigrant hometowns. Qiaoxiang studies have also contributed to a greater understanding of the processes of return migration and remittance sending.[20] Yet much current qiaoxiang research "remains imprisoned within a national narrative that emphasizes Overseas Chinese patriotism and enduring attachments and contributions to the motherland." By contrast, this study engages in "dual-sided research" (*shuangduan yanjiu*), which joins the study of Chinese societies overseas with their home areas in China.[21]

I have also been inspired by research that moves beyond politically bounded territories to take "the Americas" and the "greater Caribbean" as geographic parameters. Such work reveals migratory circuits, networks, and ideas that shaped peoples' lives.[22] I examine patterns of Chinese movement from Cuba to other regions in the Caribbean basin and the Americas. During the nineteenth century, Chinese migrants traveled through transnational circuits from Cuba to Louisiana plantations, New York tobacco factories, the Panama railroad and canal, and Mexico. In the twentieth century, additional North and South American port cities became destinations for remigration or secondary migration.

This book aims to be more than just a comparative or case study. I take a diasporic and hemispheric approach to reveal the connective nature of migrant communities and the racial systems in which they developed.[23] I show, for example, that strategies of anti-Chinese repression reverberated from the United States to Cuba and back. Some Chinese traders departed California in the 1870s, where they had experienced anti-Chinese legislation and violence firsthand, and settled in places like Mexico and Cuba. However, when the United States occupied Cuba in the early twentieth century, it promoted anti-Chinese policies there. Chinese in Cuba looked to diasporic communities in San Francisco and New York for models to assist them. The diversion of Chinese from U.S. ports during the age of exclusion (1882–1943) was never mono-directional; Chinese migrants used their networks in Caribbean port cities as "stepping stones" to enter the United States (and continue to do so today).

U.S. Southerners were linked ideologically and economically with a greater Caribbean economic and cultural plantation complex, and Cuban planters looked to them for solidarity in the preabolition period, even contemplating annexation to their northern neighbor. News of Cuba's experiences with the slavelike coolie trade reinforced the movement for the exclusion of Chinese labor in the United States. In 1862 the U.S. Congress prohibited American involvement in the coolie trade. Southern planters argued that voluntary migrants should be distinguished from coolies and reminded U.S. policy makers that Chinese workers had made possible the development of railroads, mines, and agriculture in California. Labor agents managed to import modest numbers of Chinese workers under contract from China, California, and Cuba to the U.S. South. Many of these migrants had escaped from their contracts on Cuban plantations.[24]

The hemispheric circulation of Chinese migrants calls into question the sharp distinction made between coolies in the Caribbean, most of them un-free laborers kidnapped or coerced into service, and free workers in California and the U.S. South. Chinese migrants gained entry to California through the credit-ticket system, in which credit was advanced to laborers to pay for their passage across the Pacific, and they were then constrained to a term of service until they repaid their debt.[25] Lisa Yun demonstrates the slippage of these labor systems through the case of a Californian Chinese named Yang Atian, who had lived in San Francisco since age fourteen. He worked on a ship that docked in the port of Havana, and after losing his earnings through gambling, he was forced into bondage in Cuba.[26] As Gary Okihiro states, "All of the successive systems of labor—from slave to coolie to contract to credit-ticket—were varieties of migrant labor and functioned to sustain a global order of supremacy and subordination."[27]

A Methodological Map for Transnational Migration History

Tracing the back-and-forth movement of Chinese migrants in the late nine-teenth and early twentieth centuries has demanded a course of research that also crosses national boundaries. I incorporate archival documents and oral histories of Chinese migrants, returned migrants, and their descendants in China, Cuba, and the United States. I utilize plantation correspondence, notarial, judicial, merchant, association, and civil records, remittance data, newspapers, and memoirs to trace the mechanisms and memories of the transnational migration process, drawing upon Chinese-, Spanish-, and English-language sources. In China, I concentrate on several qiaoxiang in Taishan and Xinhui, the two counties in Guangdong that produced the ma-jority of Chinese emigrants to the Americas.

Just as Asian American studies in the United States had long been domi-nated by the urban California experience, studies of the Chinese in Cuba have primarily focused on the Chinatown in Havana. While following devel-opments in Havana, this book probes the formation of Chinese communities in the provinces after the period of indenture, especially the sugar-producing region of Santa Clara Province in central Cuba. At key moments, a microhis-torical approach has enabled me to follow individual trajectories. By zooming the lens in on specific locales, in particular the town of Cienfuegos and its environs, I develop a more comprehensive picture than would otherwise be possible of the migration process and reveal the importance of everyday interactions for shaping transnational Chinese communities. I also combine a portrait of Chinese agriculturalists with one of Chinese entrepreneurs. In this sense, I echo recent developments in Asian American studies that question the assumption that the California and urban experiences set national patterns.[28]

Narrative Outline

The narrative arc of this book follows Chinese migrants as they transition from indentured to free workers in the Spanish colony, take roles in the formation of the emerging Cuban nation, and develop transnational Chinese communities.

Part I (Chapters 1–3) follows Chinese as they make the transition from coolies to free agricultural laborers and entrepreneurs. Part II (Chapters 4 and 5) examines Chinese as migrants between the collapse of the Spanish empire in 1898 and the Qing dynasty in 1911 and the formation of new Cuban and Chinese republics. On one hand, Chinese participation in the independence wars and inclusion in a Cuban national narrative provided them with a basis for citizenship in the new nation. On the other hand, restrictive immigration laws and anti-Chinese discourse at the outset of the Cuban republic continued to make belonging to that nation elusive. Part III (Chapters 6–8) explores the development of Chinese Cuban transnational communities during the Cuban republic, the process of becoming Cuban, and the devastating effects of the midcentury Chinese and Cuban revolutions on continued migration and homeland ties. This study concludes with an epilogue discussing the current situation of the fewer than two hundred native Chinese in Cuba today and the descendants of Chinese migrants. The question of the position of the Chinese in Cuba has resurfaced in official and popular discourse, now recognized as a strategic element furthering economic and diplomatic relations with China.

I

FROM INDENTURED TO FREE

This was a strange and striking exhibition of power.
Two or three white men, bringing hundreds of Chinese thousands
of miles, to a new climate and people, holding them prisoners,
selling their services to masters having an unknown religion,
to work at unknown trades, for inscrutable purposes!

—Richard Henry Dana Jr., *To Cuba and Back* (1859)

We have a new sensation on this plantation in the arrival
of a lot of Chinese laborers, called coolies, just from the vessel, after
a voyage of nearly five months. They came to labor under contract for eight
years, receiving, beyond their living, the remarkable low wages of four dollars a
month. . . . Their condition here will be, while under contract, but little better
than that of the negro slaves with whom they will labor and associate,
and they will be subject to the same compulsions and punishments
of the lash or stocks, at the mercy of their employers.

—Richard J. Levis, *Diary of a Spring Holiday in Cuba* (1872)

CHAPTER ONE

Coolies

Asian Indentured Labor in the Caribbean

For centuries the economies of Europe's Caribbean colonies had been fueled by African slave labor. The slave revolt in the French colony of Saint Domingue in 1791 and the creation of the black republic of Haiti in 1804 forever altered the Caribbean colonial landscape. In 1807 Great Britain ended the slave trade in its empire, interrupting the regular flow of Africans to Caribbean plantations. Britain pressured other European powers to follow suit, and although Spain signed treaties to end its slave trade in 1817 and 1835, a clandestine slave trade continued through 1865. With a growing abolition movement and the end of slavery looming, European powers in Latin America and the Caribbean began to experiment with different kinds of labor. The British ship *Fortitude* transported two hundred Chinese from Macao, Penang, and Calcutta to Trinidad in 1806, well before the end of slavery. However, most fled during the first year, disillusioned by plantation labor and the lack of Chinese women, and by 1825 only twelve Chinese remained on the island. For the time being, British planters could still count on slave labor. In 1810 several hundred Chinese were recruited to grow tea in the Royal Botanical Garden in Rio de Janeiro. But the experiment in labor and cultivation proved to be a failure, derailing plans to make tea a major commodity in Portuguese Brazil.[1]

Persistent agitation from the abolitionist movement and the 1831 slave rebellion in Jamaica led to the formal end of slavery in the British Caribbean colonies in 1834. As a condition for emancipation, slaves entered into agreements to serve as "apprentices" on plantations for a transitional period of six years (later reduced to four due to widespread discontent). The purpose of the apprenticeship system was to protect landholders against a mass exodus by former slaves and to minimize disruption in production. But former slaves escaped total domination by establishing small settlements or migrating to other islands, convincing landholders of the necessity of a new system of labor.[2] Through the 1830s, planters in the British colonies pushed for Asian laborers, specifically East Indians and Chinese, as a replacement for African slaves on sugar plantations. Britain's presence in India facilitated recruitment of laborers there, especially after British Crown rule was established in 1858. By the 1830s British merchants also occupied a significant position in the trading outpost of Canton and courted a population of Chinese middlemen to assist with business. From final emancipation in 1838 until 1918, almost 430,000 migrants from India and nearly 18,000 from China entered the British colonies, mostly British Guiana, Trinidad, and Jamaica. The last shipload of Chinese arrived in the British West Indies in 1884, while the importation and use of Indian laborers continued into the early twentieth century.[3]

Significant differences existed between the British and Spanish systems of indentured labor. The British government regulated recruitment of East Indians and Chinese for its Caribbean colonies, while private merchants controlled the importation of Chinese to Spain's colony of Cuba and recently independent Peru. Additionally, Britain recruited more Asian females for the West Indies, while Chinese coolies in Cuba and Peru were overwhelmingly male. Based on these differences, British authorities characterized their system as more humane. Yet, even under a government-regulated system, abuses occurred in recruitment, passage, and treatment in the British Caribbean. An 1870–71 government enquiry in British Guiana reported widespread irregularities and maltreatment.[4] Verene Shepherd exposes the particular vulnerabilities of female migrants from India in her analysis of a case of rape aboard one of the ships.[5]

Similar systems of indentured labor were established throughout Latin America and the Caribbean. The French and Dutch transported Chinese and Indians to their Caribbean colonies in much smaller numbers. Variants of Chinese contract labor operated in Brazil and other parts of Latin America such as Panama, Costa Rica, Mexico, Venezuela, and El Salvador.[6] The massive importations of Chinese indentured laborers to Cuba and Peru, however, drew the most attention and criticism, prompting decades of debate on the nature of foreign contract labor and the suitability of Asians for settlement in the New World.

The Crisis of Abolition

In the wake of the Haitian Revolution and the demise of slavery in the British colonies, sugar production shifted to the Spanish-controlled island of Cuba. French Saint Domingue had been the largest producer, but the embargo on Haitian sugar effectively ended its place in the world market. The devastation of war propelled a stream of exiled French planters and their slaves to neighboring Cuba, as well as other ports in the circum-Caribbean such as New Orleans. From the sixteenth through the eighteenth centuries, Spain had focused its attention on extracting silver, gold, and other resources from Mexico and Peru and on maintaining colonial administration. After the Latin American independence wars of the early nineteenth century, only Cuba, the Dominican Republic, and Puerto Rico remained under Spanish control, with Cuba the most dependent upon sugar production and African slave labor.

As Haiti declined, the growth of the Cuban sugar economy accelerated at a rapid pace. Cuba produced nearly 14 percent of the world's sugar supply in 1820. By the 1840s, the island surpassed its neighbor Jamaica to become the leading producer. Sugar production in Cuba had been divided into an unmechanized agricultural sector that planted, grew, and cut cane and a manufacturing sector that ground and processed it. Cuban planters began to employ new European refining techniques that increased manufacturing capacity. The technological innovations, in turn, demanded more laborers to clear land and grow cane for processing and to operate the modern machinery. Slave traders in Cuba reinvigorated their efforts to bring human chattel from Africa, even in the face of a growing abolitionist movement, and also turned to Chinese coolies. Between 1790 and the end of the slave trade in 1867 Cuba imported 780,000 new slaves, an astonishing number that surpassed the 700,000 Africans brought to all of Spanish America between 1520 and 1780. By 1870, due to slave and Chinese coolie imports, Cuba produced 42 percent of the world's sugar supply.[7]

The racial composition of Cuba's population also changed drastically. In 1775, out of an estimated total population of 171,500, there were some 96,400 whites, 36,300 free persons of color, and 38,900 African slaves, a large proportion of whom were recently imported. By 1841 the population had grown to 1,007,600, consisting of 418,300 whites, 152,800 free persons of color, and 436,500 slaves.[8] Together, slaves and free people of color comprised more than half of the island's population.

The majority of Cuban elites remained loyal to Spain long after most Spanish colonies had won independence in the early nineteenth century. Spain protected the economic interests of the landholding elites by maintaining the slave labor system and offering protection against potential slave uprisings. There was a constant threat that liberal ideas of political sovereignty and rights could filter down to slaves and free people of color to incite rebellion, which ultimately would bring economic ruin. Neighboring Haiti served as a reminder of the potential of a majority-black population for violent revolution. In 1812, hundreds of slaves and free people of color across the island were investigated for participating in a series of uprisings known as the Aponte Rebellion (named after one of its leaders, free black artisan José Antonio Aponte). Inspired by the Haitian Revolution, the rebellion aimed to destroy the institution of slavery in Cuba at a time when planters sought to further entrench it for development of the sugar industry.[9] In 1844, Spanish authorities claimed to have uncovered a widespread conspiracy known as La Escalera among slaves, free people of color, Creole whites, and foreigners. In the wake of the conspiracy, slaves and free people of color were brutally repressed, and Spain justified clamping down on its colonial institutions.[10] By promising to protect anxious white Cubans against slave revolts, Spain ensured political loyalty among planters at a time when the colonial relationship was otherwise being questioned.

Amid these revolts and the rising cost of slaves that resulted from the British ban on the slave trade and the clandestine efforts to evade it, the sense of a crisis in labor and production pervaded discussions among Cuban planters. The price for a male adult slave rose from three hundred to four hundred pesos in 1830 to over one thousand by 1855. Traditionally, adult slaves who perished or could no longer work were replaced at the market. Now planters began to encourage female slaves to give birth to more children. They also attempted to overturn the clause in the Spanish slave code of 1842 that permitted slaves to purchase their freedom from their masters. Eventually, planters turned to a "good treatment" (*buen trato*) policy in an effort to prolong the work capacity of their existing slaves. The reforms included shortened hours, a weekly rest period, and improved medical care and food. "In effect, the principle of maximum profit was replaced by that of minimal loss," notes Denise Helly.[11]

Recognizing that the "good treatment" policy could not provide a long-term solution to the plantation crisis, planters sought an inexpensive alternative to supplement and eventually to replace slave labor. The high cost of slaves, abolitionist pressure, and fear of rebellions propelled reformists to develop concrete plans for a future without slavery. Another treaty between Britain and Spain in 1835 included a clause for ending slave traffic to the island and led to a renewed interest in immigrant laborers. In order to continue growth in the face of mechanization, British opposition to slavery, and competition from French and German beet sugar, Cuban planters began to see the need for a new infusion of laborers.[12]

Labor Experiments

From the 1830s on, discussions about new labor sources focused on the question of white versus nonwhite immigrants, demonstrating the explosive potential of inserting any new group into an entrenched slave society. The economic growth of the colony lay in the hands of the Real Junta de Fomento y Colonización (Royal Board of Development and Colonization), presided over by wealthy landowner and slave trader Julián de Zulueta. With the impending labor crisis, immigration became one of its central concerns in the 1840s. The influential essayist and social critic José Antonio Saco and other Creole elites promoted abolition and white immigration, remarking on the increasing racial imbalance on the island. They perceived a significant population of free people of color as detrimental to Cuban society. The Junta de Fomento initially proposed that companies introduce white *braceros*, or contract workers, from Spain, Ireland, and Germany to sugar mills in regions considered most threatened by slave rebellions, namely, Havana and Matanzas. The reformist Spanish politician and natural scientist Ramón de la Sagra immediately recognized the potential complications of inserting free white immigrants onto plantations still dependent upon slavery.[13]

Despite these concerns, a few thousand European laborers were brought to Cuba while slavery was in full force. These early experiments with white immigrants were generally unsuccessful, as the laborers fled the sugar plantations soon after arrival. In 1837, for example, Irish and Canary Islanders were contracted to construct the Havana–Güines railroad. They worked sixteen hours each day for a monthly salary of nine pesos, under a rigid system of discipline with substandard food. In what was initially thought to be a success story for the 1840–41 sugar harvest, the owner of La Colonia Estate in Puerto Príncipe, Miguel Estorch, experimented with Catalonian contract workers. However, the immigrants fled the plantation for more lucrative work as artisans in town or settled as campesinos.[14]

Even after they had turned to China for a labor reserve, Cuban merchants continued to contract Spanish immigrants. Never abandoning his reliance on slaves, public works magnate Urbano Feijoó Sotomayor imported contract workers from his native Galicia. Under these circumstances, the treatment of European immigrants paralleled that of slaves and Chinese indentured laborers. In a notorious case, the Sociedad Patriótica Mercantíl (Patriotic Mercantile Company) proposed contracting 50,000 braceros for five years at a monthly wage of five pesos, maintenance, and two sets of clothing per year. Hunger in northern Spain facilitated the recruitment of laborers, and in 1854 the first contingent of 500 arrived in Havana. They were sent to work on the railroad in Trinidad without a period of acclimatization. After not receiving wages for the first few days of work, the Galicians abandoned the railroad. Wild reports circulated that they "disbanded like savages" from Trinidad, scattering throughout the countryside, and that hundreds of men could be heard shouting "viva la libertad" in Cienfuegos. Confronted with this lack of control, the government issued regulations authorizing the treatment of gallegos (Spanish immigrants) as runaway slaves and ordering them held in jail and put to work on public projects. With no one willing to purchase the contracts for the asking price of 200 pesos, Feijoó incarcerated about 1,800 gallegos in his barracoons. Finally, a royal order of 8 July 1855 stipulated that immigration from Galicia would be free. In total, an estimated 2,500 to 3,000 gallegos under contract disembarked. The majority remained in Havana, but some established themselves in Las Villas, mostly in towns where they found work as shop assistants.[15]

Cuban planter and business elites learned from these failed experiments that they needed a way to keep laborers bound to the workplace and that European immigrants were generally unwilling to accept such poor conditions. They sought a new work force that would essentially have the same characteristics as slave labor: "no legal protection by a Western power; a large source of supply; and significant cultural differences."[16] Along these lines, planters attempted to contract Polynesians, Filipinos, and northern

Africans through the 1870s.[17] In 1856, for example, the Compañía de Coloni-zación Africana, led by a Cuban, a Portuguese, and an Asturian, proposed to contract 60,000 Africans in Cuba and 100,000 in Brazil. The plan was met with fierce opposition from Britain and suspicion that it provided a cover for the continued slave traffic (Britain had recently prohibited the contracting of Africans in its own colonies).[18]

Closer to home, Cuban planters recruited Mayan Indians (*yucatecos*) from the Yucatán Peninsula of Mexico. Yucatecans were attractive to the island's landowners for cultural and geographical reasons, as they were nominally Catholic, knew Spanish, and were much closer at hand than Afri-cans or Asians. Prices were initially low: forty Mexican pesos per head for men, twenty-five for women, and nothing for children.[19] From 1848 to 1861, Mexican *hacendados* (landowners) sold over 1,000 Yucatecan prisoners of war to Cuban planters. Pressure from Britain and difficulties in recruitment eventually brought this traffic to an end. The 1862 census counts 786 Yuca-tecans, the majority in Havana and Pinar del Río. A clandestine traffic in Yucatecans continued through 1870, but its volume was insufficient to fulfill the needs of Cuban planters. Furthermore, Yucatecans fled plantations and assimilated into local populations of color. Juan Pérez de la Riva estimates the number at about 3,000 to 4,000 over twenty-five years. He describes the business of the trafficking of Yucatecans as "the most brilliant of all," alluding to the low purchase and transportation costs and high profits at a sale price that eventually exceeded 300 pesos.[20]

Chinese Indentured Labor

As Cuban planters and industrialists experimented with various sources of labor, they turned their attention to the coastal port cities of southeastern China. They were familiar with the use of Chinese workers in the British West Indies and in the Spanish colony of the Philippines. Since the 1830s a small number of Chinese, most likely from Manila, had established a presence in domestic service and horticulture in Cuba.[21] In 1846, the merchant Pedro de Zulueta, cousin of planter and slave trader Julián de Zulueta and in charge of the London branch of Zulueta and Company, proposed to bring Chinese contract workers to Cuba. Pedro de Zulueta had already achieved notoriety for his 1843 trial in London for contraband slave trading. As planters' quest for agricultural laborers shifted away from Europe in the 1840s, Chinese and any other non-Africans became officially classified as "white."[22] The Comi-sión de Población Blanca (Commission on the White Population) therefore approved the plan for the introduction of Chinese laborers. The first expedition would bring 600 *colonos asiáticos* (Asian colonists) who were "robust, agile, and experts in agricultural work."[23] The Junta de Fomento engaged the firm Zulueta and Company in London to enter into an arrangement with the British in Amoy (Xiamen), a treaty port in Fujian Province, and agreed to pay Zulueta the sum of 170 pesos per head.[24]

In January 1847, two ships loaded with Chinese disembarked from the port of Amoy as the beginning of an experiment to import contracted laborers for Cuban sugar plantations. The boats arrived in Cuba within days of each other. On 3 June the Spanish ship *Oquendo* docked with 206 Chinese; six had died on a journey of 131 days. Shortly after, on 12 June, the English ship *Duke of Argyle* arrived with 365 Chinese; 35 had died at sea.[25] Once in Cuba, the coolies were consigned to the Junta de Fomento and distributed in lots of 10 for the heavily subsidized price of 70 pesos per head to sugar plantation and railroad representatives. The Junta de Fomento used a government fund designated for the development of the white population to absorb the remaining 100 pesos of the cost for each colono asiático. A principal purchaser was Urbano Feijoó Sotomayor, the same industrialist who would later incarcerate his gallego immigrants. He resold the majority of the 60 Chinese assigned to him. The Compañia del Ferrocarril (Railroad Company) also acquired three lots, and several major landowners made purchases, some acquiring only one or two Chinese, most likely for use as domestic servants.[26]

Thus began the infamous "coolie trade" to Cuba. Accounting for deaths on the voyage, about 125,000 Chinese arrived in Cuba from 1847 to 1874 and 92,000 in Peru from 1849 to 1874.[27] The trade brought enormous profits to investors, as coolies cost less than African slaves and were easier to obtain. "Furthermore," as Lisa Yun states, "they could be brought in as indentured laborers, but eventually used as slaves."[28] British opposition and early negative reports on Chinese indentured laborers prompted Cuba to suspend the trade after the first agreement with Zulueta expired.[29] The British realized that the coolie trade to Cuba boosted their Spanish competitors in the sugar market. They blocked Spanish ships from entering Chinese ports and eventually ceased their own transport of Chinese coolies to Cuba. Additionally, slave traders resented the competition from this new traffic in Chinese.[30]

The trade was not resumed until five years later, in 1853. This time Cuban merchants were granted a monopolistic concession to operate independently of the Junta de Fomento. When the trade resumed, export of coolies was restricted to Macao, a Portuguese colony off the south China coast. In 1853, a total of fifteen expeditions with 4,300 coolies arrived in Havana. The years

TABLE 1 Chinese Landing in the Port of Havana, 1847–1874

YEAR	DEPARTURES	DEATHS IN TRANSIT	SOLD IN HAVANA	PERCENTAGE DEATHS
1847	612	41	571	6.7
1853	5,150	843	4,307	16.3
1854	1,750	39	1,711	2.2
1855	3,130	145	2,985	4.6
1856	6,152	1,184	4,968	19.3
1857	10,116	1,575	8,547	15.5
1858	16,414	3,019	13,385	18.4
1859	8,549	1,345	7,204	15.7
1860	7,204	1,011	6,193	14
1861	7,252	279	6,973	3.8
1862	356	12	344	3.3
1863	1,045	93	952	8.8
1864	2,664	511	2,153	19.1
1865	6,794	394	6,400	5.7
1866	13,368	977	12,391	7.3
1867	15,616	1,353	14,263	8.6
1868	8,100	732	7,368	9
1869	6,720	1,060	5,660	15.7
1870	1,312	85	1,227	6.4
1871	1,577	89	1,448	5.6
1872	8,915	755	8,160	8.4
1873	5,856	763	5,093	13
1874	2,863	373	2,490	13
TOTAL	141,515	16,578	124,793	

Sources: "Lista de los buques que han importado colonos asiáticos en la isla de Cuba desde 3 de Junio de 1847, época de la llegada del primero de ellos, con especificación de la nacionalidad, número de chinos desembarcados, días de navegación y nombres de los consignatarios," *Boletín de Colonización* 1.14 (August 15, 1873); 1.15 (August 30, 1873); 1.16 (September 15, 1873); 1.17 (September 30, 1873); Pérez de la Riva, *Los culíes chinos*, 179.

Note: Pérez de la Riva gives 1,084 as the number of deaths in transit for 1856; however, the correct number should be 1,184. He gives 141,391 as the total number of Chinese departures and 124,873 as the total number of Chinese sold in Havana; the correct total of the figures provided are 141,515 and 124,793. His figures may reflect a minor typographical or mathematical error.

1855 to 1857 were marked by large crops, higher sugar prices, more foreign investment, and a sizable expansion of credit. The volume of coolie traffic rose to over 6,000 in 1856, over 10,000 in 1857, and a record of over 16,000 in 1858. Along with the contraband slave trade, Chinese indentured laborers became the answer to the "labor question" in Cuba. Pressure from Britain temporarily limited the trade from 1860 to 1863. However, in 1864 Spain and China signed the Treaty of Tianjin, which permitted subjects of the Qing emperor to work in Cuba. That year José Antonio Saco and others promoted the "yellow trade" over the "black trade" as an immigration subsidized "by generous and progressive businessmen."[31]

A multinational network of recruiters, shippers, merchants, and investors participated in the coolie trade to Cuba and Peru. The international traffic to Cuba encompassed 342 ships from sixteen countries: 104 French, 78 Spanish, 35 British, 34 American, 21 Portuguese, 19 Dutch, and 12 Russian.[32] The same slave traders, ships, and captains involved in the Middle Passage now transported Chinese coolies.[33] Chinese referred to the clippers and steamboats that confined them at sea as "devil ships." Even new American ships were modified with iron hatches that imprisoned coolies below deck. Ship owners were confident that their investment would be returned through profits from the coolie trade.[34]

During the twenty-six-year period of the coolie trade, approximately 17,000 of the Chinese who left for Cuba died on the journey due to sickness, thirst, suffocation, cruel treatment, and suicide. Mortality rates on the "floating coffins" to Cuba reached as high as 19 percent for a given year. Coolies were crammed below deck in the hold, usually for the duration of the journey. Ye Fujun and fifty-two others later testified, "The hatchway only allowed one man at a time to come down or go up, and the stench below from the crowd of men was most offensive, and the deaths thence produced were without number." Resistance to the harsh conditions began at sea, through suicide and rebellion. Chen Aji stated, "two of those on board threw themselves into the sea because they had been flogged for taking water when suffering from extreme thirst, and for refusing to allow their queues to be cut off."[35] (The queue, or long braid worn by men to demonstrate allegiance to the Manchu Qing dynasty, represented cultural identity for Chinese men.) Mutinies also claimed lives, the most extreme example being the U.S. *Flora Temple*, which the Chinese set fire to. After being forced below deck, all 850 passengers died when the ship struck a reef and sank.[36]

The Pearl River Delta

A long-standing tradition of emigration in South China, along with new developments unique to the mid-nineteenth century, contributed to Chinese villagers' decisions to leave their hometown. Traders from China's southeastern coastal provinces of Fujian and Guangdong had sojourned in Southeast

Asia since the sixteenth century. In an effort to maintain control over its empire, the Manchu Qing dynasty (1644–1911) officially outlawed emigration. By the mid-1800s, however, European incursions, overpopulation, natural disasters, ethnic conflict, and rebellion propelled the massive emigrations of the era that lasted through the 1920s.

Britain pushed for the opening of port cities along China's coastline and rivers to international trade. By selling opium grown in India to the Chinese, the British hoped to offset the trade imbalance caused by British consumption of tea and other luxuries from China. The Treaty of Nanjing ending the first Opium War (1839–42) permitted British subjects to reside and trade in the five port cities of Canton (Guangzhou), Fuzhou, Amoy (Xiamen), Ningbo, and Shanghai and granted Britain the island of Hong Kong. Britain also pressured for the ability to recruit Chinese laborers for its West Indian colonies. In 1858, Britain and France occupied Canton, and in 1860, they invaded the capital Peking (Beijing) to force the emperor into making trade and emigration concessions. Subsequent treaties after the second Opium War (or Arrow War, 1856–60) extended commercial privileges for foreigners and led to the opening of additional ports.[37]

The Pearl River Delta region provided a plentiful source of Chinese for labor recruitment. With the opening of the ports and increased foreign presence, large numbers of Chinese males began to migrate from the countryside to urban centers, often the first step to emigration overseas. Overpopulation generated intense competition for resources and furthered dislocation in local society. In addition, ethnic conflicts arose between the minority Hakka (*kejia* or "guest people") and the Cantonese for land and jobs. Language and customs, such as the lack of foot binding among women, distinguished Hakkas from Cantonese. Large numbers of Hakkas emigrated to Hawaii and Peru, forming a significant portion of the Chinese overseas population. A local Hakka militia confederation funneled interethnic feuding into an antidynastic millenarian movement known as the Taiping Rebellion (1851–64). It nearly toppled the Qing dynasty and propelled migration, both internal and overseas. Displaced rebels escaped capture from Qing officials by emigrating to Southeast Asia, the Americas, and Hawaii. Scattered reports suggest that Taiping soldiers were also among the coolies sent to Cuba and Peru. Local Qing authorities used the coolie trade to rid themselves of hundreds of Taiping rebels. After the Taiping defeat, persistent interethnic warfare between Cantonese and Hakka propelled tens of thousands of both dialect groups to emigrate overseas.[38]

An intricate system of recruitment underlay the international coolie trade. Chinese brokers (known by Westerners as "crimps" or "runners") supplied thousands of young men in a network extending from villages to coastal cities. The opening of the ports to international trade at the end of the Opium Wars had attracted Chinese not only from Guangdong and Fujian, but also from the Straits Settlements and the Philippines, to form a class of professional middlemen and interpreters. The Qing government referred to those who cooperated with British merchants in the smuggling of opium and coolies as *hanjian* (traitors to the Han race). These "collaborators" received protection from the British government, and some were linked with secret societies (which presumably had an anti-Qing agenda).[39]

Chinese middlemen used deception and kidnapping as primary methods of obtaining recruits, known as "pigs." Recruiters lured Chinese men into gambling houses, where they were forced to sign contracts after amassing debt. Chinese who willingly signed contracts believed they were dealing with legitimate agents stationed in the ports. Zheng Amou and eighty-nine others testified, "We were induced to proceed to Macao by offers of employment abroad at high wages, and through being told that the eight foreign years specified in the contracts were equivalent to only four Chinese, and that at the termination of the latter period we would be free. We observed also on the signboards of the foreign buildings the words 'agencies for the engagement of labourers,' and believed that they truthfully described the nature of the establishments, little expecting that having once entered the latter, exit would be denied us; and when on arrival at Havana, we were exposed for sale and subjected to appraisement in a most ruthless manner, it became evident that we were not to be engaged as labourers, but to be sold as slaves."[40] Chinese migrants, however, were not completely naïve to the business of recruitment. In some cases they entered into contracts with multiple brokers, obtaining the promised food, clothing, lodging, and advance before moving on to another recruiting station.[41]

Besides farmers and vendors of agricultural products, the recruits in Macao were dockhands, fishermen, barbers, tailors, and painters.[42] In her analysis of coolie testimonies, Lisa Yun demonstrates a diversity of social backgrounds that counter the image of "coolie" laborer as "poor, unskilled, and uneducated." Among their occupations were incense shop owner, tofu maker, actor, carpenter, doctor, and translator. The majority (89 percent) were natives of Guangdong, but they came from at least fourteen provinces and included some Vietnamese, Filipinos, and Manchu bannermen. Like Tung Kun Sen, 20 percent of the coolies who testified in Cuba had been brought to the island at ages under twenty, some as young as eight.[43]

In contrast to the East Indians in the British Caribbean, Chinese coolies in Cuba and Peru were overwhelmingly male. When planters resumed the coolie trade in 1853, Spanish officials encouraged the importation of Chinese women and families to promote stability and detract criticism. They stipulated that one-fifth of the recruits be women, unless opposition from Chinese authorities made this impossible. Parents would bring children from age ten to eighteen, who would be obligated to work. Monthly wages would be three pesos for women and two pesos for children. In 1860 the tonnage allotted to females was exempted from duties. These cursory attempts to encourage the importation of women and families, however, proved unsuccessful; fewer than one hundred women came to Cuba as coolies.[44]

Details on the lives of female coolies in Cuba are difficult to come by. Advertisements for the "rent" or "sale" of young Chinese females appeared in Cuban newspapers, alongside those of black slaves.[45] One story that has passed down through generations is that of Carmen (Chiu) Montalvo, born in 1839 amid the turmoil of South China. She recalled that when she was seven, local warfare forced her family to flee their village. She clung to her mother's dress with her siblings, but unable to hold on, she got lost, and was led to a ship destined for Cuba. There she was raised in the house of the Conde de Casa Montalvo alongside other children, where she lived until she married one of the servants. The house of the well-known slave trader José Suárez Argudín also kept Chinese girls who taught her Spanish.[46]

Coolie Life

While waiting to embark on ships in Macao, the recruits were housed in jail-like barracoons, similar to the holding stations for enslaved men and women in coastal Africa. Once in Havana, the coolies who survived the journey disembarked at the port of Regla, the marketplace for African slaves across the bay from the center of the city. Chinese were locked in holding cells (*depósitos*) until their contracts were auctioned. Traders routinely used force and humiliation to subdue them. Jiang San stated, "In the Havana barracoon, for refusing to permit the removal of my queue, I was beaten almost to death." Another group of coolies testified that the practice of being stripped and examined while a price was fixed "covered us with shame."[47] Technically, the sale was for the contract of indenture, rather than the laborer, marking a legal difference from the system of African slavery. An American official reported that purchase prices for the contracts generally ranged between $400 and $500.[48]

Chinese indentured laborers in Cuba and Peru generally signed eight-year contracts. They obliged the Chinese to work twelve-hour days (with the exception of Sundays) for a monthly salary of four pesos. Contracts were transferable, as Chinese indentured laborers agreed to work "at the orders of whatever person to whom the contract was transmitted." They also agreed to accept the stipulated salary, "although recognizing the higher level of salaries received by free workers in Cuba." The difference in remuneration was supposedly compensated for by transport to Cuba, lodging, medical assistance for illness not lasting more than two weeks, a daily provision of two and a half pounds of vegetables and eight ounces of salt meat, and an annual provision of two suits of clothing and one blanket. The coolie was also obligated to accept the discipline of his employer. Yet, as Denise Helly points out, no clause in the contract specified the precise nature of this discipline.[49] Like African slaves, Chinese coolies were assigned a Hispanicized first name by masters and overseers in order to simplify administration. Once in Cuba, the majority began a path of unending labor, abuse, and confinement.

Both African slaves and Chinese indentured laborers were concentrated in the central-west sugar-producing regions. More than 80 percent of Chinese coolies were sent to sugar, tobacco, and coffee plantations in Havana and Matanzas Provinces, and some to railroads. Other areas of sugar expansion, such as Sagua la Grande and Remedios, also received large contingents of Africans and Chinese. By the 1860s and 1870s Chinese were highly visible throughout the island, especially in Matanzas. While estates continued to primarily use slave labor, some smaller, less capitalized sugar mills relied more heavily on Chinese workers. For example, the fifty-caballería Santo Domingo in Macagua, owned by Domingo García Capo, used 150 Chinese and 60 slaves.[50] The provinces of Camagüey and Oriente remained outside of the massive expansion of the sugar industry, and thus did not receive large numbers of Chinese coolies.[51] Smaller numbers of coolies were assigned to cigar factories, domestic service, and public works.

Planters and overseers blatantly disregarded the provisions of the contracts. Like slaves, Chinese were beaten, chained, deprived of food, and forced to work from fifteen to twenty hours daily. Furthermore, the wages that supposedly distinguished immigrant contract laborers from African slaves were routinely withheld.[52] Overall, Chinese indentured laborers suffered an extremely high mortality rate. Of the 223 Chinese buried by the Catholic Church in Regla, 45 percent died between the ages of twenty-one and thirty, and another 23 percent died between the ages of thirty-one and

Provinces of Cuba, 1959 boundaries

forty.[53] The investigatory commission of 1874 estimated that over 50 percent of Chinese who arrived in Cuba perished before the end of their contract.[54]

From the outset, contradictory images of Chinese circulated. Opponents of the importation of coolies believed they were physically weak and morally corrupt, while promoters perceived them as more intelligent and skilled than African slaves. These positive attributes, however, were not met with better treatment on Cuban sugar estates, where the most blatant abuses occurred. Travelers frequently commented on the weak constitution and submissive nature of Chinese laborers. In 1872, Richard Levis wrote, "They look remarkably neat, in dress of Chinese style, with hair in a long plaited tail. They have rather dull, submissive faces, and their smiles are, as is reputed, 'childlike and bland.' They are rather slightly formed, and, with their small hands and feet, with long finger-nails, I have been wondering what kind of occupation they have been accustomed to at home. It will take some time to inure them to the hard labor they are destined for." Levis, who visited large plantations in Santa Rita, Flor de Cuba, and Tinguaro, noted that Chinese coolies "are preferred for all kinds of skilled labor, but do not bear field work in the hot sun so well as the negro."[55]

Chinese coolies worked alongside African slaves in the cane fields, but were housed in separate quarters. The overcrowded barracoons generally had poor ventilation, no windows, and dirt floors. On San José sugar mill in Matanzas Province, the slave barracoon was subdivided into interior rooms, while the Chinese one consisted of a single large room with cots and a washroom. Both the Chinese and slave quarters opened onto a central courtyard.[56] The door to the barracoon was locked at night to prevent coolies from running away. On some estates, Chinese were required to build their own thatch huts. While constructing their own dwellings provided Chinese with an opportunity to improve their living conditions, it became an onerous financial burden. Testifying with twenty-three other coolies, Liang Axiu stated, "On the plantation also there were no habitations for us, and we were told to provide them ourselves. Our monthly wages were but $3, and as even a grass hut for two would cost $10, it was not in our power to obey. We explained this to our employer's son, who became very wrathful, struck us indiscriminately, and together with certain negroes, seizing knives killed one of our number, a native of Hiangshan [Xiangshan], and wounded the remainder."[57]

Chinese were forced to adjust their diet in Cuba, as a typical meal in South China consisted of rice with meat and vegetables. Richard Levis described a standard meal on a sugar estate with African slave and Chinese coolie laborers: "The breakfast for the laborers was brought to the field about eight o'clock, and consisted of boiled jerked beef and boiled sweet potatoes, in a large wooden box or trough. Folding some cane leaves into a sort of basin, each laborer supplied himself liberally with the food, and sitting in the shade of the uncut cane, ate large quantities. This diet is varied at other meals with the plantain and rice, with sugar and water for a drink; and at all moments of idleness the negroes are seen gnawing and sucking the sugar-cane."[58] Plantation owner Eliza McHatton-Ripley attempted to quell dissatisfaction by importing low-grade rice from India "frequently issued to the Chinese in place of mush."[59] However, Chinese who complained about their food or other conditions risked the wrath of the estate owner or manager. Ye Ayao deposed: "For refusing to eat maize I was almost beaten to death. My entire person was lacerated; on it there was not a single spot uninjured."[60] Some masters, rather than providing food, forced coolies to purchase provisions at the plantation store with wage deductions. The plantation store, similar to the company store in the export economies of Central and South America, sold a limited supply of goods such as cooking utensils, clothing, and opium at inflated prices, on credit or with a currency that was only valid on the estate.[61] This tactic from the slave regime further indebted Chinese laborers to plantations.

Chinese experiences on Cuban sugar plantations consisted of a litany of horrors, documented through their own testimony and accounts by others. Plantation owners in Cuba were often absentee, leaving the work of the day-to-day operations and discipline of slaves and indentured laborers to overseers and administrators. In a few cases Chinese contrasted the cruel treatment at the hands of intermediaries with the benevolence of masters.[62] Both planters and overseers used corporal punishment, a pillar of the slave system, to discipline, punish, and control Chinese. Runaways were shackled or placed in the stocks upon their capture. The "good treatment" toward African slaves during this period did not extend to Chinese coolies. To the contrary, planters perceived Chinese as easily replaceable. Thus, flogging and other forms of punishment, even to the point of death, were common. Xie Asi deposed: "The owner has urged the administrator and the overseers to flog us. He has said that it matters not if one is beaten to death as he is rich enough to buy ten others."[63]

The arrival of Asian indentured laborers across Latin America and the Caribbean disturbed the social and racial hierarchy on plantations. Chinese coolies and African slaves worked alongside each other in the cane fields in Cuba, and masters and overseers quickly learned to manipulate the divisions between the two racial groups.[64] Across plantation societies, Creole slaves put into "driver" positions were used to control field hands. Their privileged status within the slave population ensured the continuation of the system. Indentured Chinese worked under black low-level overseers in Cuba, even though regulations prohibited it. Knowing that they were technically free workers who had signed a legal contract, Chinese thought it untenable to be under the control and whip of a black slave. Li Ahui stated, "when, on the plantation, I was incapacitated for work by sickness, four negroes were directed to hold me prostrate, whilst I was being flogged on my naked person."[65] Furthermore, Chinese believed that black slaves received better treatment. Huang Ade reported a murder of a Xiangshan (Zhongshan) native by a black. Although an official examined the body, he did not arrest the offender, and the master "simply inflicted on him a slight chastisement, and the matter was then considered terminated. Negroes indeed receive better usage than the Chinese."[66]

Planters and overseers exploited animosities to further humiliate the Chinese into submission and to prevent incipient cross-racial alliances from developing out of common oppression. When Eliza McHatton-Ripley and her former confederate officer husband purchased the sugar plantation Desengaño in Cuba after the war, she noted a separation between the two groups: "The Chinese did not mingle with the negroes, either in their work or socially, though subject to the same rules and regulations in regard to their hours of labor and hours of rest."[67] At times slaves protected the interests of sugar estates in the wake of coolie rebellions, a phenomenon that Benjamin Narvaez emphasizes was more common in Cuba, with its large slave population, than Peru, where planters depended more on Asian laborers. Masters in Cuba and Peru also promoted divisions within coolie ranks by offering rewards to Chinese who reported subversive behavior or assisted with the capture of runaways. Chinese *contramayorales* (low-level overseers) charged with disciplining field laborers received privileges such as extra wages and plots of land for personal use.[68]

Planters applied techniques from the African slave regime to instill a process of psychological and cultural humiliation upon Chinese coolies. The dehumanization began with Chinese standing naked at auction, allowing purchasers to examine them like a herd of cattle.[69] The queue, an object of curiosity and fascination for the gaze of American and European travelers, became one of mutilation during the coolie period. By cutting off the queues of Chinese workers, planters denied them a visible marker of identity as a male subject of the Qing dynasty. This process of cultural humiliation intersected with racial exploitation by white slave owners. On one estate, Chinese workers who claimed to be sick were forced to drink the urine of a female black slave. The perverse logic of domination was that if the coolie were truly sick, he would drink the urine, and if he refused, he would be forced to go back to work.[70] In other cases, coolies were put on display and forced to imitate animals. Wu Asan stated that "the Chinese in chains were beaten severely if they did not imitate the cries of sheep and dogs."[71] In 1860 the American abolitionist and writer Julia Ward Howe recounted the use of coolies for entertainment of the masters. With pity, she describes a blind coolie on a coffee plantation forced to perform: "'*Canta!*' says the master, and the poor slave gives tongue like a hound on the scent. '*Baila!*' and, a stick being handed him, he performs the gymnastics of his country, a sort of war-dance without accompaniment. '*El can!*' and, giving him a broom, they loose the dog upon him. A curious tussle then ensues,—the dog attacking furiously, and the blind man, guided by his barking, defending himself lustily. The Chino laughs, the master laughs, but the visitor feels more inclined to cry, having been bred in these Northern habits which respect infirmity."[72]

Coolies beyond the Plantation

Sugar production spawned a host of related industries fueled by slave and coolie labor. Beyond plantations, Chinese worked in urban centers in warehouses and docks, in factories, and on the expanding network of railroads across the island. Sugar was transported from the interior of the island to enormous storage facilities at the port of Regla, across the bay from Havana.

Samuel Hazard noted that "all the labor is done by Chinese coolies, who work there on contract" with "no clothing on them except a pair of pants."[73] Hazard also toured the nail factory at Puentes Grandes outside of Havana, observing that all sixty workers were Chinese, under an English supervisor. The factory churned out one hundred barrels of nails daily, sold at six dollars per barrel and used primarily for securing boxes of sugar.[74]

The Cuban railroad system heavily depended on Chinese labor, especially during a period of expansion through 1868. As on the sugar plantations, Chinese developed a reputation for skilled and methodical labor on railroads as brakemen, furnace attendants, and in other jobs. In 1856 Caminos de Hierro de La Habana used 98 Chinese, a number that tripled within five years. Ferrocarril del Oeste maintained the largest Chinese workforce, reaching 751 in 1859. This number is not surprising, considering that the railroad's promoters, the Pedrosos, were directly involved in the coolie trade. Throughout the 1860s, railroads came to rely less on slaves and free wage laborers and more on Chinese coolies in order to reduce costs. In 1862 the directors of the Matanzas Railroad, for example, reported that the monthly salary for Chinese was 4.65 pesos, compared with 20.25 pesos for hired slaves and 21.30 for free day laborers. When Ferrocarril de La Bahía began construction on a new line in 1859, its workforce consisted of 197 convicts, 42 emancipados, 526 slaves (owned or rented), 273 Chinese indentured laborers, 15 free blacks, and 20 white day laborers. By the time it completed the line in 1865, the workforce consisted of only 1 slave and 446 Chinese.[75]

Besides sugar, shipping, and railroads, key sectors of the Cuban economy that used Chinese labor included mining, tobacco, road and building construction, and domestic service. Coolies in Cuba's eastern provinces were fewer in number and arrived later than in the sugar-producing provinces of the central-west. But they were significant for the development of industries such as copper mining. According to 1859 census statistics, 715 Chinese populated the Eastern Department (from Puerto Príncipe to Baracoa), compared with 16,386 in the Western Department (from Pinar del Río to Trinidad). They were spread among several jurisdictions in the east, with the overwhelming majority in Santiago de Cuba and many in Puerto Príncipe.

In the 1830s and 1840s, Cuba had become one of the primary exporters of copper worldwide, especially to England. Near Santiago de Cuba in the east, the town of El Cobre developed in conjunction with its famous copper mines. By 1864, the majority of the 387 Chinese men in El Cobre lived in town, with only four working in sugar mills. The remainder of El Cobre's population consisted of 1,798 whites, 3,587 free people of color, 583 slaves, and 52 emancipados.[76] Even before slave emancipation in Cuba, the eastern provinces had become a haven for free people of color, including refugees from Haiti.

When Samuel Hazard descended into the Consolidated Copper Mines during his travels, he portrayed the perils of the industry. Out of the 250 men employed by the British company, eleven captains and assistants were mostly English and the laborers black and Chinese. Hazard observed coolies at work in the extreme conditions as much as one thousand feet below ground with temperatures reaching 140 degrees Fahrenheit: "Three or four perfectly naked Chinese were at this work, the perspiration pouring off them as they used their picks and gads in prying out the pieces of somewhat soft rock."[77] In 1866, after the death of several English operators from yellow fever, the chief engineer of the mines authorized the placement of blasts by "some Chinese known for their experience and skill."[78]

Treacherous conditions in the mines led to frequent accidents, often resulting in death for slaves and coolies, but also for some English. In January 1862, a cable broke, killing twenty Chinese and two English who were inside the attached cage. In August 1858, a Chinese named Chang Heng, but known as Braulio, fell asleep in the mine while waiting for the balance to lift him to the surface. He fell into the funnel where the copper was deposited, becoming literally entombed in the mineral, and his body was not discovered until the next morning by two other Chinese.

In the subsequent investigation, according to statements made by other coolies, including the contramayoral Carlos, this deathly fall was not an isolated case. Nevertheless, the deputy of mines in El Cobre declared that blame for the misfortune belonged to Braulio himself. The engineer inspector traced the accident to the practice of working in the dark, something the Chinese did frequently "with the aim of selling in town their candles." The official report sent to the governor and general commander of the department stated that the fall and death of the colono asiático Braulio was an accident, similar to other incidents in the mines "when workers forget the necessary prudence." As Oscar Luis Abdala Pupo comments, not once in this report did "the real cause of the death of the Chinese" gain mention: the exhaustion of the workday.

In subsequent cases from 1858 to 1871, the Spanish government functionary repeated his argument that the practice of saving candles for later sale was the cause of the accidental deaths. However, in 1863, his conclusion that a slave's death was "purely accidental" did not convince members of the Tribunal de la Audiencia Territorial, who in a communication to the captain general called attention to the repeated "misfortunes" in the mines and the actions of the inspector of mines. Despite criticism for the number of deaths in the mines, the inspector remained in his position until 1871.[79]

The inspector's accusation about selling candles hints at Chinese participation in an informal economy, even while under indenture and despite the poor working conditions. They had easier access to town than the Chinese on sugar plantations in the west, facilitating the kind of activity that represented resistance to the company's regime and the possibility of earning extra money. The Chinese must have been willing to risk accidents in order to compensate for low wages.

As on the sugar estates, mining companies housed Chinese coolies in prisonlike barracks. After finishing their shift, they were directed to their dwelling, known as the *casa de chinos*, a barracks with endless rows of cots. A Chinese guard was chosen from among them to keep watch during the night and prevent their exit. The constant vigilance, however, failed to prevent runaway attempts. In January 1860, a coolie named Ciriaco escaped, only to be captured in nearby Santiago after several days. In July 1868, the Chinese Asin was captured in Nuevitas and returned to his master Pedro Ferrer y Landa. Before securing his coolie's return, Ferrer had to pay the sum of $21.70 for the costs of the holding cell (a sum that ultimately came out of the coolie's salary).[80] In October 1859, the Chinese who worked in the English mines of El Cobre protested against maltreatment and poor conditions by stopping work, abandoning the mine, and heading en masse toward the city of Santiago de Cuba. They were intercepted by Spanish troops, and the head of forces ordered twenty lashes to four Chinese (Lucio, Fermín, Teodoro, and Roque) considered responsible, afterward escorting them to the jail.[81]

Chinese laborers were also used in Cuban cigar factories. Like today, the superior reputation of Cuban tobacco in Europe and North America compelled tourists to tour factories. A room filled with Chinese piqued Samuel Hazard's curiosity when he visited La Honradez: "Each workman has a small table to himself, at which he folds, fills, counts, and does up in packages the little cigarettes; and it is astonishing what facility and dexterity they acquire from long practice in handling and counting these small bits of paper."[82] In 1872, Richard Levis also toured the factory, which produced over two million cigarettes daily, "mostly by the labor of Chinese operatives, who have acquired great dexterity in the manipulations." Levis also noted the new machinery by American manufacturers, commenting that "all that represents ingenuity, invention, and the progress of intelligence, may be referred for its origin either to the United States or England."[83]

Travelers passing through the island commented on the prevalence of coolies in domestic service, especially as cooks or butlers on sugar estates and in towns. Richard Henry Dana noted that two of the cooks in his hotel were Chinese coolies.[84] From the original group of thirty-five coolies on her plantation, Eliza McHatton-Ripley chose "one with a good countenance and neat appearance" for a cook. She came to rely heavily on her cook for the duration of his term: "I never saw any servant so systematic, so methodical, so quiet, so solemn, so intent, so clean. During the eight years he was in the kitchen, there was not an hour in the day when Ciriaco could not be found. He brought his wood from behind the sugar-house at the same hour every afternoon, drew the water from the cistern with the same regularity, carrying it Chinese fashion in pails swung at each end of a pole."[85] Like African slaves, coolies who worked in these positions often became trusted members of plantation society who gained access to privileges.

In addition to domestic service, Chinese coolies could also be found in towns standing behind counters or laboring in construction projects. Chinese were sentenced to public works for running away or refusing to agree to another term of contract. American and European travelers commented with surprise at their presence in urban centers. Edwin F. Atkins, a Massachusetts businessman who eventually purchased a sugar estate in Cuba, made his first trip to the island in 1866. He described the streets being "cleaned every night by chain gangs made up mostly of Chinese and negroes, who were often sentenced for light offences, as the Government was glad to get their services."[86] Urban slavery was a common phenomenon throughout Latin America. As Lisa Yun comments, cases of coolies sold to small businesses and households overturn portrayals of Chinese in urban centers as merely disadvantaged "immigrants." Huang Qiutai, who had been a tailor in China, was sold to a candy shop, and the former grocer Wu Asi was sold to a tailor's shop, where the manager abused and restrained him. Yun states, "The Chinese 'shopkeeper' behind the counter, in such instances, was actually a slave."[87] During the coolie era even Chinese market-gardeners, generally associated with entrepreneurship, could be trapped within a system of perpetual re-contracting.[88]

Enforcing the Coolie System

Two years after the first coolie ships arrived in Cuba, the Spanish colonial government issued a set of regulations to reinforce the contracts. The 1849 regulations limited mobility and permitted corporal punishment, with disciplinary measures such as flogging, leg shackles, and confinement in stocks derived directly from the world of slavery. Certain articles explicitly addressed the tensions between Asians and blacks. Whenever there were ten coolies on an estate, they must be assigned a white overseer. The overseer could deliver corporal punishment, but not in the presence of slaves, as such a physical subordination of Chinese to slaves could produce an unwelcome backlash. Despite these provisions, Juan Pérez de la Riva and others conclude that the legislation, based on a slave code of 1842, reduced the Chinese to a state of bondage.[89]

With the resumption of the coolie trade in 1853 came a new set of regulations in 1854, supposedly intended to correct some of the abuses of the system as practiced. They prohibited corporal punishment and granted coolies limited civil rights. A new clause addressing the practice of forced recontracting stipulated that coolies were not obligated to extend the contract beyond the eight-year term, even if they were in debt. Chinese were thereby granted the same right to settle as other foreigners, including Spanish, upon completion of their contracts. They could also contract marriage, assume parental authority over children, and acquire and dispose of property. Furthermore, they could file charges against masters for failure to comply with the new regulations and appeal to colonial authorities in cases of abuse. The 1854 regulations also granted coolies who reached age twenty-five or completed six years of service the right to provide an indemnification to masters in order to have their contracts rescinded.

Even under the new regulations, masters retained great power over coolies' lives. Confinement in the stocks and withholding wages were still permitted as punishments. One provision prohibited them from leaving the workplace without written permission from the master. Those found without this document were to be apprehended by the authorities and jailed or returned at the master's expense, effectively making the Chinese laborer a prisoner. Marriage and the acquisition of property also required the master's approval.[90]

The new civil rights granted by the regulations were limited in practice. Their self-purchase was neither encouraged nor facilitated. Their situation was similar to that of Cuban slaves, who also had access to the process of *coartación*, or gradual self-purchase. As Rebecca Scott notes, while self-purchase was important for the development of Cuba's large free population of color, given the increases in slave prices, it affected only a small percentage of slaves in the 1860s.[91]

Again, masters and overseers routinely ignored the ban on corporal punishment and continued to force coolies to recontract after the initial eight-year period. Evelyn Hu-DeHart points out that the sale, purchase, and renting out of coolie contracts in practice differed little from slave transactions. The laws "were flagrantly disregarded, the contract a mere piece of paper."[92] This paper accumulated a certain value, however, when masters forcibly imposed the contracts of dead coolies on other Chinese who had completed their contracts.[93]

Chinese indentured laborers were required to carry a *cédula* at all times. The cédula was a document of identification and legal status, indicating whether a slave had been emancipated or a Chinese indentured laborer had completed his contract. While in theory this requirement protected Chinese against fraud (making it difficult for masters to claim a Chinese was someone else in order to add time to the contract), it also curtailed their mobility. Without a cédula, Chinese were subject to arrest and detention until reclaimed by their masters. Local officials routinely withheld the coveted document from Chinese, transforming it into a vehicle for profit and corruption.[94]

Former coolies who desired to remain in Cuba had to endure what Lisa Yun calls "the paper chase." They were required to produce evidence of the completion of their contract, a certificate of baptism, a "freedom paper," a letter of domicile/residency, and a "walking paper." Chinese needed white godparents to sponsor them for the baptism certificate. In addition, licenses were required for opening a small shop or practicing certain trades such as medicine. Even those who became beggars had to purchase a "begging paper."[95] Zhu Jixun and ten others testified about the financial and social obstacles to procuring a letter of domicile, which required conversion to Catholicism: "An outlay of $50 or $60 and baptism and adoption by a foreigner were indispensible, so that it was useless for a poor man to endeavour to obtain these documents."[96]

Despite all the power masters had over coolies under the 1854 regulations, they continued to encounter difficulties in controlling Chinese indentured laborers. In response to planter complaints, Spain in 1860 issued new regulations. A key clause reversed the prohibition on recontracting, thereby sanctioning what had become a common practice. The new law required coolies who arrived after 15 February 1861 and completed their original term of service to sign another contract, either with the same master or with another. If they did not recontract, they were obligated to leave the island within two months or were detained in holding cells originally intended for runaway slaves.[97] Once there, they were forced into public works such as construction and road repair. Ye Fujun and fifty-two others petitioned: "When the completion of the eight years term was approaching, every one was consoled at the prospect of speedy liberty, of saving money, and going back to China, but our employer was so heartless as to insist on our binding ourselves for other six years, sending those who refused to the dépôt, where they had to labour on the roads the whole day, with chained feet, receiving no wages, and not having enough to eat, whilst the severity of the toil was augmented by the burning sun."[98]

With the recontracting clause, the royal government clearly intended to make it difficult, if not impossible, for a Chinese indentured laborer to become free on Cuban soil. Reporting on Cuba's labor history, U.S. Special Commissioner Robert Porter commented that most Chinese on the island were forced to recontract for another term. However, he noted that new contract conditions were for a shorter term at a higher wage, four years at seventeen dollars per month, though twelve of these dollars would be retained by the municipality and supposedly remitted to the Chinese at the end of the contract period.[99]

Coolie Resistance and Rebellion

Like African slaves, from the outset Chinese indentured laborers engaged in both overt and covert resistance to abuses in the system. Their actions ranged from suicide, sabotage, homicide, and armed revolt to legal appeal to Spanish authorities.[100]

In the middle of the nineteenth century, Cuba had the highest suicide rate in the world, one for every 4,000 inhabitants, a statistic largely due to the Chinese and comparable only to that of coolies in Peru. Because under Spanish law suicide was a crime, Chinese suicides appeared regularly in criminal statistics. In 1862, half of the recorded suicides on the island were Chinese, 173 out of a total of 346. Proportionately, the suicide rate for Chinese was one hundred times greater than for whites and fourteen times greater than for slaves.[101] One coolie corroborated the statistics and impressions of observers, testifying that at the end of eight years half of the number of his group had died, many from suicide.[102]

Suicide, particularly rampant on Cuban sugar plantations, served as both a means to protest the labor regime and to put an end to the misery of a seemingly endless bondage.[103] By leaping into hot sugar cauldrons, for example, Chinese coolies fulfilled a dual aim of stopping production and finding relief. Chen Mingyuan stated that the Chinese "endure hunger and chains, hardships and wrongs of every class, and are driven to suicide to the extent that no count can be made of the number of those who have thrown themselves into wells, cut their throats, hanged themselves, and swallowed opium."[104] On a Saturday morning in March 1872, traveler Richard Levis reported the sensational news from Santa Barbara Estate in Villa Clara: "One of the newly arrived Chinese laborers was found dead, having committed suicide by hanging himself to a beam across the bathing-house. The self-murder was effected in a determined manner, as the feet were almost touching the floor, a ledge was within their reach, and objects of support could have been readily seized by the hands."[105] Cuba's famous runaway slave Esteban Montejo solemnly recalled Chinese suicides on plantations: "They did it silently. After several days passed, they appeared hanging from a tree or lying dead on the ground."[106] The practice of recontracting, in particular, led Chinese to turn to suicide as a means to escape the system. He Asi testified: "At the end of the eight years no cedula was supplied to me, and I was forced to work for another term of four years. A few days ago I asked my master for a cedula, and was told by him that I had to serve for other six years. If this be the case, suicide is the best course open to me."[107] For Chinese, the hope of returning to their native land, albeit in spirit form, outweighed the humiliation and harshness of life in Cuba.

Some Chinese committed suicide in groups, indicating collective protest. In December 1870, for example, fourteen Chinese contracted on Dos Marías were found hanging.[108] This form of protest is reminiscent of resistance by indigenous peoples during the initial years of the colonial conquest, in which families and entire villages protested enslavement through group suicide.[109]

Planters, travelers, and others who commented on the prevalence of Chinese suicide attributed it to maltreatment but also to flawed cultural and character traits. José Antonio Saco speculated that the "corrupt and perverse" Chinese character led them to commit suicide "for the pure purpose of vengeance."[110] Some believed the practice of corporal punishment to be an underlying cause of both homicide and suicide. During his morning walk in February 1859 in Matanzas, Richard Henry Dana encountered a New York shipmaster and related the fellow North American's belief that "it would not do to flog a Coolie. Idolaters as they are, they have a notion of the dignity of the human body, at least as against strangers, which does not allow them to submit to the indignity of corporal chastisement. If a Coolie is flogged somebody must die; either the Coolie himself, for they are fearfully given to suicide, or the perpetrator of the indignity, or some one else, according to their strange principles of vicarious punishment."[111] Traveler Julia Ward Howe also commented on the high rates of suicide among Chinese. She contrasted the

Chinese indentured laborer's proclivity for suicide with the African slave's determination to suffer through hardship. "So many of them emancipated themselves from hard service by voluntary death, that it became matter of necessity to lighten the weight about their necks, and to leave them that minimum of well-being which is necessary to keep up the love of life. The instinct itself is shown to be feeble in the race, whereas the Negro clings to life under whatever pains and torment."[112] Here Howe indicates that conditions may have actually improved for the remaining Chinese as a preventative measure against future suicides.

Planters used tactics of mutilation and cultural humiliation in an attempt to prevent suicides. In March 1872 Richard Levis noted that after six coolies were discovered hanging one morning, "further instances were prevented by making in the presence of their comrades a complete dissection and mutilation of one of the bodies." In other cases the bodies were burned on a pile of wood. "These horrible sights, it is said, took from the Chinese their romantic ideas on the subject of self-destruction." At best, the corpses of Chinese who committed suicide would be buried unceremoniously in a ditch. In one case of a newly arrived coolie found hanging from a beam in the washroom, Levis reported: "The body of the Chinese suicide has been interred outside the walls of the little enclosure which, by church regulation, must receive the remains of those only who have been baptized in the Catholic faith. In digging the shallow grave to receive the body, another sleeper was unceremoniously turned out by the spades, and I saw the decaying remnants of mortality, including a skull with some matted hair and portions of clothing, scattered on the ground, and they were left so to remain."[113]

Although opium ingestion constituted one of the main ways Chinese committed suicide, from a planter's perspective, the substance became a necessary evil. As Evelyn Hu-DeHart notes, planters in Cuba and Peru permitted and promoted the sale and consumption of opium. They strategically deployed opium "as a largely effective mechanism of social control of the Chinese coolie labor force."[114] While opium was used to bind Chinese indentured laborers to the sugar estate, it could also be a means of resistance to the labor regime on plantations and in mines, as its use resulted in premature death, lowered productivity, and absenteeism. By causing overdoses (intentional or accidental) and slowing work, it disrupted production. For Chinese who distributed the substance, opium also served as means to gain capital. In El Cobre, the governor of the Eastern Department became alarmed by the use of opium after two related deaths in March 1857 and November 1858. He sent the following official notice to the *capitanía* of El Cobre on 13 December

1858: "The use of opium among the Asian workers of the Consolidated Mines has caused new misfortunes among them and convinced this Government that someone brings that substance to that town and profits by selling it to Chinese miners." He implored overseers and other employees to increase vigilance at the mines in order to expose the culprit, who was certainly Chinese. One coolie earned enough profit from the sale of opium to buy himself out of his contract. His master released him, apparently to get rid of what had become a nuisance.[115]

Far from being passive recipients of their hopeless situation, coolies also rebelled, individually or collectively, by killing foremen and administrators. In cases of Chinese uprisings, work tools such as hoes and spades became deadly weapons. Like their commentary on the predilection of Chinese for suicide, observers linked Chinese who committed homicide with an innate character trait. Richard Levis viewed attacks by Chinese as an aberration from their passive nature. "The Chinese laborers are of mild and tractable temperament, seem to be contented with their humble duties, and are submissive to the abuse to which they are on some plantations subjected; but when once their revengeful nature is aroused, they mutually combine with each other and have proved dangerous in their rage. I saw yesterday an officer of a plantation whose arm had been severed in an attack, and in another neighborhood a white employer was murdered by them, his skull having been hacked to pieces by their hoes, each one of the infuriated coolies striking a blow at him."[116]

The report generated by the 1874 investigation into the conditions of Chinese in Cuba cites numerous instances of rebellion and attacks, some resulting in homicide. Between 1856 and 1874, 445 Chinese indentured laborers participated in 312 recorded homicides, and 96 percent were convicted.[117] Most of these homicides took place in the western and central districts, especially the sugar-producing core Matanzas. While spontaneous attacks against white overseers predominated, coolies also targeted low-level black and Chinese overseers who withheld wages or administered beatings. Some of the homicides were carried out together with slaves, both African-born and Creole, even if only a temporary alliance. Joseph Dorsey states, "These contract workers killed in the name of liberation, stabilizing self-improvement, or temporary relief. Despite hardships, a strong sense of ethics prevailed; most resorted to homicide only when pushed to the brink of despair."[118]

As they did with suicide and rebellion, groups of coolies used homicide as a strategy to escape the plantation regime. Several Chinese interviewed for the 1874 report declared that life in prison was preferable to the plantation regime. Xie Agou testified, "We stabbed to death the administrator, on account of his cruelty. We, 24 in all, proceeded to the jail and surrendered ourselves. Our master, by an outlay of $680, induced the officials to order 12 of our number to return to the plantation, and on our refusal, an officer of low rank discharged fire-arms, wounding nine and killing two. There are 22 still in jail, and we consider it preferable to the plantation."[119] Joseph Dorsey finds a pattern of coolies accused of homicide testifying that jail conditions were an improvement over the cane fields. A conviction for nontreasonous homicide rarely resulted in a death sentence, but it did terminate the coolie contract. Many Chinese were sentenced to labor in Puerto Rico under minimum security as road builders, machine operators, cooks, gardeners, tobacconists, and farm hands. From 1867 to 1895, of the fifty-five Chinese deaths registered in the cemetery of the Cathedral of San Juan, all but one were coolies from Cuba who had been convicted of a crime.[120]

At times individual grievances culminated in collective attacks on plantations and factories. Eliza McHatton-Ripley describes a Chinese uprising on Desengaño Estate in Matanzas prompted by dissatisfaction with food shortly after their arrival. Eliza and her husband Lamo (nickname for "el amo" or master) encountered difficulty in understanding the complaints, but held firm to their food rations: "A moderate allowance was meted out three times daily, which disappeared with marvelous rapidity, leaving them muttering and discontented." One morning, when McHatton-Ripley was alone on the plantation, her black servant Zell (who had accompanied the family from the U.S. South to Cuba) rushed into the house informing her of disturbances by the Chinese. "The Chinese were in full rebellion: stripped to the middle, their swarthy bodies glistening in the hot sun, they rushed with savage impetuosity up the road, leaped the low stone fence that surrounded the cluster of plantation-buildings, of which the massive dwelling-house formed the center, brandishing their hoes in a most threatening manner, and yelling like demons, as with hastily grasped rocks from the fences they pelted the retreating overseer."[121] After the doors and windows of the house were barred, she ordered her Chinese servant Ramón to give the 900-pound plantation bell a rapid ring, signaling danger to the district captain and neighbors. Zell fired his gun at the Chinese. Order was restored, with interventions from McHatton-Ripley's black and Chinese domestic workers, as well as the Civil Guard.[122]

From the outset, Chinese protested their condition of bondage by fleeing, and Spanish colonial newspapers were filled with notices of runaway Chinese alongside those of runaway slaves. Some masters permitted indentured laborers temporary mobility from the plantation or factory, and Chinese also engaged in the practice of *petit marronage*, leaving the work site for a short period of time.[123] The tradition of Chinese running away accelerated with the onset of the anticolonial armed conflict in Cuba from 1868 to 1878 known as the Ten Years' War. Like slaves and free blacks, Chinese indentured laborers joined these struggles in the eastern part of the island in an attempt to gain freedom or improve their condition, especially when many faced recontracting.

The legal contract itself became a mechanism by which Chinese indentured laborers asserted their rights. According to promoters of the system, rebellion was a product of maltreatment and failure to fulfill contractual obligations. Ramón de la Sagra commended the owner of Candelaria Estate for his experiment with employing only coolie labor. He noted the ability of Chinese in multiple tasks beyond the cane fields and mill yard, such as masonry, carpentry, and locksmithing. The master had not lost a single one of his forty-seven Chinese to suicide or flight.[124] The Chinese in Cuba were well aware of their legal status as free workers. They filed complaints against masters and local authorities for violation of contracts or regulations, such as those forbidding corporal punishment.[125] From their home villages, Chinese peasants were familiar with tenant contracts and a long-standing legal tradition of appeal to local magistrates. In Cuba, however, these appeals were often stifled by the power of planters and the widespread corruption of local officials, who often benefited financially from the illegal exploitation of coolies.

"A Trip with No Return"

Despite efforts to keep Chinese coolies under bondage through recontracting and official corruption, a significant number attained "free" status. In 1872, the Comisión Central de Colonización recorded 58,400 Chinese on the island, of whom 34,408 (59 percent of the total) were still under contract. According to this census, 14,046 Chinese were free, either naturalized or foreign subjects; 7,036 had fled from their masters; and 1,344 runaways were detained in depósitos. Another 1,508 were detained, either pending recontracting, awaiting judicial proceedings, or completing sentences.[126] Through most of the 1870s, the majority of Chinese were serving their original contracts or recontracts. By the time of the census of 1877, the proportion of free Chinese had increased. Although the majority of Chinese were still indentured (25,226), 46 percent (21,890) had fulfilled their contracts.[127]

The majority of free Chinese were too poor to return to their home villages. According to one announcement from 1865, passage to China cost six ounces of gold.[128] In the provincial archive of Santiago de Cuba, Oscar Luis Abdala Pupo has located only one case, among the hundreds who worked in the eastern region of the island, of a Chinese coolie who returned to China. On 6 February 1872, the governor of the Eastern Department and the jurisdiction of Santiago de Cuba granted permission for a forty-one-year-old Chinese named Mariano Segundo, a cook who most likely worked in the mines of El Cobre, to return to China through England. Abdala comments: "For the majority, almost absolutely, the trip to Cuba would be a trip with no return."[129]

Ironically, the first Chinese who returned to China did so by means of coolie ships headed to China for new recruits. Ships bound for Hong Kong competed for Chinese passengers in the pages of *Diario de la Marina*. Their advertisements emphasized convenience and good treatment. After the completion of the U.S. transcontinental railroad in 1869, steamship companies offered new routes: by boat to New York or St. Louis followed by rail to California.[130] However, all told, between 1865 and 1874, only about 2,000 Chinese returned from Cuba to China, though after 1874, more were able to go home. A Chinese study calculated that from 1880 to 1885, 1,885 Chinese returned.[131]

Some indentured laborers escaped Cuba for sugar plantations in the U.S. South, cigar factories in New York, and elsewhere in Latin America and the Caribbean. The first Chinese cigar makers in New York came from workshops in Cuban ports.[132] Chinese fled to other Caribbean islands such as neighboring Hispaniola or Trinidad. One Chinese in Cárdenas, for example, escaped reindenture in Cuba in 1862 and boarded an American ship. He lived in Halifax, Nova Scotia, for four years before making his way to Trinidad, attesting to the significance of shipping routes in the Americas in linking Chinese diasporic communities in the nineteenth century.[133]

The Qing Dynasty and the Cuba Commission Report

Although Western nations widely reported on the rampant abuses in the Cuban system of indentured labor, the coolie trade did not come to an end until 1874. The Qing government's inaction in protecting its overseas subjects stemmed from a traditional conservatism regarding emigration, bureaucratic inefficiency, unwillingness to engage in foreign entanglements, and poor communication from the southeastern provinces. Negative attitudes toward foreign trade and emigration were deeply rooted in Chinese society. Despite their growing wealth, merchants held a low social position in the Confucian hierarchy, based on the belief that trade corrupted traditional values. Furthermore, emigrants who sojourned for long periods of time would be unable to fulfill their filial duties toward parents and ancestors, such as burial of the deceased. Nevertheless, a flourishing trade between coastal China and Southeast Asia sent generations of sojourners overseas.[134]

When the first Manchu Qing ruler ascended the imperial throne in 1644, the dynasty inherited these negative images of Chinese overseas and maintained discriminatory policies toward merchants and traders. As the Manchus attempted to shape their own image into one of Confucian rulers (rather than alien usurpers), commentary on Chinese overseas took on new overtones. For the next several decades, as the Qing solidified territorial control over the Chinese empire, descriptions of the Chinese overseas as "political criminals," "conspirators," and "rebels" emerged in government documents. During the more politically stable eighteenth century, government fears of conspiracy among Chinese overseas had somewhat dissipated. However, Qing rulers increasingly adopted a Confucian and paternalistic outlook and continued to portray Chinese overseas as materialistic "deserters." By not fulfilling their obligations toward family, clan, and country, Chinese overseas forfeited their rights to government protection. When the governor of Fujian memorialized the throne with a report of a 1740 Dutch massacre of Chinese in Java, the Qianlong emperor bluntly responded: "These people are deserters of the celestial empire, they deserted their ancestral tombs and sought benefits overseas, and the court is not interested in them."[135]

Contrasting with this lack of attention from the imperial palace, the abuses of the coolie trade generated fear and outrage among local society in Fujian and Guangdong. Chinese officials in the port of Amoy, the initial center of the coolie trade, generally adopted a policy of noninterference in order to protect their own interests. In 1852, Fujianese rioted over the massive kidnappings, compelling authorities to adopt a more proactive stance. Seeking to prevent another antiforeign movement, the subprefect of Amoy suppressed the riots and prohibited the circulation of antiforeign placards. At the same time, he ordered the police to apprehend coolie brokers.

When recruitment activity shifted to Guangdong after 1852, it continued to generate popular protest toward the methods of kidnapping and deception and the maltreatment of victims in the barracoons. According to one placard, the coolies were "to serve either like baits for fish in catching birds, or as horse and oxen in the labour of reclaiming waste land, or perhaps they are placed in front of armies to be shot down by cannon."[136] As Yen Ching-hwang suggests, these wild speculations about the eventual fate of coolies may have been used as a warning to those who desired to emigrate. In 1858, for example, news spread through Canton that abducted Chinese were to be eaten by Cubans. It was rumored that English Protestant missionaries had spread this story in order to discredit their Catholic competition.[137] Chinese officials began to take notice, executing "crimps" who collaborated with the trade. In 1855, the governor of Guangdong became the first high-ranking official to make a public statement advocating its suppression.[138]

The protection of Chinese abroad became an important component of an emerging Chinese nationalism in the late nineteenth century. As part of the "self-strengthening" programs in business, education, and diplomacy, progressive officials in China sought to selectively adapt elements of Western learning and technology while preserving elements of traditional Chinese culture. Officials involved in foreign affairs such as Li Hongzhang, commissioner of trade of northern ports and governor-general of Zhili, made the status of Chinese overseas a central concern. After China's defeat at the hands of European powers in 1860, they began to link the construction of a strong, modern nation-state with its ability to protect Chinese migrants abroad. Chinese officials in the treaty ports were forced to approach the issue of emigration more realistically, recognizing that many migrants, far from being "deserters," were pushed by poverty and deceived by coolie brokers. Chinese diplomats also learned about the conditions of Chinese migrant communities during their visits to ports in Southeast Asia and the United States.[139]

As demonstrations of resistance to the coolie trade stirred South China port cities, public criticism found its way into the pages of newspapers and political debates in the United States and Britain. Protests against Chinese contract labor stemmed from nativist and anti-Chinese sentiment as well as reports from U.S. consular officials in China. The 1862 Prohibition of Coolie Trade Act banned coolie imports to U.S. territory and American involvement in the coolie traffic.[140] Britain also condemned the coolie trade to Cuba and Peru, even as it safeguarded its own recruitment efforts in Canton and Hong Kong through the 1880s. While Britain professed to protect its contract laborers, Portuguese-controlled Macao did not operate under the same regulations. With U.S. support, Britain continually pressured the Portuguese to shut down recruitment operations in Macao.[141]

A combination of popular protests, proactive Chinese officials, and international pressure led to an official investigation into the abuses of the coolie trade in Cuba and Peru. In 1872, Spanish and Peruvian delegations met in

China to negotiate a new emigration agreement. International ministers representing Russia, Britain, France, Germany, and the United States recommended an official investigation into the treatment of Chinese contract laborers in Cuba. Portugal decreed the end of the coolie trade from Macao in December 1873, effective the following March. The 1874 investigative commission to Cuba consisted of a French official and a British official of the Imperial Maritime Custom Service, both under the authority of Qing functionary Chen Lanbin. As special commissioner of the Chinese Education Mission to the United States, Chen was responsible for the educational and cultural welfare of Chinese abroad. On 18 March 1874, Cuban newspapers announced the arrival of Chen Lanbin in Havana from New Orleans. His delegation launched their investigation into Chinese indentured labor in Cuba over the course of the next six weeks.[142]

The commission took individual depositions, received petitions from groups of Chinese laborers, and investigated conditions on plantations.[143] Of the 2,841 Chinese coolies who gave oral and written testimonies of their experiences in Cuba, only 90 said they had emigrated freely, only 2 attested to humane treatment by their employers, and only 2 said they had signed a second contract freely. The workers describe in detail their recruitment through capture and deception, conditions on plantations, and rampant abuses at the hands of planters, overseers, and corrupt officials. The report condemned traffickers and recruiters in Macao and Cuban and Spanish authorities. Sent under the auspices of the Chinese government, however, the commission was unwilling to examine the social and economic pressures that helped produce emigration from China. Instead, the report criticized the naiveté of the coolies, remarking, "Industrious men who work willingly and well, can support themselves at home, and do not emigrate voluntarily."[144]

In entering their testimony, Chinese coolies drew upon traditional conventions of petitioning the government in China. As Lisa Yun notes, the use of flowery and formal, respectful language was a strategy to establish authority and persuade their superiors to read the petitions. For example, ninety-six Chinese closed their petition with the phrase: "We, as ordinary civilians, are humble and foolish laborers with misfortune. Youths trapped in a land faraway from home; adults wasting their lives in a foreign country."[145] When asked about maltreatment, the common refrain "We bowed our heads in submission" as a response to maltreatment is misleading. As Joseph Dorsey states, the commissioners may have purposely construed Chinese responses as docile, as "too many references to militant behavior" may have agitated an international audience, especially those from the United States healing from the divisions of the end of slavery and the Civil War.[146]

Months later, a similar investigation took place in Peru. In October 1873, the Peruvian government had sent naval captain Aurelio García to negotiate a treaty with China to increase the supply of laborers. García met in the port city Tianjin with Commissioner Li Hongzhang. In the early phase of the negotiations, Li referred to petitions from Peruvian Chinese in 1869 and 1871 alleging abuse. García denied the charge, maintaining that the petitions were generalizations based on false evidence. Li pressed for the repatriation of coolies before signing a new treaty. Eventually, however, to avoid a direct confrontation with foreign powers and a rupture of the existing relationship with Peru, Li reached an agreement with García in June 1874. As part of the treaty, the Peruvian government agreed to permit a Chinese mission to investigate the conditions of Chinese coolies in Peru. When Li sent Yung Wing to Peru in August 1874, the investigative report confirmed abuses there similar to those in Cuba. The investigations in Cuba and Peru armed Li with the necessary evidence to counter Peruvian claims that coolies were given adequate protection. During negotiations for the Sino-Peruvian treaty the following summer, Li advocated delaying ratification and reinforcing the prohibition of the Chinese coolie trade to Peru.[147]

The investigations of the coolie trade to Cuba and Peru marked a turning point in Chinese diplomatic history and signaled a major shift in the Qing government's attitude toward Chinese overseas from one of scorn for "deserters" to sympathy for maltreated coolies. The Zongli Yamen (foreign affairs office) published and circulated the report and supporting evidence. It confirmed the opinion that many Chinese were indeed unwilling emigrants, kidnapped or deceived by coolie brokers, who faced abominable treatment abroad. After making the commission's findings public, the Zongli Yamen was able to force Spain to make concessions, and the Chinese emperor immediately decreed the end of the coolie trade. Shortly after the investigations in Cuba and Peru, high-ranking officials of the coastal provinces and diplomats who had direct contact with Chinese overseas began using different language, reflecting a change in attitude toward Chinese abroad. They employed the terms "Chinese subjects" (*huamin, huaren,* and *zhongguo renmin*) and "Chinese merchants" or "Chinese merchant-gentry" (*huashang* and *huaqiao shenshang*), an indication of the growing complexity of Chinese communities abroad and an understanding of that complexity on the part of Qing officials. These terms filtered up to the Zongli Yamen, gradually finding their place in official records. The official view now held that Chinese subjects abroad, if protected, could remain culturally Chinese and politically loyal. Over the next several decades, the Qing government sought to enlist the wealth and expertise of its subjects overseas.[148]

In November 1877, Spain and China signed a formal treaty that terminated the coolie traffic and limited future recruitment of Chinese laborers. The Qing government subsequently established consulates throughout the Americas, four of them in Cuba, to enforce treaties and protect Chinese interests.[149] This diplomatic achievement in Cuba established a precedent for Chinese consular representation, one that was later used by Qing officials and Manila's Chinese merchant elite in another Spanish colony, the Philippines.[150] As a reflection of its new attitude, in 1893 the Chinese government finally lifted the long-standing official ban on emigration.

Chinese Coolies and African Slaves

Within the context of African slavery and abolition, the significance of Chinese indentured labor to the increase of sugar production in Cuba is undeniable. In 1866, the last year of the slave trade to Cuba, coolie imports reached over 12,000, followed by an all-time high of 14,000 the next year. For the next decade, as coolie imports continued, sugar production maintained a steady increase. Evelyn Hu-DeHart observes that coolies replenished the labor supply, "delaying the crisis that would have set in with the end of the slave trade and making it possible for the plantation economy to continue to prosper."[151] After 1875, when both the slave and coolie trade had ended, sugar production in Cuba declined.

In his analysis of Cuban slave society, Franklin Knight remarks, "Chinese labor in Cuba in the nineteenth century was slavery in every social aspect except the name."[152] The wretched record of maltreatment and official corruption corroborates this point of view. Subsequent scholars have debated to what extent Chinese indentured laborers in Cuba were a continuation of slavery or a step toward free labor.[153]

An examination of the institutions regulating the indentured labor system in Cuba yields insights into how, at least theoretically, it differed from the system of slavery, as well as the ways in which it replicated slavery. The terminology used by Spain regarding Chinese indentured labor suggests immigration and colonization, rather than employment.[154] In contracts and Spanish government documents, Chinese were officially referred to as *colonos asiáticos*, and the contract itself was entitled "Emigración china para Cuba" (Chinese Emigration to Cuba). But, as Juan Pérez de la Riva argues, the term *colono* belied the fact that "the coolie everywhere, and the Chinese especially in Cuba, was none other than a cheap laborer subjected to forced work."[155] Indeed, the language referencing Chinese workers evokes the paternalism and control of slavery. Rather than employers, purchasers of contracts were referred to as *patronos* (patrons or masters), and escaped coolies were referred to as *cimarrones*, the same term for runaway slaves. Employers of coolies discussed buying and selling property rather than hiring laborers or transferring contracts.[156] In 1873, for example, Antonio Gallenga commented that a Cuban contracting a Chinese coolie "bluntly says he is *buying* a Chino. And the poor Chinaman, here the most unhappy of beings, seems indeed to bear the brand of slavery on his dejected brow."[157]

The discrepancy between, on the one hand, the contract and the regulations pertaining to it and, on the other, the actual experiences of laborers on the ground has prompted contemporary observers and modern-day scholars to characterize the system as another form of slavery.[158] Colonial Spanish slave society inscribed contradictory racial identities and legal statuses upon Chinese indentured workers, who were nominally free. Although the terminology, contract, and regulations issued by the Spanish government give the impression that Chinese coolies were legally free immigrants, in practice planters modeled the system on the slave trade and plantation regime. The regulations issued by Spain generally protected the interests of masters, more so than the physical and mental well-being of the laborers. In addition, local authorities responsible for upholding the laws colluded with merchants and planters to attempt to keep coolies in a perpetual state of bondage. Juan Pérez de la Riva concludes that the coolie system was merely a thinly disguised form of slavery intended to prolong slave labor. In particular, the practice of forced recontracting after 1860 perpetuated bondage indefinitely, blurring the distinction between indentured labor and slavery.[159] Arnold Meagher suggests that the nineteenth-century coolie trade to Latin America can be categorized within the expanded definition of slavery adopted by the United Nations in 1956.[160]

Lisa Yun also challenges the supposedly free nature of Chinese coolies. Yun questions liberal assumptions about the nature of the contract, stating that the case of coolie labor in Cuba reveals how "the *contract institution* itself, if taken to its logical extreme, is capable of being one of enslavement." She argues that the contract in fact became a tool by which to enslave Chinese: coolies did not willingly enter into contracts, it was difficult for them to escape recontracting, and they were disempowered when violations occurred. Contracts of dead Chinese were transferred to other coolies, and coolies were continually bought, sold, and circulated in a series of practices that resulted in a system of what Yun calls "mobile slaves."[161]

There were, nonetheless, key differences between slavery and indentured labor. Unlike slavery, indentured labor was not inheritable and in many cases came to termination.[162] The Chinese were in a distinct category from slaves, who were chattel for life. Coolies were legally allowed to, and did, file complaints against their masters and local authorities for violation of contracts or regulations. While recognizing the abuses in the coolie system and the abject material condition of Chinese, scholars such as Manuel Moreno Fraginals, Juan Jiménez Pastrana, and Denise Helly view Chinese contract labor as an essential step in the development of a skilled, free labor force and the development of the working class in Cuba. In this view, even the *existence* of formal legal rights, however much they were abused in practice, could change the structure of labor relations and influence the actions of oppressed individuals. Coolies became aware that their contractual rights were being denied and pushed the limits of the legal system.[163] Additionally, Moreno views Chinese indentured labor as an essential component of the transition from slave to wage labor and capitalist development.[164]

Contracts could also serve as a tool for demanding an improvement of conditions and, eventually, freedom.[165] A closer examination of the process by which Chinese completed their contracts sheds some light on these issues. While the coercion in recontracting has been well documented, the variation in subsequent contracts suggests that "planters were not able to dictate uniform terms, and that, more importantly, the coolies appeared to have had some leverage in negotiating the terms."[166] For example, recontract agreements from 1868 indicate shorter terms, generally six months or one year. Pay ranged from four pesos, two reales monthly to thirteen pesos monthly. In addition to wages, some Chinese were provided with food, clothing, and medical attention. In at least one case, two Chinese who recontracted with the same master were offered different wages (8½ pesos and 12 pesos).[167]

Yet the rise of the indentured labor system did not produce the end of slavery, nor was the coolie system the only half-way house to free labor in Cuba. The increase in coolie imports came just at the time that slaves were gradually moving toward freedom. As the number of slaves on plantations declined during the 1870s, hiring gangs of *libertos* (freed slaves), renting slaves, and experimenting with soldiers, immigrants, and other forms of labor provided planters with some economic flexibility. While in one sense the Chinese occupied an intermediate position in the labor hierarchy, between slave and free, many of the features of the indentured labor system that hinted at free labor practices already existed in the slave regime. Receiving gratuities for additional work on Sundays or at the beginning of the harvest or earning profits from the sale of produce from garden plots (*conucos*), for example, were common practices among the slave population.[168] Evelyn Hu-DeHart concludes that "a lack of agreement on the question of whether they were slave or free, and whether and how they contributed to the transition from a slave mode of production to a capitalist mode, only points up the ambiguity of the coolie situation: indentured labour implanted in the midst of very entrenched slavery."[169] As Cuban sugar interests adapted to the imminent decline of bonded labor by using Chinese indentured labor, they continued to rely on slaves until the last possible moment through final abolition in 1886. Planter adaptations to the system were therefore not equivalent to a repudiation of slavery, which came "not from planters but from the slaves and Chinese indentured laborers themselves, through self-purchase and through flight."[170]

The last vestiges of the coolie system remained into the early 1880s. The Chinese who were unable to leave Cuba continued to populate sugar estates and towns for the remainder of the nineteenth century and into the first decades of the twentieth century. As they settled in Cuban society, the essential questions raised during the coolie period about Chinese character and assimilability and impact on the population continued to surface and remained open to debate, especially as Cuba moved toward independence from Spain.

Here he is, now, a regular thorough going "John Chinaman,"
who, after having served out his term as a Coolie on perhaps some
large sugar estate, has become imbued with the ambitious desire of being a
merchant, and no longer remaining in his hard working way of life as a *"trabajador"*
in the hot sugar fields. Having saved sufficient money from his hard earnings, or,
what is more likely, made his capital by gambling with his more verdant and
less fortunate fellows, he has started in trade, with a bamboo yoke carried
over his shoulders, and pendant from the ends of which hang two
large, round baskets filled with crockery of all kinds.

—Samuel Hazard, *Cuba with Pen and Pencil* (1871)

The place was thoroughly organized and everything went like clockwork.
One reason for our steady work was the number of Chinamen employed on
the place. They were faithful men and never missing from their places.

—Edwin F. Atkins, *Sixty Years in Cuba* (1926)

CHAPTER TWO

Free Laborers

Like Pastor Pelayo, tens of thousands of Chinese who survived indenture and remained on the island during the 1870s and 1880s now had more physical, occupational, and even social mobility. They joined gangs of agricultural laborers, grew vegetables in the countryside, peddled goods, and worked as artisans or at unskilled jobs in town.

After the 1877 treaty between Spain and China, coolies completing their term of service could no longer be forcibly recontracted, and the entry of new Chinese contract labor was prohibited. This change in the official status of the Chinese overlapped with the gradual end of slavery in Cuba. For years slaves had been gaining their freedom through a variety of mechanisms, including self-purchase. The 1870 Moret Law granted liberty to any child born to a slave mother after 1868 and to any slave over the age of sixty. Slaves were freed by the emancipation law of 1880 but obligated to serve their owners under the *patronato*, or apprenticeship system, until final emancipation, scheduled to occur in stages between 1884 and 1888. As in the British Caribbean colonies half a century earlier, the apprenticeship system proved impracticable due to former slave resistance and planter unwillingness to relinquish control. It was terminated early, and Spain decreed final abolition in 1886.[1]

As slavery stood on its last legs and Chinese indentured labor came to an end, major transformations occurred in the Cuban sugar economy. Beginning in the 1870s, the separation of growing and processing sugarcane altered the structure of the industry. New mills increased the amount of juice extracted from cane stalks, and centrifugals improved the appearance and quality of sugar crystals. As the technology of sugar production improved, along with the transportation infrastructure, large mills known as *centrales* emerged. The central mills purchased cut cane from multiple sources, including independent planters who could no longer afford to maintain their own mills and small-scale *colonos* (cane farmers). Heavy investment financed the modernization of plantation methods, the installation of expensive equipment in the mills, and the construction of railroads for transportation of cane. But the demand for field labor remained high. Workers were needed for cutting cane and loading it onto the new railway cars that ran from fields to central mills.[2]

In the mid-1870s, eight mills in Matanzas, the heart of slavery and sugar production, were designated as centrales. The four largest ones (Perla, La Paz, Santa Petrona, and Victoria) were located in Hanábana, a frontier region under development. The owners of almost all of them were relative newcomers. As Laird Bergad states, "Most of the prominent families who had built ingenios [sugar mills], constructed railroads, imported slaves and Chinese, and modernized mills would be vague memories by the early twentieth century." With the decline of Cuban planter families such as the Diagos, Arrietas, Pedrosos, Montalvos, and Aldamas due in part to a failure to adapt to the structural changes, newcomers were confronted with the challenge of producing sugar without slave labor.[3]

While planters continued to rely on African slaves and Chinese coolies for sugar production through the 1860s and 1870s, they turned to Spanish immigrants during the 1880s and 1890s. Over 250,000 nonmilitary Spaniards entered Cuba between 1882 and 1894. After an initial decline during the reorganization process, sugar production in Cuba soared in the early 1890s. The highest levels of Spanish immigration corresponded with the million-ton harvests of 1892 and 1894. The broad-based labor force for sugar expansion in postemancipation Cuba thus consisted of former slaves and former indentured laborers, Spaniards and Canary Islanders, and, to a lesser extent, native-born white Cubans.[4]

TABLE 2 Population of Cuba, Santa Clara Province,
and Cienfuegos District, by Race, 1899

	CUBA	PERCENT	SANTA CLARA	PERCENT	CIENFUEGOS	PERCENT
Native white	910,299	57.9	214,945	60.3	32,209	54.5
Foreign white	142,098	9	29,823	8.4	6,376	10.8
Negro	234,738	14.9	48,524	13.6	7,468	12.6
Mixed	270,805	17.2	58,050	16.3	11,888	20.1
Chinese	14,857	0.9	5,194	1.5	1,187	2
TOTAL	1,572,797		356,536		59,128	

Source: U.S. War Department, *Report on the Census of Cuba 1899*, 194–95, 198–99.

Economic opportunities in Cuba and Peru after indenture, and in Mexico beginning in the 1860s, coupled with increasing anti-Chinese hostility in the U.S. West after the end of the gold rush, led to the influx of thousands of new Chinese immigrants to these regions by the 1870s, including many from California.[5] Some of the new migrants in Cuba were contractors who recruited former coolies for work gangs. By the end of the nineteenth century, Chinese in Cuba worked as domestic servants, shopkeepers, peddlers, cigar makers, charcoal burners, launderers, masons, and carpenters. However, at least initially, most former coolies who remained in Cuba continued working in the sugar industry, only now as free wage laborers. In 1872, the majority of free Chinese worked in agriculture (about 10,600 out of a total of 14,000).[6] By 1899, well after the period of indenture, most Chinese were still employed as day laborers (8,035), followed by domestic servants (2,160) and merchants (1,923).[7]

Cuadrillas, or work gangs, became the most important mechanism by which Chinese made the initial transition from indentured laborer to free agricultural wage earner. Along with new infusions of Spanish immigrant labor, these work gangs were integral to the late-nineteenth-century Cuban sugar boom and played a key role in the colony's gradual transition from slave to free labor.

Among the newly liberated Chinese who dispersed from the cane fields of Havana and Matanzas Provinces, some were attracted to economic activities in the capital, while most migrated to central and eastern Cuba. By the end of the century, 13,676 laborers from Spain and 2,924 from China resided in Santa Clara Province.[8] Evidence from Santa Clara suggests that, in addition to Spanish immigrants, Chinese were integral to sugar production in Cuba in the 1880s and 1890s, especially during times of labor "scarcity." One can

TABLE 3 Selected Occupations by Place of Birth,
Males, Santa Clara Province, 1899

OCCUPATION	TOTAL	CUBA	SPAIN	ASIA
Apprentices	355	349	6	—
Bakers	1,108	843	251	9
Barbers	824	719	70	31
Blacksmiths	563	399	155	—
Carpenters	3,180	2,550	566	29
Clerks and copyists	489	407	64	—
Draymen and hackmen	497	339	146	—
Fishermen	716	505	199	6
Harness makers	344	331	13	—
Hucksters	289	153	53	76
Laborers	94,622	75,374	13,676	2,924
Launderers	172	97	56	17
Lawyers	153	128	19	—
Masons	1,185	992	152	34
Mechanics	1,037	831	167	6
Merchants	8,430	3,628	4,030	631
Operatives, cigar factories	2,460	2,252	105	94
Painters	196	161	29	3
Physicians	186	149	25	1
Policemen and watchmen	1,183	959	215	3
Printers	210	198	11	—
Sailors and boatmen	1,091	601	455	2
Salesmen	2,092	907	1,012	165
Servants	3,497	1,990	570	843
Shoemakers	1,855	1,629	217	7
Tailors	628	530	89	6
Teachers	269	194	69	1

Source: U.S. War Department, *Report on the Census of Cuba 1899*, 504–5.

Note: Although the census did not list any of the 22 Chinese females in Santa
Clara as employed, it listed 11,584 Cuban and foreign females as hucksters, laborers,
laundresses, merchants, operatives of cigar factories, saleswomen, seamstresses,
servants, shoemakers, and teachers; most Cuban women worked as laundresses (3,789),
servants (3,784), laborers (1,568), and seamstresses (1,340). Besides Cuba, Spain, and
Asia, places of birth were classified in the census according to the following categories:
Porto Rico, West Indies, South America, Central America, Mexico, United States, Canada,
Great Britain, Germany, Africa, Australia, and Other Countries.

better understand the significance of Chinese workers for sugar production and the process of their transition from indentured to free through a local study of work gangs in the sugar district surrounding the town of Cienfuegos.

A View from Soledad Estate

Situated on the southern coast of Cuba in Santa Clara Province, Cienfuegos served as a major center of sugar production and export. Numerous estates surrounding the town were connected by roads, railroads, and rivers that transported sugarcane, machinery, food, supplies, and laborers from place to place. Cienfuegos was also linked to Havana by railroad and to U.S. port cities such as New Orleans and New York by steamer.

In 1884, just two years before final abolition, the Boston businessman Edwin F. Atkins finalized the purchase of Soledad Estate in Cienfuegos. Despite some *patrocinados* (apprentices) remaining on the estate, he viewed his business venture as an endeavor in free labor and modern technology. For most of the year, especially the hot summers, Atkins lived in Boston and maintained daily correspondence with his manager in Cuba (J. S. Murray from 1884 to 1894, J. N. S. Williams from 1894 to 1898, and L. F. Hughes after 1898). The letters between Atkins and these administrators comment on the day-to-day operation of the estate and provide an in-depth view into transformations in the sugar industry and living and working conditions for laborers in the world of sugarcane. Soledad Estate came to rely heavily on free Chinese workers.

With the end of slavery, transformations in the Cuban sugar industry disrupted the operations of small-scale planters, who now sold their cane to large centralized mills. The new cane farmers were forced to compete with other colonos and adjust to a drop in socioeconomic status, as they were no longer independent mill owners. Managers encountered difficulties in their contract negotiations with colonos for cane delivery. During his first year as manager of Soledad, J. S. Murray butted heads with Leopoldo Villegas of Josefa Estate. In a letter to Atkins, Murray succinctly captured his view of the root of the problem: "Villegas don't like coming down from a planter to become a colono."[9] Colonos demanded large advances for planting cane and, like smallholders, subordinated the needs of the estate to nurturing their own crops. In May 1884, Atkins responded to Murray's repeated complaints: "I am sorry to hear you are having such trouble with Colonos, they are useful factor on an estate if you can control them but pretty troublesome; it will not do to let them get the upper hand, if they will not come to terms

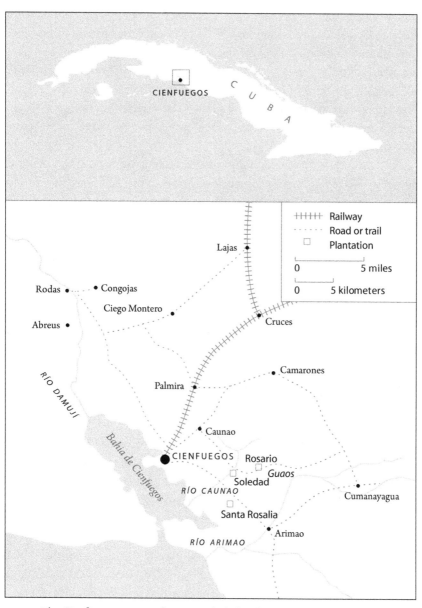

The Cienfuegos region, showing Soledad and neighboring plantations
(Source: Rebecca J. Scott, "Reclaiming Gregoria's Mule: The Meanings of Freedom
in the Arimao and Caunao Valleys, Cienfuegos, Cuba, 1880–1889," *Past and Present*
170 (2001): 181–216, by permission of the Past and Present Society.)

you can keep them short of money and hold them to present contract of $3 per 100 @ [*arroba*, or 25 pounds]."[10] Later, some cane farmers turned their attention to cultivating their own vegetables, which management perceived as a threat to the estate's productivity. Longtime employee Captain P. M. Beal wrote to Atkins in June 1887 that with only two exceptions, the colonos "are doing nothing for the interest of the Estate, while they are weeding and caring for their corn and potatoes, their cane never see a hoe, and is getting in a pretty bad condition."[11]

Compounding the unreliability of cane farmers, labor shortages continually plagued Cuban sugar estates, primarily due to planters' resistance to paying higher wages. Laborers often refused to work under extreme conditions and abandoned the estate after payday, during holidays, and when better wages or opportunities were offered elsewhere. Although planters made informal pacts to hold down wages, competitors occasionally raised pay rates to attract workers. Word of the higher pay quickly spread, compelling other estate owners to follow suit or risk losing their employees. In December 1885, Murray reported: "I was obligded to increase wages of laborers to keep them here as they are paying on some estates—'Parque Alto' one of them—as high as $20. I have agreed to pay $15 and $17 until grinding begins when we will have to pay the same as other estates."[12] By the following year workers seeking better pay had become a familiar pattern, and Murray reported, "As usual just before grinding begins the laborers commence moving round from one estate to an other asking for an increase of wages."[13]

In addition to higher wages on other estates, opportunities to work on railroads and the French construction of the canal in Panama attracted Cuban laborers. Chartered ships docked in the port of Cienfuegos, poised to take workers to the canal zone. In September 1885, Murray wrote to Atkins: "There is an agent in Cienfuegos offering high wages for laborers for Panama Canal and a number of our men have left, I am afraid this will again put up wages and make labor scarce for crop season."[14] Atkins responded with a suggestion to get the editor of a Cienfuegos daily newspaper "to write up an article on the terrible death rate [in Panama] and uncertainty of pay— which is all true, he will be doing a service to his country."[15] On 22 December 1885, at the critical beginning of the grinding season, Murray reported that 900 laborers in Cienfuegos were recruited to the eastern town of Santiago de Cuba and 500 to Panama, and a week later he reported 500 laborers to Santiago de Cuba and 318 to Panama.[16] In July 1889, Murray expressed his hope that although the railroads could pay somewhat more than he could, superior conditions on Soledad would deter laborers from migrating to the railroad industry: "We give them better food than in other places, and I am carefull to keep dry and in good order their quarters for sleeping; good workmen appreciate this more than a dollar or two advance in wages."[17]

Finally, every year as the Christmas and Easter holidays approached, Murray bemoaned the interference of the festivities with the cane grinding schedule: "It would be only loss of time to commence [grinding] between the 25th and 1st as it would be difficult to keep laborers to work. Almost all go off during the Christmas holidays."[18]

When Atkins purchased Soledad in 1884, the bulk of its workforce consisted of former slaves and patrocinados, still bound to their masters until final abolition in 1886. Unwilling to lose the book value of these laborers, management confronted head on the issue of how to control the remaining patrocinados. Murray believed that kinship ties among recently freed slaves would create a more stable, reliable workforce. He wrote to Atkins: "They work better, cost less and are much easier to manage than white men and they all more or less have fathers, mothers, sisters and aunts that attach them to the estate."[19] However, as elsewhere among slave societies in the Americas, former slaves were reluctant to subordinate the rhythm of their lives to the regimen of sugar production.

From the planters' viewpoint, therefore, alternate sources of labor were necessary to keep up with the increased demand for cane cutting and processing. Throughout the years, the owner and managers of Soledad echoed discussions at the national level as they tossed around various proposals for a labor supply, including government soldiers and immigrants from Spain, the Canary Islands, and Italy. Chinese never faded from view. In September 1885, Edwin Atkins implored his manager to contemplate solutions to what many called the "labor question": "Our labor has given, and will continue to give, more trouble than any other thing and calls for a good deal of study, I am of the opinion that we shall have to depend very largely upon Chinamen for field work what do you think? I am also strongly in favor of a moderate number of soldiers for the conductors [conveyer belts] & other batey [mill yard] work."[20]

Based on his experiences the previous year, Murray agreed to recruit Chinese laborers, but pointed out the difficulties of keeping them bound to the estate: "Regarding chinese I think I can get plenty of them . . . but it is very uncertain as chinamen are not fond of staying long in one place."[21] Murray's observation hints at the frequent movement of Chinese from estate to estate and from cane fields to towns. The seasonal nature of sugar production required a highly mobile work force. As a result, management preferred Chinese day laborers, who were mostly bachelors or had families back in China. At the same time, however, unattached men could easily leave the estate when better wages or opportunities were offered elsewhere, even in other Caribbean ports. In such an atmosphere, Chinese contractors assumed even greater importance as recruiters.

Cuadrillas

Given the conflicts with colonos and the erratic labor supply, Chinese continued to be integral to sugar production in late-nineteenth-century Cuba. Now, however, they worked not under contracts of indenture but as free laborers in cuadrillas, or work gangs. Mostly from Guangdong emigrant regions, they were familiar with collective responsibility systems and labor brokers in the recently opened port cities. In Hong Kong and Canton a class of compradors achieved wealth and status by serving as middlemen between Western businessmen and Chinese markets and labor, recruiting "skilled" workers from Guangdong for factories as far away as in Shanghai.[22] While contractors in the Americas likely drew on their knowledge of similar systems in China, the cuadrilla system in Cuba also developed from the experiences of indentured laborers on sugar plantations since 1847.

In 1870, two Chinese, Domingo Ramírez and Antonio Chuffat, recruited and organized the first successful cuadrillas under Chinese management. The existence of free Chinese workers compromised planter control over both coolies and slaves. While work gangs provided economic flexibility for planters, they removed Chinese from under the direct supervision of estate overseers and masters. Before long, planters complained that cuadrillas had become a natural hiding place for coolies fleeing their contracts. One Chinese contractor testified that he was falsely accused of accepting runaways into his gang (although they all possessed cédulas).[23] In 1871, in the midst of the anticolonial rebellion known as the Ten Years' War (1868–78), the Captain General banned cuadrillas, "choosing the necessity of control over economic flexibility." An 1873 editorial in the *Boletín de Colonización* charged that cuadrillas encouraged runaway coolies and "demoralized the workers."[24] Lisa Yun suggests that cuadrillas "constituted competition for the most profitable brokers of Chinese labor on the island—the officials and police themselves."[25] The ban was not lifted until after the end of the war in 1878. By this time, the coolie trade had ended, and cheap labor was in short supply. Several Chinese contractors began operating cuadrillas from 1883 to 1885, and after the abolition of slavery in 1886, these work gangs multiplied.[26]

Chinese quarters on Soledad Estate in Cienfuegos, Cuba, 1884.
(Courtesy of the Massachusetts Historical Society)

Large planters hired cuadrillas for a period of time or a specific task. The contractor, who was often a former coolie, served as a liaison between estate administrators and hundreds of potential workers in the towns and countryside. He negotiated competitive contracts, supervised and disciplined Chinese laborers, obtained tools and supplies, and provided food and lodging.[27]

Soledad Estate relied heavily on a Chinese contractor named Damián Machado. It is unclear from the documentary evidence whether Machado had been an indentured laborer or a more recent arrival from California, Mexico, or China. Generally, newer arrivals retained a Chinese surname, while those who had been baptized on Cuban sugar plantations used the surname of their former master. If not an indentured laborer, it is possible that Machado had been a contractor in the Philippines (another Spanish colony). Machado was proficient enough in Spanish to serve as a cultural broker between his men and management, and he put down roots in the Cienfuegos community, eventually marrying a white Cuban woman and establishing several businesses and a Chinese mutual aid association in town.[28]

Chinese performed a variety of seasonal tasks on Soledad Estate and were perceived to be more efficient, dependable, and flexible than other groups, especially during periods of labor shortages. Most importantly, Chinese cuadrillas provided planters with a somewhat steady labor supply during the grinding season. As on other estates, sugarcane dictated the labor cycle on

Soledad. Machado and his gang cleaned fields and planted new cane in the spring and summer, cleared woodland during the "dead" season, and cut and loaded cane during grinding season, which usually began in December or January and often lasted through May. On sugar estates throughout western and central Cuba, Chinese were also employed in the technical tasks of sugar production, such as the hot and difficult work in the *casa de calderas* (evaporating room). Chinese contractors organized the movement of laborers from one estate to another, and within one estate, from one task to another. On Soledad, Damián Machado was particularly successful at maintaining a steady work force. Throughout the years the estate administrator repeatedly reported that Machado was able to meet his quota of cut cane when the colonos were lacking. In April 1890, for example, Murray wrote to Atkins: "As usual after the holidays it is up hill work to get started to grinding again, Machado is the only one that is delivering his full tarea [piecework] of cane and Piñol [a colono] has only delivered 4000 @s. [*arrobas*, or 100,000 pounds] of cane in 2 days, he says his men have not returned yet."[29] During the grinding season, it was critical to process the cut cane immediately or risk spoilage.

The 1891 Foster-Cánovas reciprocity treaty between the United States and Spain propelled Cuban sugar production. From 632,000 tons in 1890, sugar production in Cuba reached 1 million tons in 1894.[30] Edwin Atkins described the period from 1888 to 1894 as one of intensive growth for Soledad, spurred by the reduced tariff, installation of new machinery, and streamlining of labor. In his memoir *Sixty Years in Cuba*, Atkins described the importance of Chinese workers at Soledad to the estate's efficiency: "They were faithful men and never missing from their places."[31] How did Chinese cuadrillas come to occupy such an important role on Cuban sugar plantations?

Contractors and Estate Managers

The Chinese contractor assumed a key role as liaison between estate administrators and newly mobile Chinese workers. In the competitive environment of sugar production, both managers and contractors employed tactics for maximizing profit. From one season to the next, the bargaining process between J. S. Murray and Damián Machado filled the pages of correspondence from Soledad. In the fall of 1886 Murray and Machado engaged in an extensive period of haggling over the contract for cutting and loading cane. Murray reported the contract proposals on 26 October: "Machado and other contractors insist on prices nearly as high as last year for cutting and loading cane; his basis for calculating is $15 for labor and $8 for feeding total $23 or 77¢ per day."[32] He claimed that Machado made a profit on feeding his men. While Atkins expressed preference for another contractor, Murray seemed to hold out for Machado on the basis of character: "Machado is not as active but I think him more honest."[33] Machado refused to lower his price for cutting and loading cane, but for work in the boiling house he proposed a different kind of arrangement in which he would furnish "all the men we may require he to feed them at $8 per month the estate paying all other expenses." The gang foremen would be under Murray's orders, and Murray would pay the contractor $500 at the end of the crop. Murray reported: "I think I will close with Machado or his partner for the sugar house as theirs is the most reasonable offer I have received. So far I find Machado honest which is to be considered, there is so little of that stock in this Island."[34] When grinding of the 1886–87 crop began on 16 December, Murray had still not closed with a contractor for cutting and loading cane. He wrote to Atkins on 4 January, "Machado will not agree to take less than 70¢ [per day] and we are cutting the cane our selves and so far it is costing us more, as we have not worked regularly, but in future I think it will cost less."[35] For the rest of that month Murray frequently reported slow grinding due to a shortage of laborers. However, on 27 January he wrote, "We now have all the hands required for work . . . and have no trouble getting all the cane we want for grinding." But at the beginning of February fieldworkers were again scarce.[36]

Labor relations on Cuban sugar estates had clearly changed. The process begun during the period of gradual abolition accelerated in the 1880s with the imminent demise of slavery. No longer banned, Chinese contractors now negotiated with managers of more than one estate. In addition to engaging in intensive bargaining with estate managers, Chinese contractors competed with each other. The availability of multiple contractors could work to the estate's advantage. Murray wrote to Atkins: "I put the chinamen for centrifugals to work in boiling house, cleaning and painting as the contractor fears they otherwise will not wait, being able to get work on other estates. Our advantage is that this estate is known to be good pay and give good treatment and I do not anticipate much difficulty in getting labor."[37]

In September 1886, Murray heard that the Chinese contractor on Caledonia had entered into an agreement to cut, haul, and manufacture sugar, giving the estate 28 hogsheads for every 100 produced and depositing $7,000 as security for fulfillment of the contract. Murray expressed awe at the amount of cash the contractor had at his disposal: "The chinaman must have more money than he knows what to do with if this is true."[38] Judging from Murray's reaction, this arrangement was unique. In this case, the Chinese contractor surpassed arrangements made by area colonos by agreeing to process the sugarcane. Furthermore, he risked a large amount of capital as security deposit. The contractor must have been fairly confident in his ability to retain workers and complete the task from beginning to end. By 2 December, just over a week into grinding, Caledonia had produced 80 hogsheads of sugar, shipped to Cienfuegos before being purged.[39]

While not altering the plantation hierarchy, the cuadrilla system provided an opening for some Chinese contractors to achieve a similar economic (if not social) position to that of the colonos. As has been seen, Soledad Estate managers often juxtaposed their commentary on the two groups, viewing the colonos as less reliable than the Chinese. Several Chinese even purchased their own sugar estates in Matanzas and Santa Clara during the colonial period.[40]

Contractors and Laborers

Planters depended on contractors for a supply of field hands and sugarhouse workers, and contractors, in turn, depended on a pool of day laborers. Chinese contractors ensured a relatively steady supply of agricultural workers through a variety of mechanisms. Drawing on experiences from both South China villages and Cuban sugar plantations, contractors and laborers developed a system based on mutual dependency and collective responsibility, one that generally benefited both parties. Laborers could be employed for a greater part of each year by allowing contractors to locate work and transport them from one estate to another. Sucheng Chan demonstrates a similar role of Chinese contractors in California agriculture in the late nineteenth and early twentieth centuries. Chan compares this system in California to the bao jia system of collective responsibility in Chinese villages: "Several employers had noted that the Chinese laborers all seemed to 'share in the contract,' whether they were doing reclamation work or picking fruit."[41] By making each member of the gang responsible for his share of work, all would reap the benefits.

Besides wages, issues concerning food and housing permeated daily conversations and negotiations on the estate.[42] Throughout his years as manager at Soledad, J. S. Murray frequently dealt with worker complaints about the poor quality and lack of variety of food. He attempted to balance economy with the need to satisfy the palate of his laborers. For example, in September 1886, Murray proposed raising hogs for fresh meat and jerky (*tasajo de puerco*). He also wrote, "We are harvesting corn and as we have quite a large crop I suggest you send a small mill, no doubt we could save something on rice by giving the people more corn meal."[43] The contractor's social and economic networks in the town and countryside made it possible to feed (and feed well) large groups of Chinese laborers. Speculating on how the Chinese contractor was able to retain men, Murray declared that "they always feed their men better than the ordinary white contractor does."[44] Damián Machado obtained supplies and provisions from shopkeepers in town, on credit if necessary. Fresh vegetables were typically an important element of southern Chinese cuisine as an accompaniment to rice and pork. In Cuba, hired Chinese cooks moved from estate to estate with the gangs of workers. At least one of the Chinese workers on Soledad was employed in *hortaliza*, or garden produce.[45]

The experiences of Chinese in the U.S. South also testify to the importance of food to Chinese migrants in their new settings on plantations in the Americas. Beginning in the 1860s, escaped coolies from Cuba had begun to make individual contracts with planters or joined gangs of free Chinese workers in Louisiana. Food rations were generally ten pounds of rice and three and a half pounds of pork per week, but Chinese gangs supplemented this base provision. In May 1867, when the editor of *Planter's Banner* encountered a group of former indentured laborers from Cuba who had made their way to Bayou Lafourche plantation in Assumption Parish, he wrote, "They abhor corn bread, and will nearly starve before they will touch it." The Chinese grew vegetables in garden plots, both to add flavor and nutrition to their meals and to sell for extra profit. The report from Louisiana continued, "They cook careless weed, and other weeds for greens, and are fond of potatoes and other vegetables. They hang up an opossum till it is juicy and mellow, and then cook it and stuff it with raisins."[46] On Millaudon plantation, which occupied 1,700 acres in Jefferson Parish, near New Orleans, two or three Chinese cooked and one served tea to laborers in the fields. In order to satisfy his workers, the Chinese headman had charged thirty dollars worth of vegetables to the estate. The owner grudgingly paid the debt, but informed the headman that the agreement for food was limited to meat, rice, and tea. Later the headman requested a garden plot to raise cabbages and pumpkins "not for their own consumption but to sell."[47]

Planters generally preferred contractors who arranged food and lodging for their men, but were wary of their charging the estate for supplies. Allowing contractors to secure provisions meant relinquishing potential profits from the plantation store, a common fixture during slavery and the export boom. Murray wrote to Atkins in August 1885:

> I have repeatedly protested against Machado's buying supplies in Cienfuegos, but he insists he can purchase them cheaper than we sell them to him, he defends his charging $8 per month for food, saying I oblige him to furnish a certain number of men and to do so he is oblidged to keep a reserve and that he seldom gets paid for their food while idle and that he makes but little at $8. There is more or less truth in what he says and I could do without him during the dead season, but will want him during the crop. One of his methods for keeping men is that he feeds them well, undoubtedly better than we do, as chinamen have a happy faculty of economizing where others can't.[48]

Continuing trends from the period of indentured labor, Chinese working in agriculture were usually housed separately from other estate workers, including former slaves. In June 1887, P. M. Beal complained to Atkins about Machado's use of lumber for construction of bunkhouses known as *ranchos*: "We can not well spare any, we shall be short of all kinds of lumber particularly white pine boarding and yellow pine planking."[49]

Cuadrillas, Conflict, and Control

While the cuadrilla system benefited both the contractor and his men, it could also represent a new form of control over laborers. As Sucheng Chan notes about the situation in California, many believed "that all Chinese were inalienably bound to their 'bosses,' who kept them under perpetual bondage."[50]

The contractor, inserting himself as an agent in between his Chinese gang and the estate management, generally paid his men after the task was completed. At Soledad Estate, the manager concluded that the Chinese contractor must be withholding wages in order to retain his gang. Murray wrote to Atkins in October 1885, "On all estates where they have a chinese contractor they have been more successfull in obtaining and keeping laborers than where they employ other systems, probably . . . [the contractors] do not pay them and they can't get away."[51]

By controlling wages, food, opium distribution, and gambling, contractors could keep laborers in long-term debt. On Sundays the Chinese on Soledad could be found relaxing, gardening, or gambling in their huts. When

Edwin Atkins's sister Grace visited the estate in 1892, she wrote to her mother back home: "Sunday is a leisure day for every one. All through the forenoon I heard a voice calling numbers. The Chinamen were spending their Sunday in gambling."[52] Gambling or playing the lottery could provide a short-term diversion from work. In July 1888, Murray wrote, "Labor is still unsteady men going and coming, then some 6 or 8 of our best men drew promissaries of $500 each in the lotery and of course they have all gone off."[53] Earlier that year exaggerated rumors that the Chinese contractor had won a large sum of money in the lottery circulated on Soledad estate. On 7 May 1888, Murray wrote to Atkins: "We are having some excitement over the supposed appearance on the Estate of 9 bandits. They stopped at Machados ranchos last night asking for him, but he was in town. . . . It is reported that Machado drew $10,000 in the Madrid lotery, but in reality only $400. My theory is they were some of Machado's discharged men who had heard of his good luck and wished to participate in it."[54] Contractors also provided opium to their workers. An American cane farmer in Cuba interviewed by U.S. Special Commissioner Robert Porter in 1899 stated that many of the Chinese he employed smoked opium: "we calculate on sixty per cent. only being at work, while forty per cent. are resting in their barracon."[55]

While former indentured laborers now worked under a new kind of regime, they were able to resist contractor abuse by using the legal system or by abandoning work gangs altogether. During the 1880s, the municipal court of Cienfuegos heard numerous cases of workers accusing fellow Chinese in the cuadrilla business of fraud. In 1883 individuals of a cuadrilla on La Pastora Estate accused their Chinese foreman, Pedro Pascual, of swindling them.[56] The same year the Chinese Luciano Valle demanded $115.15 pesos gold from the Chinese Alejandro Acuré (known as Celestino) for his work as foreman of a cuadrilla that Acuré contracted to Vega Vieja Estate. However, a letter from the administrator of Vega Vieja supported the defendant's claim that he never had a cuadrilla on that estate, and the municipal judge declared that Acuré was not obligated to pay. Acuré owned the *fonda* (inn) La Luna in town, attesting to a dual role as contractor and merchant.[57] In addition to this commercial establishment, he earned income from cuadrillas he employed on surrounding sugar estates.

The Chinese contractor was the principal figure behind the numbers and effectiveness of Chinese workers. Yet contractors were not immune to the difficulties of retaining men on sugar estates. On Soledad, Machado's men sometimes left on payday and when work conditions were unfavorable. Toward the end of the grinding season in May 1886, Murray frequently reported that Machado was unable to obtain sufficient workers for cutting and loading cane. He wrote: "Notwithstanding my constant urging and threatning Machado he has not been able to increase his gang in fields, a large number of his men will not work afternoons and what makes it more aggravating is the unusual fine day weather for grinding. I have tried in every way to obtain laborers, as 'Andreita' finished grinding Saturday I sent Machado there and he brought 25 men to Cienfuegos where the half of them deserted him, on his arrival here 9 of his old men went off."[58] Eventually Murray sent all available batey hands to the fields to cut and load cane in the afternoons and charged Machado for their wages.[59]

Even with financial incentives, Chinese refused to work under extreme conditions. In 1889 at the end of the grinding season, Murray, desperate because the Chinese laborers he needed were leaving Soledad before the work was done, "offered all the men a gratuity if they would continue work until all the cane was cut and loaded." With few exceptions, however, "they refused."[60] In the spring of 1890, Machado consistently kept up with his tarea while the colonos were short of hands. But the volatile labor situation changed within a matter of days, and a wage raise proved to be insufficient incentive for Machado's gang. On 26 April 1890, Murray informed Atkins, "We are still making poor tareas although I am employing all the means available to get cane. A number of Machado's men went off yesterday saying the days were too long, yet he offered them an increase of $2 per month. . . . There are plenty of men idle in town from estates that have finished, but they refuse to work saying they want to rest."[61] Five days later he reported that "Machado in the mornings has sometimes as many as 180 men at work and in the eavening only 140." With labor so "demoralized," "we cannot count on any regularity in delivery of cane."[62]

In a seasonal labor system, the "faithful" Chinese workers who Atkins commended were also vulnerable and could be dismissed at a moment's notice. After grinding, the labor needs of the estate changed, and fewer men were needed for cleaning the fields and planting spring cane. In May 1885, Murray reported, "our chinaman has to-day from 60 to 70 men cleaning cane fields, I wish to have this work done as early as possible as it is of greate importance; will reduce force as fast as we can get fields in proper order."[63] In a letter to Murray before the start of grinding in December 1893, Atkins advised, "You must do what you can to reduce labor, more particularly in the field & in the factory good men are worth their wages, but I think some of our last year's chinamen could be spared without loss to us."[64]

The Chinese were attractive to the Soledad management because they were considered less costly than white laborers, in part due to the feeding arrangements. Murray wrote to Atkins, "I hope to still economize in expenses considerably, as soon as possible do away with gang of white laborers, leaving only a few of the oldest and best."[65] However, evidence from Soledad indicates that, while they may have been less expensive to maintain than white workers, the Chinese commanded competitive wages from Cuban employers. The number of days that Chinese worked each month depended on the task and the season. In January 1890, the asiático Tomás worked in the batey for all thirty-one days for a wage of 18 pesos. Chinese under Damián Machado generally worked all days of the month in January, February, March, and April of 1890 in the factory, where wages ranged from 23 pesos for a laborer to 34 for the foreman, with most Chinese receiving 28 or 29. The number of days worked only slowed when grinding itself tapered off in May of that year.[66] Chinese continued to work on Soledad after Cuban independence from Spain in 1898. In February 1899, Machado employed his men in cart driving, manual loading, vegetable produce, road repair, factory work, and in the fields cleaning new cane. Wages for these varied tasks ranged from 16 to 33 pesos, with most at 23.[67] In December 1905, out of the 48 Chinese Soledad employed cleaning the *casa de purga* (purifying house), one was paid a monthly wage of 30 pesos (silver), one 20, and the rest 18. The Chinese employed in this task worked from as few as four days to as many as seventeen.[68]

In California and the U.S. South, while less expensive than white workers, Chinese also commanded competitive wages in agriculture. According to Sucheng Chan, Chinese agricultural laborers in California generally worked for an average of one-third less than white workers. There was a minimum wage below which, however, they would not accept work. Chan concludes that "the Chinese had a firm idea of what was an acceptable wage and saw to it that their countrymen did not violate it."[69] A recruiter of Chinese in California for Louisiana sugar plantations also expressed that, contrary to rumor, the Chinese were not inexpensive labor.[70] As in other regions of the Americas, Chinese agricultural workers were attractive in Cuba more for being reliable and efficient (through recruitment networks) than for being cheap.

Racial Divisions of Labor

Both as indentured and free laborers in Cuba, Chinese were concentrated in the processing sector of the sugar industry, where they developed a reputation for precise and methodical work habits and ability with machinery. The

TABLE 4 Chinese Wages on Soledad Estate, December 1905

NAME	DAYS	WAGE	TOTAL IN SILVER
Felipe Díaz	17	30	16.45
Tomás García	17	20	10.97
Manuel Asan	11	18	6.39
Andres Cantón	13	18	7.55
José Luis	13	18	7.55
Nicolás Rodríguez	14	18	8.13
Domingo Luis	17	18	9.87
Carlos Terry	17	18	9.87
Manuel López	17	18	9.87
Enrique Ajay	17	18	9.87
Santiago Alfonso	14	18	8.13
Julian García	15	18	8.71
Francisco Sixto	16	18	9.29
José Atay	17	18	9.87
Manuel Silva	17	18	9.87
Atilano Lan	15	18	8.71
Esteban Marquete	11.5	18	6.68
Manuel García	16	18	9.29
Adolfo Achón	8	18	4.65
Bonifacio Montaña	14	18	8.13
Ygnacio Alfonso	13	18	7.55
Alejandro Achón	10	18	5.81
Pedro Sigüanea	14	18	8.13
Laureano Martínez	15	18	8.71
Juan Moliner	14	18	8.13
José Acosta	12	18	6.97
Tomás Cárdenas	13	18	7.55
Rufino Pablo	11	18	6.39
Elias Moré	8	18	4.65
Lorenzo Achón	11	18	6.39
Arcadio Truffin	9	18	5.23
José Cantón	10	18	5.81
José Zulueta	11	18	6.39
Blas Aman	6	18	3.48
Manuel Oña	10	18	5.81
Pedro Luis	9	18	5.23
Marcelino Martínez	7	18	5.52
Abelardo Achón	8	18	4.65
Pablo Primero	8	18	4.65
Domingo Niqueta	7	18	4.06
José García	8	18	4.65
Francisco Rodríguez	7	18	4.06
Agustín Casanova	6	18	3.48
Matias Loraine	6	18	3.48

TABLE 4 (Continued)

NAME	DAYS	WAGE	TOTAL IN SILVER
Francisco Sarría	4	18	2.32
Lucas Rodríguez	5	18	2.90
Gabino Cotera	4	18	2.32
Francisco Martínez	4	18	2.32

Source: "Chinos en Limpa. Casa Purga," December 1905, Libro 704, Libros del Central Soledad, ICEA, ANC.

use of coolies for mechanized jobs correlated with the development of positive characterizations of them as able workers. Ramón de la Sagra described double columns of Chinese operating machinery in the evaporating room of a large estate "with the mathematical regularity of a pendulum."[71] Planters and observers viewed Chinese as physically weaker, but possessing superior skill. However, as Rebecca Scott points out, many coolies performed the same tasks as slaves in the fields.[72]

The demise of slavery and influx of immigrant laborers in the late nineteenth century supplied new racial meanings to occupational roles on plantations throughout the Americas. In the postindenture period, tasks continued to be racially segmented on Cuban sugar estates, with blacks and mulattos concentrated in field labor and Spanish and Chinese in the sugar house. The introduction of new technology and equipment, foreign investors, and large numbers of Spanish immigrants (categorized as white) added a new dimension to these dynamics. During Soledad's first grinding season, Edwin Atkins advised his estate manager on the use of labor, suggesting that the most skilled jobs need not go to Cubans: "[We] have all the world to draw skilled labor from; while you will be dependent upon Cuban labor for field work it is not so to any great extent regarding factory and mill hands. I would not put any machinery how ever simple in charge of an estate negro, but would suggest Chinamen for sugar house, . . . negroes as fire men in boiler house, and some white man as machinist and second engineer."[73] Murray, writing from the estate, responded with a critique of even the skilled American and European white men who came to Cuba to work with new machinery: "My very long experience in this country has made me mistrustfull and it appears as if the way of doing work here is contagious and that the best men degenerate"—adding, perhaps in jest, "of course I include myself."[74]

By 1899, Soledad employed 121 Chinese, representing 10 percent of the total work force of 1,183 men. The remainder of the employees consisted of

TABLE 5 Racial Composition of Labor Force on Soledad Estate, 1899

SOLEDAD	SPANIARDS	BLACKS	CHINESE	NATIVE WHITES	TOTAL
Factory	215	10	48	37	310
Railroad	34	—	—	4	38
Belmonte	71	88	69	43	271
Rosario	27	35	1	22	85
Guabairo	17	231	3	71	322
Josefa	12	98	—	17	127
Martínez	—	6	—	24	30
TOTAL	376	468	121	218	1,183
PERCENT	32	40	10	18	100

Source: Edwin F. Atkins to General John C. Bates, 29 January 1899, Edwin F. Atkins Papers, Atkins Family Papers, Massachusetts Historical Society, Boston.

Note: Belmonte, Rosario, Guabairo, Josefa, and Martínez refer to *colonias* that supplied Soledad with sugar cane. Josefa and Rosario had earlier possessed their own mills.

468 blacks (40 percent), 376 Spaniards (32 percent), and 218 Cuban-born whites (18 percent). Spaniards were clearly favored for the more technical work, with 215 in the sugar mill and 34 on the railroad. Blacks, on the other hand, were concentrated in fieldwork on the various *colonias*. In the factory, Spaniards represented 70 percent of the work force, Chinese 15 percent, native whites 12 percent, and blacks only 3 percent.[75] Continuing trends from the coolie period, the Chinese worked in the cane fields, but were preferred over blacks for the more technical positions in the sugarhouse. However, whites were chosen for supervisor positions and preferred over both blacks and Chinese for those positions deemed to require advanced technical skill.

Managers' continually shifting and contradictory perceptions of character and ability according to race became a guiding factor in their allocation of tasks. In his daily correspondence Murray repeatedly described the Chinese as sharp and able workers. In October 1885, he wrote: "I yesterday engaged a crew of chinamen for boiling houses and centrifugals. The head man appears to be very inteligent if no good we can get others as I keep at work here all the inteligent looking chinamen especially those who say they have worked on centrifugals."[76] Just a few years later, no group completely satisfied Murray's quest for "good character" on Soledad. In June 1888, he bemoaned, "It is a shame and a greate misfortune that in this Island we are obligded to mistrust every one and that they have so little respect for truth and honesty that the two words would hardly be missed out of the spanish language."[77] Chinese workers were portrayed as physically weaker than blacks, Spanish immigrants, or native whites. Referring to conditions in the boiling house, Murray wrote, "Last Sunday several chinamen took sick overcome by the heat in pans, yet they were twice filled with cold water and the men entered them 15 hours after the apparatus was stopped. They only worked 5 hours refusing to go back into pans. I will see if we can get white men for this work next Sunday."[78] Tellingly, Murray had previously written that many whites were sick from the "excessive heat" and that others had left.[79]

Both during the period of indenture and afterward, the racial division of labor could exacerbate tensions in the cane fields or sugarhouse. Murray perceived Damián Machado and the Chinese in general to be honest and intelligent and thus suitable for work in the sugarhouse. At the same time, they had not completely earned the manager's trust. In November 1884, Murray wrote, "I was thinking if it would not be best to educate two or more of the most inteligent spaniards for defecators and centrifugals, as chinamen are in general very tricky, if they are more inteligent, I have been talking it over with Rigney [mechanic] and he is of my oppinion and will employ spaniards at 'Parque Alto.'"[80] Atkins concurred: "Your idea of putting two intelligent Spaniards in sugar house is well if you can find reliable men, Chinamen are as a rule excellent for such work if under a careful sugar master."[81] Managers preferred white men for supervisory positions. In 1894, Atkins wrote to his new manager J. N. S. Williams, "I think your suggestion in regard to putting on two white men (I suppose you mean one for each watch) for the filter press gang is a good one, provided it does not upset all the Chinese labor in the house."[82]

In 1899, when Special Commissioner Robert Porter prepared a report on the condition of labor in Cuba, his field notes from planters and overseers confirm a racially segregated labor force. An American who operated a prosperous cane farm in Cuba described the classifications of labor, from Cuban blacks to Chinese to Canary Islanders, with all of the associated stereotypes and contradictions: "During the crop time we employed from one hundred and fifty to two hundred Chinamen; of the balance of the labourers, probably there were more negroes than Spanish, with the white Cubans in a distinct minority. The Chinamen we have here now make very steady workmen, but they are weak, and not able to do as much work per day as either a negro or a Spaniard can do in the field."[83] The American believed black Cuban workers to be the most capable, superior to the Chinese in strength and productivity, but bemoaned their scarcity on the island shortly after emancipation. He continued with his views on importing immigrant laborers from elsewhere:

The best workmen we have, if we can get enough of them, are the negroes. One negro in cutting cane, can do as much as two of any other class; but I do not think this country is adapted for the American negro, from what I have heard of him, as he would have to put up with hardships here, and as a style of eating and living which, I imagine, is not as good as he has in the southern part of the United States. The immigration of Chinese is prohibited, although a few manage to get in at a time. I do not believe the Jamaica negro would make a good workman; for, from what I have heard of him, he is very lazy, and would not be at all a desirable laborer. Thus our only hope for labour is to retain here the Canary Islanders, because they are harder working and can stand the climate better than the others. They are men who can save money here, and that in itself is proof that they must be steady workmen, because they earn so little. Galicians are also good workers, but so far as I know of the men working here, the Canary Islanders are the best. The white men are mainly employed as stevedores in the batey, though they are also good labourers in the field.[84]

The American's impressions of Jamaican workers as lazy and undesirable came from the experiences of British government officials and planters, who had been importing Asian indentured laborers for its Caribbean colonies since final emancipation in 1838. Chinese were considered desirable, but by 1899, many of the former Chinese coolies were aging, and new Chinese labor immigration was restricted by the occupying U.S. forces.[85]

The racial division of labor on Cuban sugar estates demonstrates how skill was socially constructed. Even back in China, workers from a particular region who entered guilds in Shanghai became identified with certain types of skilled labor.[86] From the perspective of the estate administrator, the "honest" and "intelligent" Chinese were preferred over blacks for the technical aspects of sugar production. Such a definition of skilled labor was slippery; thus the Chinese, who were also described as "weak" and "tricky," were not preferable to immigrant whites. However, one must keep in mind that Spanish immigrants were attractive to planters foremost because they were considered capable of serving the needs of the estate rather than some innate character trait. Echoing the same stereotypes used to describe Chinese workers, Cuban planters in Matanzas sought "uneducated peasants with a history of docility and stoicism" from the interior of the Spanish province of Galicia.[87]

Farmers and Peddlers

Throughout the Americas, Chinese agricultural laborers moved into truck gardening and itinerant peddling. Chinese peddlers carrying produce in baskets on a bamboo pole or in a cart became a familiar sight. Typically Chinese leased land for farming and hauled their produce to local markets. Duvon Corbitt notes, "The production and sale of vegetables passed almost completely into their hands, where it long remained."[88] In addition to fruits and vegetables, Chinese hawked meat, garments, dry goods, and china.[89]

The growing of vegetables and peddling of wares were tasks that could be performed on and around Cuban sugar estates, especially on days off or during the dead season. Like labor contracting, truck gardening required comparatively little capital—tools, access to small plots of land, and knowledge of growing vegetables that are harvested at different times of year. Chinese obtained this expertise both from their experiences in rural Guangdong and with garden plots on sugar plantations, where they grew vegetables both for their own meals and to sell. Sucheng Chan aptly calls the vegetables produced by truck farmers in California "green gold." She notes that "vegetables mature in only a few months, so even persons who stay in a locality for only a short time may engage in truck gardening."[90] Other types of businesses in town such as shops, restaurants, pharmacies, and inns required greater amounts of capital for rent, products, and employees.

Throughout the diaspora, Asians were credited with introducing fresh vegetables to local diets and turning wasteland into productive plots. The 1907 Cuban census comments that before the arrival of the Chinese it was difficult for even the wealthy to obtain vegetables for consumption.[91] That year the Australian Chinese market gardener Ah Louy decided to return "home" to China after twenty-five years in his Victorian town. In recognition of his contributions, the local Australian population held two farewell parties in his honor at the town hall and presented him with a gold watch.[92] Fantastic descriptions of Asian-grown vegetables circulated into the twentieth century. In the 1950s, a writer commented on the market gardens of San Francisco: "The ant-like labor of the Chinese has transformed the sterile sand into the most fertile black earth. . . . The fruits and vegetables, raspberries and strawberries under the care of the Chinese gardeners grow to a fabulous size. I have seen strawberries as large as small pears and heads of cabbage four times the size of European heads, and pumpkins the size of our wash tubs."[93]

As blacks and Chinese in Cuba moved off of the estates and settled on nearby lands, small communities took root. In the Cienfuegos region, an area known as "puente de los chinos" developed across from the community of Paisito, populated by descendants of slaves. Former Chinese indentured workers also settled there to plant vegetables along a creek that feeds the Caunao River.[94] Throughout the countryside, Chinese cultivated parcels of low-lying land close to streams or canals for irrigation.[95] Among the Chinese workers at Soledad, at least one was exclusively engaged in garden produce, an activity that meshed with peddling. Selling vegetables or other wares could also lead to the establishment of shops. In 1931, a Hawaiian-born Chinese described a progression in the hawking business: "The peddler gets a little money and buys a box of fruit, some peanuts, and then he carries them around selling them. When he has been at it a while, and has saved some money, he gets a cart and increases his stock. Eventually he may set up a small shop."[96] Chinese who deserted their work on estates in Louisiana also became peddlers (and in the process carried news to communities where other Chinese had settled).[97]

Contractors and Social Mobility

Being a labor contractor was a path to social advancement for Chinese in late-nineteenth-century Cuba. Some former indentured laborers were able to move up the "agricultural ladder" from day laborer into truck gardening or leading a gang of workers. Contractors required little capital to begin an enterprise, since they typically paid their laborers' salaries only after being paid by employers. Necessary skills included knowledge of Spanish, familiarity with local conditions, networks with merchants in town to acquire provisions and supplies (often on credit), and expertise in negotiating with estate administrators.

In the late nineteenth and early twentieth centuries, most Chinese in the Cienfuegos region lived in smaller neighborhoods around sugar estates, as opposed to in town. By the time of the 1907 electoral census, 64 asiáticos eligible to vote lived in rural Guaos (the neighborhood that incorporated Soledad Estate), out of a total of 611 of all races. The Chinese were overwhelmingly agricultural laborers, several of whom had worked under the contractor Damián Machado at Soledad. In contrast, the list for residents of the center of town named only nineteen asiáticos whose occupations included merchant, cook, servant, police, night watchman, seaman, farmer, agricultural laborer, day laborer, and cart driver.[98]

Chinese agricultural workers frequently moved between rural and urban areas. Migration from sugar estates to town was daily, weekly, and seasonal.

As demonstrated by Machado's excursions from the Chinese quarters on Soledad, the roles of agricultural labor contractor and small merchant could blend. Machado's network extended to neighboring estates, where he exchanged news with other contractors and negotiated with managers, and to the streets of Cienfuegos, where he purchased supplies and rounded up men. With his base on one sugar estate, Machado maintained a family and invested in other enterprises in town. In 1890, he established a commercial banking house patronized by Chinese "of social standing" and constructed a *casino asiático*, or Chinese association, and in 1898, he opened a store of Asian products.[99] Machado further profited as a moneylender to both Chinese and non-Chinese.[100] When he died in 1902, Machado left behind seven urban properties (three in Cienfuegos and four in Rodas) and a horse. He had diversified his business interests between his cuadrilla on Soledad, his properties, and his moneylending activities. He also held shares in two enterprises in Cienfuegos, the Jagua line of Boullón and Company Steamships and the Electric Light Company.[101]

By the 1880s social relations on Cuban sugar estates had become more fluid, as the case of Pastor Pelayo reveals. Pelayo's time on Rosario Estate, adjacent to Soledad, brought him into contact with the domestic slave Wenceslaa Sarría. Under the patronato system, Wenceslaa and two brothers were freed by the emancipation law of 1880 but obligated to enter into work arrangements with masters until their final emancipation in 1886. With Chinese contractor Pastor Pelayo's assistance, they were released several years earlier. In addition to his Chinese cuadrilla, Pelayo maintained a gang of black workers, and in order to avoid conflict, he placed his wife's two brothers at the head.[102] For Pastor Pelayo, cross-racial alliances, as much as Chinese networks, informed his postindenture social mobility.

Cuadrillas in Transnational Context

Cuadrillas were an integral component to the transition of Chinese from indentured to free wage laborers in nineteenth-century Cuba. No longer indentured, Chinese agricultural laborers engaged in a range of actions to resist unfair labor practices and enhance their quality of life. They earned competitive wages and left the estate when they judged working conditions to be too unfavorable. The Chinese contractor faced competition from other contractors and negotiated with management for competitive prices. Cuadrillas even advertised their services in local newspapers.[103]

Chinese cuadrillas in Cuba were similar to the African and Indian independent task gangs that developed after emancipation in British Guiana in 1834. Walter Rodney describes these laborers as follows: "They moved from estate to estate in the search for better rates; they haggled over the definition of given tasks; and they sought to use the state of the weather or the necessity of the planters to extract some advantage. Above all, village labor aimed at subordinating the requirements of the estate to the rhythms of village life. Their own garden plots, their minor subsistence endeavors and their estimate of necessary relaxation came before the time and motion of the plantation."[104] The Chinese *jornaleros* (day laborers) who worked in gangs formed a changing, mobile workforce that frequently moved between rural and urban spaces in Cuba. The men Damián Machado rounded up in town were not unlike today's day laborers who gather on street corners, empty lots, busy intersections, and home improvement stores. Through a survey of Los Angeles day laborers, mostly unauthorized Latino immigrants, Abel Valenzuela challenges definitions of entrepreneurship that emphasize factors such as firm size and location, innovation, proprietorship, and capital start-up, pointing out that "marginal" workers such as day laborers are also a type of entrepreneur.[105] Without access to the voice of Chinese workers in late-nineteenth-century Cuba, it is impossible to determine how they chose whether or not to work on a particular estate during a particular day, week, or month. But from the Soledad Estate correspondence a portrait emerges of these workers pursuing economic strategies they considered advantageous and pursuing a quality of life unknown during the indentured period. They negotiated wages, conditions, and length of work with the gang leader; the gang leader, in turn, negotiated with estate management.

The postindenture experiences of Chinese, in particular patterns of occupational mobility, differed throughout plantation societies in the Americas. The fact that slavery ended in the British West Indies much earlier than in Cuba accounts in part for differences in Chinese settlement by the late nineteenth century. Beginning in the 1870s, forty years after the end of slavery, Chinese in Trinidad had gravitated from plantations into small farmer and trader positions, and by the late 1880s they had become "an overwhelmingly small-trader community."[106] According to the 1891 census, 60 percent of the 1,006 Chinese in Trinidad were small traders, including both shopkeepers and clerks. The forty-five or so Chinese involved in agriculture were mostly small farmers, and only seven resided on sugar estates.[107] During roughly the same period in Cuba, by contrast, most Chinese were still classified as jornaleros.[108]

On the surface, the structure of the contract labor system in rural Louisiana was more reminiscent of Chinese indenture than the free cuadrillas in Cuba. Beginning in 1867, Chinese from Cuba who were recruited as laborers for Louisiana sugar plantations initially signed contracts directly with planters for a period of eighteen months. They worked under Creole (rather than Chinese) headmen who served as interpreters.[109] However, despite the existence of a contract with planters and a non-Chinese headman, the abuses of the indentured labor system in Cuba were not replicated in Louisiana. The Chinese had learned harsh lessons from their experiences in Cuba, and they refused to endure the same treatment once having fled Cuban sugar estates for other regions. The eighteen-month (as opposed to eight-year) contract in Louisiana was indicative of the more flexible nature of contract labor agreements.

Scholarship on international migration tends to demarcate labor immigrants from entrepreneurial immigrants.[110] For the Chinese overseas in particular, Wang Gungwu has identified four patterns of Chinese migration: trader (huashang), coolie (huagong), sojourner (huaqiao), and descendant or remigrant (huayi). Wang states that in general the coolie pattern of migration was transitional because a large proportion of contract laborers returned to China at the end of their contract and because it was relatively quickly put to an end.[111] In the case of the nineteenth-century coolie trade to Cuba and Peru, however, only a small number were able to return to their home villages. For those who remained in Cuba, their coolie status continued to shape their adaptation and integration into society. For some Chinese, the transition from agricultural laborer to entrepreneur began not long after fulfilling their contract of indenture. The first stage of the transition often took the form of growing fruits and vegetables for sale in towns or becoming a contractor of Chinese workers. As ex-coolies earned wages and moved from estate to estate and to and from the countryside, they participated in the social and cultural life of the towns and helped to build the foundations for Chinese communities in Cuba.

In Sagua la Grande they had their own clubs. They gathered there
to speak their languages and read newspapers from China out loud. They
probably did it to be annoying, but since nobody could understand them,
they kept right on with their reading as if nothing else mattered.

—Esteban Montejo, *Biography of a Runaway Slave*

Lucrecia kept her money in an account at the
Chinese bank on Calle Zanja. She'd opened the account after
Chen Pan had gone off to deliver machetes to Commander Sian. Little
by little, she deposited her profits there. A year after Chen Pan returned
from the war, Lucrecia gave him the seven hundred pesos she'd saved to
buy her freedom. He took the money. What choice did he have? He knew
she couldn't have loved him otherwise. But instead of leaving, Lucrecia
told Chen Pan that if it pleased him, she preferred to stay.

—Cristina García, *Monkey Hunting*

CHAPTER THREE

Families and Communities

Local histories in Cuba tend to focus on the most prominent Chinese, recognized for their service in the wars for independence (1868–98) and transnational businesses. According to a history of the sugar town of Placetas,
for example, the best-known Chinese in the region by the 1880s were contractors, merchants, and owners of fondas, or small restaurants and inns—
all founders of the first Chinese association there in July 1887.[1] Similarly,
while sympathizing with the plight of coolies, Antonio Chuffat Latour's 1927
community history *Apunte histórico de los chinos en Cuba* focuses primarily
on transnational Chinese merchants, in particular those who came from
China in the late nineteenth century with capital and Qing diplomatic titles.[2]
Scholarship has generally followed this trend, emphasizing a narrative of
Chinese coolies who died, fled, or blended into the Afro-Cuban population
after the period of indenture.

Alongside transnational merchants and diplomats, however, were thousands of former coolies who, like Pastor Pelayo, continued to work on sugar
plantations or as employees in Chinese-owned businesses. Far from disap-

pearing from view after indenture, they were integral to the early formation of Chinese Cuban family and community life. By the 1880s slaves in the
final years of emancipation and former indentured laborers followed similar
paths, as both sought a livelihood and increased social status through informal and formal means. The Chinese who survived their contracts and remained in Cuba settled into local society by marrying, having children, purchasing property, and engaging in business, often alongside former slaves.
The traces they left behind in notarial, judicial, merchant, and association
records indicate an accelerated engagement with the legal and governmental
system for the purpose of making claims to status, identity, and belonging
in Cuban society.

Former coolies, now wage laborers and small-scale traders, laid the foundations for the development of Chinese communities throughout Cuba,
characterized by small shops, eateries, inns, and ethnic associations. As early
as 1858, Chinese entrepreneurs established the beginnings of Havana's Barrio
Chino, or Chinatown. Luis Pérez (Chung Leng) opened a café on the corner of Zanja and Rayo Streets, Abraham Scull (Lan Si Ye) a fruit and fried
food stand on Zanja, and Pedro Pla Tan (Chi Pan) a grocery on Calzada del
Monte.[3] Other Chinese businesses followed on the main artery Zanja, near
the railroad.[4]

The Chinese gradually established themselves on the outskirts of the colonial core known as Old Havana, north of the black working-class neighborhood Jesús María and south of an emerging white residential zone. Proximity
to frontier land and water as well as a large central market proved conducive
to truck farming. Selling goods and lending services "in a zone of contact
between the black and white neighborhoods," the Chinese occupied a role
common throughout the Americas.[5]

By the 1870s, an influx of Cantonese merchants and craftsmen from California and China joined the emerging Chinese communities in response to
economic opportunities. These new migrants, many with capital and transnational connections, altered the social and class structure of the existing
Chinese communities. They established institutions typically associated with
Chinatowns: transnational businesses, banks, theaters, ethnic associations,
and newspapers.[6]

Because most coolies had labored on sugar estates, small Chinese communities also began to develop throughout the provinces. As in Havana,
Chinese settled just beyond town centers, near central markets and railroads. One of the first Chinese zones developed in Regla, the port where
African slaves and Chinese coolies had initially disembarked. By 1881 the

Regla census counted 225 Chinese, not including day laborers from surrounding areas.[7] Other towns known for long-standing Chinese populations were Sagua la Grande on the northern coast of central Cuba and Santiago de Cuba in the east. The runaway slave Esteban Montejo recalled, "Their stores sold great numbers of strange things. They sold paper dolls for children, perfumes, and fabrics. The whole of Tacón Street in Sagua la Grande was Chinese. They also had tailor shops, candy shops, and opium dens there."[8]

In the sugar hinterland, Chinese initially settled in small rural towns rather than provincial capitals. In Santa Clara Province, for example, the nucleus of emerging Chinese community life formed in towns such as Cruces, Lajas, Rodas, and Abreus that bordered sugar estates. In the provincial capital of Cienfuegos, the first Chinese establishments were located around the central plaza, near the docks (on Santa Clara Street, intersected by Paseo de Arango, Casales, and Velasco). The more prominent Chinese import firms were situated on the main commercial artery of San Fernando Street, alongside Spanish-owned businesses.

Overlapping Diasporas of Slavery and Freedom

During the decades that spanned the wars for independence, the U.S. occupation in 1899, and the establishment of the Cuban republic in 1902, recently freed slaves settled around plantations, purchasing and selling property, formally marrying and recognizing children, voting, and establishing themselves as Cuban citizens.[9] Chinese no longer under contract were doing the same, at times in conjunction with former slaves.

The new kind of access to the legal system that former slaves and indentured laborers experienced beginning in the 1880s is reflected in an increase in notarized transactions in which they are subjects (*otorgantes*), rather than objects, or property, being sold or transferred.[10] For example, on 3 April 1883, a group of individuals who predominantly worked in agriculture came before a notary in Cienfuegos formally to lend power of representation to two legal agents (*procuradores*). The membership of the group provides a sample of the kind of multiracial, multiethnic society that had formed in the countryside of Cuba. Among them were four Spaniards, two Chinese, and three black women. The two single Chinese males who resided in Santa Clara Province were a thirty-eight-year-old carpenter, Antonio Farray, and a forty-year-old farmer, Antonio Sardiña. All except the women were given an honorific title "Don," in this period usually accorded to those who could claim whiteness.[11]

Power of attorney (*poder para pleitos*) granted the agents, "representing the people, rights, and actions of those present," the ability to "assist and defend them in their cases, causes, and business transactions both civil and criminal." Specifically, it enabled individuals, as legal actors, to request subpoenas, certifications, recognition of legitimate children, deposits, evictions, pensions, seizures of goods, and the sale or auction of property. Increasingly, native Cubans, former slaves, former Chinese indentured laborers, and European immigrants entered into the official record activities such as marriage, the recognition of a child, property purchases and sales, and pension requests for service in the wars for independence. For marginalized individuals, like some of those who came before the notary on that February day in 1883, the process of seeking official documentation signified a shift in their social status.

Despite the new legal identities former slaves and coolies possessed, authorities continued to inscribe their histories of bondage into the official record. Michael Zeuske notes that before 1880 it was standard practice for a slave's given name to be preceded by the color term *moreno/a* (black) or *pardo/a* (brown) and followed by a "cultural, ethnic, or corporal marker" such as "*criollo/a* (creole), *congo/a*, *lucumí*, or *delgado* (thin)."[12] Former slaves were often described in official documents as *moreno/a libre* (free black) or *pardo/a libre* (free brown). Similarly, Chinese no longer under indenture were described as *asiático libre* (free Asian). A notarial document from February 1880, for example, granted power of attorney from the free Asian Juan Galve to a solicitor. Juan Galve was described as a forty-year-old single native of Canton who works in the countryside and resides on Santa Clara Street in Cienfuegos. His cédula of personal identification had been issued on 20 January 1880.[13] The additional descriptor *de contrata* (contracted) was sometimes applied to ex-coolies who after 1874 negotiated the terms for their labor on an individual basis. The forty-five-year-old married "asiático libre de contrata" Antonio Rubio recorded the sale of a house with a notary in 1880.[14]

The cédula continued to be a coveted document in Cuban society immediately after the end of the coolie trade and during the period of gradual abolition of slavery. This card of identity and legal status indicated whether a slave had been emancipated or a Chinese indentured laborer had completed his contract, and thus determined an individual's physical mobility and ability to engage in transactions. Official corruption and illegal business transactions sprang up around these documents, at times reminiscent of the falsification of "paper identities" for Chinese entering the United States after the passage of the 1882 Exclusion Act. In April 1883, for example, the court of Sagua la Grande summoned the asiático Saturino Campos three consecutive times in the criminal case against the asiático "Malvino Baltazar (á) Bacalao" for *portación* or use of an identity card issued for another individual.[15]

In the 1880s, notaries and public officials continued to employ racial descriptors such as *moreno* and *pardo* for former slaves, but after final abolition in 1886, the juridical marker *libre* was no longer meaningful. According to Zeuske, during the phase of gradual abolition from 1880 to 1886 new "hidden markers" began to appear in official documents: *sin segundo apellido, sin más apellido*, and *sin otro apellido*, abbreviated *s.o.a.* ("without a second surname" or "without another surname"). Notaries seemed to add these initials after the names of subjects of lower social status and/or a nonwhite racial category.[16] By contrast, when dealing with Americans or Europeans of higher social status, notaries explicitly stated that these foreigners chose not to follow the custom of using a second surname.[17]

In colonial Spanish society, children were considered "legitimate" if they were born to two married parents or subsequently formally recognized by a father. Their double surname consisted of the father's first surname and the mother's first surname. Generally, while the father's surname was used in day-to-day social interactions, both surnames were employed in legal transactions and official documents. Children born into slavery, on the other hand, bore only the surname of their mothers (often derived from the plantation owner). While not explicitly racial, the new marker s.o.a. indicated social illegitimacy. Former slaves purchasing property in the 1880s lacked the second surname signaling legitimate birth or recognition by a father. As Rebecca Scott and Michael Zeuske argue, "Not for the first time, the holders of legal authority responded to initiatives on the part of Afro-Cubans by labeling them as deficient and out of place. Property was gained, but stigma was attached at the moment this victory was achieved."[18]

Not surprisingly, notaries began to employ similar markers for Chinese who were no longer working under contract alongside slaves, but who had remained in Cuba. As Chinese moved out of indenture and began small businesses, the social stigma of coolieism lurked not far behind. The Chinese Marcelino Hernández initially came as an indentured laborer to Cuba, where he was baptized in Sagua la Grande. Hernández managed to become part-owner of a grocery store, and on 19 September 1878, at the age of fifty, he gave his last testament before a notary in Cienfuegos. At the beginning of the testament, the notary refers to Hernández as a "free Asian, contracted," marking into the official record an indentured labor past, just four years after the end of the coolie trade. Hernández is also described as working in business (*del comercio*), indicating occupational flexibility.[19] When fellow Chinese Juan de la Torre and Ramón Moya liquidated their inheritance from Marcelino Hernández in 1887, the notary described them as "without second surnames."[20] By now all indentured laborers were free. But the marker *sin segundo apellido* called attention to their status as Chinese immigrants (who, like other non-Castillian ethnic groups, used only one surname) and possibly former coolies.

In official records, Damián Machado, the Chinese contractor on Soledad Estate, is given the title "Don," suggesting whiteness, but his surname is followed by the label s.o.a., indicating social illegitimacy and a possible link to a coolie labor background. Machado had amassed a substantial amount of property and capital by the 1890s. When he declared his last testament in November 1902, the notary described him as "Señor Don Damián Machado, without a second surname, who states he is the legitimate son of Conchinf and of Pienlión, deceased, natives of Canton in the Chinese Empire, sixty-four years old, widower, property owner, and of this neighborhood."[21] Juxtaposed to the notary's description of Machado as "without a second surname" (and thus not legitimate) is Machado's own declaration that he is, indeed, the legitimate son of two Chinese parents.[22]

In addition to s.o.a., other markers of race and class came into usage during the period of abolition of slavery and the end of Chinese indenture. Such markers in documents included mentions of an individual's dress, facial features, and birthplace. In April 1883, a circular in Santa Clara Province summoned the asiático Adolfo, "of regular stature, fat, intelligent, and accustomed to wearing a shirt and slippers."[23] Adolfo apparently defied the stereotype of a Chinese coolie: a shirtless laborer who spoke in broken sentences and was unable to read or write Spanish. Although indentured labor as an institution had ended, the coolie image persisted in both official and popular discourse.

The descriptor *achinado* was used to indicate presumptively Asian facial features, whether or not the individual was of Chinese descent. By the end of the nineteenth century the first generation of Cuban-born Chinese, many of mixed African descent, were coming of age. In September 1897, the court of Cienfuegos summoned the "pardo Leandro Garrido, achinado" to appear at the public jail to clear himself of the charge of swindling.[24] Those who reported the incident described Garrido as having Asian features. In July 1907, authorities in Colón were in pursuit of the *mestizo* Nicolás Herrera, "18 to 20 years old, achinado, short in stature, beardless."[25] By 1907, the more benign term *mestizo* often replaced the mulatto category of the colonial era to indicate someone of mixed African and European or African and Asian descent.

Race, Color, and Resistance to Chinese Settlement

By 1860, as large numbers of coolies neared the end of their contracts, the potential for a substantial free Chinese population loomed over Cuba. The introduction of Asians into Cuban slave society had upset both the racial and class ideology of Creole elites, who divided society into black and white, slave and free. Rather than creating a new category, official Spanish censuses in the nineteenth century generally classified Asians as white and slaves and *libertos* as black.[26] In her analysis of marriage, race, and class in colonial Cuba, Verena Martínez-Alier describes the Chinese and Yucatecan laborers as "a classificatory embarrassment." Although their skin color was lighter than that of many Spaniards, public opinion and custom positioned them as inferior to whites, largely due to their occupational status as coolies.[27] Lisa Yun's analysis of coolie testimonies corroborates that, from the perspective of planters and overseers, there was no "intermediate" category in the racialized labor hierarchy. Chinese coolies were generally treated as slaves, at times worse than slaves.[28]

An examination of how the Chinese were identified in social arenas in which skin color was considered important, such as baptism and marriage, lends insight into how the Cuban racial hierarchy operated during the period of gradual emancipation of slavery. Despite their legal status of "white," in local parish records Chinese coolies were usually recorded in the baptismal registry for blacks (*libro de bautismo de color*).[29] Furthermore, in colonial Spanish society the Chinese were routinely restricted from certain public spaces. In 1874, a group of ex-coolies described being subject to discrimination: "When traveling by rail we are not allowed on the better cars, and in the hotels and in the shops we are kept apart in the same manner as the black slaves."[30]

While Spanish colonial priests went to great lengths to convert African slaves to Catholicism, their efforts to convert Chinese coolies, who were not expected to settle, paled in comparison. However, baptism became a common practice among indentured laborers, especially those who sought certificates of residence upon completion of the contract or permission to marry. As such, baptism turned into a profit-earning business opportunity, with some individuals charging coolies for serving as godparents.[31] If baptized, a Chinese acquired a Spanish surname, usually that of his master. Tung

Kun Sen adopted the name of the master of San Pelayo Estate, becoming known in Cuba as Pastor Pelayo. The Chinese Von Ayen was given the name Cirilo Zoilo during his eight years under contract. In 1867, when he was baptized in a Trinidad church by Don Manuel de Mena, he added the surname Mena, becoming Cirilo Zoilo Mena.[32]

White elites who considered themselves protectors of traditional Spanish society in the colony were uneasy with the increasing numbers of Chinese in Cuba, especially as they completed their contracts. The growing population of mobile Chinese became an issue for officials in Santa Clara Province, as the number of Asians rose from 6,274 in 1861 to 15,878 in 1872.[33] In 1863, the governor ordered that those not under contract be conducted to the depository for reindenture under new patronos.[34] Concerns about free Chinese settlers in Cuba merged with issues of controlling people of color. In 1864, the government circulated a royal order promoting "Christian morality" among the Asian and colored races "as the only method of avoiding criminality in them." The Cienfuegos town council named Don José Gregorio Díaz de Villegas, Don Gabriel Montiel, and Don Manuel Suárez del Villar to a commission charged with informing the government of the best way to propagate morality on plantations.[35]

The commission claimed to have observed "better behavior" among slaves than among the free class of color. They attributed the difference to the guiding benevolence of masters and to the practice of slaves raising their own pigs and crops during free time and on Sundays, so that they "do not have time to engage in vices unfortunately so common among the heterogeneous free class."[36] The commission recommended limiting regular contact between slaves and free blacks and mulattos, as the latter supposedly infused slaves with pernicious ideas and seduced females. The commission also called attention to the practice of white overseers living together with female slaves and recommended penalties for those guilty as well as the owners and administrators who looked the other way. Among the "heterogeneous free class" to be feared were the small numbers of Chinese who managed to escape indenture and settle in towns.

Turning to "the immorality of the Asians," the commission stated that the Chinese "brought from their country a rooted vice" of sodomy, but that "punishment will not be sufficient to destroy it." It attributed the high numbers of suicides and murders among the Chinese population to the masters' and overseers' failure to comply with the terms of their contracts. The commission then acknowledged there had been abuses on the plantations, including providing coolies with substandard food and forcing them to work more hours than stipulated, and it stated that "they are not treated as free men but are whipped by the hand of a black."[37] Joseph Dorsey argues that the "racialized homosexual stereotypes" attributed to Chinese coolies "were constructed as noncriminal, more an innocuous curiosity than a menacing social peril." The practice of homosexuality among Chinese was largely accepted "as a social by-product of sexual imbalance . . . and welcomed if not promoted as a reassuring ritual of contraception."[38] In other words, it did not threaten traditional Cuban society, since the colonial government never intended for them to settle and form families.

Chinese Cuban Families beyond Slavery and Indenture

Despite official and social opposition, Chinese men did settle and form families. From their time as coolies on plantations, through their transition to freedom in Cuban society, Chinese mixed with local women. In her novel *Monkey Hunting*, Cristina García evokes the possibilities for interracial marriages between Chinese ex-coolies and black slave women. The relationship between Chen Pan and Lucrecia begins with the former indentured laborer purchasing the enslaved woman for help with domestic chores and business and gradually evolves into a lifelong partnership. Although Chinese coolies mostly formed common-law unions with women of African descent, there were exceptions. In particular, positions as domestic servants seemed to gain Chinese access to lighter-skinned women.

Chinese who worked on estates earning wages could be instrumental in the emancipation process for African-descended slaves. Rebecca Scott argues that free male workers employed by sugar estates "provided visible evidence of the possibility of freedom" and contributed "funds for their partners' and children's freedom." Slaves increasingly purchased their freedom with money from the sale of crops and pigs or with wages that had been paid to other members of the estate population, including Chinese. The daybook of Angelita Estate recorded the births of at least two children described as asiático to female slaves. One of these women purchased her freedom shortly thereafter.[39] Antonio Chuffat relates that after the Chinese coolie Crescencio was baptized, he married a slave from Africa known as "Ma Cristina" in Jovellanos. While we do not learn the fate of the female slave, the coolie eventually became a manager of a Chinese work gang. His compliance with his master's promotion of marriage among slaves as a moralizing, educating principle likely assisted with his own social mobility on the plantation.[40]

The handful of Chinese women in Cuba during the period of indentured labor presented the Spanish colonial government with the possibility of locally born Chinese children and the disruption that families ultimately brought to the plantation regime. According to regulations, any children of a female coolie would inherit the status of the mother, a norm from slavery. The 1874 commission reported that two Chinese who completed their contracts, obtained letters of domicile and cédulas, and won the lottery went on to marry Chinese women. They remained on the island, however, unable to afford the cost of return passage.[41]

In 1863, the asiática Teresa Sopena (Hu Hi), most likely a domestic worker, requested termination of her contract in order to marry another Chinese. After giving birth to a child, Teresa came into conflict with her masters over work duties. The child's father, asiático Agustín la Piedra, filed a complaint on her behalf against her master, Juan Sopena. He claimed that Teresa was forced to neglect her son when she worked and that he had indemnified the master for the contract, which was due to expire in four months. Juan Sopena responded that the contract was under the name of his wife, Enriqueta Danjón, "who never impeded Teresa from lactation"; Teresa, however, "abandoned work entirely." He had acquired the contract with the understanding that it was for a period of ten years, according to a handwritten note at the bottom. The two parties thus disagreed with respect to the lactation hours of Teresa's child, the length of the contract, and the sum for which it could be transferred. An authority reviewing the case believed that "there exist sufficient reasons for the nullification of the contract in question because it is not in accordance with the existing regulations."[42]

By law, Chinese coolies had the right to contract marriage. Nineteenth-century Cuban elites generally opposed Chinese intermarriage with whites but were more permissive toward their mixing with people of color. If a baptismal certificate classified a Chinese as white, authorities did not have grounds for dismissing a petition to marry a white women. But legal status did not automatically transfer into social acceptance. Commenting on a Chinese-white marriage, the lieutenant governor of Colón undermined the classification of asiáticos as white, claiming that "the Chinese race is assimilated to the black race" and "although it is thought to be purer than the African race, it is nonetheless looked upon with a certain aversion by whites." Furthermore, he noted, the majority of whites "reject this kind of marriage."[43] The 1874 commission reported two instances of Chinese who married white women but faced opposition from Cuban society.[44]

In a rare case, the thirty-three-year-old Chinese Julián Güisen married a white Cuban woman in April 1861. Because he was unable to demonstrate completion of his eight-year term, a couple of months later he was sent to the *depósito* of Bejucal (outside Havana) for recontracting. The local priest, Don Rodrigo Alonso Delgado—who had also baptized him, served as a godparent, and named him Julián—now made the required deposit of 306 pesos to secure his services. As a domestic servant, Julián had cultivated a wider social network than that of a typical field laborer. On 23 November, the priest transferred the contract to Doña Cruz Crescencia Pérez, who replaced the priest's deposit. Crescencia Pérez was the "legitimate daughter" of Don José and Doña Concepción Hernández, and her marriage to Julián was inscribed in the registry for whites and consented to by her parents. Julián Güisen is described with the honorific "don" as a "native of Canton in Asia, resident of Bejucal, single, the son of Confú and Aquien."

Fifteen months later, on 23 February 1863, Crescencia Pérez de Güisen appealed to the Captain General, requesting that an exception be made to the regulation that Asians either recontract or be deported at the end of the eight-year period. She described the hardship incurred by Julián in "his condition of colono under my patronage." With no legal autonomy, he needed his wife's authorization for all matters, including leaving the house. Since six months had passed and his former master Alonso had not reclaimed him, she requested that Julián remain free of all colono obligations and that he have access to the 306 pesos deposited in the royal coffer.[45]

In both of these cases the petitioners—a Chinese male and a white woman—made claims rooted in the institutions of marriage and family, as well as traditional gender roles, in order to free their partners from the bondage of indenture. Teresa Sopena sought to marry and care for her child, and Julián Güisen to leave the house without permission from his wife.

Cuban government and elite attitudes toward Chinese unions with people of color were somewhat more relaxed. Class status influenced a Chinese migrant's marriage options. According to Cuban scholarship, Chinese testimonies, and folklore, former indentured laborers mostly intermarried with black and mulatto women.[46] The statistical details of this generalization await a thorough analysis of ecclesiastical records. Even with such an analysis, however, one must keep in mind the prevalence of common-law marriages that may not have generated a paper trail. Given the difficulties of returning to China and scarcity of Chinese women, ex-coolies could be expected to have formed unions with slaves or free people of color for mutual assistance, especially during the age of emancipation. The social spaces through which Chinese men and Cuban women of color moved—sugar estates, markets, and "marginal" neighborhoods—provided opportunities for daily interactions that could anchor more permanent partnerships. Among the new arrivals of Chinese transnational merchants, some sent for wives from China, while others married Cuban women, both white and black (and often maintained families back home).

Although Chinese unions with black or mulatto women were more common than with white women, they did not necessarily go unopposed. In Havana, an 1873 petition by a young mulatto woman to officially marry a former Chinese indentured laborer reveals the vehement opposition to these unions, sometimes from black or mulatto parents themselves. The eighteen-year-old mulatta Nicolasa Hernández initiated the case by soliciting a license to contract marriage with the asiático Ciprian Bernal. Nicolasa was the "natural daughter" of the free black María del Rosario López and of an "unknown father."[47] She earned from twenty to twenty-five pesos monthly as a seamstress. Her thirty-four-year-old mother, also a seamstress, refused to grant her daughter permission to marry Ciprian simply because he was Chinese. She disapproved of the marriage "because she wants her daughter to marry one of her class and not an Asian—without having other motives for denying her the license."[48] The mother's opposition to the union stemmed from her desire for her family's upward mobility. As a recently freed black, she aimed to prevent her lighter-skinned daughter from marrying someone considered socially inferior. Her perception of Ciprian as an unworthy match for her daughter owed more to his former occupational status than to his skin color or racial categorization, since officially he was "white."

Ciprian had been baptized on 3 March 1864, while under contract to his patrón Luiz de Cárdenas. He was named José Cipriano, and he adopted his surname from his godfather, Juan Bernal. Ciprian's baptism was inscribed in the book for mulattos and blacks (*libro de pardos y morenos*). By the time of the marriage petition, the twenty-nine-year-old Ciprian had been free from his contract of indenture for five years, since 1868. Although the documents do not reveal precisely how Ciprian obtained his liberty, by 1873 he was a salaried worker earning thirty pesos monthly. This former indentured laborer was now free, but he faced new limits on his social mobility due to his race and past occupational status. Facing such opposition to his marriage, Ciprian depended on the support of his employer and on references from neighbors attesting to his good moral conduct. Despite her mother's objections, Nicolasa's petition to marry a Chinese was ultimately approved.

Ciprian and Nicolasa were married by a parish priest. As a group, parish priests were thoroughly confused as to how to classify Chinese baptisms and marriages. The Consejo de Administración debated the question and ruled that children of Chinese were to be registered in the book for whites for the purpose of baptism, as long as none of the parents were *de color*. Unlike whites, however, Chinese did not need to obtain an official license to marry a woman of color. As Verena Martínez-Alier notes, by exempting them from this regulation, "the authorities betrayed their innermost doubts about the true racial status of the Chinese" and in effect classified them as nonwhite.[49]

The cases of Julián Güisen, the coolie who married a white woman in 1863, and Ciprian Bernal suggest a linkage between positions in domestic service and access to freedom and social mobility. Ciprian and Nicolasa lived near each other, and both were domestic workers.[50] "Frontier" neighborhoods, between town and countryside, became spaces where social networks and business alliances between Chinese and other people of color could form. The Bernal case, initiated just months before the end of the coolie trade, also opens a window on the process of transition from coolies to salaried workers and the interracial alliances between blacks and Asians that assisted this transition.

Free Chinese who managed cuadrillas or owned shops and thus had moved into a higher economic stratum were at times able to marry white Cuban women. Damián Machado, the contractor from Soledad Estate in Cienfuegos, entered into a common-law union with the white María de la Caridad Pérez y Espinosa in 1877, and together they had four children. When they formalized their marriage in 1890, the registry listed Caridad as the daughter of Doña Antonia P. Espinosa, but did not include her father's name.[51] Caridad's use of two surnames came directly from her own mother, rather than both a mother and a father. We can infer that she did not receive a formal education, as another witness signed for her. Her own status as white, but illiterate and not the product of a legitimate marriage, perhaps facilitated the union in 1877 for the twenty-year-old with a property-owning entrepreneur who was able to write, yet who was Chinese. Another case is that of Antonio Rubio, a former coolie who had moved off the plantation and settled in Abreus. After fulfilling his contract, Rubio entered commerce and married the white Mercedes García y Barros, a native of Santa Cruz (in Puerto Príncipe Province) and resident of Cienfuegos. The couple had three children whose surnames were derived from both parents (Rubio y García).[52]

Newly arrived Chinese merchants also married Cuban women, both white and nonwhite. Wilfredo Lam, one of Cuba's most celebrated artists, descended from an Afro-Asian union. In the late nineteenth century Lam Yam followed a common route from Guangdong to San Francisco, then Mexico, and finally Cuba. He established a business in Sagua la Grande, the site of a sizeable Chinese community. As a man of letters familiar with several Cantonese dialects, Lam Yam fulfilled a key role writing letters on behalf of his compatriots to their relatives in China. For a hobby he brushed calligraphy with the sayings of Confucius and Laozi on colored paper, which he hung in his home. Toward the end of the century, Lam Yam politically supported the Chinese revolutionary movement of Sun Yat-sen. He married a mulatta of African, Spanish, and Indian descent, and together they had seven children. In 1902, when Lam Yam was eighty years old, his son Wilfredo Oscar de la Concepción Lam y Castilla (Wilfredo Lam) was born.[53]

Future Generations and Social Standing

As they formed families, Chinese and Cubans shared the goal of elevating their children's social status through formal recognition and acquisition of property and land. By the 1880s those who had children born outside of marriage made use of the legal action *reconocimiento de hijo natural* (recognition of a natural child), which gave children the right to use two surnames in official transactions.[54] The Chinese contractor Damián Machado had "maintained marital relations" with the Cuban Caridad Pérez y Espinosa since 1877. Yet, they did not formalize their union with a marriage contract and have their children recognized as "legitimate" until 18 January 1890, when Machado was fifty and his wife was thirty-three. Caridad Pérez y Espinosa died just six months after their civil marriage, on 18 July 1890.[55] Machado linked his marriage and official recognition of his children to improving their status. Perhaps Caridad was ill, and the couple wanted to have their children declared legitimate before she died.

Twelve years later, when Damián Machado was ready to give his own last testament, two of his children were adults of marrying age. His four children were twenty-four-year-old Norberto de Jesús (known familiarly as Alberto Amancio), twenty-two-year-old María Gregoria de la Natividad, twenty-year-old Catalina, and seventeen-year-old Lucia Dominica Julia. Machado declared that 300 pesos Spanish gold should go to Catalina and 132.50 to Lucia when these two youngest daughters became adults or contracted marriage. As he stood before a notary, leaving behind legal minors without their mother must have been worrisome to Machado. But some peace of mind must have come from knowing that he had been able to leave them property, pesos, and a legitimate name.[56]

The ex-coolie and Chinese contractor Pastor Pelayo also took measures to formally recognize his children with the former slave Wenceslaa Sarría. The

Blas and Santiago Pelayo in front of their Chinese grandfather's house in
Cienfuegos, Cuba, March 1999. (Photograph by Shannon Dawdy)

baptismal record inscribed his first-born child Blas as the "son of unknown
father and of the black patrocinada Wenceslaa criolla [lowercase in original],
native of this city." Wenceslaa's parents were listed as "Justo and Consolación
Criollo," the marker *criollo/a* used to distinguish Cuban-born slaves from
African-born slaves. However, she was known as Wenceslaa Sarría, after the
owner of Rosario Estate, and her son Blas also took the surname Sarría. A
note in the margin of his baptismal record indicates that on 9 September
1910, Pastor Pelayo formally recognized Blas Sarría as *hijo natural* (natural
son) before a notary.[57] Blas had, however, been using his father's surname
"Pelayo" for other official interactions even before this legal recognition. At
the time of the 1907 electoral census, the mestizo Blas Pelayo was a twenty-
six-year-old seaman (*marinero*) able to read and write.[58] His aging Chinese
father Pastor Pelayo officially recognized him as *hijo natural* just a few years
before his own death in 1913.[59]

Names and surnames hint at changes in the social status of Chinese beyond the coolie period. While under indenture, most Chinese were given
Spanish names, even if not baptized. Lists of Chinese often refer to them by
first name only, such as "Santiago 2nd," "Juan 3rd," and "Pedro No. 44" in the

burial records at Regla.[60] At times a geographical marker, such as "Cantón" or "Manila" was appended to a first name. The practice of assigning numbers and other identifying descriptors in cases of duplicate names derives from the world of slavery. In addition to serving an administrative purpose on sugar estates, it was intended to strip African slaves and Chinese indentured laborers of identities associated with their names. It subsumed the cultural identity of the laborer to the organizational regimen of the estate or industry, adding an additional layer of control over the subject.

For Chinese coolies, baptism and conversion to Catholicism constituted a step toward social legitimacy and freedom. Upon being baptized, Chinese took the surname of their master or a godparent, at times choosing one based on a patron-client relationship. However, they could retain their Chinese names for inner social circles. Pastor Pelayo ensured that his Chinese name (Tung Kun Sen) continued to be used and passed down through family generations; it appears in his burial record. Some Chinese created new hybrid surnames. For example, in Cuba after the period of indenture, multitudes of men used the surname Achón, most likely derived from the common Chinese family name Chen.[61] Common Chinese surnames in Regla include: Afak, Elay, Añi, Atán, Asón, Achoín, Moyle, Luis, Asen, and León.[62]

As a further claim to legitimacy, some Chinese sought to enter their parental lineage into an official record. In notarized documents former indentured laborers Marcelino Hernández and Antonio Rubio explicitly named their two Chinese parents. Hernández declared he was the "son of Allon and Chon Quian, both deceased," and Rubio the "son of Cama and Aná, named such in his country and deceased."[63] In his last testament Damián Machado also named his Chinese parents. Although at this stage of their lives, these men knew that they were unlikely to return to China, they deemed it important to formally record the names of their parents. Former slaves also engaged in this practice of creating an ancestral heritage for posterity.[64] In other cases, Chinese simply listed Spanish first names as parents, such as the common "José y María."[65]

Doubling a surname constituted another means through which one could create legitimacy. After independence, when the Constitution of 1901 granted universal male suffrage in Cuba, several Chinese ex-coolies became eligible voters. Pastor Pelayo is registered on the electoral list of Santa Clara Province in 1907 as Pastor Pelayo y Lunchon, a sixty-five-year-old asiático who had been in the province working in agriculture for twenty-four years. Pelayo lent himself a marker of legitimacy by adding the second surname "Lunchon," most likely derived from his Chinese mother or father. By combing the electoral register for Guaos (the area of the province that encompassed workers on Soledad Estate), one finds that sixteen out of sixty-four asiáticos listed two surnames. Some of these eligible Chinese voters seemed to simply double a first surname, such as José Achón y Achón. Some took on two Spanish surnames, such as Juan García y Valladares, while others named two Chinese parents, such as Miguel Apen y Funsen.[66] By doubling a surname, migrants made claims to status and citizenship as Chinese within Cuban society. Naming also had implications for assimilation. In the post-indenture period, pairing a Western first name with a Chinese surname facilitated their ability to engage in business and social transactions.

Like former slaves, then, Chinese chipped away at the markers of past status by marrying, formally recognizing children, and taking on a second surname. At the same time, many sought more tangible expressions of upward mobility, such as purchasing property and establishing small businesses. The case of Antonio Rubio indicates how, in anticipation of death, some Chinese went to great lengths to secure their possessions for posterity. After his period of indenture, Rubio had eventually entered trade and married the young Mercedes García y Barros in Cienfuegos. The couple had two children, Dominica and Lino Rubio y García, and Rubio made home improvements to his property on Real Street in Abreus. When the forty-seven-year-old Rubio declared his last testament before a notary on 7 February 1883, his wife was seven months pregnant. Rubio's property was held by the firm Castaño and Yntriago with a stipulation for repurchase (*pacto de retro*). When he swore his last testament, Rubio must have felt a sense of urgency as he officially declared the property to be his upon payment of 300 pesos and named his family as heirs. He left as his beneficiaries his minor children Dominica, Lino, and the (at the time unborn) Luz Rubio y García.[67]

Antonio Rubio called upon men from his social networks in the community to validate his claim. The men he gathered bear witness to an integrated, networked Chinese community in a Cuban sugar town, as opposed to an enclosed ethnic enclave. The Chinese contractor Damián Machado served as a witness for Rubio's last testament, along with two other non-Chinese, shoemaker Juan Pérez y César and merchant Antonio Vidal y Español. Rubio named as the executor of his will his father-in-law José García y Viamonte. Eight months later, Rubio's twenty-five-year-old widow appeared before the notary officially to claim the house in Abreus for her children. It was described as an urban property "made previously of wood and thatch and today of wood and tile, divided into 2 rooms, on land of 25 yards front by 40 back." Rubio's father-in-law ultimately provided the 300 pesos to acquire the property for his grandchildren.[68]

Planting Roots

By the time the coolie trade had ended, Chinese businesses in Cuba ranged from fruit stands to major transnational import firms. In 1900, during the U.S. occupation, Chinese merchants were obligated to register their shops, groceries, taverns, bakeries, and laundries.[69] Contrary to the image of an enclosed Chinatown, seething with hawkers and vice, that has been portrayed in travelers' descriptions of San Francisco and Havana, Chinese settlements in the Cuban provinces were rather porous. The Chinese interacted with native Cubans, European immigrants, blacks, mulattos, and other Chinese on a daily basis.

Both the interracial tensions and cross-racial alliances that existed during the period of indenture continued as blacks and Asians interacted in the market for labor and services. The Chinese Federico Valdés was proprietor of the inn El Gallito on Velasco Street in Cienfuegos, in a neighborhood made up of people of color. In August 1883, one of his non-Chinese employees, Marcelino Guerrero, filed a suit against Valdés. Guerrero testified that he had placed in a safety deposit box $156.60 in cash that had not been returned and was also owed $14 in wages (for a total of $170.60). Valdés claimed that he "did not owe one cent" to Guerrero, besides $8.50 for fifteen days of work. The court ruled for Guerrero regarding the cash and Valdés regarding the wages, ordering Valdés to pay within three days $165.10 ($156.60 plus $8.50 in wages) plus court costs. When Valdés did not comply, an embargo was placed on goods from his fonda. By September, Valdés and Guerrero reached an agreement whereby Valdés would pay 85 pesos, about half of the original claim.[70]

In June 1902, Ygnacio Hernández, an ex-slave born in Africa, demanded from Lorenzo Chao of the Chinese-run shop La Niña Julia on San Fernando Street, the payment of fourteen pesos for ploughing soil. Chao denied the claim, stating that he was not the owner of the establishment. The court found the suit groundless, as Hernández was unable to produce a written document to prove the existence of a contractual arrangement.[71] The former slave Hernández was now working at least part-time as a day laborer, finding odd jobs in the countryside or in town.

Instances of cooperation between blacks and Asians were as common as those of strife. In 1878 the Chinese Marcelino Hernández pledged in his last testament to the black Julieta Montalvo, "for one time and as demonstration of thanks for services that she has lent, the quantity of 100 pesos in gold."[72] Hernández was a former indentured laborer, now free of his contract and operating a grocery in Cruces, and it is not unlikely that he and Julieta Montalvo had formed a friendship, in addition to a business relationship.

Chinese starting their own businesses made use of Cuban credit. Between October 1882 and March 1883 the Chinese Antonio Joff had accumulated a debt of ninety-two pesos gold with the warehouse (*almacén*) of Álvarez Castaño y Compañía. The provisions he purchased in bulk on credit—grapes, apples, and potatoes—were for his own small business. Joff admitted that he had not been able to pay the debt due to other obligations.[73]

Another means of raising capital was to invest with other Chinese. Former indentured laborer Marcelino Hernández formed a partnership with fellow Chinese Ramón Moya to acquire property. Hernández and Moya each invested 1,025 pesos gold for a grocery (*pulpería mixto*) they ran in Cruces. On 1 June 1878, Hernández and Moya purchased a house in Cruces situated near the railroad for 150 pesos gold. When on 19 September of that year Marcelino Hernández declared his last testament before a notary, lacking "legitimate or natural children," he named Ramón Moya and another Chinese partner, Juan de la Torre, as his sole beneficiaries. He died just two days later.

The three Chinese business associates all belonged to the main mutual aid association in Cruces, the Casino Asiático. Although not officially registered with the government until 1901, the organization had been functioning at least since 17 March 1880, when Juan de la Torre purchased the building on Heredia Street for 325 pesos from a native of Asturias. This property was near their house and business and also bordered the railroad to Santa Clara. Years later, in 1887, Ramón Moya and Juan de la Torre appeared before a notary to liquidate their inheritance. After calculating funeral costs and outstanding debts, the total remaining inheritance was 1,440 pesos, with each beneficiary receiving 720 pesos. The youngest of the three, Ramón Moya, remained a leader in the Chinese community of Cruces and became president of the mutual aid association in 1900.[74]

In August 1880, the two Chinese sold their house to the thirty-three-year-old single black female Matilde O'Bourke, a native of Cienfuegos and resident of Cruces, for 150 pesos.[75] The sale of the house in Cruces to an Afro-Cuban woman is representative of a larger pattern. As slaves purchased their liberty or were emancipated and as Chinese completed their contracts, both settled just outside of plantations, away from the centers of sugar towns and often close to the railroad tracks. These newly formed neighborhoods, populated by people of color, became known as "Ferrocarril" after the railroad they bordered. In Lajas several Afro-Cuban women living in the neighborhood Ferrocarril formed unions with Chinese who worked, now as free laborers, on the large Caracas Estate.[76]

New migrants who came to Cuba in the late nineteenth century also entered small businesses. In June 1893, José Asan (Chang Nan Ko) of Jiujiang, Nanhai County took charge of the inn El Gallo on the main commercial artery, San Fernando Street, in Cienfuegos.[77] Asan also invested in a charcoal factory in Caimanera de Cienfuegos and was a labor contractor for the cane farm Guabairo, one of Soledad's suppliers. He brought four sons from China and gave them Spanish names: José, Andrés, Guillermo, and Pedro. José Asan was known for providing food to insurgents during the 1895 war, and afterward his well-known inn became headquarters of the Liberation Army.[78]

In 1897, another new migrant, the twenty-five-year-old Rufino Achón who lived in Abreus, purchased a laundry (tren de lavado) on Argüelles Street in Cienfuegos from fellow Chinese Luis Achón for one hundred pesos, with fifty pesos as a down payment. The remaining half of the purchase price was due on 30 June. When Rufino Achón failed to pay, Luis Achón filed a juicio verbal demanding the money, and a month later the two reached an agreement. Luis Achón's claim was supported by testimony from two young, recent migrants to Cuba who worked in the laundry.[79]

Chinese engaged in a wide array of occupations by the turn of the twentieth century, among them herbal medicine. While the 1899 census recorded only one Chinese doctor in Cuba, literary and material evidence provides a different portrait. In October 1996, a hurricane damaged the building that three Chinese businesses (Las Californias, La Niña Julia, and Wen On Long) in Cienfuegos had previously occupied. The demolition crew discovered artifacts on the second floor, which had been boarded up for decades. Among them were some Qing dynasty coins, bunches of dried herbs stuck in the floorboards or in tins that hung from the ceiling, and a mill, indicating traditional pharmaceutical activity.[80]

Chinese doctors were present on coolie ships and practiced on plantations and in towns in Cuba, despite some local opposition. The Cuban press and popular imagination portrayed Chinese doctors with a mixture of fascination and revulsion toward their strange techniques. Nineteenth-century fictional works describe Chinese doctors in typical orientalist fashion, exotically dressed, wearing long braids, and commanding flocks of people to benefit from their herbal miracles. Chinese medical practitioners developed a reputation for curing illnesses such as yellow fever and tuberculosis. The general fascination for Chinese fans, silks, and porcelains extended to paintings of the Chinese "medicine man" known as Saanci, a top seller in Cuban shops. Saanci apparently had arrived on a coolie ship in 1847 and was held in the depósito of Cimarrones. He escaped the fate of other coolies through his skill with Chinese medicine, and he eventually left Cuba on a ship bound for New York. Another doctor, Dhin Fua Sin, had reportedly performed miracles in Puerto Príncipe, Camagüey. In 1838, when authorities denied Dhin Fua Sin a license to practice medicine, sixty residents of Puerto Príncipe signed a complaint to the captain general. The best-known Chinese doctor was Chan Bom Bia, who arrived in Havana in 1858 and operated in Matanzas and Cárdenas. He developed a reputation for treating even those who were unable to pay.[81]

The "Californians"

With the arrival of the new transnational merchants, many from Hong Kong and San Francisco, an upper stratum of Chinese inserted themselves into the nascent communities, altering class dynamics. Juan Pérez de la Riva argues that the "Californians" in particular "destroyed the coolie tradition," rendered as proletarian, rebellious, and anti-imperialist. He juxtaposes the corrupt merchant who financed gambling and opium with the authentic coolie, "the one of the docks, the factories, the cane fields."[82] The picture of early Chinese communities, however, is more nuanced than a simple dichotomy between pure coolie and corrupt Californian. Divisions among migrants began much earlier, as some ex-coolies took advantage of economic opportunities by selling contracts of those still under indenture or establishing cuadrillas to profit from Chinese labor.

Transnational Chinese merchants from San Francisco and Hong Kong established branches of their firms beyond the capital of Havana to provincial towns across the island, especially major centers of Chinese population such as Cienfuegos and Santiago de Cuba. They imported luxury products such as silk and lacquerware to sell to Cubans and specialty foods, medicine, and tea to sell to Chinese. In 1873, the first Cantonese restaurant for wealthy patrons opened, and in 1878 a Chinese newspaper began publication. Chinese merchant and banking interests proliferated, and they became moneylenders and financed gambling on a large scale. Pérez de la Riva characterizes this level of prosperity by 1880 as "totally negative for Chinese and Cubans."

A new social class was formed, "a hybrid mixture of Americanism and Orientalism," imbued with "capitalist spirit."[83]

Hong Kong–based transnational firms established branches in major diasporic cities in the Americas, such as San Francisco, Lima, and Havana. Typical of the most prestigious Chinese import firms in Cuba was Yan Wo Chang, begun in February 1872 with a capital of 80,000 pesos. Tung Kong Lam of Nanhai County sailed to California in 1870 and the following year to Havana to manage the Cuban branch. The Afro-Chinese Antonio Chuffat delivered mail for the firm when he was twelve years old and describes it as one of the most respected businesses in Havana and abroad (as opposed to other firms that he identifies as opium importers). In the aftermath of the Spanish colonial government's assassination of Cuban medical students in 1871, Tung Kong Lam publicly cried out against the injustice and published a statement of protest in a Guangzhou newspaper.[84] Contrary to later Cuban scholars' depiction of transnational Chinese merchants as "antirevolutionary," Chuffat views them as contributing to an anticolonial Cuban identity.

In February 1879, the first major Chinese firm headquartered in Cuba opened. The import house of products from Asia, Weng On y Compañía, opened its doors on Galiano Street in Havana under Chinese merchant Loy Kay. The firm, which operated until 1912, introduced porcelains, satins, silks, ivory, cosmetics, and perfumes that "became fashionable in the capital of the Island of Cuba, as in all cities."[85] Members of the Cuban elite frequented the shop, as it gained a reputation for importing quality luxury products from France, England, and Germany. At its peak the firm did around three million pesos worth of business through its multiple branches.

Owner Loy Kay is representative of the upper tier of transnational Chinese merchants who became integrated into Cuban society while maintaining ties to China. In addition to his native Chinese, he "spoke and wrote English and Spanish correctly" and "considered Cuba his second country."[86] In 1886, Loy Kay brought three nephews from China to work in the firm: Luis Chung, Luis Po, and Luis Yong, all educated in Havana. The young Luis Chung's movements illustrate the cycles of transnational migration. He traveled across the island, establishing branches of the firm in Cárdenas, Colón, Cienfuegos, Sagua la Grande, and elsewhere. The branch in Cienfuegos, called Weng On Long, began in 1888 on Velasco Street.[87] In 1890, after acquiring some capital, Luis Chung returned to China and married. He later brought his own two sons to Cuba, replicating the pattern established years earlier by his uncle Loy Kay.[88] Another one of the nephews, Luis Po, became known for his transnational political activities, supporting Sun

Yat-sen's nationalist movement that led to the fall of the Manchu Qing dynasty in 1911.[89]

The development of Chinese businesses throughout the provinces generally followed a pattern in which merchants established companies in Havana, followed by branches in the provinces. At times, though, merchants started their own business directly in one of the provincial towns. In June 1887, Antonio Bu (Bu Fan Son) came from China to work in the Havana firm Weng On y Compañía. He eventually opened two shops of his own in Cienfuegos, selling products from Asia. Located in the heart of town on San Fernando Street, the shops were named Las Californias and La California, reflecting connections between Cuban Chinese and San Francisco Chinese.[90] Antonio Bu settled in Cienfuegos, and in 1901 he established a Chinese association there.[91]

Culture and Community

Chinese working under indenture and later in cuadrillas spoke different dialects and came from different areas of South China, with their primary attachments to their home village or region. Their self-identification as "Chinese" developed in the face of maltreatment in Cuba, where they formed communities based on common needs. Like enslaved Africans, indentured laborers brought religious and cultural traditions from their homeland to their new environment. Samuel Hazard described some of the cultural artifacts among indentured Chinese in a Cuban cigarette factory, "curious articles of Chinese life and habits" such as musical instruments and gambling boards.[92]

During the Spanish colonial period, religious authorities organized Catholic brotherhoods, or *cofradías*, of Africans for proselytizing, engaging in charitable acts, and promoting African culture. The Spanish government viewed these organizations and the fraternal societies known as *cabildos de nación* as a means to control laborers, since Africans joined according to their ethnicities.[93] While out of necessity Chinese converted to Catholicism, they also maintained popular religious practices from China and adopted some Afro-Cuban traditions. In February 1867, a "brotherhood of Asians" (*cofradía de asiáticos*) serving some two hundred Chinese, both indentured and free, operated in an establishment owned by Francisco Clasaola on Santa Rosa Street in Regla. Not all were baptized, and they paid homage to Chinese traditional deities and celebrated religious festivals. Unions between Chinese men and African-descended women facilitated religious syncretism. According to Pedro Cosme Baños, local historian and director of the Museum of

Regla, Chinese accepted religious traditions of African origin such as *santería* and *el Palo*, and some members of the Afro-Cuban fraternal organization Abakuá were of Chinese descent. Abakuá societies originated in Regla and took root in Matanzas, which was heavily dependent on slaves and coolies.[94]

A syncretic form of worship combining Chinese with Afro-Cuban traditions developed around the Chinese deity San Fan Con. The Chinese god of war, Guan Gong, already associated with honor, became a protector of immigrants in Cuba. According to legend, Guan Gong's spirit entered the body of Chung Si in Cimarrones, Matanzas, to deliver wisdom to his compatriots in an oration that combines Confucian and Catholic wisdom. Thus, Guan Gong developed into the Afro-Chinese-Cuban Sanfancón, associated with Changó in santería and Santa Bárbara in Catholicism.[95]

The interplay between economic and cultural initiatives is embodied in Chinese contractors and entrepreneurs who established *huiguans* (mutual aid associations) in their neighborhoods, as well as Chinese from California who invested major capital in theater companies and schools. Although the circumstances of their migration made it difficult for former indentured laborers to remain connected to their hometowns, they attempted to re-create elements of Chinese culture in their new environment. Chinese ethnic associations, known in Cuba as *casinos asiáticos*, provided mutual aid, assisted with employment, extended credit, maintained hostels, mediated disputes, represented the Chinese "colony" in the nonimmigrant community, and initiated and coordinated fund-raising and charitable projects. In addition to their important social function in Cuba, associations helped Chinese maintain homeland ties through remittance sending, return passage, and burial arrangements.[96]

Both former indentured laborers and new arrivals founded associations and theaters. As early as 1867, a group of five Chinese in Havana formed the first Chinese society Kit Yi Tong (La Unión), with the mission to unite all Chinese residents in Havana. Shortly afterward, at the beginning of 1868, another group of Chinese established Hen Yi Tong (Los Hermanos) on Estrella Street at the corner of Campanario and Manrique, uniting all Chinese "brothers" in Havana, "some slaves and others free." Later that year, the ethnic minority Hakka Chinese formed Yi Seng Tong (Segunda Alianza, or Second Alliance) on Maloja Street. One source traces its founders to the first boatloads of coolies in 1847.[97] During the coolie period, merchants pooled money to assist Chinese who were harassed by colonial authorities for not recontracting.[98]

New Chinese ethnic associations developed with the arrivals from California. Pérez de la Riva contends that organizations that proliferated after 1880 lost "the esoteric and combative character of the brotherhoods of the previous decades." They became Westernized, and converted to the model of the lyceum. He cites as a typical example the Casino Asiático de Placetas, founded in 1882. Although nominally a mutual aid society, education and recreation predominated "over solidarity and class struggle," and the regulations expressly prohibited political and religious debate.[99] It is important to keep in mind, however, that the associations were required to register and submit bylaws to the Spanish government, which only recently had been enmeshed in an anticolonial uprising. By basing their external structure on the model of other *sociedades de instrucción y recreo*, Chinese mutual aid organizations improved their odds of survival and mitigated the risk of government intrusion. The liberalization of Spanish laws on assembly after the end of the Ten Years' War led to a proliferation of associations, including many for Spanish immigrants as well as Chinese and African-descended populations.

In 1883, the Chinese society "La Caridad" in Havana was formed primarily to benefit "the moral and material interests of the working and agriculturalist classes" and to "protect the destitute." In addition to mutual aid, the association supported instruction in reading and writing both Chinese and Spanish, games such as billiards, chess, dominoes, and the lottery, a library with national and foreign newspapers, and weekly performances of Cantonese opera. The flag of China was raised every Sunday, accompanied by the flag of Spain on festival days. When the association's executive committee convened in 1886, it addressed the importance of continued participation and dues from the remaining members. The committee emphasized that the Chinese "do not have in this country another center where in their language and according to their customs they can meet and remember their native land."[100]

Publicly adopting names of Catholic saints facilitated acceptance of Chinese ethnic associations, while internally they retained a Chinese name. In Cruces in Santa Clara Province, the Chinese Ramón Moya established the Casino Asiático Nuestra Señora de la Caridad del Cobre (Chinese Association Our Lady of Charity of Cobre). As the patron saint of Cuba, Caridad del Cobre resonated at all levels of society. Devotion in China to the Buddhist deity Guanyin, goddess of mercy, facilitated the use of Catholic saints as the outward representation of these early Chinese associations in Cuba.[101] According to legend, an apparition of the deity appeared in Caibarién to rescue her sons from the hands of slavery. Chinese from all over the island made pilgrimages to the statue of the Virgin in the Chinese association there.[102]

The Chinese theater became a diasporic link circulating people, capital, and news to Chinese communities across American cities. Chinese theater managers in Cuba imported professional actors and acrobats from California and from China. In March 1873, four Chinese from California (Carlos Chang, Li Weng, Wong Yot Sen, and Lay Fu) formed a theater on Zanja and San Nicolás Streets in Havana with a capital investment of 15,000 pesos. Francisco Gasso officially represented the theater on Zanja Street and generally defended Chinese interests, along with Agustín Chuffat, Pedro Pa, Abraham Lan, and Luis Pérez, by now longtime Chinese residents in Cuba.[103] Two years later Chinese comic performers from California established another theater on Lealtad Street, which held shows in the evenings and on Sunday afternoons.[104]

In the 1870s and 1880s, Chinese ethnic associations and theaters proliferated across the island. In Cienfuegos, for example, eight societies of education and recreation were registered: three for whites (Casino Español, Liceo, and El Artesano, the latter two with a theater); three for people of color (El Progreso, La Amistad, and La Igualidad, all with a theater); and two for Chinese, one in 1875 and another in 1883, "a great center of instruction and recreation for the Asian race, with more than 500 members, called La Gran China." During its inauguration, the new Chinese association publicly presented a five-hundred-peso donation for the hospital to the mayor, who presided over the ceremony.[105]

Theater companies in Havana regularly traveled to Chinese communities in the provinces. In April 1875, the Havana theater on Zanja Street established another one in Cienfuegos on Paseo de Arango, managed by businessman Loo Pan. The theater company performed the famous Cantonese opera set in the Tang Dynasty "Shik Yan Kuey" (The Legend of Xue Ren Gui) for fifteen days. Chinese from the neighboring communities of Ranchuelo, Cruces, Lajas, Palmira, Rodas, and Abreus attended the premier.[106] In 1883 another Chinese theater opened in Cienfuegos on Santa Clara Street.[107] Opera performances provided a respite for agricultural and factory laborers, who flocked to theaters and festivals, especially during Lunar New Year. Sagua la Grande boasted an immense three-story wooden theater on Tacón and Caridad Streets, popularly known as the "teatro de los chinos." In 1876 a company of ninety-four Chinese actors premiered. According to Mauro García and Pedro Eng, "It was so successful that Chinese workers left the fields and workshops and flocked to the theater, where they hid among the artists. The landowners complained, and the local authorities ordered the theater to open only on holidays."[108]

During the summers throughout the Cuban countryside, Chinese celebrated the festival of Guan Gong. For sugar workers, the "dead season" after grinding provided an opportunity for mobility, following celebrations as they ended in one town and began in the next. Chinese associations hosted the festivals. In July 1882, Agustín Chuffat (an elder relative of Antonio Chuffat Latour) and Perfecto Díaz (Jamock) coordinated the inauguration of their association Chen Chi Weng Kueng in Jovellanos with a four-day festival that drew Chinese from across the island, local authorities, and a Chinese diplomat. In 1890, the contractor Damián Machado established a Chinese association in Cienfuegos. In June of that year, delegates from all of the Chinese associations of Santa Clara and Matanzas flocked to the Guan Gong festival he hosted. After the celebration ended in Cienfuegos, the Chinese association in Colón began hosting its own festival.[109]

While the presence of local notables indicates the good standing of Chinese community leaders in the late nineteenth century, at times association activity directly clashed with local mores and the Catholic Church. In Jovellanos, for example, the local parish priest opposed the association's activities when participants chanted the "rite" of Guan Gong at the inauguration ceremony.[110] Chinese theaters similarly confronted restrictions from local laws and opposition from Cuban neighbors. Like Damián Machado and others, former indentured laborer Pastor Pelayo had acquired capital and social standing within the Chinese community in Cienfuegos as a contractor of Chinese laborers for area sugar estates. In 1884, Pelayo became president of the Chinese association La Gran China in Cienfuegos, and the following year he petitioned the town council for permission to establish a theater on Santa Clara Street. When his plans were derailed by municipal ordinances prohibiting wood construction, Pelayo constructed a small theater on the patio of his association, where a company rehearsed during the evenings.[111]

Antonio Chuffat recalled the splendor of the Chinese theater for Cubans, who were fascinated by the exotic music.[112] However, the theaters did not escape criticism from their non-Chinese neighbors. In Havana, the Chinese association Cristóbal Colón (Christopher Columbus) on Zanja Street was formed for three major purposes: dramatic performances, a private school for the children of members, and legal games. In November 1888, thirty-two neighbors signed a complaint to the civil governor, declaring that the drums, cymbals, and violins of the theater disturbed the peace. The petitioners further stated that Asian music was particularly "inharmonious" and "deafening," much worse than the prohibited dances of black urban-dwellers. Association president Facundo Campo responded to the complaint, stating that the noise level "will never reach that which the meat vendor produces beginning at 2 in the morning, whacking his products with an ax, interrupting the sleep of the neighborhood."[113] His response asserted the right of the Chinese community to carry on everyday activities, much as the local butcher did.

In addition to mutual aid, Chinese associations were spaces for congregating, reading newspapers, drinking tea, and celebrating festivals. At times they formed the backdrop for heated arguments between members. Pastor Pelayo remained a force within his Chinese association, known by Cubans as the *casa de socorros* (house of mutual aid). In May 1894, he was accused of inflicting a three-centimeter-long wound upon Nicolás Aside, an association member who had not paid his dues. The court concluded that Aside had fallen against an empty case and hit his head against a sharp corner as he was backing away from Pelayo, causing the wound himself. Pelayo was therefore not fined.[114]

The Californian Chinese in particular became linked with vice by Cuban law enforcement, and later in folklore and historiography. The Chinese lottery filtered into Cuban society by end of the nineteenth century, inspiring new concerns about social customs and morality. In 1894 the pamphlet *Los chinos y su charada* (The Chinese and their charade) was published in Havana by Ramón de Perseverancia, who warned readers of the "pernicious, immoral, and dangerous" Chinese lottery to the greater Cuban public. According to the author, during the years 1876 to 1878, the lottery was popular among domestic workers and messengers in Havana and nearby towns. From 1879 to 1882, however, it corrupted the broader Cuban public, regular customers of Chinese fruit stands and laundries.[115]

In the early twentieth century, the Chinese Cuban Antonio Chuffat echoed the concerns expressed in the pamphlet. He remarks that in 1873 only the Chinese played the *chi-ffá*, keeping the inner-workings of the game closely guarded. This traditional Chinese lottery was based on 36 symbols (such as gold, mountain, and warrior), each with a corresponding number. Chuffat distinguishes this authentic Chinese lottery from "the semi-Creole" and "pillaged" game known among Cubans as "la charada." He condemns the "hardened gamblers" who fabricated the popular version of it in order to swindle the unsuspecting.[116]

Chinese workplaces and residences were constantly subject to police raids for suspected gambling and opium use. From 1867 to 1880, for example, Havana police inspector José Trujillo often fined Chinese and others for playing the Chinese lottery. Most were cooks, day laborers, or itinerant vendors.[117] Across Santa Clara Province throughout the 1880s and 1890s, Chinese were formally charged with *juego prohibido* (illegal games), sometimes individually and other times in groups. In May 1881, for example, the court in Remedios summoned the asiáticos Daniel Vaqué, Tomás Ariosa Asan, and José Lay "to present themselves within nine days to clear themselves of the charge of illegal gambling."[118] Around noon on 25 July 1898, the public health warden in Cienfuegos raided a Chinese association located on Santa Clara Street between Casales and Arango. Stuffing money into their pockets, the Chinese fled down the stairway and scattered onto the street. Police confiscated several items that had been used for the game of *botones*. When interrogated by the authorities, the association president Jacinto Manuel responded that the charges of gambling were dubious, as the majority of members were poor and had no money. When asked why some forty Chinese were gathered at noon, Manuel replied that they were unemployed.[119]

The picture Jacinto Manuel painted of his organization in 1898 was common among many of the Chinese huiguans established during and immediately after the period of indenture. They were populated by aging Chinese men, either unemployed or too old to work, and they lacked new members to sustain the organization. Without sufficient membership dues, the associations were unable to keep up with rent payments. In 1903, the association that had been founded by Pastor Pelayo, "La Gran China" on Velasco Street, had fallen into such a dilemma. President Celestino Sarría was ordered to remit 114 pesos silver in back rent to the building's owner.[120]

An official list generated from 1903 to 1904 reports twelve Chinese associations in Santa Clara Province alone.[121] Eight of these associations were established before independence, and four during the first U.S. occupation (1899–1902). Only three of them were in Cienfuegos, while the remaining were in surrounding sugar towns such as Cruces, Rodas, Sagua la Grande, Santo Domingo, Remedios, Camajuaní, and Placetas. By 1899 these towns also were home to the majority of Chinese shops, reflecting the interconnection between sugar estates and the development of small communities.

Merchant Communities and the Qing Dynasty

As Chinese planted roots in Cuba through their small businesses, property, and families, China itself may have seemed increasingly distant for them. Yet many, especially the transnational merchants of large import firms, attempted to pass Chinese culture and education on to their Cuban-born children and remain connected to their homeland. Chinese consulates, chambers of commerce, and associations served these interests. Up until the 1911 revolution in China, the Qing government remained the institution that best supported these organizations overseas (although often more symbolically than financially). With the exception of a handful of diplomats, Chinese migrant communities lacked the scholar-gentry class that occupied so prominent a position in China. Instead, the recently formed consulates bestowed similar honors and titles upon merchant community leaders overseas, in order to retain their loyalty and to attract investment.[122]

Not until after the end of the coolie trade and the establishment of a Chinese diplomatic presence in Cuba did a general huiguan representing the interests of all Chinese on the island develop. Under the direction of the consulate in Havana, Chinese merchant community leaders formed the umbrella organization known as the Casino Chung Wah (Zhonghua Zonghuiguan) in 1893 and the Chinese Chamber of Commerce (Zhonghua Zongshanghui) in 1897.[123] The Casino Chung Wah was equivalent to the Chinese Consolidated Benevolent Association (CCBA) or Chinese Six Companies in San Francisco, which by 1882 had been established from the various district associations. The CCBA developed transnational commercial and political networks and became the most influential of the Chinese organizations in the Americas.[124]

Similar in organization and charged with representing the interests of the Chinese community in Spanish colonial society, the Casino Chung Wah in Havana engaged in charitable, welfare, cultural, and educational missions. In addition to facilitating bureaucratic procedures for migrants returning to China, it became a conduit for Chinese seeking entry to the United States.[125] Leaders of the Casino Chung Wah came from the highest strata of Chinese merchant society in Cuba. In 1902, the first year of the Cuban republic, Chinese consul general Tan Qianchu purchased a new building for the Casino for $40,000.[126] Unlike nineteenth-century associations founded by former coolies, the Casino Chung Wah, supported by the wealthy Chinese merchant elite, remained intact throughout Cuba's republican period.

Distinctions of race and class among Chinese extended to burial grounds, where the location of tombs for the dead indicated their social status while living. Upper-class Chinese took measures to ensure that their remains would be transferred back to their native land. For example, in December 1886, Quong Sang of Havana received authorization from the governor general to transfer the bones of Antonio Jam Chung Sanz, buried in the cemetery of Colón in June 1881, back to China via the United States.[127] Former Chinese indentured laborers who had converted to Catholicism were buried in La Reina Cemetery in Cienfuegos, but relegated to the "second patio." Here we find the gravesite of Pastor Pelayo.[128] In Regla, Chinese were initially relegated to a cemetery at Punta Blanca, rather than the church cemetery. Later, as the community of free Chinese developed and more adopted Catholicism, they were buried in the church cemetery near the Chinese district.[129] Although Chinese had been dying in Cuba since midcentury, it was not until 1893 that the consul general inaugurated the Chinese General Cemetery (Zhonghua Zongyishan) with donations from community members.[130]

Educational institutions reflected transnational merchants' desire for Chinese cultural attachments to form among the second generation. In the late nineteenth century, Qing diplomats, merchants, and missionaries developed institutions in the Americas to promote Chinese and Western education, a goal that dovetailed with China's path to modernization. Chinese-Western academies (*zhongxi xuetang*) for the sons of Chinese merchants developed in Havana in 1886 and in Lima and San Francisco in 1888. The academies aimed to educate talented overseas Chinese youth in Western technology and science so that they might contribute to China's national wealth and power, while enabling them to retain their cultural heritage through the study of the Confucian classics. The schools' principal founder envisioned a generation of Western- and Chinese-trained youth positioned in shipyards and arsenals along China's coast. Chinese teachers were brought directly from China to the Americas to teach the Confucian classics, and English- or Spanish-language teachers were hired locally. The Chinese-Western academies also prepared students to take the traditional Chinese civil service examinations, thereby providing access to a bureaucratic career in China. Confronted with shortages of funds and enrollments, the academy in Havana closed after five years.

Cuban-born youth struggled with acquiring sufficient Chinese language ability and with competing demands on their time. Of the sixteen successful candidates of the Chinese-Western academy in Havana in 1889, eight passed both the Chinese classics and Spanish exams, four passed only the Chinese classics exam, and four passed only the Spanish exam. They ranged in age from eight to fifteen, with an average age of ten. In a formal inquiry in 1891, the consul general learned that enrollment had dropped due to Chinese New Year festivities, children working for their fathers' businesses, and families returning to China.[131]

Some nineteenth-century transnational Chinese merchants in Cuba sent their sons back to China for school. Among these returnees were mixed children born to Chinese men and Cuban women. In 1881, Pedro López (Lion Fat) had established the American product import firm Con Yin Long. He married a Cuban woman and sent their son to China for education (his son was given the Chinese name Lion Chuk Yin and Spanish name Pedro López).

The younger Lion eventually returned to Cuba and settled in Camajuaní, where according to Antonio Chuffat, he "admirably speaks and writes Chinese." In 1893, the Chinese Andrés Robau established La Perla, the "famous and luxurious café and pastry shop" in Sagua la Grande. He married Julia Glean, and they sent their eldest son to China to study Chinese.[132]

Other children of Chinese merchants attended local (non-Chinese) schools in Cuba. For example, the mixed Antonio Chuffat Latour, who was from a Chinese merchant family background on his father's side, had been educated at the Colegio Los Desamparados (The Defenseless) "for the colored race" in Jovellanos in Matanzas Province. Second-generation children of merchant families such as Chuffat became especially significant as "cultural brokers" with Cuban customers and South American contacts.[133]

In addition to the maintenance of hometown ties in China, toward the end of the nineteenth century Chinese began to engage in transnational activity at higher levels. The intellectual momentum of early Chinese nationalism seeped into Chinese communities overseas. In the face of late-nineteenth-century foreign incursions into China, some migrants displayed spontaneous expressions of patriotism in the bodegas and cafes of Havana. Although at least one Chinese newspaper circulated in the 1880s, Spanish-language Cuban newspapers also served as conduits of news that fueled late-nineteenth-century Chinese patriotism in Cuba.[134] Groups of Chinese gathered to learn about the progress of the Sino-French War (1883–85) through *Diario de la Marina*, *La Discusión*, and *El País*. Vendors of *Diario de la Marina* were known to raise prices on days when the paper carried favorable news for the Chinese, who celebrated Qing military victories over the French by holding banquets, setting off fireworks, and inviting Cubans and Spaniards to drink "fine liquor." Fights broke out in cafés between Chinese and French patrons.[135] By beginning to identify as Chinese, these migrants lay the seeds for the nationalism that took root in overseas communities during the twentieth century.

The planters who initially brought coolies to Cuba and Peru did not intend for them to settle and form families, as indicated by official debates and the lack of females imported. Yet, remaining in Cuba was often the only option for the Chinese who survived indenture. The fact that Chinese indentured laborers in Cuba worked side-by-side with slaves produced a social dynamic different from that elsewhere in the Americas. Slaves in the final years of emancipation and former coolies followed similar paths, moving off large sugar estates and settling in small towns, at times in conjunction with each other. They employed a range of mechanisms to increase their social status and improve their quality of life, including engagement with the legal system, marriage and godparenthood, and participation in ethnic and cultural associations. As Chinese made claims to a place in colonial Spanish society, they formed interracial alliances with local Cubans. Collaborations between Chinese and Cubans of color came from common experiences on the plantation, such as Pastor Pelayo's purchasing the freedom of an enslaved woman, entering into a common-law marriage, and employing her two brothers as cuadrilla heads. Business arrangements in the neighborhoods and towns that developed beyond the plantation could be mutually beneficial for Cubans and Chinese.

Chinese merchant elites arriving from California or directly from China with capital and connections transformed the urban landscape with their transnational businesses, associations, and theaters. As Chinese communities developed around these institutions in Havana and throughout the provinces (in a less concentrated manner), class stratification developed. The late-nineteenth-century developments in Chinese migrants' diplomatic, economic, cultural, and educational life were brought about by joint initiatives between Qing officials and wealthy, transnational merchant elites, who attempted to define a Chinese "community" that served their interests. Chinese of lower economic strata — those who staffed the restaurants, laundries, shops, and import firms — were effectively in a patron-client relationship with these community leaders. But some former indentured laborers also became leaders of the emerging Chinese Cuban communities and led similar cultural initiatives.

While connections to China weakened for those former indentured laborers who started families in Cuba, they were not severed completely. As Spain began to gradually lose its grip on its prized Caribbean possession, thousands of Chinese, either by choice or lacking an alternative, planted roots in Cuban soil. Antonio Chuffat comments, "After thirty years of residency, in which they had spent their youth enslaved, they had lost the affection toward their country, and they were considered Cubans."[136] Some expressed loyalty to an incipient Cuban nation, most vividly portrayed by the Chinese *mambises*, or freedom fighters, who participated in the Cuban struggles for independence from Spain.

II

MIGRANTS BETWEEN EMPIRES AND NATIONS

There was not a single Chinese Cuban deserter;
there was not a single Chinese Cuban traitor!

—Gonzalo de Quesada, *Mi primera ofrenda* (1892)

Once they had achieved their goal, they peacefully and silently
retired to their homes, without great displays or propaganda that might call
into question their good faith toward the Cuban motherland, whose creation
was the sole interest that animated them in serving it. *And they served.*

—Guillermo Tejeiro, *Historia ilustrada de la Colonia China en Cuba* (1947)

CHAPTER FOUR

Freedom Fighters

It is said that one of the men eligible to serve as president of the first Cuban republic in 1902 was José Bu Tak (Hu De), a celebrated Chinese mambí and veteran of all three wars for Cuban independence from Spain (1868–98). In 1869, José Bu and sixty other Chinese indentured laborers rose up to join the insurgents in Sagua la Grande. Bu guided Cuban forces through the mountains of Trinidad, delivering messages for General Máximo Gómez across the fortified ditch constructed by Spain and earning the rank of captain. Those who knew Bu on the battleground during the 1895 war describe him as ferociously charging with a machete and shouting "¡Cuba yat pa' carajo!" (For Cuba! Spanish go to hell!).[1] How is it possible that just a few decades after the end of the coolie trade one of the lowly Chinese laborers would be spoken of with such high esteem in Cuban nationalist discourse?

During the thirty years of struggles for independence from Spain, Cubans were forced to reconsider the relationship between race and the emerging nation. The independence movement advocated the abolition of slavery and embraced Cubans of color. The Spanish, however, represented it as nothing more than a lawless insurgency with the potential to turn Cuba into a black republic, thus evoking old fears of another Haiti. In the interim between the end of the Ten Years' War (1868–78) and the onset of the War of Independence (1895–98), an idealized portrait of the black insurgent emerged in public discourse. Ada Ferrer argues that this figure, "dreaded emblem of race war and black republic, was neutralized and made an acceptable—and indeed central—component in the struggle for Cuban nationhood."[2] Intellectuals and activists of all socioracial backgrounds forged a conception of a raceless Cuban nationality as the ideological foundation of the movement.

Chroniclers of the wars for independence wove stories of black mambises into narratives of the birth of the Cuban nation. These stories about the feats of average soldiers for the cause of "Cuba libre" also reference patriotic actions by Chinese. The recent history of the Chinese as coolie laborers who had suffered the same atrocities as slaves made them a natural choice for the construction of a cross-racial discourse about Cuban revolutionary soldiers. Both slaves and coolies shared a common trajectory from bound laborers to cimarrones (runaways) to freedom fighters. During the late nineteenth century, daily interactions with Cubans, ethnic networks, and legal claims facilitated the Chinese transition out of indenture. But it was their participation in the Cuban struggles for independence from Spain that enabled the Chinese to be included as an integral component in the public discourse on the Cuban nation. Nationalist writings on the role of the Chinese during Cuba's shift from colony to nation further cemented their position. However, while on the surface Cuban nationalist discourse glorifies Chinese contributions to the independence struggles, qualified portrayals of their roles indicate a deeper ambivalence toward their full inclusion in the new republic.

Throughout Cuban history, the story of the Chinese mambises has been told and retold, from an 1892 treatise by a Cuban statesman to a recent memoir by three Chinese Cuban generals who fought in the 1959 revolution.[3] While war narratives highlight moments of ferocity and courage on the front lines of battle, they also emphasize the Chinese role in noncombat auxiliary activities. Chinese delivered messages, prepared food, and acquired medicine and clothing for the rebels—auxiliary roles that have also been associated with Cuban women and Afro-Cuban men. A discourse of Chinese freedom fighters as returning peacefully to work after the war promotes the ideal of a certain kind of Chinese immigrant in the Cuban nation, one who helps with the rebuilding process through manual labor. The selective glorification of the "contributions" of the Chinese to the Cuban nation becomes especially significant in light of the immediate aftermath of independence, when Cubans of color protested the unequal distribution of power, some refusing to turn in their arms.

The Ten Years' War

The independence momentum that resulted in the birth of new Latin American republics in the early nineteenth century failed to reach Spain's Caribbean possessions. In Cuba, the colonial government catered to Spanish planters and merchants amid debates over issues such as autonomy and the institution of slavery. Creole elites increasingly made demands on the colonial government for liberal trade and taxation policies, the gradual abolition of slavery, and greater representation in government. Spain's unwillingness to reform fostered a growing independence sentiment that erupted into war in 1868.

Carlos Manuel de Céspedes (1819–74), owner of a sugar mill in Manzanillo, set off the armed struggles on 10 October 1868 with a proclamation of Cuban independence, known as the "Grito de Yara" (Shout of Yara). The immediate goals of separatists were limited in scope, as they attempted to win the support of western planters in Cuba and authorities in the United States, both of whom were concerned about economic disruption and race rebellion. On 10 April 1869, Céspedes and other rebel leaders met in Guáimaro in Camagüey Province to approve a constitution that provided for representative government and declared all inhabitants of the new Republic in Arms to be free. The insurrection quickly gained momentum, attracting tens of thousands of volunteer soldiers from among all races and classes in Cuba within a few years. With the outbreak of war, planters followed the lead of Céspedes in emancipating their slaves and indentured laborers. Those freed, however, were subject to recruitment for the insurgent army.

The 1874 commission to investigate Chinese indentured labor arrived under Spanish escort in the midst of the anticolonial struggle and therefore did not reach rebel camps in the eastern provinces. Lacking testimony from Chinese insurgents, the report concluded: "The probability is that the Chinese are unwilling to take part in aiding the insurrection."[4] However, evidence from war memoirs and other sources suggests that up to 5,000 Chinese fought in Cuban rebel ranks. Their presence was considerable, as in the case of the 400 Chinese incorporated into General Thomas Jordan's column in May 1869 (comprising three-quarters of the total) or the 500 Chinese among 1,300 Cubans in the Battle of Las Guásimas in March 1874, precisely during the time of the commission's investigation.[5]

For African slaves and Chinese indentured laborers in colonial Cuba, joining the insurgents offered a means of emancipation. Both sides in the struggle enticed them with promises of freedom in exchange for military service and loyalty. Spanish officials offered them financial incentives.[6] Some Chinese followed a particular master or cuadrilla head in joining the anti-colonial struggle, and experiences on the plantations could pave the way for leadership roles. An officer who enlisted a group of fifty-four Asians in 1869 predicted that one of them who had led a labor gang would prove a capable sergeant.[7] Others may have been influenced by recent military experiences in China, especially the midcentury Taiping Rebellion in China. Lam Fu Kin (Juan Sánchez) "knew warfare" from his experience with the antidynastic movement in China and became a captain of insurgents in Cuba.[8] Contemporary observers attributed Chinese involvement in the insurrection to the Spanish government's policy of requiring them to either recontract or leave the island. In 1878, the English consul commented on the policy as "probably the chief, if not the only cause, why Chinese are found in the rebel ranks."[9]

Many slaves and coolies escaped their masters to join the uprising in Camagüey and Oriente. News of Chinese participation in the struggles reached the Cuban diasporic community abroad. On 9 May 1870, *Estrella de Cuba*, a revolutionary publication in New York, commended the patriotism and good behavior of Chinese soldiers. Spanish colonial authorities were concerned enough about their swelling numbers in the rebel army to suspend further Chinese immigration by royal decree on 27 April 1871, portraying them as subversive elements fomenting disorder and blocking the pacification of the island.[10] Free Chinese also joined the ranks of local heroes. In 1869 Liborio Wong (Wong Seng) abandoned his herbal medicine practice near Manzanillo to join the rebel cause. Early in the war, Captain Wong became known for his heroism in the battles of Cauto Embarcadero, Mina de Tuna, and Guáimaro.[11]

Not all coolies flocked to insurgent camps, however. The 1874 commission reported on dozens of Chinese who testified to forced recruitment. Zhang Luan, petitioning with thirty others, stated, "The rebellion in Cuba is one of Spanish subjects against the Spanish Government; many instances have occurred of planters, when joining the rebels, endeavouring to induce the Chinese labourers to do likewise, and of the latter, even at the risk of death, refusing, or, if constrained to go, at once returning." Rather than being commended, Chinese bore the brunt of their refusal to associate with "disturbers of law and order." Some fled to Havana, while others joined cuadrillas. Some reported the occurrence to Spanish officials, only to be forced to labor without wages. Wu Ajing stated, "I was carried away by the insurgents, but in a few days I succeeded in escaping, and was subsequently conducted to a dépôt."[12]

Spanish generals responded to the guerrilla warfare by constructing "La Trocha" in 1873, a defense zone that attempted to separate insurgent regions in the east from the rest of the island, and by establishing martial law in the cities. The fortified ditch extended from the northern to southern coasts of Camagüey Province, which bordered Las Villas and the massive sugar plantations of central Cuba. Spanish officials sent thousands of captured Chinese runaways to work on the project. One Chinese testified that "for the work of the Trocha, a locality most unhealthy and close to the insurgent districts, the Government dispatched 1/10th negroes and 9/10ths Chinese. Of the latter a third perished, and those who survived, instead of receiving on their return the freedmen's papers which had been promised to them, are now confined in the various dépôts."[13] Spain's promise to grant cédulas to Chinese who remained loyal to the crown often remained unfulfilled, and many escaped the wretched work of the trocha to join rebels in the east.

Over the course of the Ten Years' War, Generals Antonio Maceo and Máximo Gómez led bands of guerrillas through the countryside. Highly mobile, immune to disease, and familiar with local conditions, the rebels defeated Spanish soldiers in key battles and burned sugarcane fields in order to destroy the source of Spain's economic power. Although much of the fighting occurred in the east, Chinese troops also engaged in military efforts in Santa Clara Province. In the November 1877 battle of Nuevas de Jobosí, rebels under the command of Generals Carlos Roloff, Francisco Carrillo, Serafín Sánchez, and others defeated Spanish troops. The Chinese captain José Bu "demonstrated his warrior qualities" in this battle.[14]

Ultimately, the war did not expand beyond the eastern regions of Cuba, far from the centers of sugar production. Colonial troops multiplied in Cuba, and after a prolonged period of fighting, Spain prevailed. When the 10 February 1878 surrender at Zanjón officially ended the Ten Years' War, Cuba remained a Spanish colony. Article Three of the Pact of Zanjón granted unconditional freedom to insurgent slaves and indentured laborers registered in the Liberation Army at the end of the war. In the peace settlement Spain also pledged to enact a range of political and administrative reforms. Although ultimately not successful in overturning colonial rule, the battles undermined the institution of slavery on the island.[15]

For many insurgent leaders, the treaty provisions fell short of their demands for independence and abolition. Just a month later, with 1,500 men assembled in the eastern town of Baraguá, General Antonio Maceo publicly repudiated the peace settlement and renewed the commitment to armed struggle for independence from Spain, continuing the fighting for ten more weeks. During these battles associated with the "Protest of Baraguá," Chinese insurgent leaders were noted for staying the course. By May, however, the protesters were forced to surrender.

Unresolved issues lent continued life to a separatist movement of exiles in the United States and throughout Latin America and Europe. They remained committed to an independent Cuba and to armed struggle, leading to intermittent battles until the final war for independence began in 1895. General Calixto García led returned exiles from abroad and war veterans into the Guerra Chiquita (Little War), named for its short duration of nine months in 1879 and 1880. Like the Ten Years' War, fighting began in the eastern part of the island but also took root in the central provinces.

The rural communities that had developed at the edges of sugar plantations and in the foothills of the Escambray Mountains in Santa Clara Province became key regions of insurgent activity. The mixed population of these communities provided new recruits for the growing independence movement.[16] In Santa Clara, Generals Serafín Sánchez, Francisco Carrillo, and Emilio Núñez led the Guerra Chiquita struggles, with contingents of Chinese soldiers under their command. Prominent Chinese veterans of the Ten Years' War, such as José Bu and José Tolón, also joined. According to one estimate, some eighty Chinese battled under Carrillo in the Remedios region against the Spanish general Polavieja. The captain general intentionally emphasized the race of the insurgents to instill fear among elite Cubans, reporting that "with four blacks and twenty Chinese" Carrillo passed through the zones of Sagua la Grande, Remedios, Cifuentes, Camajuaní, Corralillo, and Los Quemados and made bold incursions through the Cienfuegos region during the course of the campaign. At the same time, in Santa Clara, published edicts and posters in both Spanish and Chinese offered slaves and Chinese contract laborers a reward of 500 pesos for handing over Francisco Carrillo.[17]

The Chinese and the Making of the Cuban Nation

Alongside these feats in battle, Cuban narratives emphasize the Chinese in auxiliary roles as an essential component of the emergent Cuban nation. Emancipated slaves incorporated into the rebel army generally filled subordinate positions at the lowest ranks. By laboring productively and serving as assistants to officers, libertos aided the rebellion materially and quelled the fears of leaders wary of social unrest.[18] Like freed slaves, Chinese participants in the independence struggles were often relegated to noncombat tasks, such as digging trenches, growing and cooking food, and acquiring provisions.

During the Ten Years' War the rebel army drew upon the knowledge of Chinese herbal healers, and in 1871, they were able to contain an outbreak of cholera and smallpox on several sugar estates in Sagua la Grande.[19]

One narrative of Asians as auxiliaries involves an encounter between Cuban insurgents from Key West and a group of charcoal makers. On 4 April 1884, veteran general Carlos Agüero Fundora disembarked his expedition force in Varadero, on the northern coast of Cuba. Hoping to evade Spanish forces, Agüero guided his men through the surrounding mangrove swamps and into the wooded hills. The next morning, Agüero found himself in front of a Chinese charcoal factory (*carbonera*) and cluster of huts. Colonel Rosendo García approached the Chinese with a small group, hoping to obtain information about Spanish forces.

As any hospitable Cuban would do, the Chinese greeted their visitors with coffee, asking where they had come from and what they wanted. García explained that they were separatists from Key West who urgently needed food prepared for forty-seven men. He offered fifteen pesos to Andrés Chiong, the head of the Chinese workers, to make the necessary purchases in the nearest store. But Chiong declined the money and offered to feed the men. García thanked Chiong and quickly returned with his group to the camp in the woods.

Moments later, at 8:30 in the morning, a Spanish commander led 100 cavalry of the Civil Guard on the road from Cárdenas, stopping in front of Andrés Chiong's hut and asking him if he had seen a group of armed insurgents. Chiong evaded the commander with his response "I didn't see armed insurgents in the morning. No sir, I don't know, I was working, burning charcoal." The commander angrily ordered his men to "get out of here": "This *chino* is an idiot, nobody understands him."[20] When Colonel García returned to the Chinese huts, another Chinese named Ambrosio Tang reported that the Spaniards had come by several more times looking for the insurgents, but that the charcoal makers had protected them.

Colonel García thanked Ambrosio Tang and the rest of the Chinese. Now that García had successfully evaded Spanish forces, he turned his attention to satisfying his soldiers' hunger. When he asked the Chinese if they could prepare food for the force and bring it to their camp, "the Chinese did not hesitate; they prepared a magnificent meal: rice with chicken, fried pork, plantain and sweet potato: a Creole meal [*arroz con pollo, cerdo frito, plátano y boniato: una comida criolla*]."[21] After eating, the two Cubans embraced Chiong and Tang with gratitude for the good treatment they had received.[22]

The description of this meal, which was first published in a history of

Cuban Chinese by the Afro-Chinese author Antonio Chuffat and later reproduced in the work of other Cuban writers, encapsulates the link between food and an emerging national culture. Shannon Dawdy argues that "Cuba developed a national cuisine (i.e., a countrywide system of food meaning and food production) in the mid-nineteenth century that became a *nationalist* cuisine during Cuba's revolutionary moments."[23] The foundations of this national cuisine were *viandas* or starchy roots and tubers such as sweet potatoes, yams, and manioc, as well as plantains. These vegetables were native grown and produced on small-scale farming plots. The Cuban independence movement itself became associated with similar values—against both foreign control and large-scale agricultural regimes.[24] In this story, the Chinese, who were relatively recent arrivals on the Cuban scene, prepared what was considered a quintessential Cuban meal. They are portrayed, in other words, not only as defenders of Cuban independence, but also as eligible for integration into Cuban national culture. The Chinese themselves were "imports," but they had endured against both the colonial and plantation systems. By the time of the independence movement they were also potential Cuban citizens.

In the ideal-typical version of these kinds of dynamics, the common struggle against Spanish colonialism had produced a union of whites and blacks. In the words of Ada Ferrer: "The nation—born of the physical, moral, and spiritual embrace of black and white men—transcended race and converted white and black into Cuban. That image and that idea—developed jointly by white, mulatto, and black activists and intellectuals—provided a counterargument to dominant colonial claims about the impossibility of Cuban independence."[25] Through an examination of stories portraying Chinese in war, an analysis of the multiracial dimensions of the birth of the Cuban nation can be expanded beyond white, black, and mulatto. In the charcoal factory episode, the physical embrace between the Chinese civilians and the insurgent leaders sealed a more symbolic union—one of men of all races working together toward the common goal of national unity. Racialized descriptions of the Chinese circulating in the late nineteenth century were replaced by neutral, even positive traits. The Chinese are now portrayed as having assimilated mainstream culture through their adoption of Cuban food and the Spanish language. Furthermore, the Chinese had developed a reputation for quality charcoal production, a contribution to the Cuban wartime economy. Antonio Núñez Jiménez's grandmother, describing the process by which they constructed earthen furnaces to slowly burn charcoal, remembered the Chinese as "the best charcoal makers."[26]

Stories of Chinese heroism reached the ears of the intellectual leaders of the Cuban nationalist movement. Known as the father of Cuban independence, José Martí (1853–95) espoused unity to counter colonialism and its legacies of injustice and racism across the Americas. The ideological foundation of Cuba's independence wars deepened alliances between Chinese coolies and black slaves. While mambises struggled on Cuban soil, exiled leaders waged battle through the international press. José Martí imagined the souls of whites and blacks who died together on the battlefield rising to forge a transracial Cuban union. His writings on race in Cuba focus on blacks and mulattos, with scant mention of the Chinese coolie past. However, Martí's approach does not amount to a full-blown "Orientalist erasure" of the Chinese presence and role in Cuban society.[27]

While José Martí avoided the particularities of the Chinese experience in Cuba, his essays written in exile on "North American Scenes" (*Escenas Norteamericanas*) include detailed passages on Chinatowns in the United States. His descriptions are typical of Orientalist representations of Asians at the time: "little men with almond eyes, bony and hairless faces, and long braids."[28] Yet, Martí's portrayals of the sights, sounds, and scents of funerals, weddings, and theater in New York's Chinatown reveal an animated interest in whatever he deemed representative of Chinese culture. As an advocate of the liberation of oppressed peoples everywhere, Martí defended Chinese immigrants against abominable treatment and racial attacks in the United States. He condemned the 1882 Chinese Exclusion Acts, expressing astonishment "that the nation that prided itself on calling all men to its breast" would "close its doors and deny its fields to an entire race of respectful, useful, and peaceful people."[29] Shortly after the passage of the law, a conflict between workers for Union Pacific Coal at Rock Springs in Wyoming Territory resulted in a white mob firing at unarmed Chinese miners and burning their huts, killing twenty-eight and wounding fifteen. Martí wrote a letter to the Buenos Aires newspaper *La Nación* condemning the massacre.

However, embedded within his defense of Chinese workers, Martí perpetuated stereotypes of them as passive and exotic. He described them as "cheap, perfect labor," writing: "They are docile and submissive, no less skilled and energetic than workers of other races, so the companies are pleased to employ them."[30]

Shifting to Cuba, Martí referenced the Chinese reputation for loyalty in the Cuban struggles for independence: "The Chinese were great patriots; there is not one case of a Chinese traitor: even if they catch a Chinese, there is no danger: 'I don't know,' no one can get him to say more than 'I don't know.'"[31] Here he reproduces the grammatically incorrect Chinese response as "no sabo," simultaneously highlighting both their loyalty and foreignness. Martí also relates the story of a captain who requested to be relieved from his command of unmanageable Chinese soldiers. After a meeting with General Ignacio Agramonte, the captain agreed to return to his troops, declaring with teary eyes that the diplomatic leader could persuade him to "become a father to these Chinese."[32] This paternalistic gesture, and Martí's inclusion of this narrative, underscores the suitability of Chinese "freedom fighters" to be welcomed within the Cuban nation, but under the guidance of white Cubans.

Martí's mentions of the Chinese in Cuba are scant because they are peripheral to his main discursive goals: Cuba's independence and the related promise of racial equality between blacks and whites. The Chinese were a potential threat to racial harmony (an "other" that complicated the ideal of black-white unity and mestizaje or racial mixing). The few mentions he makes of the Chinese in Cuba are an attempt to impose order on the potential chaos from large numbers of foreign workers brought in to undercut native labor, a dynamic with which he was familiar from observing conflicts in the United States.

One of Martí's contemporaries and confidants, Gonzalo de Quesada y Arostegui (1868–1915), was the first to highlight the Chinese positively in the emerging Cuban nation. The Cuban statesman's 1892 work *Mi primera ofrenda* contains a section celebrating the participation of the Chinese in the struggles for Cuban independence.[33] Gonzalo de Quesada sympathetically discusses the Chinese coolie trade within the history of colonialism and indigenous and African slavery. It is significant, however, that he begins his essay by glorifying free Spanish immigrants and the potential of a new generation of Cuban-born whites for the developing nation. Only then does he present Chinese motivations for joining the Ten Years' War and their record of unfailing courage, loyalty, and assistance.

Like his black counterpart, the Chinese insurgent is portrayed in such texts as heroic, selfless, and—to a certain extent—raceless. In one anecdote, he relates that Chinese Lieutenant Pio Cabrera steadfastly held his position to enable the safe retreat of his fellow Cuban insurgents. "The Spanish troops were coming; in the highway a soldier, a Chinaman, awaits them, head uncovered, knee on the ground, rifle shouldered. Every time he shoots, an enemy falls. Almost upon him are fifty men; Pio unmoved, charges, aims, shoots with mathematical regularity. A bullet breaks his leg, and Pio lying in the red and damp earth, with the same calmness, with the same deadly certainty charges, aims, shoots. Every time the detonation of his arm is heard, one more uniform falls. He ceases to shoot."[34] Even while being pounded with a hailstorm of bullets in his final moments, Pio threw his rifle at the Spanish soldiers.

The Chinese who fought in the Cuban wars for independence were aware of the significance of their actions beyond seeking relief from the unjust system of coolie labor. The Chinese Captain Tancredo came to Cuba at age ten and received an education in Villa Clara. Gonzalo de Quesada describes him as "never ill dressed" and interested in continuing his learning during moments of rest under the guidance of Eduardo Machado, one of the leaders of the Ten Years' War. "More than once, under the shade of some luxuriant 'mango,' the blonde Representative of Las Villas gave lessons to the Chinaman, the humble Lieutenant of the Army. What a beautiful picture of brotherhood, the work of our Revolution!" When Tancredo was wounded and taken prisoner, a Spanish officer scornfully called him a "chino de manila." In nineteenth-century Cuba, the label referenced coolies and corruption, as some Chinese brokers from the Philippines profited from the trade. Tancredo took to his feet, pulled his officer's diploma from his breast, and replied that he was "not a Manila Chinaman, no," but "a Lieutenant of the Army of Liberation of Cuba! . . . Shoot me!"[35]

Such anecdotes about Chinese heroic participation in the struggles for independence abound in Cuban war memoirs and in recent historiography. Beneath this surface, questions emerge as to how the Chinese presence shaped the racial and class dynamics of the Liberation Army and of a Cuban society in transition. Insurgent commanders, both white and black, led soldiers who hailed from among the lowest stratum of Cuban society and who had only recently emerged from bound labor. The wars for independence proved to be, to a certain extent, a social leveling ground. Ada Ferrer notes that although the movement was initially led by "a handful of prosperous white men," it "placed free men of color in local positions of authority. It also freed slaves, made them soldiers, and called them citizens."[36] Service in the Liberation Army was one means by which former slaves, ex-coolies, and their descendants could raise their social and economic status. Juan Jiménez Pastrana comments that to serve in General Antonio Maceo's forces "constituted a recognized stamp of honor." When others referred to a particular Chinese under Maceo's command merely as "José" or "Chino," he was known to respond, "Careful, I am Corporal José."[37] At this moment, his self-identification as a soldier for the Liberation Army was paramount.

From 1868 onward, men of all classes became citizens of a Republic in Arms. In the mountains and woods of Cuba, the Chinese interacted with blacks, mulattos, and whites whose rank ranged from foot soldier to general. In Havana Province, General Adolfo Castillo reportedly attempted to learn some Chinese in order to converse with all of his troops. Castillo's regiment included "a group of brave Chinese," among them Víctor, Genaro, and Francisco Arocha. On many occasions the general was observed practicing Chinese "in democratic conversation in the camp with one or another Asian soldier," usually Victor Arocha, who "rode a horse extremely fast" and wore "a long braid."[38] Retaining the Manchu queue in a display of loyalty to the Qing dynasty and to his homeland did not preclude his participation in the Cuban independence movement or hinder his battlefield heroism. Arocha and the black Domingo Mendoza joined forces to rescue the general in hand-to-hand combat with a Spanish officer.[39]

Accounts of and praise for Chinese heroism may have been overstated. Yet, they demonstrate how in the unique setting of battle, former distinctions of color and class could give way to those of skill and valor. Chinese forged comradeship with Cubans in camp and on the battlefield. The Chinese Captain José who served under General Máximo Gómez was described not only as dashing in looks but also helpful and good-humored. During periods of rest in the camp, Captain José lightened the mood by "amusing his brothers in arms with his witty remarks." One day, he shot a Spanish captain who had surprised him on horseback. José took the reins of the fallen captain's horse and headed back to the camp. In the horse's saddlebags, he was surprised to find a roasted chicken and an abundant ration of crackers. "Over several days, José ate the chicken in pieces and shared some of the delicacy with various comrades. When not one muscle of the chicken remained, José, in his characteristic jovial tone, showed it to his comrades" and said, "You want chicken? Kill a Spanish captain."[40]

The War of 1895

In 1895, Cuban rebels renewed the war of independence under the inspiration of José Martí and the leadership of Generals Máximo Gómez and Antonio Maceo. By all accounts, fewer Chinese participated in the War of 1895 than in the previous struggles.[41] By the onset of the final war for independence, the majority of former indentured laborers who had remained in Cuba worked in agriculture or as traders. Most were of an advanced age, and some had even achieved a degree of social and economic success in the Spanish colony. Thus, there were fewer incentives for Chinese, especially for the new arrivals from China and California, to join rebel forces than there had been during the Ten Years' War (1868–78), which overlapped with the coolie period.

Damián Machado, the Chinese contractor from Soledad Estate in Cienfuegos, continued work as usual in 1895. He avoided insurgent camps, even becoming a target of rebels who gradually encroached upon Soledad and nearby estates. Writing from his sugarcane farm Guabairo on 2 November 1895, a panicked P. M. Beal described rebel forces taking control of boat transportation to Soledad: "I was informed there would probably be no boat for Soledad, as the rebels would not permit her to pass unless she paid her port charges; on her way down she had been stopped, the rebels took the Chinaman Damian out of her and kindly informed him that he would immediately be conducted to the nearest guasima where the solemn ceremony of hanging a Chinaman would be proceeded with in due form." Damián Machado used his skills at negotiation to get himself out of this sticky situation. Beal continued: "However, he made some kind of compromise with them, gave them his nickel-watch and I don't know what else—and he was landed right side up at Cienfuegos never again to return to Soledad while these dreadful people held the situation."[42]

In an effort to remove the rebels' economic and social base of support in the countryside, in mid-1896 Spanish Commander-in-Chief Valeriano Weyler instituted the infamous reconcentration policy that forcibly enclosed the rural population in towns and sugar mills, resulting in starvation and death. When Damián Machado eventually returned to the estate, he met with difficulties in obtaining new workers. In December 1896, just before grinding was to begin, Machado was contracted to cut and deliver cane from the colonia Belmonte. He informed the estate manager that "he had been refused the necessary permits that were required at that time to allow work people to leave the town of Cienfuegos."[43] Machado's short-term interests lay in maintaining his cuadrilla of Chinese workers and earning a profit, rather than to some broader realization of Cuban independence and conception of a Cuban nation. Other factors keeping him in Cienfuegos were his family and several businesses in town. When Machado opened a shop of Asian products in 1898, however, he named it La Cubana, a gesture toward the emerging Cuban nation.[44]

Although fewer in numbers than in previous struggles, Chinese participated in the independence struggles throughout Cuba in 1895 both as combatants and in key auxiliary roles.[45] In addition to the many veterans of the Ten Years' War who reenlisted, new recruits joined the ranks of the Liberation Army. One of the first rebel victories during this war was the 13 May

1895 battle at Jobito, led by Generals Antonio and José Maceo, Jesús Rabí, and Periquito Pérez against some 400 Spanish troops in the east. In a bitter struggle that lasted six and a half hours, Spanish forces abandoned their camp after suffering numerous losses, including the death of Colonel Joaquín Bosch. General Pérez's forces in this campaign included twenty Chinese. War veterans attest that Captain José Tolón and his twelve Chinese soldiers reportedly "battled at the level of the strongest natives" under General Rabí.[46] Chinese troops also concentrated in Matanzas and Santa Clara Provinces. The Chinese are described as participating "gracefully" in the 18 November 1896 battle at Paso de las Damas that resulted in the death of insurgent General Serafín Sánchez. One group of Chinese belonged to the guard of General Francisco Carrillo. Another, headed by the Chinese Captain Facundo, belonged to the infantry of General José González Planas. The third and "heartiest" contingent of Chinese, headed by Captain Andrés Lima, battled under General José Miguel Gómez (who later served as the second president of the Republic of Cuba from 1909–13). At the vigil held at Pozo Azúl for the fallen Serafín Sánchez—whose last words were "Continue the march"—"the eyes of those hardened natives and Chinese insurgents could not evade the furtive tear."[47]

In addition to such battles, the Chinese have been especially noted for their contributions in bringing food, medicine, clothing, and shoes from the towns back to the camps and for offering refuge to insurgents. The majority of those who assisted in this manner were not included in the official registers of soldiers in the Liberation Army. Nicasio, "a valiant and astute Chinese" who served under Colonel Eladio Bacallao, for example, lived in a hut on the southern coast of Havana Province. One night, while in a deep sleep after fulfilling his daily "Cuban journey" (*cubanísima jornada*), Nicasio was killed by Spanish troops and his rustic dwelling was burned.[48] Antonio Simón, who entered and exited Remedios with goods and correspondence, was one of many Chinese who served in auxiliary roles there.[49]

Even some wealthier Chinese merchants lent economic aid to the independence movement. The sugarcane farmer and merchant Pan Wu (Justo Peña) in Villa Clara committed "almost all of his fortune" to the independence cause and later contributed five thousand pesos to Sun Yat-sen's republican revolution in China. Pan Wu is also remembered for being a friend of Marta Abreu and her husband Luis Estévez, well-known separatists and benefactors connected to Cuban generals and politicians.[50] In Cienfuegos, José Asan's business "El Gallo" served as general headquarters for the Liberation Army. Its key location and function as a place for soldiers to eat, rest, and converse made the Chinese inn an ideal spot for the base. This choice of headquarters also attests to preexisting community ties between the Chinese owner and members of the multiracial army. Antonio Chuffat commends José Asan's "serious and kind character; he never denied food to any Cuban during the war of independence."[51] During reconcentration, Chinese played a key role in alleviating hunger in towns. The Hakka Chinese Carlos Cartaya Chung, a well-known philanthropist and president of the Sociedad Asiática in Remedios, set up a canteen during reconcentration and donated eight hundred bowls of Chinese soup each morning and evening. After 1902, Cartaya Chung established a shop of merchandise from China, a restaurant, and a currency exchange business in Remedios. He married a Cuban woman and sent their four children back to China for school.[52]

Like other merchants, Chinese shopkeepers did not always voluntarily offer food and provisions to soldiers. Insurgents routinely requisitioned shops and were aided in the looting by local residents. On 22 January 1896, for example, a black officer raided the town of Sabanilla del Encomendador in Matanzas Province with about three hundred men, predominantly black and mulatto. The town was known for being the birthplace of independence leader Juan Gualberto Gómez. The insurgents burned some buildings, stole some horses, and looted several grocery stores owned by Chinese and Spanish. Before departing, they distributed a portion of the goods among a gathering of black onlookers in town.[53]

Documenting Chinese Freedom Fighters

Despite the widespread recognition of Chinese participation in the wars for independence, an analysis of their role remains peripheral to scholarship on the social composition of the armies. Appointed inspector general of the army, Carlos Roloff compiled a register of surviving and deceased soldiers between 1899 and 1900. The massive list indicates whether a soldier was native to Cuba or foreign-born, but in keeping with the democratic ideal of the rebel army, it does not further classify combatants by color or birthplace.[54] Thus, it is impossible to ascertain the exact number of Chinese combatants. The occasional Chinese surnames in the register are one indicator of ethnicity. However, without a racial marker, the widespread use of Spanish names among the Chinese during this period makes it difficult to distinguish Chinese participants from whites, blacks, and mulattos.

Historians can only roughly estimate the percentage of soldiers who either identified themselves or were classified by others as persons of color. Drawing on available sources, Michael Zeuske suggests that blacks comprised anywhere between 40 and 90 percent of the Liberation Army.[55] Recent studies have attempted to reconstruct the social composition of rebel forces during the 1895 war from a local perspective. Orlando García Martínez demonstrates that kinship networks aided recruitment among former slaves and their descendants, who maintained a strong presence in the Cienfuegos region.[56] Among the recruits were numerous men surnamed "Sarría" (from the same plantation as Chinese contractor Pastor Pelayo's wife). According to oral tradition, both Pelayo and his Afro-Chinese son Blas participated in the final war.[57] Even more difficult to count than Chinese immigrants are the second generation of Chinese Cubans who participated in the independence struggles. Born in Cuba to a Chinese man and Cuban woman, the veteran Ramón Estrada lived in Santa Lucía in the Holguín region of Oriente. A photo of him in mambí attire, with his gun at his shoulder, and inscribed to his aunt as a "memento of the war of '95" has been proudly passed down through his family.[58]

Once officially discharged from the Liberation Army, soldiers acquired the status of "veteran" of the Cuban war for independence, which eventually enabled them to claim back pay and a pension. In 1902, a commission was formed under the direction of General Máximo Gómez to determine the definitive lists of veterans and the amount of pay accrued according to their rank and duration of service. Among the foreign-born combatants who applied to this commission for back pay were 1,361 Spaniards, 139 Africans, 67 Puerto Ricans, 39 Americans, 37 Dominicans, and 36 Chinese. Of the 36 Chinese applications, 30 were awarded compensation, including 6 for which payments were made posthumously to the veteran's surviving family members.[59]

The small number of Chinese applicants to this commission belies their actual degree of participation in the 1895 war. However, even from this small sample, regional and demographic recruitment patterns emerge, which show that the recruits mirrored the general population of Chinese in Cuba. Out of the 36, 15 were from the Fourth Corps and 9 from the Fifth Corps, units situated in Santa Clara and Matanzas Provinces, which were centers of large-scale sugar production where former slaves and former indentured laborers had been concentrated.[60] Most of the Chinese applicants to the commission were listed as unable to read and write, and working in agriculture or as cooks, carpenters, and vendors. Most were also listed as single, although a civil status of single does not indicate whether a Chinese man had entered a common-law marriage (or whether he had a wife in his home village in

China). Nineteen of the applicants were between forty-five and fifty-four years old, and 13 between fifty-five and sixty-four, while the oldest was seventy. Their relatively advanced age suggests that they had been in Cuba since the coolie period.[61]

Many known Chinese veterans do not appear in the official registers because they did not apply for a pension. One was the celebrated captain José Bu. After the end of the Guerra Chiquita, Bu had established himself as a trader in Sagua la Grande and eventually in Cienfuegos, where he married a Cuban woman. With the outbreak of war in 1895, Bu sold his business and moved to the Barrio Guadalupe (today the Barrio Chino), dividing the proceeds from the sale between his wife and the liberation cause, and subsequently joined the army. Bu finished the final war of independence with the rank of lieutenant colonel under the command of General Higinio Esquerra, in the Cienfuegos brigade.[62]

Notwithstanding the example of José Bu, limits on opportunities for advancement within the army ranks replicated old social hierarchies, particularly for those formerly under bondage.[63] Like blacks and mulattos, most Chinese were simply soldiers; 30 of the 36 Chinese applicants to the commission were designated as such, while two were noncommissioned officers (one sergeant and one corporal). However, four achieved officer status: two second lieutenants, one lieutenant, and one captain—Pablo Jiménez, the Ten Years' War veteran who had fought under the command of the American general Thomas Jordan and General José Sanguily.

Six Chinese who died during the war were officially recognized after family members solicited the army on their behalf. Of these, four died in combat, one due to illness, and one of an unspecified natural cause. Another six were denied official recognition because they did not present sufficient evidence of active service or remunerable civil service. However, the petitioners may have contributed nonremunerable efforts to the independence movement. For example, the sixty-eight-year-old José Bruzón joined the Third Corps in 1896 and remained until 24 August 1898. Bruzón declared that he had served as assistant to an officer for one year and five months. He was excluded from the register because he had not proven active service.[64]

Postindependence Citizenship

After the explosion of the USS *Maine* in Havana harbor in February 1898, when it became more certain that the United States would intervene and that Spain would lose the war, new recruits joined the rebel army. Many were white, urban, and educated, and they automatically superseded the majority of soldiers of color in rank. In April 1898, the United States declared war against Spain. Within four months, U.S. and Cuban troops emerged victorious, bringing thirty years of Cuban struggles for independence from Spain to an end, although the U.S. army would occupy the country for the next three years. During this period, the status of officers of color in the postwar distribution of power remained highly contested. White independence leaders were well aware that rank in the army would affect postwar social status and so attempted to limit the social leveling effect of service in the rebel army. Ada Ferrer comments, "An army of rustic men defending a just cause was one thing; quite another was the exercise of power, authority, and responsibility by those same men in time of peace."[65]

When Chinese soldiers returned to their former occupations after the war, many did so with a new sense of identity. They were among the honored mambises (freedom fighters) who had won national independence; they were citizens of the new Cuban republic. Yet they were still vulnerable to the partiality and clientage that pervaded the preparation of the final lists of veterans in 1902–3.[66]

It took much determination for an individual to persevere with a claim. On 10 January 1903, the Chinese Manuel Jiménez wrote a letter from his association in Cárdenas directly appealing to General Máximo Gómez. He detailed his military service from 1896 to 1898 and requested his back pay. In 1896, he had enlisted at Hatuey Estate in San José de los Baños under Colonel Clotilde García, ultimately finishing the war under Colonel Aguilar. In addition to combat, from 1897 to 1898 he had entered towns "incognito" to take provisions "without appearing before any authority, as my being Asian permitted me impunity." He emphatically wrote to the esteemed general, "I have witnesses who can certify my services."[67] In the aftermath of the independence wars, the very act of writing a letter to Máximo Gómez signified a claim to citizenship in the new republic.

Cuban independence narratives generally praise Chinese soldiers who, after leaving the Liberation Army, simply returned to work, thereby contributing to the restoration of the land and economy after decades of war. In part, these narratives reflect the postwar fear of Cuban elite politicians and U.S. authorities that there might be an uprising by former rank-and-file soldiers. These narratives in effect promoted an ideal type of Cuban citizen, one who peacefully contributed to the rebuilding process, rather than joining Cubans of color in protesting the U.S. occupation or the unequal distribution of power after independence.

This discourse persisted well into the twentieth century, as in the portrayal of Chinese in a local history of Remedios, published after the Second World War. One case in the book is that of a Chinese surnamed Cuan, who in 1870, at age twenty-two, was brought to Cuba as an indentured laborer, where he worked on Chavasco Estate in Sagua la Grande. Cuan "threw himself into the revolution years later" and was wounded three times. He converted to Catholicism in Placetas and was baptized as Agapito Fortún. After the war, he returned to working in sugarcane on San Andrés Estate, and from there he made his way to Remedios. The local history praises him as "an exemplary citizen" who "left behind many children, *remedianos*, who distinguish themselves as professionals, teachers, and artists."[68] Another case is that of the Chinese captain Luis Lima, who had guided an "intrepid company" of Chinese in the defeat of Spanish troops in Arroyo Blanco, Las Villas. After the war, Lima acquired a modest sugarcane farm in a remote part of Morón, Camagüey, and "devoted his days honestly to agricultural work."[69] Still another Chinese captain, Facundo, had headed a contingent of his compatriots in the battle at Paso de las Damas on 18 November 1896, led by the black general José González Planas. After the war, Facundo established a shop in Yaguajay, Las Villas, "where he devoted himself in an exemplary manner to commercial occupations."[70]

Perhaps the most well-known case of a Chinese who simply returned to work, but also a precautionary tale of the cost of doing so, is that of the famous José Bu. No available evidence indicates that Bu applied for his record of discharge and pension after the end of the 1898 war. In June 1897, at the age of forty-six, Bu married the twenty-year-old white Ana Justa Suárez in Cienfuegos. Their young daughter, Josefa Bú y Suárez, died in November 1898.[71] In 1900, Bu registered a shop of imports from Asia called La Niña Julia, located on the main commercial artery, San Fernando Street, in Cienfuegos but sold it a year later.[72] Antonio Chuffat, writing in 1927, painted a depressing picture of Bu's final days in Havana: "He currently lives in the Capital of the Republic, forgotten by his friends, those whom in another era, in his good times, he had protected."[73] Bu ended his days working as a porter in a theater on Zanja Street in Havana, with no pension to fall back on. He died on 28 July 1928.

At his funeral, however, he received military honors. In a moving ceremony, veterans of the Liberation Army escorted Bu's corpse to the General Cemetery of the Chinese community in Vedado, placing his remains in the pantheon of the association On Ten Tong (of which Bu was a founder).[74] Subsequent chroniclers, especially those writing after the Cuban Revolution of

1959, celebrate José Bu, adding the Chinese mambí to a pantheon of heroes recognized by all Cubans.

Race and Protests in the New Republic

Cubans began the New Year in 1899 with a formal military occupation by U.S. forces, one that circumscribed the ability of nationalists to shape their own political future. In particular, Cubans of color who made claims to voting and property rights as citizens of the new nation were quickly confronted with obstacles. These barriers came from both U.S. military rulers and Cuban leaders, unwilling to endanger political stability in a time of transition from colony to republic. In the name of public order, the U.S. occupation government imposed limits on suffrage and land distribution and ownership. Rebecca Scott and Michael Zeuske describe the result as "a complex, multi-sided struggle to define the boundaries of freedom, the content of citizenship, and the pattern of access to resources."[75]

Limits on Cuban political participation and access to resources stemmed not only from the U.S. occupation, but also from internal political struggles that had developed among Cubans during the final war for independence.[76] The political consensus between black, white, and mulatto revolutionaries was fragile. José Martí, the white son of a Spaniard and a Cuban, had supported the argument that the continued use of racial labels was detrimental to national unity. However, Ada Ferrer demonstrates that "as nationalist writers called for racial silence, as they argued that nationality superseded race, and as they propounded the image of a passive and politically malleable black insurgent, the recent history of anticolonial rebellion and slave emancipation encouraged not political passivity but rather political action—and often political action organized explicitly on the basis of racial identification."[77]

In order to overcome the limits on power for people of color, a cluster of intellectuals began to advocate racially organized political engagement. Journalist Juan Gualberto Gómez y Ferrer (1854–1933)—who self-identified as mulatto—was born free to slave parents, received an education in Paris and Havana, and emerged as a leader of this group.[78] He advocated political representation and advancement of black citizens, even as he attempted to reconcile this stance with the concept of a raceless nation. Other prominent proindependence intellectuals of the same generation included Martín Morúa Delgado (1852–1910), who communicated with Gómez and other leaders about the best way to ensure that blacks in Cuba enjoyed their rights, but, like the popular mulatto general Antonio Maceo, "eschewed the establishment of separate black organizations and insisted that their rights had to be won, not as blacks, but as Cubans."[79]

Juan Gualberto Gómez cultivated relationships with other Cubans of color, including Chinese. The veteran Juan Chao Sen, for example, was known as a friend of Gómez. Juan Chao Sen was born in Zhongshan just before the end of the coolie trade, and he came to Cuba through the port of Veracruz in Mexico to work for a relative in Las Villas. From there he joined the insurrection. According to García and Eng, "Juan Chao Sen frequently complained that the new Republic was not what José Martí had intended, so he had no wish to avail himself of the benefits available to veterans." Like other patriotic Cubans, he paid homage to José Martí in a small corner of his Barrio Chino home through "a photo of the leader, a Cuban flag, and a clay vase filled with fresh flowers."[80]

Gómez and Morúa both corresponded with the prominent Afro-Chinese Antonio Chuffat Latour.[81] The son of a Chinese man and a Cuban woman of African descent, Chuffat identified himself publicly as a member of the *raza de color*. Although he was part of a Chinese merchant family, Chuffat had received a formal education in a school for people of color. In December 1898, two weeks before the beginning of the U.S. occupation, Chuffat wrote a letter to Juan Gualberto Gómez in his capacity as "president of the race of color of the district of Colón and Yaguaramas."[82] Their relationship with Morúa had ruptured due to differences regarding the role of race in the new nation. Chuffat lamented that Morúa "went astray from us." He appealed to Gómez for "a good reconciliation for the future of our race." Finally, he commended Gómez for his sacrifice and struggle: "There is not a black in Cuba who does not recognize and celebrate your worthy opinion."[83] Within this context, Chuffat's understanding of the *raza de color* is inclusive, as he himself was the mixed-race son of a Chinese man of merchant status and a woman of African descent.

Around the same time that Antonio Chuffat was in communication with Cuban independence leaders and working on behalf of people of color, he also endeavored to protect Chinese interests in Cuba. Just a few years later, in 1901, Chuffat became secretary of the Chinese Commercial Union of Cienfuegos, and during the first Cuban-led administration, he served as inspector of sanitation in Cienfuegos.[84] Rather than excluding him from participating in the nation-building process, Chuffat's mixed racial background, self-identification as a member of the "race of color," and merchant-class status permitted him to make a particular intervention in the discourse surround-

Afro-Chinese translator
Antonio Chuffat Latour.
(From Chuffat Latour, *Apunte
histórico de los chinos en Cuba*.)

ing the role of race in the new Cuba. Chuffat would continue his activities
on behalf of the interests of both Chinese and blacks into the early Cuban
republic, eventually becoming the target of U.S. intelligence officials during
the occupation.

Despite their gains in access to the vote, men of color who exercised a new
sense of rights as citizens of the republic were perceived as a potential threat,
both by Cuban authorities and by occupying U.S. forces. In towns throughout Cuba, the occupation government's obsession with order and sanitation
often provoked demonstrations in protest. In Cienfuegos, where blacks and
Chinese settled in neighborhoods near town centers, daily interactions between Chinese and non-Chinese underpinned more substantive alliances in
the face of oppression.

In 1899, toward the end of the first year of the U.S. occupation, war veteran General Dionisio Gil, a native of the Dominican Republic, had been
staying at a Chinese-owned inn on the main commercial artery San Fernando Street. The mayor of Cienfuegos had named hygiene inspectors to
regulate the cleanliness of fondas and cafés. Inspector of Hygiene Enrique
Quintana had apparently been "harassing" the Chinese owners of the inn
for some time. They complained to their guest General Gil, who in turn con-

veyed the situation to the mayor. On the evening of 29 December, the inspector came to the inn to confront the owners once again. Gil, who was eating at the time, rebuked the inspector, and an altercation between them resulted in the "violent expulsion" of the inspector from the inn. Gil fled to a friend's house, where a pair of mounted police apprehended and shot him. The general subsequently died, sparking a protest movement the next day in which demonstrators assembled outside the Center for Veterans. Local police dispersed the crowd by charging with sticks, leaving three wounded.[85]

A convergence of forces were in play to bring about Dionisio Gil's untimely death: the U.S. occupation of Cuba in 1899 and its emphasis on sanitation, targeting poor and immigrant neighborhoods; a war veteran's sense of entitlement to rights as a citizen of Cuba at the turn of the century; and the relationship that had developed between Gil and his Chinese hosts over the course of time that propelled him to speak out on their behalf. A year later, a commission began collecting funds to build a park and monument in Cienfuegos to commemorate the fallen general. The town council demonstrated a marked lack of enthusiasm for the project. Despite council members' reluctance, a small park was finally inaugurated — without a statue — on 29 December 1902, the second anniversary of the general's death.

Marial Iglesias Utset suggests that the debate surrounding the park is evidence of the complex racial and class prejudices at play in the "institutionalization of historical memory." Yet, she argues, the fact that the park was eventually built "tells us about the real capacity of the popular sectors to exercise pressure and assert, despite all of the obstacles, their own alternative memory."[86] Furthermore, she states, "the circumstances surrounding the death of the mambí general, not in the course of battle against enemies of the Nation, but at the hands of its own municipal police formed in its majority by members of the Liberation Army, anticipate a conflict repeated many times after. Old comrades in arms for the independence cause would confront each other in different groups: workers against owners, liberals against moderates or conservatives, members of the National Army against insurgents of the Independent Party of Color."[87]

The 1901 Constitution and Universal Manhood Suffrage

As an assembly convened in Cuba to prepare a constitution for the new nation in 1900, Washington aimed to secure U.S. interests in Cuba after the withdrawal of troops. Under the proposed Platt Amendment, the United States retained the right to intervene in Cuban affairs when deemed necessary to preserve Cuban independence and stability. The legislation also circumscribed Cuba's ability to enter foreign treaties and to contract public debt. The hegemonic nature of the U.S.-Cuba relationship underpinning the amendment directly contradicted the basic principles of the Cuban independence movement. News of the legislation generated opposition among Cubans of all social classes, with protests and public anti-U.S. demonstrations springing up across the island. The U.S. government made clear that it would not withdraw its occupying forces until Cuba incorporated the amendment into the new constitution. In June 1901, the constituent assembly voted by a narrow margin in favor of the Platt Amendment.[88]

Given this political atmosphere, the push among Cubans for voting rights was remarkable. After the fighting broke out in 1895, Spain had enacted a last-ditch reform effort that included universal male suffrage. During its occupation in 1899, in an attempt to maintain political stability, U.S. military authorities imposed literacy and property requirements on voters for the 1900 municipal elections. Their experiences with cross-racial, cross-class alliances, both during and after the war, in part account for Cubans' insistence on full voting rights. In an expression of what has been called "the right to have rights," the grassroots support for suffrage was "an assertion of entitlement to respect" and thereby "was itself expressive, communicating something about the nature of the new nation."[89] Unlike their counterparts in the United States, all men in Cuba—including Chinese—were eligible to vote at the dawn of the twentieth century. The Cuban Constitution signed by delegates in February 1901 eliminated the U.S.-imposed voting restrictions. It established universal adult male suffrage in Cuba without any reference to color or birthplace. When Cuba became a republic in 1902, adult males needed only to establish residency to be eligible to vote in a municipality.[90] This stipulation opened the vote up to thousands of Chinese men and their Cuban-born sons.

By 1907, the electoral census of the municipality of Cienfuegos listed 64 Chinese eligible voters out of a total of 611 in the barrio of Guaos, where the majority of agricultural laborers were concentrated. War veteran José Bú, now a merchant who resided on Santa Elena Street in the town of Cienfuegos, registered as a married voter in his barrio of Mercado. He was one of the few Chinese classified as able to read and write. Former indentured laborer and contractor Pastor Pelayo of Guaos, and his first son Blas Pelayo of Paradero, also became eligible voters at the dawn of the new republic. Another voter was Antonio Chuffat (listed as Carlos A. Chuffat y Latour), registered as a mestizo who had entered into a common-law marriage. Now fifty-seven years old, he worked as an interpreter and resided on Rafael Cabrero Street in the barrio Aduana.[91]

Three treaties signed in 1903 sealed the relationship between Cuba and the United States. The Platt Amendment, which bestowed upon the U.S. government the right to intervene politically and militarily in Cuba's domestic affairs when deemed necessary, was formalized in the Permanent Treaty. The Reciprocity Treaty stipulated trade concessions favorable to the United States. Finally, Cuba leased the sites of Bahía Honda and Guantánamo to the United States for the construction of a naval base.

In a highly contested election, Moderate Tomás Estrada Palma won a second term as president, setting the stage for a Liberal backlash. In a multiclass, multiracial alliance resembling that of the Liberation Army, between 1904 and 1906 Cubans publicly demonstrated against the abuses of power in Estrada Palma's government. An armed revolt known as the "August Revolution" pitted disgruntled Liberals against the government. Liberal leaders depended on what Lillian Guerra terms "veterans-turned-labor-and-race-activists" such as Quintín Banderas and Evaristo Estenoz, who had developed a radical vision for social change in Cuba, in order to secure the broad, popular constituency necessary for overthrowing the administration. Unable to defeat the insurgents and fearful of the implications for the future of mobilized popular classes, the Cuban government requested U.S. military intervention. The result was a second formal U.S. occupation from 1906 to 1909. The U.S. intervention, authorized by the Platt Amendment, was also enabled by Liberal leaders who feared opposition and social revolution from Cubans.[92]

During the second intervention, U.S. occupying forces continued to watch Cubans of color. In the fall of 1907, a U.S. intelligence officer focused his interest on Juan F. Latapier, assistant to the chief of prisons in Havana. According to the officer's report, Latapier was "spending a great deal of his time traveling around the island making political trouble among the negro people."[93] The report suggested that Latapier was politically aligned with Alfredo Zayas, the anti-imperialist Liberal Party leader who had voted against the Platt Amendment and the granting of naval bases to the United States (he was elected vice president the following year and president in 1920). The intelligence officer also surmised that Latapier was an "agent" of Juan Gualberto Gómez, the black veteran leader and activist in Havana: "His real purpose here seems to be that of organizing the negroes into one party for the purpose of securing a more equal distribution of government positions between blacks and whites. He is not at all satisfied with the present government or the outlook for the near future. The Americans, he says, must not be allowed to remain here longer." The report continued with a list of nineteen "negroes of this vicinity" associated with Latapier who "are considered to be very bad agitators and citizens."

Among the men listed was Antonio Chuffat, the Cuban-born activist of Afro-Chinese descent. Chuffat, despite his merchant-class background, had drawn on the history of black and Chinese workers in Cuba to shape his political consciousness. What makes Chuffat's involvement with these protests even more remarkable is that in 1902 he had been given a local government post in sanitation, a position usually bestowed only upon members of the educated classes. Chuffat resided in a racially mixed neighborhood and associated with other men of color seeking increased black representation and a change in the balance of official power. Chuffat's activism in 1907 is consistent with his 1898 written appeal to Juan Gualberto Gómez to continue the struggle for black political voice in republican Cuba.

Whites, blacks, mulattos, and Chinese participated side by side in the thirty years of Cuban struggles for independence from Spain. The discourse surrounding independence incorporated the Chinese into the conception of a new raceless, classless citizenry. As early as 1892, the famous words of statesman Gonzalo de Quesada seemed to have relegated the coolie status of the Chinese to the past: "There was not a single Chinese Cuban deserter; there was not a single Chinese Cuban traitor!"[94] Chroniclers of the era and later scholars note that under the Constitution of 1901, regardless of their foreign birth, the Chinese José Bu Tak and José Tolón (Lai Wah), for having served more than ten consecutive years in arms for Cuban independence, shared the right to be elected president of the new republic with the esteemed Generals Máximo Gómez (Dominican), Carlos Roloff (Eastern European), and Juan Ríus Rivera (Puerto Rican).[95] Yet, the improbability of a Chinese, let alone a former coolie, serving as president of the new republic becomes evident in the immediate aftermath of independence. As nationalistic writing continued into the twentieth century, Chinese veterans were cast as patriotic, but also as apolitical and cooperative.

The renewed entry of Chinese immigrants became a topic of much debate in the early republic. Political elites balked at the potential ramifications of power among illiterate, undisciplined masses, and a campaign to whiten the nation through immigration was accompanied by anti-Chinese policies and sentiment. With restrictions on new Chinese immigrants and continued pressure by Cuban authorities on shops and associations, the actual incorporation of the Chinese into the Cuban nation remained open to debate during the republic. Racial attitudes from the colonial era persisted, and with later periods of political turmoil and economic hardship, new anti-Chinese prejudices surfaced. The imperial interventions by the United States reinforced these anti-Chinese attitudes, in particular by demanding Cuban acceptance of Chinese exclusion laws in order to quell U.S. fears of the "yellow peril" approaching its shores.

The Chinese race does not mix with the white race, nor with
the black, without producing . . . descendants whose vitality is poor.

—Cuban commissioner of immigration F. E. Menocal (1909)

Cuba needs immigrants who come with the intention of becoming citizens and who
will conform to the laws, usages, and reliable customs of the country, and not those
who come to merely get work and return to their homes with the fruits of their toil.

—*Havana Daily Post*, 2 October 1913

CHAPTER FIVE

Yellow Peril

In 1920, the Cuban fishing boat *Remplazo* was stopped off the coast of Tampa,
Florida, on suspicion of transporting contraband alcohol. Inspectors discovered $50,000 worth of liquor hidden in a hold for fish below the deck. In
addition, they apprehended seventeen Chinese who claimed they had paid
a middleman to take them from Havana to Tampa. Authorities believed the
Remplazo affair to be just one component of a massive immigrant smuggling
scheme and one scheme among many in the circum-Caribbean region. Such
cases highlight the need to examine Chinese migration to Cuba through a
hemispheric lens, one that focuses on port cities and commercial and social
networks. The frequency of commercial transportation and lax regulations
made Caribbean ports a convenient "stepping stone" to the United States in
the age of official Chinese exclusion, 1882 to 1943. Testimony from customs
officials, captains, crew, and migrants themselves reveals the complex networks stretching from Cantonese villages to Hong Kong to Caribbean and
U.S. port cities that enabled Chinese to evade entry restrictions. Through
Creole middlemen, migrants navigated linguistic, national, and racial borders during their journeys abroad. As Chinese circulated in the hemisphere,
so did discourses of a "yellow peril" approaching the shore. The use of port
cities as centers of smuggling operations and their linkage with opium, gambling, and secret societies generated and reinforced anti-Chinese sentiment
and campaigns to restrict new immigration across the Americas.

After three decades of Cuban struggle, the treaty ending the Spanish-
American War of 1898 guaranteed independence from Spain. But the birth

of the Cuban nation was midwifed by U.S. imperial interventions in the years 1899–1902 and 1906–9. The Platt Amendment ensured the right of the United States to intervene in Cuba's domestic affairs when deemed necessary and sanctioned its continued surveillance. After 1898, the United States applied its own anti-Chinese immigration policies to newly acquired or controlled territories, including Cuba. U.S. officials sought to prevent Cuba from serving as a springboard for what it considered to be racially undesirable immigrants, among them Asians, and especially Chinese. One contingent sought to halt the importation of braceros into Cuba, which would undercut sugar production in the U.S. South. During the first few decades of the twentieth century, U.S. policies oscillated between protection of domestic sugar planters and support for large American sugar companies in Cuba.[1]

"El Norte," as the United States was known, held an undeniable influence on Cuban politics and society throughout the nineteenth and twentieth centuries. Under the Platt Amendment, Cuba had little choice but to comply with U.S. policies. The United States therefore played a significant role in shaping anti-Chinese sentiment and policies in Cuba. But although the origins of anti-Chinese restrictions in Cuba can be found partly in the U.S.-imposed legislation, equally if not more important was a deeply ingrained ideology among white political and intellectual elites concerning the ideal composition of a progressive and prosperous nation. U.S. demands for restrictions on Chinese immigration to Cuba coincided with debates in the aftermath of independence on what kind of citizens would make up the nation. Cuba looked to other Latin American countries that were attempting to reconcile their indigenous and African colonial heritage as models for a civilized nation, "whitened" through European immigration. Chinese exclusion resonated with this vision, one that had been articulated by Creole elites such as José Antonio Saco in the early nineteenth century.

Extending Exclusion: Order No. 155 of 1902

Since the mid-nineteenth century, industries in the United States had recruited Chinese to develop their Western territories through work on railroads, in mining camps, on fields, and in towns. However, in the white settler imaginary, neither "alien" Chinese nor former slaves of African descent belonged in a territory dedicated to small production free of the stains of industrial wage and chattel slavery. Furthermore, the unfree, servile Chinese "coolie" threatened the white American working family. Decades of Chinese migration to the United States resulted in protests by nativist labor movements and local anti-Chinese ordinances, policies, harassment, and violence, most pronounced in California.[2]

On 6 May 1882, anti-Chinese sentiment and incidents culminated in Congress's passing the Chinese Exclusion Act, which prohibited the immigration of Chinese laborers to the United States for a period of ten years. Subsequent legislation extended and broadened the reach of the law. The Exclusion Act should be considered both the culmination of smaller-scale anti-Chinese laws and the beginning of a modern policy of restricting immigration at the federal level and transforming the United States into a "gatekeeping nation."[3] After 1882, U.S. government officials were charged with protecting the nation's land borders and seaports from the illegal entry of Chinese.

Just five days before the end of the U.S. occupation government, on 15 May 1902, Military Governor Leonard Wood issued Order No. 155 of the Headquarters Division of Cuba. This concise document applied the immigration laws of the United States to Cuba. With modifications, it served as the official basis of Cuba's immigration policy through the first half of the twentieth century. The document declared the usual prohibition on the entry of idiots, paupers, polygamists, and felons. Sections Seven and Eight excluded the Chinese, with the exception of those classified as merchants, students, diplomats, and tourists. Chinese workers who had resided in Cuba since 14 April 1899 were also exempt. Furthermore, the law prohibited the entry of contract laborers from any nation.[4]

Despite the law, Chinese continued to enter Cuban ports, either with falsified documents or through smuggling operations. Official government statistics indicate that no Chinese entered Cuba between 1908 and 1917, but seven did in 1918, and eleven hundred in 1919.[5] However, newspapers, contemporary accounts, and Chinese institutions of the time tell a different story. The Chinese Consulate in Havana recorded 6,258 Chinese entries between 1903 and 1916, along with data such as name, date of entry, name of ship, and category of immigrant. One day in September 1913, for example, the Ward Line steamer from New York to Havana carried eighty Chinese passengers who claimed to be students and merchants.[6] Duvon Corbitt notes that "the entry of Chinese between 1902 and 1917 was about equal to that of the closing days of Spanish rule, with nearly enough arrivals to replace losses from death and emigration."[7] In her travelogue, Irene Wright observed a connection between unauthorized Chinese immigration and "day laborers in the sugar houses where managers ask no questions as to where the constant supply afforded them is procured."[8] Clearly, U.S. attempts to extend the exclusion of Chinese to Cuba were ineffective.

TABLE 6 Chinese Population of Cuba according to Official Census Figures, 1861–1970

CENSUS	TOTAL	MALES	PERCENT	FEMALES	PERCENT
1861	34,828	34,771	99.83	57	.17
1877	40,327	40,261	99.84	66	.16
1887	28,752	28,694	99.80	58	.20
1899	14,863	14,814	99.67	49	.33
1907	11,217	11,166	99.55	51	.45
1919	10,300	10,016	97.20	284	2.76
1931	24,647	24,445	99.18	202	.82
1943	15,822	15,657	98.96	165	1.04
1953	11,834	11,350	95.91	484	4.09
1970	5,892	5,710	96.91	182	3.09

Source: Baltar Rodríguez, *Los chinos de Cuba*, 90.

Promoting White Settlers: The 1906 Law of Immigration and Colonization

Cuba approved a new Law of Immigration and Colonization on 11 July 1906, which allocated one million dollars for a massive project to develop white settlement. Eighty percent of this sum was to be used for bringing families from Europe, in particular the Canary Islands, and the remaining $200,000 for the importation of braceros from Sweden, Norway, Denmark, and Northern Italy. José de J. Monteagudo, a former officer in the Liberation Army and head of the census, commented that inhabitants of these nations "more easily adapt themselves to the climate of the country and more readily familiarize themselves with the work of Cuban agriculture."[9]

A rapidly rising demand for labor, driven by expansion of the Cuban sugar industry, propelled the new legislation. An influx of U.S. capital on the island resulted in a nearly tenfold increase in sugar production between 1900 and 1913.[10] Cuban planters and industrialists pushed for state-sponsored immigration to provide the cheap, imported labor deemed necessary for sustaining the nation's economic growth. Employers also preferred to hire immigrants over native workers because immigrants were thought to be less likely to engage in labor politics.[11]

The renewed debates within the Cuban government echoed the prior century's discussions on immigration as a solution to the labor crisis that would set in with the end of slavery. President Tomás Estrada Palma emphasized the benefits of European immigrants not only for the development of agriculture, but also for the improvement of Cuban national culture, while other supporters of the whitening project justified their positions with current racial theories in social science. As Lillian Guerra states, "By inoculating society with new blood and new cultures that augured a prosperous, united future, the project promised to neutralize continuing conflicts over a past shaped by slavery and revolutionary struggle."[12]

A major strand of thought within these debates linked Cuba's future to Spanish America, even more so than to the United States. The bill's proponents noted the backwardness and poverty of fellow Latin American nations. However, they claimed, nations such as Mexico, Chile, Argentina, and Brazil "opened their doors to European immigration, which has begun to leave its benevolent influence on the progress of those peoples of our race."[13] The law, then, aimed to make Cuba as economically and racially stable as North America and the prosperous nations of South America.

Chinese laborers had been officially excluded by the 1902 military order, but the 1906 Law of Immigration and Colonization reinforced sentiment among leaders in the administration that Chinese were racially undesirable for settlement in the new Cuban republic. Within the debates, Cuba's experiences with Chinese indentured laborers surfaced. Creole writer Ramón Meza y Suárez Inclán, one of the leading proponents of immigration from Spain, believed that "the vile shackle of a contract" lay behind Cuba's problems with Chinese.[14] As in the United States, Chinese laborers would always be associated with coolieism, and therefore bondage.[15] In 1906, President of the Academy of Science Juan Santos Fernández supported the government's proposal for Spanish laborers as a means to achieve cultural progress and economic modernization. Santos contrasted Cuba's slow development to that of Germany and the United States, which paid attention to the physical characteristics of their populations. Cuba, in his view, had relied on inferior races from Africa, Yucatán, and Asia to fulfill its need for cheap agricultural labor. He attributed Cuba's low population density to the inability of its mixed races to reproduce. Echoing the arguments behind the caste system of colonial Spain, he claimed that the positive aspects of "purer" races mutated in mixed descendants, generating the "impulsive forces that produce the political crime of rebellion."[16]

A state-sponsored project committing funds to the importation of white immigrants directly contradicted the multiracial vision of Cuba forged during the recent struggles for independence from Spain. Afro-Cuban leaders and their newspapers, as well as the labor press, denounced the proposal. Due to the efforts of black congressmen to halt passage of the law, the final version did not mention specific races to be excluded. However, by clarifying that the funding was earmarked for Canary Islanders and Northern Europeans, considered white, the language of the law excluded West Indian and Asian immigrants. The passage of the immigration law denied the viability of a native workforce, regardless of race. Guerra comments that "a new Cuban nation would emerge, embodied by new Cubans: white, docile, and energetic servants of their masters' republican state."[17]

Transnational Merchants and National Borders

By the late nineteenth century, there had emerged a Chinese transnational migrant circuit linking key ports in the United States such as New York, San Francisco, and New Orleans with those in Mexico, Jamaica, and Cuba. The diasporic Chinese merchant community maintained business networks that transported goods and people across the Americas, including smuggling operations to the United States through Canada, Mexico, and the Caribbean. A host of recruiters and middlemen, from home villages in China to destination cities in the United States, formed an apparatus that moved Chinese migrants from one port to another, aided along the way by corrupt immigration officials. In addition to smuggling, Chinese utilized "paper identities," false documents, and "in transit" status to enter Cuba and the United States.[18]

The Cuban laws passed in the early twentieth century excluded further Chinese labor immigration, but also constricted the mobility of merchants and their transnational business operations. Chinese merchant organizations, chambers of commerce, and consulates launched campaigns in opposition to exclusion laws in the Americas. In their defense of Chinese subjects, diplomatic representatives in Cuba focused their attention on distinguishing merchants from common laborers. Initially they directed their efforts toward loopholes in the law, rather than the injustice of exclusion itself. Immediately after the promulgation of Order No. 155, some Chinese migrants were literally stranded between nations. Those who had left China before the passage of the decree were refused entry by the time they reached the Havana harbor. On 11 June 1902, when the ship *Monterey* docked in Havana, forty-three Chinese aboard were refused the right to disembark and were forced to continue on to Mexico. Eighteen months later, the Chinese subjects remained in Mexico "without resources or work." The Chinese chargé d'affaires in Cuba petitioned the Cuban government on their behalf, basing his appeal on "international custom" and a U.S. legal precedent that established a grace period of ninety days.[19]

Throughout the period of U.S. exclusion, prominent Chinese community members and merchants relied on their exempt status to freely cross borders between the United States, Canada, and Mexico. Those who stopped in Cuba while in transit to another country were adversely affected by the new rules. The Chinese legation emphasized that the United States, despite its exclusion laws, permitted Chinese laborers to travel through its territory to another nation. This privilege extended to Chinese—including laborers—traveling from Mexico or Cuba to Canada or back to China through American seaports (as well as those making the reverse trip).

The "in transit" category of travel had been used for decades as a means of illegal entry to the United States. U.S. customs agents required Chinese laborers to produce evidence of a through-ticket and a penal bond of at least $200 posted by the transportation company or by an individual on behalf of the laborer. Under a common scheme, a Chinese passenger traveling through a U.S. port swapped places with another Chinese. The passenger blended into the city, and the Chinese who had been residing in the United States, in addition to a payment, gained free passage to Mexico, Cuba, or even back to China. If the "substitutes" were legal residents, they could reenter the United States at a later date.[20]

From 1882 onward, Chinese had used Cuba as a springboard to circumvent U.S. exclusionary policies. Officials in Cuba were therefore reluctant to allow transit passengers entry, regardless of their status. On 17 May 1908, the merchant Wong King Yong of Torreón, Mexico, arrived in the Havana harbor on his way to Jamaica for business. Aware of the restrictions against Chinese entry, Wong had obtained a document from the Cuban Consul in Tampico requesting that he not be detained upon arrival or during the days in which he would be in Cuba before his boat departed for Jamaica. However, once docked in Havana, Wong was not permitted to disembark. He complained to the Chinese legation, which pushed for his release. Several other Chinese merchants in Cuba knew Wong personally and were willing to provide him the security deposit necessary during his stay on the island to guarantee his departure for Jamaica. The Chinese envoy reminded the Cuban Department of State that the intention of the legislation "was simply to limit the right to reside in Cuba to certain classes" and did not apply to individuals in transit.[21] By advocating exclusively for Chinese merchants, he reinforced the division made by the government between merchant and laboring classes.

This pattern of Chinese defense continued through the second U.S. occupation from 1906 to 1909. Rather than petitioning for the wholesale elimination of Order No. 155, the envoy repeatedly pushed for modifications that would facilitate the entrance of Chinese merchants. He requested that Chinese legally entitled to enter Cuba be allowed to disembark in other important ports, besides Havana. The ability to disembark directly at ports such as Cienfuegos on the southern coast and Santiago de Cuba in the east would facilitate the operations of Chinese transnational merchants, who by the early twentieth century had established branches of their businesses throughout the island. The envoy also requested that evidence submitted by Chinese witnesses be accepted when Cuban officials solicited information to enforce immigration regulations. He further petitioned that Chinese not be subject to requirements other than those established by the law and that nonlaborers not be subject to personal examination, bertillonage (a method of identifying individuals by means of body measurements, colorings, and markings), or similar measures. The Department of State in Cuba supported these requests, but in an official response denied that bertillonage was employed.[22]

A "Yellow Peril" in Cuba

Anti-Chinese racialist constructions had circulated throughout the Americas since the nineteenth century. Northern Mexican newspapers recycled images of the Chinese as a "yellow plague" and a "locust invasion," morally inferior, criminally inclined, and completely unassimilable to mainstream society.[23] By early in the twentieth century, the perception of Chinese as a threat to the economy and culture of the dominant population of Cuba, defined as white and with a Spanish heritage, became particularly pronounced. Anti-Chinese stereotypes surfaced in official correspondence, scientific reports, newspaper editorials, and popular magazines.

These kinds of attitudes crystallized in an official statement by the Cuban head of immigration in 1909. The end of the second U.S. occupation on 28 January left Cuba in the hands of foreign interests, with the issue of a steady source of labor unresolved. On 27 July, the Interim Chinese chargé d'affaires in Cuba petitioned the Cuban Congress to overturn Order No. 155. The Cuban commissioner of immigration, F. E. Menocal, used this request to outline his arguments for continued exclusion of the Chinese. On 1 September, he wrote to the secretary of the treasury, urging that this Chinese petition be rejected. His arguments suggest intimate knowledge of U.S. immigration policy and a desire to use it as a model for Cuba. Menocal began his memorandum by stating that the governments of the United States, Canada, England, Australia, "and other countries of Caucasian race" had dismissed similar petitions. He then elaborated four general grounds for rejection of the Chinese petition: "economic or social, ethnic or racial, sanitary, and diplomatic." In his elaboration of these themes, he repeatedly turned to the United States and Hawaii for examples of what should be avoided in Cuba.

In promoting the economic and social well-being of the Cuban nation, Menocal invoked a fear of race riots such as those brought on by the importation of thousands of Chinese coolies into the United States for the construction of the transcontinental railroad. Only after "years of violence and disorder" did the United States implement the Chinese Exclusion Act. Like José Martí, Menocal alluded to the 1885 "bloody incident" at Rock Springs in Wyoming Territory, in which a white mob attacked unarmed Chinese coal miners. But whereas Martí had expressed sympathy for the Chinese, Menocal used the incident as a lesson for Cuba: "Nations, like people, should take advantage of the teachings or experiences of their neighbors." From an economic point of view, he argued, the unrestricted importation of Chinese was counterproductive because the Chinese did not invest in the nation; they "consume" and "do not produce," and these limited aims are detrimental to the native worker and the country.

According to Menocal, Chinese coolies accept salaries so low, just enough for subsistence, with the result that "they evict the white worker" and reduce the capacity of natives to be able to afford "the necessities that a more advanced civilization demands." Chinese immigration might produce "the violent protest of the damaged classes," leading to "bloodshed and international complications," or the lowering of the "moral and material level of this class of workers." Menocal referred to recent protests and diplomatic difficulties brought about by the passage of discriminatory anti-Japanese legislation in California. In 1906, the San Francisco Board of Education ordered Japanese and Korean students in public schools to transfer to the "Oriental School" for the Chinese. The Japanese government protested, and out of respect for Japan's rising military power, President Theodore Roosevelt intervened. Under the 1908 Gentleman's Agreement, in exchange for the school board's willingness to permit Japanese students to attend public schools reserved for white children, the federal government would persuade Japan to stop issuing passports to laborers.[24]

As ethnic/racial justifications for restricting Chinese immigration, Menocal cited "differences of language, religion, and customs that impeded the assimilation of the Chinese element" into Cuban society. Rather than assimilating, the Chinese clustered in the suburbs of major population centers, "forming colonies where they live a semi-savage existence, engaging in all kinds of vice, and constituting centers of infection." Menocal was aware of the interracial unions between Chinese and blacks, mulattos, and even whites, and he elaborated that Chinese who mix with the Cuban population "produce rickety descendants, weak, in their majority predisposed to tuberculosis." In addition to the specter of racial tensions in the United States, Menocal invoked the coolie trade "and the disaster with which it ended," an allusion to the international scandal generated by the 1874 commission of enquiry.

The immigration commissioner called China "the mother of plagues." He mentioned outbreaks of bubonic plague "imported directly from China" that spread throughout the Americas to San Francisco, Chile, Peru, and Mexico. Chinese communities were "a constant source of anxiety for the sanitation authorities." Menocal purposely referred to the new waves of Chinese immigrants as "coolies." In addition to reminding Cubans of the abuses of contracts of indenture, his use of the term was intended to conjure up images of Chinese workers living in crowded, unsanitary conditions. He stated, "The way of life that the coolies observe completely dispenses with hygiene; they crowd together in unhealthy rooms, with excrement and rubbish piled up inside and out." Menocal also linked sanitation with the economic well-being of Cuba. He noted that when the bubonic plague hit Hawaii in 1900, the Board of Health burned down Honolulu's Chinatown.

Finally, Menocal offered diplomatic justifications for continued restrictions on Chinese entry. With the U.S. occupations and the passage of the Platt Amendment as a condition for independence, Cuban politicians were compelled to placate the American government in its international and domestic policy. Menocal proposed that Cuba, "for its commercial and political relations with the United States, should obtain laws that are, inasmuch as possible, homogenous with the American laws." Furthermore, if Cuban ports were open to Chinese immigration, the United States would adopt retaliatory measures against Cuba "every time that the Chinese come to the island as the next stop to the American coast." Menocal ended his statement on a strong exclusionary note. He recommended that the Chinese request for the overturn of Order No. 155 be denied, and that, furthermore, the current law be more rigorously enforced, for "although it restricts Chinese immigration to a certain point, it does not prevent it as it should." He acknowledged that Chinese laborers, "undoubtedly disguised as merchants or students, come to Cuba in great numbers."[25]

Coming in the aftermath of a second U.S. intervention, at stake in the immigration commissioner's statement and subsequent debates on "the Chinese question" was Cuban national identity, sovereignty, and internal stability. For the next several years, Cuban officials continued to juggle the interests of the U.S. government and Cuban planters and industrialists as it tackled the issue of a steady labor supply. As they attempted to block Chinese immigration, Cuban officials continued to propose new schemes for the entry of Europeans. A law of 23 June 1911 appropriated three hundred thousand dollars for colonizing frontier regions of Cuba with "desirable" immigrant families.[26]

Cuban newspapers criticized President José Miguel Gómez (1908–12) of the Liberal Party for not enforcing the anti-Chinese immigration laws, contrary to his political promise to protect native workers. Multiple loopholes in the law facilitated illegal entry. In October 1911, *El Día* denounced "the secret door through which so many Chinese are introduced," a policy that gave the Chinese legation in Cuba responsibility for verifying immigrant status. Within two days of arriving with false certificates, the editorial declared, Chinese were making charcoal or working in laundries, creating "ruinous competition" for Cubans.[27] In March 1913, the Department of Sanitation, "convinced that many Chinese are obtaining admission into Cuba by falsely representing themselves to be students or tourists," announced a stricter investigation of new arrivals. The main English-language newspaper in Cuba, the *Havana Daily Post*, echoed U.S. exclusion policy.[28] *El Mundo* critiqued the ineffectiveness of another decree with the sarcastic but dire warning: "Prepare yourself for an invasion of students and merchants."[29]

As they had earlier, Chinese merchants protested the restrictive decrees and accompanying discourse. The reorganized Chinese Chamber of Commerce in Cuba, which since 1912 recognized a new Chinese republic, couched its arguments in notions of equality among citizens of progressive nations. Chinese merchants petitioned against the Cuban government's passage of a new law, Decree No. 603 of 13 May 1913. In a letter of 6 June, Chamber of Commerce President Wong Chiu Sen reiterated that the history of the Chinese community in Cuba from colonial times to the present "always has been distinguished for its good relations with the natives of the country, with whom they shared the harshness of war and the labors of peace." The letter then expressed "the alarm and surprise" caused by the new law, which had been promulgated in the past under different names. Wong described Cuban immigration law as "a constant shame for our people, who, like Cubans, have paid with blood for their liberty and the right to be counted among the most worthy and progressive." This depiction of Chinese who fought for freedom invoked and conjoined two patriotic histories: the Chinese participation in the Cuban struggles for independence and the more recent overthrow of the Manchu Qing dynasty in China's Revolution of 1911.

Wong argued that "in reality the Decree represents a politics of exclusion of the Chinese even more radical than that which has ever existed in the United States," as it burdened transnational merchants who traveled frequently for short periods of time. Furthermore, a clause requiring Chinese residents in Cuba to register with the Department of Immigration singled out the Chinese, treating them differently than foreign residents of other nationalities. The commissioner of immigration responded that although the decree may be "mortifying and offensive for the Chinese," it was not identical to previous decrees, nor did it deserve the name "enemy of the Chinese community." The exclusion clauses of the immigration law would remain in effect.[30]

A Wartime Renewal of Chinese Labor Migration

Despite the call for white, European settler families, the needs of the sugar industry eventually propelled an actual migration of nonwhite, single contract laborers, again paralleling the mid-nineteenth century. Sugar industry magnates continued to push for foreign laborers, primarily Spaniards. Between 1900 and 1929, approximately nine hundred thousand Spanish immigrants entered Cuba. However, like native Cuban workers, they were often unwilling to labor in the fields for low pay and under adverse conditions. While the flow of Spanish immigrants continued, Cuba also turned to West Indians, in particular Haitians and Jamaicans. Sugar interests convinced Cuban government officials "that the economic 'necessity' of cheap labor outweighed the supposed evils of black immigration."[31] In 1912, President José Miguel Gómez authorized the United Fruit Company to import fourteen hundred Haitians, and the following year President Mario G. Menocal (1912–20) authorized the Nipe Bay Company to import a thousand laborers from other West Indian islands. Employers agreed to return the laborers to their homes after the harvest (although this often did not happen). The parties signed the contracts after the immigrants disembarked, thereby evading the legal restrictions on the entry of contract laborers. Planters also continued to propose Chinese labor during the period before Cuba's entry into World War I, in April 1917.

Demand for agricultural workers to boost sugar production for the war effort officially opened the gates for a new wave of immigration. Cuba played a key role in providing sugar, alcohol, and manufacturing explosives for the Allied forces. Sugar planters insisted that they needed immigrants laboring under contract, especially Chinese. After Cuba entered the war, Chinese labor immigration was temporarily reinitiated. Despite protests from some politicians, on 3 August 1917, President Menocal approved a law permitting the entry of contract laborers, without distinction by race, until two years after the termination of the war. The deadline for reimposing the ban on Chinese laborers came and went, and planters continued to use Spanish, West Indian, and Chinese immigrants. Koreans from Mexico also came to Cuba to develop the sisal-growing industry. One sugar estate even experimented with East Indians, who had been continuously transported to the British Caribbean.[32] Although official statistics for Chinese entry as contract labor during this period are not available, daily newspapers in Cuba announced thousands. The Chinese Consulate in Havana recorded a total of 16,005 entries from 1917 to 1924, a figure that only accounts for those who entered as merchants and students, exemptions to the 1902 regulations. Duvon Corbitt's sample in 1920 from the shipping pages of the *Havana Post* reveals the entry of 2,084 Chinese in just ten days.[33]

After the end of the war, in 1918, political and economic conditions at home propelled large numbers of European migrants to the Americas. Cuba continued to serve as a "stepping stone" to its northern neighbor, and the United States maintained concern that its own exclusionary laws would be compromised if certain types of immigrants entered Cuba. Asians, as always, were unwelcome. But the postwar environment also brought political refugees. In August 1922, Washington demanded that Cuba prevent the immigration of Chinese and "undesirable" Europeans (namely, Communists and other political radicals). The U.S. government declared that such immigrants only went to Cuba in order to enter the United States illegally.[34] Many Jewish refugees who had planned a temporary stay in Cuba were now deemed undesirable for entry into the United States and faced the reality that Cuba would be their new home.[35] The U.S. Immigration Act of 1924 aimed further to restrict Southern and Eastern Europeans with reduced quotas based on the 1890 census. It effectively prohibited entry of Middle Easterners and Asians, as these "nonwhite" immigrants were ineligible for naturalization.

Sugar and Smuggling in the Age of Prohibition

During the postwar period, Chinese continued to use Cuba as a springboard to enter the United States. In addition to the usual schemes, migrants were smuggled aboard vessels transporting sugar to U.S. shores. Throughout 1919 several attempts at bringing Chinese into the United States on boats from Santiago de Cuba came to the attention of authorities, who advised immigration commissioners to be on alert. The frustrated commissioner in Philadelphia responded that as many as three or four sugar cargo vessels arrived from Cuban ports daily and that his office lacked sufficient resources to search them all.[36] In December, a Cuban schooner destined for New York with a cargo of molasses "foundered off the Virginia Capes." The inspector reported that "19 Chinese coolies were being smuggled into the United States on that schooner, 17 of which number perished, while 2 were among the rescued and returned to Havana." The investigation determined that shipmaster Francisco Alonzo Riveron worked with a smuggler in Cuba and would likely make further attempts to bring Chinese into the United States.[37]

Thus, when seventeen Chinese were discovered aboard the fishing boat *Remplazo* in 1920, a well-established tradition of smuggling products and people through Caribbean port cities had been in place.[38] All of the Chinese apprehended were only in Cuba with the intention of entering the United States, aided by a recruiter known simply as the "Mexican." This middleman's background is cloudy: several migrants described him as a Chinese from Mexico, while one called him a "halfbreed" with a Chinese father and Cuban mother. He had connections in Havana's Chinatown and in Chinese and U.S. port cities, as well as a command of the Spanish language. Tom Sing stated, "I met him on the street in Havana. He is among the Chinese very often." In this particular operation, for $100 the "Mexican" ferried Chinese in a small rowboat to a schooner: "He took one and two at a time to the boat and some of us did not know each other until we got to the boat." In each port the operations relied on locals, not necessarily co-ethnics. The inspector in Tampa implicated a group of Greeks on the U.S. side of the smuggling operation. Once in Tampa, the Chinese would find work or make their way through kinship and huiguan networks to other U.S. cities.

At least one of the migrants was attempting to repeat a route that had proven successful in the past. Ng Bow of Xinhui County, in Guangdong Province, had entered the United States from Cuba twenty years earlier. After a decade working as a laundryman in New York City, he made a return trip to his home village, a desire shared by nearly all Chinese migrants living in "bachelor" societies in the Americas. When he decided to return to the United States in 1920, he boarded a steamship from Hong Kong to San Francisco, and then to Havana, where he made arrangements in the Barrio Chino to be smuggled back into the United States. This time, however, his journey coincided with the increased vigilance that came during the Prohibition era, and he was one of the unfortunate migrants caught on the fishing boat filled with contraband alcohol.

As in the nineteenth century, Chinese migrants to the Americas continued to come from a few areas in Guangdong Province. Of the Chinese apprehended aboard the *Remplazo*, nine were from Taishan County alone. Although Cuba's sugar boom made possible their entry, only two of the migrants reported actually working as estate laborers. The others had worked in laundries, restaurants, shops, or were unemployed. Most had families back in China, and only three reported being single.[39]

Some Chinese in Cuba, rather than attempting to stay in the United States, apparently used the U.S. exclusion laws as a means to return to China with free passage. The U.S. State Department noted that after the steep drop in sugar prices in 1921, many attempted to enter the United States, "evidently with the idea that they will be detained here and deported to their native country at the expense of this government."[40]

Post-1917 Immigration Debates

As Chinese came to Cuban shores by the thousands and smuggling operations to the United States escalated, debates in Cuba about Chinese immigration were renewed and recast. White politicians and intellectuals grouped the Chinese together with West Indians in their linkage of immigrants and disease. In 1915 the new monthly cultural magazine *Cuba Contemporánea* featured an essay titled "The Yellow Danger and the Black Danger," which pitted both groups against "Cuban solidarity."[41] Beliefs about the racial inferiority of Chinese and blacks remained prominent in the minds of native-born whites and Spanish immigrants. In particular, fears of witchcraft, criminality, disease, immorality, and proclivity for revolt among Afro-Caribbean laborers surfaced. A 1922 editorial in *La Prensa* questioned the utility of preventative measures "as long as the ports of the country are wide open to Chinese, Haitian, and Jamaican immigrants, who bring in malaria and smallpox."[42] In Cienfuegos, a 1923 editorial opposing "the yellow invasion" warned its readership of the dangers posed by the stream of Chinese immigrants and praised government efforts to halt the flow.[43]

The immigration issue became intertwined with national political campaigns and U.S. hegemony over the island. From 1920 to 1924, President Alfredo Zayas of the Liberal Party officially governed Cuba. However, U.S. special envoy General Enoch H. Crowder in fact controlled the first three years of the Zayas administration; he complained that despite the similarities between the U.S. and Cuban restrictions on Chinese labor, many Chinese still managed to enter Cuba, and demanded revision of immigration laws and tightening of enforcement. Cuban officials attempted to uphold the existing immigration restrictions. As Adam McKeown points out, in the age of U.S. expansion abroad, a nation's obvious failure to enforce local immigration restrictions made it vulnerable to foreign intervention.[44] As Chinese laborers continued to pour into Cuba (some gaining entry into the United States), Cuban officials attempted to clarify the law through new decrees. Despite their efforts, loopholes in the law, corruption on both the Chinese and Cuban sides, and lax enforcement made the 1902 exclusion law relatively ineffective at preventing the entry of Chinese. Furthermore, a powerful sugar lobby repeatedly pressed for the lifting of the law.

A major police investigation in April 1924 implicated fourteen prominent Chinese merchants in Havana in the illegal trafficking of Chinese migrants. The police report declared that over fifteen thousand Chinese had entered the ports of Cuba illegally through an arrangement between Cuban consular agents and Chinese merchants. Based on false sworn declarations they bestowed the status of student and merchant to Chinese emigrants. The Chinese minister in Cuba, P. C. K. Tyau, publicly expressed his surprise at the accusations and the detention of the merchants, stating that all of the Chinese "have come to Cuba with correct documents" and those detained are well-known merchants who have been established in Cuba for years, "long-time residents and owners of commercial houses."[45] One of the merchants, Luis Po, had come to Cuba in 1886 to work in his uncle's transnational firm Weng On y Compañía, established in Havana in the late nineteenth century, with branches throughout the provinces. Luis Po also held the esteemed position of president of the Guomindang (Chinese Nationalist Party) in Cuba.[46]

On 10 May 1924, *El Mundo* published an editorial "La invasión amarilla" (The Yellow Invasion) that estimated a population of one hundred fifty thousand Chinese in Cuba. The article described Chinese as "so little desirable for the ethnic composition of our population," in contrast to Spaniards. The newspaper criticized President Zayas's message to Congress that reported only three Chinese entries to Cuba during the past year. It called attention to the multitudes of Chinese who enter with false documents, "grouped in cargoes like that of nearly five hundred which was recently dumped on Cuban soil from the hold of a single ship." The editorial referenced hemispheric exclusion policies: "When the entire world rejects yellow immigration, when the United States decides to refuse not only that of the Chinese but also of the Japanese," the continued entry of Chinese into Cuba debilitated national customs, morality, and racial composition. It condemned the corruption of those who profited from immigration schemes, casting it as a grave threat to Cuba's future: "Already Cuban youths are accumulating in our hospitals, victims of the infernal blue poison, opium. To speak plainly, we are dealing with a crime of high treason."[47]

President Zayas, determined to halt the criticism, on 12 May 1924 issued an order to Cuban consuls not to approve visas for Chinese passports. *Diario de la Marina* responded with an article, "La inmigración china," that included the historical background to the Chinese presence in Cuba. While the article commended the presidential decree restricting Chinese immigration, it implored Zayas to enforce it.[48] His successor, General Gerardo Machado y Morales (1925–33), passed a new immigration law in April 1926 to tackle "the Chinese question" and eliminate loopholes in the existing exclusion policy. Decree No. 570 exempted diplomats and their households and permitted Chinese merchants and laborers who were residents of Cuba on 14 April 1899 to visit China and return. Chinese tourists could also enter for six months with a deposit of $1,000.[49] It officially shifted responsibility for the issuing of certificates of residence to the Department of Immigration in Cuba. The maximum period for a valid certificate was now twenty-four months, and a larger guarantee was required. Despite public outcry from members of the Chinese merchant community, the decree went into effect, and the Department of Immigration became the only authority to issue certificates.

That fall a police investigation revealed an elaborate scheme by which potential emigrants sent photographs to agents of Chinese merchants in Cuba, where they were placed on certificates of other migrants. The falsified certificates made legal entry into Cuba possible for hundreds of Chinese migrants, who were now able to prove prior residence in Cuba. The scheme involved cooperation between Chinese transnational merchants and Cuban immigration officials and a total circulation of 400,000 Cuban pesos. According to the police report, all of the Chinese who arrived in Cuba declared they had contracted to work for Chinese commercial houses, which provided travel costs and documentation, and were unaware that the certificates had been falsified.[50] Although the 1926 law, like others before it, proved ineffective at halting the entry of laborers, Chinese immigration did slow toward the end of the decade. A combination of economic depression and the tumultuous politics of the Machado administration propelled many Chinese to leave Cuba.[51]

A transracial conception of the Cuban nation and universal manhood suffrage marked the emergence of the Cuban republic. Yet, at the outset of the twentieth century, Chinese were depicted in public discourse as a "yellow peril" to be avoided, along with black immigrants, in the making of the new Cuban nation. Under the constraints of the Platt Amendment, Cuban officials applied Chinese exclusion laws from the United States. But anti-Chinese attitudes in Cuba also stemmed from the debacle of the coolie trade half a century earlier. The ever-present desire for white, European immigration reinforced anti-Chinese regulations in Cuba. While adopting U.S. exclusion laws, Cuba also looked to some of their Latin American neighbors as models for a progressive, prosperous nation. Events in Mexico demonstrate how discourses of yellow peril could have an extreme outcome in the context of revolutionary nationalism. In 1911, bands of soldiers attacked Chinese residents in the northern town of Torreón, resulting in over three hundred deaths and extensive property damage.[52]

Whether coming from Chinese diplomatic representatives or community organizations, protests against the anti-Chinese exclusion laws in Cuba were made, to a large extent, by merchants in defense of their own interests. Chinese transnational merchants needed to enter and exit frequently for their businesses, which included the smuggling of migrants. They argued for equal treatment with other resident foreigners and emphasized their contributions to progress and modernity through commerce. While using the well-known and frequently extolled participation of the Chinese in Cuban independence to their advantage, these merchants were far removed from the ex-coolies who had fought on the battlefield. In the process of defending their interests, then, they distanced themselves from the thousands of Chinese laborers also entering Cuba and promoted an image of an apolitical entity that could bring prosperity to the nation.

The temporary lifting of the ban on the entry of Chinese labor in 1917 brought tens of thousands of new immigrants to Cuba. For the next four decades of the Cuban republic, as the Chinese settled in Cuban towns, worked in Cuban enterprises, and married Cuban women—while maintaining transnational ties to China—the dichotomous issues present at the outset of the republic continued to shape the discourse on Chinese immigrants in the Cuban nation.

III

TRANSNATIONAL AND NATIONAL BELONGING

You bid farewell to the village well, setting out for overseas.
It's been eight years, or is it already ten, and you haven't thought of home.
Willow branches are now brilliant, fields exuberantly green;
In her bedroom, the young woman's bosom is filled with frustration and grief.

—Hom, *Songs of Gold Mountain*

On Santa Clara and Esperanza Streets the industrious Asians
Antonio Gong, Fernando, Manuel, Alfonso, Mario, Benito, Ramón and
Martín, all of the surname Jhon, have a magnificent vegetable garden and
dedicate all the hours of the day to extract what is necessary to live
and to save "a little something" for when they go to Canton.

—*El Comercio*, 23 March 1923

CHAPTER SIX

Transnational Connections

Former indentured laborers who remained in Cuba had laid the foundations for the development of Chinese communities across the island. The arrival of merchants and craftsmen from China and California and the establishment of Chinese consulates in Cuba further opened the way for the strengthening of ties between migrants and their homeland in the late nineteenth century. Throughout the era of exclusion, Chinese used Cuba as a springboard to the United States. However, with their networks and business opportunities, many also viewed Cuba as a destination for sojourning or settlement. The major wave of free Chinese migrants in early-twentieth-century Cuba sustained ties to China through letters, remittances, investments, and return trips. In the process, they transformed life in the Guangdong countryside and developed Chinese transnational communities in Cuba.

Thousands of Chinese entered Cuba under the 1917 provisions for agricultural laborers. Soledad Estate in Cienfuegos recruited Chinese laborers and continued to concentrate them in the technical aspects of sugar production. In January 1921, for example, the following Chinese worked in the factory: Benito Díaz, Chon Chu, Chan Chau, Cun Chin, Sen Gui, and Ra Leon.[1] The use of Chinese names in plantation records indicates the improved social and legal status of Chinese workers over the previous century. No longer were they indentured laborers, given a Spanish name upon arrival or baptism and bound by contract to work long years on sugar plantations. Rather, they were free men who kept their names. Chinese took advantage of temporary laws allowing the immigration of contract laborers for sugar production. However, most quickly moved on or evaded the sugar estates altogether. Chinese increasingly made their way to Havana or provincial towns, where they worked in shops, restaurants, and laundries or engaged in small trade.

With the second major wave of Chinese labor migrants to Cuba, new businesses and associations proliferated across the island. Havana, the nation's capital and the principal port for immigrants, maintained the largest population of Chinese. By the 1920s, fruit and vegetable stands, restaurants, groceries, tailors, shoe and watch repair shops, and photography studios lined the streets of Havana's Chinatown, one of the best known in the Americas.[2] In 1927, Chinese owned 535 fruit and vegetable stands, 293 laundries, and 63 groceries in Havana.[3] These commercial establishments were complemented by ethnic institutions—associations, theaters, four newspapers, a cemetery, language schools, a hospital, and a residence for the elderly. Chinese political, economic, social, and cultural life flourished through these transnational institutions. Shops continued to serve as centers for informal gatherings of immigrant men, providing remittance and letter-writing services and public space for discussions of business, circulation of hometown news, and socializing. Together with the more formal associations, shops became central nodes linking a Chinese migrant's life at home and abroad.[4]

Remittances and Return

Chinese in Cuba developed a "transnational social field" linking their places of origin and settlement.[5] They maintained ties with home communities, corresponded with relatives and business associates in other overseas locales, and increasingly became part of the fabric of Cuban society. Like other movements of people past and present, migration between Guangdong villages and Cuban towns can be more accurately described as "translocal." The patterns of Chinese transnationalism were based on sustaining ties with specific localities in Guangdong province. Luis Guarnizo and Michael Smith use the term "translocal relations" to describe the connection between "historically and geographically specific points of origin and migration established by transmigrants."[6] Chinese migrants carried out transnational activities at three basic levels: family, village, and nation. They maintained relationships

TABLE 7 Third-Order Businesses on the Principal Artery of Barrio Chino, Havana, 1926

STREET ADDRESS	ESTABLISHMENT	OWNER
Zanja 10	inn	Santiago Bú
Zanja 18	tailor	Andrés Li
Zanja 22	tinsmith	Jok Mon Lluke
Zanja 22	carpenter	Julio Jun
Zanja 32	tailor	Can Wa
Zanja 17	bodega	Guillermo Lin
Zanja 17 (by San Nicolás)	eatery	Yat Pon San
Zanja 17 (by San Nicolás)	fruit stand	Chung Son
Zanja 19	tailor	Chiún Chin
Zanja 23	eatery	Juan Lang
Zanja 25	shoe store	Wa Chen
Zanja 27	bodega	Sun Ma Wo
Zanja 37	shoe store	Antonio Chung
Zanja 37	tailor	Julio Chin
Zanja 111A	tailor	Fo Con
Zanja 41	fruit stand	Manuel Wong
San José 35 (by Zanja)	photography	Lai Lan
Campanario 101 (by Zanja)	shoe store	José Aquin
Rayo 36	café	León Tan Leu
Rayo 19	chop suey	Chin In Lan
Rayo 11	chop suey	Alfonso Wong
Rayo 21 and 22	eatery	Chang Tin
Rayo 24	miscellany	Weng Chen
Dragones 54	inn	Alfonso Lúi
Dragones 66	shoe store	Juan Chen
Dragones 66	fruit stand	Mario Lujo
Dragones 29	eatery	Ley Pin
Dragones 27	fruitstand	Domingo Lain
Manrique 81B	shoe store	Gustavo Wong
Manrique 100	tinsmith	Antonio Lai
Manrique 100	tailor	Luis Chí
San Nicolás 108	eatery	José Chang Claat
San Nicolás 114	fruit stand	Martin Chong
San Nicolás 85	fruit stand	Juan Chen
General Casas 1	fruit stand	Cué Long
General Casas 3	tailor	José Chi
General Casas 5	eatery	Mi Giam Chi
General Casas 7	eatery	Chan Chon
General Casas 9	fruit stand	San Sen Lung
General Casas 79 and 81	fruit stand	Quong Cheon Long

Source: Exp. 51, leg. 25, Secretaría de la Presidencia, 28 August 1926, Archivo Nacional de Cuba, Havana.

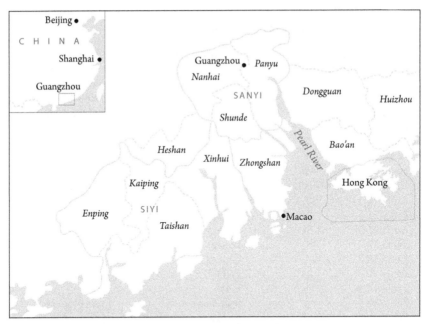

The Pearl River delta region

with home villages in the early twentieth century by sending remittances to relatives, funding local and regional modernization projects, and supporting and defending the emergent Chinese republic.

During the late nineteenth and early twentieth centuries, most Chinese migrants to the Americas came from the Pearl River delta region of Guangdong Province, particularly the overwhelmingly agricultural Siyi (four counties) of Taishan, Xinhui, Kaiping, and Enping, as well as nearby Zhongshan. In Cuba, more than half were from the single county of Taishan. Significant numbers also came from the Sanyi (three counties) of Nanhai, Panyu, and Shunde, more urbanized and commercially developed areas located closer to the city of Guangzhou. These patterns continued into the 1940s and 1950s. By 1942, 41 percent of the 18,484 Chinese registered with the Chinese Consulate were from Taishan, and only 43 individuals were from outside of Guangdong Province.[7]

Migrants from the same dialect groups in China tended to settle in the same regions and occupations overseas. Although numerically in the minority, Sanyi migrants played prominent roles in the economic and cultural life of Chinese communities overseas. Merchant-class migrants from Nanhai became known for their development of the import/export sector and for labor contracting in the Americas. Tensions between the Sanyi and the

Siyi communities in California propelled some Sanyi Chinese to seek opportunities in Mexico, Cuba, and other Central and South American countries, where they developed successful enterprises.[8] Writing in the 1920s, Chinese Cuban author Antonio Chuffat reported that from the more urbanized Sanyi came merchants, grocers, butchers, and tailors, who dominated the powerful Chinese Chamber of Commerce in Havana. Chinese from the town of Jiujiang (Kow Kong) in Nanhai County were well represented among the economic elite of the community.

The new waves of Chinese in early-twentieth-century Cuba brought more migrants from villages in Taishan, Xinhui, and nearby Zhongshan Counties. Men from the rural Siyi mostly began as laborers but rapidly moved into other occupations. According to Chuffat, the Taishanese sold fruits and vegetables and worked on sugar estates, while migrants from neighboring Xinhui owned shops in Havana and worked as confectioners, cooks, vendors of meat and fish, and itinerant peddlers elsewhere. He emphasized that the Xinhui Chinese never had luxury-goods shops for the sale of perfume, household wares, and silk.[9] Zhongshan migrants generally were businessmen in Cuba and maintained two district associations in Havana by 1950.[10] Although migrants from Taishan and Xinhui typically inhabited the lower socioeconomic strata in Cuba, the actual patterns of occupational mobility were much more fluid than Chuffat describes. As in other global migration flows, those who left China did not come from among the poorest classes of society. They required a degree of capital and connections to be able to make a journey overseas.

By the early twentieth century, Chinese migration to Cuba had become a dual-sided, network-driven process. Men working abroad maintained strong ties to their home villages through remittances, investments, and return visits. They saved their earnings, however meager, in suitcases or under the floorboards of their homes, for a trip back to their villages in China. Return trips were a goal even for lower-income Chinese in Cuba, and a sudden stroke of fortune could accelerate the process. In April 1934, for example, after winning the Cuban national lottery, "two humble Chinese" from Rancho Veloz gave their fruit stand to "a fellow countryman" before they embarked on a train to Havana and from there continued on a journey back to China.[11] Chinese migrants abroad defined economic and social achievement by the ability to contribute to home villages. With enhanced wealth, expertise, and social standing, some formerly marginal Chinese who had worked as laborers or merchants abroad became increasingly influential in China. Back in China, they became local political leaders, school principals, and

Typical *qiaoxiang* in Guangdong Province, China, August 2001.
(Photograph by author)

newspaper editors.[12] Of course, few migrants related the harsh realities of life abroad, opting instead to be hoisted on a chair and escorted through the village upon their return, hold banquets for family and friends, improve their homes, and display the latest Western products such as sewing machines, radios, cameras, jewelry, and suits.

Migration overseas as an economic strategy affected entire villages in the southeastern coastal provinces of Guangdong and Fujian. They became known as *qiaoxiang,* or "overseas Chinese home areas," where returned migrants and their dependents were (and still are) concentrated. Adam McKeown captures the uneven effect migration had in South China: "In some villages, all the able-bodied men were sent overseas, leaving behind agricultural fields gone wild, and women, children, and elderly people living on remittances. A village two kilometers down the road without any significant advantages or disadvantages in local economic circumstances may have produced no emigrant families at all."[13]

Different migration chains lent distinct character to these villages. Several villages in Taishan and Xinhui Counties, for example, historically sent the majority of their men to Cuba, rather than the United States or Southeast Asia, in the early twentieth century. Earlier settlers facilitated the migration of relatives and fellow villagers (*tongxiangren*) by providing housing, employment, and support. Once abroad, migrants preferred to work with fellow kin, purchase food and supplies from them, and borrow money and sell businesses to them.[14] Today, village elders in Guangdong aptly describe this network-driven migration process with the phrase "one brings another" (*yige dai yige*). Sons followed fathers, nephews followed uncles, and younger brothers followed older brothers. From 1919 to 1930, over seven hundred men from the town of Dulian in Xinhui County migrated to Cuba to work on plantations and in road construction. During this period almost every Dulian household had a relative in Cuba. Interestingly, this migration chain shifted after the Depression and World War II, when opportunities in Cuba became scarce, and Dulian Chinese in Cuba resettled in Venezuela to work in the oil industry.[15]

Given the expense of return trips, letters and remittances were the primary means of maintaining ties to China, forming the glue for transpacific family and business relationships. Shops and associations on both sides of the ocean unofficially managed most remittances from Cuba. With the assistance of professional writers, letters to relatives back home served as the unofficial receipts for remittances. Migrant letters were often brief, relating the state of the business and alerting family members to the amount of money sent home. Letters from China reported important events in the village and household, detailed children's progress in school, and confirmed receipt of remittances. One Chinese mother pleaded to her overseas son, "For many months there has arrived no letter or money. My supplies are exhausted. I am old; too infirm to work. . . . Hereafter, my son, change your course; be industrious and frugal, and remit to me your earnings; and within the year let me welcome home both your father and yourself."[16]

A deportation case from the United States demonstrates the role of family networks in Chinese migration. During the age of Chinese exclusion, U.S. authorities seized a batch of letters from two detained migrants (Louie Lit and Louie Fong). A letter from their father, Louie Quong Kee, explained that another brother, Wah Tang, had borrowed $133 and left Hong Kong for Havana several months earlier, but has not yet been heard from. The father also provided an accounting for the $70 he had received from his son in the United States: "I paid $30 to Ah Hing for interest and $20 for your family and the other $20 for me."[17] In some cases, Chinese migrants went beyond the formulaic reporting of general conditions and amounts of remittances sent. Huang Baoshi, a Chinese migrant known as Francisco Wong in Sagua la Grande, consistently wrote descriptive, detailed letters commenting on the economic and political situation in Cuba to his son Huang Zhuocai in China. To this day, Huang Zhuocai maintains a connection to Cuban society and history through the preserved letters from his father, although he has never been to Cuba.[18]

With the remittance business mainly in private hands, detailed records are sparse for the 1920s and 1930s. A record from the Guangdong post office during the postwar period lists migrants from Southeast Asia and the Americas who sent remittances through official channels and those who received them, county by county, town by town. Chinese from all over Cuba sent money home. In addition to Havana, where the largest number of Chinese were concentrated, official remittances came from Matanzas, Cárdenas, Jovellanos, Colón, Cienfuegos, Santa Clara, Remedios, Camagüey, Bayamo, and Santiago de Cuba. The majority of official remittances from Cuba sent through the Guangdong post office in 1948 were from the Chinese of Jiujiang (Nanhai County).[19] Although migrants from the "four counties" of Taishan, Xinhui, Enping, and Kaiping were numerically stronger, they sent fewer remittances through the post office that year than migrants from Nanhai. The imbalance is likely due to the preference of the wealthier, more urbanized Jiujiang Chinese for using official government remittance services. These official government numbers do not include the thousands of remittances sent annually through traditional immigrant organizations.[20]

Along with money, information and goods traveled to China via migrant circuits. Migrants from the town of Dulian filled their letters from Cuba with news about the state of business, wages for manual labor, and safety conditions abroad. Products with cultural significance also crossed the ocean. Chinese in Cuba sent Western-style suits, vests, leather shoes, and hats to their relatives back home, and Dulian elders still proudly wear these articles of clothing.[21] Men from the town of Meige worked on sugar plantations and in restaurants in Cuba in the 1920s. At times, along with letters and money, they sent packets of coarse white sugar back home.[22]

Chinese abroad also shaped local Guangdong society by building railroads, hospitals, schools, ancestral temples, and houses and establishing modern banks, mining ventures, land reclamation projects, and steamship lines. Through these investments, Chinese overseas transformed the physical landscape of Cantonese villages. Today, residents of the town of Shadui in Xinhui County point out the two- and three-story houses built by Chinese who returned from Cuba in the early decades of the twentieth century. Towering above the rest of the village, and incorporating Western architectural traits, these houses are typical of Guangdong qiaoxiang in the 1920s and 1930s.[23]

Transpacific Families

Although Chinese migrants lived in "bachelor societies" in the Americas, the majority of them were married or intended to marry upon their return to China. Economic strategies and cultural norms produced a migration to Cuba that was almost exclusively male, even long after the end of the period of indentured labor.[24]

The long-standing tradition of migration altered notions of family and kinship in the Pearl River Delta. Divided households developed from long-term separations between Chinese migrants and their wives. Evelyn Nakano Glenn uses the term "split-household family" to characterize situations in which production by males abroad was separated from other functions by relatives in home villages, while the family remained "an interdependent, cooperative unit."[25] In a typical scenario, Chinese men working overseas provided financial support through remittances and ensured continuation of the family line through return trips. Chinese women who remained in their villages often became heads of household. Specifically, they tended to the fields, raised livestock, performed chores, engaged in cottage industries such as weaving and silk spinning, and were responsible for the education of children. Often facing loneliness, alienation, and hardship, these women demonstrated flexibility and endurance in adapting to south China village life without their husbands. The *qiaojuan,* or "overseas Chinese dependents," who remained in Guangdong represented a critical component of the transnational migration process.[26]

Laishui Village in Guanghai, Taishan County, is a typical qiaoxiang, in which the majority of households have long depended on remittances from relatives overseas. Laishui traditionally consisted of thirty households. Of these, eleven sent men to Cuba, four to the United States, four to Burma, three to Canada, three to Hong Kong, two to Australia, and one to India. Thus, 93 percent of the village households had relatives overseas, and 37 percent had immediate relatives in Cuba. The market town Guanghai provided a convenient point of departure for emigrants, who proceeded through Hong Kong or Macao to board foreign ships destined for the Americas.

A meeting in Laishui with local historian of Taishan, Liu Chongmin, uncovered the experiences of one overseas Chinese dependent and her son. Liu's mother and other women in the village became known as "lifelong widows" (*shoushenggua*). While her husband Liu Kongjiu sojourned abroad, she remained in Taishan, passing on family history to her son. Liu Chongmin recorded extensive interviews with his elderly mother, before she died in 1995 at the age of 104. In 1911, well before Chinese labor immigration restrictions were temporarily lifted in Cuba, Liu Kongjiu migrated to Cuba at age eighteen along with three brothers. He waited until 1926 to make his first return trip to Laishui, where he married and built a new house adjacent to the ancestral dwelling. Liu Kongjiu's letters to his wife departed from typical migrant custom of not reporting the difficulties of life abroad. She learned about the harsh treatment he received at the hands of sugar estate foremen and the hardship of carrying loads of laundry on his back until after midnight.

Long-term absences of immigrant men made producing heirs back home difficult. Although not ideal, adoption was a viable strategy for maintaining the family line. After their child died at a young age, Liu Kongjiu and his wife formally adopted the six-year-old Liu Chongmin in Laishui Village. In this case, the adopted son (and only heir) remained in China with his mother. He developed an especially close relationship with her based on mutual dependence in the absence of his father. As the only son, Liu Chongmin and his mother "leaned on each other" (*xiangyi weiming*) for survival. Like many other women in Guangdong emigrant communities, Liu Chongmin's mother had lived most of her life without her husband. Out of the eleven men who went to Cuba from Guanghai, only two were able to reunite with their families in old age.[27] As an adult, Liu Chongmin channeled the village's collective stories of separation into a local history of Taishan qiaoxiang.[28]

Distance and long stretches of time without communication had the potential to devastate transpacific family relations. As Madeline Hsu notes in her study of Taishanese transnational migration, "Even when letters and money crossed the Pacific at regular intervals, years of separation distanced husbands from wives, and children grew up ignorant of the contours of their fathers' faces."[29] Families of Chinese migrants to Cuba faced such hardships.

The Lui family, divided between Xinhui County in Guangdong and the town of Cienfuegos in Cuba, offers a portrait of a Chinese migrant and his descendants who maintained transpacific relations, despite distance and time. Through earnings from his fruit and vegetable business in Cienfuegos, Lui Fan was able to make three return trips to Lui Village and send money home to support his wife and two daughters. On several occasions Lui Fan asked his wife in China to join him in Cuba with their two daughters to help with cooking, cleaning, and the tasks of domestic life. She refused, unwilling

Liu Chongmin in his home in Guanghai, Taishan County, China, August 2001.
(Photograph by author)

to settle in a place with an unfamiliar culture and language. She also wanted to remain in China to care for her elderly mother. This refusal to join her husband abroad indicates another reason behind the skewed gender ratios in Chinese migration: women's ability to make decisions based on their own interests.

The decision for males to migrate and females to remain in China can be viewed as part of a family-based economic strategy. Confucian ideals mandated that after marrying, a woman would move to a husband's village, living among his parents and fellow villagers. Because they were expected to take care of their in-laws, Chinese women in China were considered better brides than those born abroad, who were often "assumed to be of uncertain character and moral values." With knowledge that marrying a "Gold Mountain guest" usually meant long-term separations, marriage in early-twentieth century Guangdong villages took on unique characteristics. For example, although it was considered improper (or, better said, scandalous) for women to engage in an extramarital affair, it was more tolerable for a woman to seek out another husband if her immigrant husband neglected his familial responsibilities by not sending home remittances. The worst fate was abandonment by an overseas husband, signified by a lack of letters, remittances, and return visits.[30] The following excerpt from a Taishanese folksong evokes the challenges faced by migrants' wives:

> My husband, pressed by poverty, took off to Gold Mountain.
> With a petty sum of money, he cannot make the journey home.
> The road to Gold Mountain is extremely perilous and difficult;
> At home, in grief and pain, my longing eyes pierce through to the
>   horizon, waiting for his return.
> O, no way is such a life better than that of farming at home:
> Toiling for half a year, relaxing the rest;
> You greet parents in the morning;
> You are with your wife at night;
> Everyone is happy, with smiles all over their faces;
> Festivals, parties, New Year's Eve celebrations—
> You and I, husband and wife, O, how loving would that be![31]

Many such songs only tell one part of the story—alienation and anguish. Lui Fan's wife in China maintained a practical attitude toward the hardships she endured in the village while her husband worked abroad. Meanwhile, Lui Fan entered into a common-law marriage with a local woman in Cuba. Asked if their mother envied Lui Fan's Cuban wife, his Chinese daughters responded with a shrug, "There was nothing she could do about it."[32]

Patriarchy in village life and in migration patterns did indeed shape daily life and relations between men abroad and their wives left behind, but often in complex ways. In the absence of men, women could take on the dominant position at home. Their management of the family, fields, and finances was crucial in maintaining the *jia*, or traditional household, and continuing the family line. In his discussions of Asians in American history, Gary Okihiro advocates a repositioning of women from the margins to the mainstream, one that "stretches the boundaries of that past to encompass both the bachelor societies in the United States and their counterpart communities of women in Asia."[33] The role of women in Chinese migration history thus encompasses women who did *not* migrate, but who held as crucial a role in the family economic strategy as the men who went abroad.

Non-Chinese women were also affected by transpacific family arrangements, as Chinese men customarily could have multiple wives. While the primary wife usually remained in the home village, some migrant men, such as Lui Fan, also married local women abroad. In certain circumstances, non-Chinese wives accompanied their husbands on journeys back to China. In the early twentieth century, reports circulated of Peruvian women begging on Hong Kong streets to earn passage back to Peru. Adam McKeown notes, "They all told the same story of marrying a Chinese man in Peru, accompanying him to China, and then being left there as a secondary wife when the husband returned abroad."[34] Perhaps the most extreme case involved Mexican women who were deported with their Chinese husbands from Mexico in the 1930s, at the height of the Mexican anti-Chinese movement. Mexican Chinese couples formed a distinct enclave in Macao, from where they appealed for repatriation and for the inclusion of their mixed-race children in the Mexican nation.[35]

The Japanese occupation of China from 1937 to 1945 cut off communication and transportation, with devastating effects on family members who were dependent upon remittances. Cantonese women whose husbands sojourned abroad became especially vulnerable. During the occupation Liu Kongye's wife resorted to begging in her Taishanese village and died "prematurely."[36] The Lui family in the adjacent county of Xinhui faced similar difficulties. In the absence of a male head of household, the Lui women were "bullied" by other villagers.[37]

Transnational Community Institutions

Even while maintaining hometown ties through remittances, investments, and return visits, Chinese overseas settled into the daily routines of life and established transnational migrant organizations to assist with navigating their new environments. The immigration wave of the early twentieth century produced a plethora of organizations and clubs in Havana as well as provincial towns. Between 1900 and 1929, thirty-five Chinese associations were registered with the Provincial Government of Havana (twenty-six between 1921 and 1929).[38] The umbrella organization Casino Chung Wah, established in 1893, continued to engage in charitable, welfare, cultural, and educational projects and to serve as the main organization representing the Chinese community to outsiders. With the increase in the Chinese migrant population, branches were established throughout Cuba. In addition to the traditional clan and regional associations, new occupational, mutual aid, political, cultural, and sport organizations developed.[39] Chinese associations served a dual function, pivoting between homeland issues and those particular to the Chinese in Cuba. They regularly celebrated the Chinese New

Year and the Qing Ming festival. As spaces for socializing, networking, and receiving financial, legal, medical, and burial assistance, these associations were central to a typical migrant's experience abroad.

Social relationships in South China were underpinned by kinship and native place, and to the extent possible, migrants reproduced these networks through associations abroad. The first clan association in Cuba was the Lun Con Cun Sol (Longgang Qinyi Gongsuo), established in 1900 to unite migrants with the surnames Zhao, Zhang, Liu, and Guan. Typically, a Chinese migrant's first stop would be the clan or native place association, where he would find kin from his hometown. A member of the huiguan met immigrants at the docks and escorted them to headquarters, where they would receive assistance with housing and employment. When Lui Cuon Chong (Lü Qiantong) arrived in Havana in 1926, he rented a room on Cuchillo Street in the association for those surnamed Lui. The association gave Western names to new Chinese migrants, and Lui Cuan Chong became known as Felipe Luis.[40] Once migrants were overseas, considerations of mutual assistance often overshadowed those of common surname or home district.[41] For example, the Lui kinsmen formed an association with two other surname groups on Cuchillo Street in the heart of Havana's Barrio Chino.

One of the most well known regional associations represented the wealthier migrants from Nanhai County. In 1924, the Kow Kong Association (Jiujiang Gonghui) established a medical clinic for Chinese residents in Cuba known as the Quinta Benéfica de Kow Kong (Jiujiang Qiaoshang Gongyiyuan). Members, who hailed from all parts of Guangdong, paid modest monthly dues to receive treatment at the modern facility. Nestled in the suburb of Lawton in Havana, the hospital specialized in dentistry, tuberculosis, bone grafting, autopsy, internal and external medicine, pediatrics, and women's health.[42] The association spent the considerable sum of $60,000 pesos to construct the modern facility.[43] Shortly after the clinic's opening, the Chinese merchant paper reported on its "considerable success."[44]

Occupational, money-lending, and rotating credit associations assisted Chinese immigrants in Cuba with starting a business. The Lui migrants in Cienfuegos, including Francisco Luis, belonged to an occupational association. In November 1926, ten Chinese who cultivated and sold fruits and vegetables met at No. 157 Santa Clara Street to form the Asociación Cienfueguera de Agricultores Chinos for the promotion of the members' collective and individual interests. Its purpose was to develop agriculture and systems of cultivation as well as to facilitate contracting. The same building also served two other Chinese associations, allowing the produce growers to tap into these networks for business.[45]

The laundry association developed into one of the most extensive Chinese trade organizations. First established in the late nineteenth century in the Americas, Chinese laundries were typically dispersed throughout cities according to the concentrations of their customer base, usually non-Chinese. Chinese from California set up laundries in northern Mexico, Peru, Panama, and Cuba, forming a transnational network cemented by the laundry association. The Chinese dominated the laundry business in Havana, with 293 establishments in 1927. Although by 1954 the number decreased to 130, Chinese laundries maintained a significant presence throughout the city. In September 1933, the Asociación de Lavanderos Chinos was formed with its center on Dragones Street in the Barrio Chino. Mario Castillo and Miriam Herrera demonstrate that the concentration of Chinese laundries in Havana coincided with the formation of new working-class neighborhoods near developing industries, such as the municipalities of 10 de Octubre, Marianao, and Cerro. Chinese laundries also proliferated in the central parts of Havana, with a range of social classes and business activity. The middle- and upper-middle-class Cubans of Plaza (Vedado) were likely more disposed toward dry cleaners.[46] In Cuba, the Chinese-operated laundry was referred to as a *tren de lavado* (washing train), signifying the line formation of washers and ironers. According to Mauro García and Pedro Eng, "Clothes were rarely lost or mislaid, since each item was marked with a Chinese character taken from eighty that appear in the works of Confucius."[47]

The primary purpose of all of these huiguans was mutual aid. Along these lines, Triad lodges became the best-known fraternal organizations among Chinese in the Americas, as they catered to working classes and were considered to be adept at dealing with the needs of migrants in their new settings. The Triads traditionally were secret societies in China that advocated the overthrow of the Manchu Qing dynasty and the restoration of the Ming dynasty. Members of these sworn brotherhoods underwent an elaborate initiation ritual underpinned by a rhetoric of fraternity and comradeship.[48]

The Chee Kung Tong (Zhigongtang) maintained the broadest membership of Chinese migrants overseas. In Cuba it developed from a pre-existing Triad organization known as the Hongmen Sanhehui, founded in 1887. In 1902 it became the Partido Republicano Chee Kung Tong in response to a call to organize from the North American branch.[49] Despite its label *partido* in Cuba, the Chee Kung Tong was not a political party and did not develop detailed political programs for China, beyond the overthrow of the Qing dynasty. Over time, Triads overseas became less revolutionary and more involved with concerns particular to Chinese migrants, such as mutual aid, bypassing immigration barriers, and importing opium.[50] As a fraternal organization that appealed to the lower strata of Chinese migrants, the Chee Kung Tong maintained the strongest membership rosters in Cuba. Branches multiplied throughout the provinces and attracted small traders, itinerant vendors, laundrymen, tailors, barbers, gardeners, fruit stand operators, and restaurant employees. According to one report, the association maintained 10,000 members across the island in 1928.[51] Vegetable vendor Francisco Luis was a founder and treasurer of the Cienfuegos branch in 1924. He was one of fifteen members with the surname "Luis" in the branch, attesting to the link between kinship networks and settlement patterns.[52]

Rituals associated with ancestor worship and filial piety remained paramount for Chinese overseas in the twentieth century, and associations on both sides of the ocean managed burial and "bone repatriation." Chinese migrants went to great lengths to ensure that bones of the dead were shipped back to families in China, or, if they remained interred abroad, that basic funeral rituals were practiced and maintained. Even Chinese who had converted to Catholicism arranged for their bones to be sent home if possible, in one case prompting objections from the archbishop of Lima in Peru.[53] Him Mark Lai points out the level of commitment fellow migrants maintained in fulfilling their burial obligations. In 1909, three partners of the Tuck Lee Yuen Store in Pierce City, Idaho, informed their burial association (*shantang*) that they had sold their business to "a white man" and were planning to return to China. Before departing, however, they left detailed information about the deceased Chinese who had deposited funds with them to ensure proper exhumation and shipment of their remains back to China.[54]

The Chinese cemetery in Havana, managed by the Casino Chung Wah, continued to served as a key node in the burial process. Plots and mausoleums were organized by district and clan associations. Chinese throughout the provinces arranged for bones of their deceased relatives or fellow association members to be transferred to the Chinese cemetery in Havana or back to China. Bones from La Reina Cemetery in Cienfuegos, for example, were transferred to Havana or directly to China through the Tung Wah Hospital (Donghua Yiyuan) in Hong Kong.[55] Exhumations and shipments of bones back home were scheduled at intervals several years apart. In November 1916, the local sanitation headquarters in Cienfuegos authorized José Jhulay to exhume the remains of the Alfonso Pons for transport to Hong Kong. Jhulay was a leader in the Chinese community who in 1924 founded the Sociedad Long Kuan (Gran China), where Pons was a common surname.[56] During times of warfare and political disruption in China, shipments of bones were temporarily halted. Although the Chinese cemetery in Havana was considered a temporary resting place, its importance became highlighted during the Japanese occupation of China (1937–45), when sea transport was cut off and shipping the remains of deceased Chinese proved impossible.[57] Besides the Chinese cemetery in Havana, local cemeteries in the provinces served as final resting spots for many migrants.[58]

Transnational networks brought Cantonese opera to San Francisco, Havana, and other cities in the diaspora.[59] In Havana, the building of the restaurant El Pacífico in the Barrio Chino formed the nucleus of Chinese Cuban cultural life. It housed the Club Cultural de Música China (Zhonghua Yinyue Gongsuo), which contracted Chinese actors and musicians directly from China and from North America. Also, martial arts clubs representing different styles were formed.[60]

Overseas Chinese Nationalism

Toward the end of the nineteenth century, as Cuba moved toward independence from Spain and U.S. imperial ambitions in the Caribbean and Pacific expanded, Chinese migrants in Cuba were pulled into the orbit of another struggle back home: a revolution against the 250-year-old Manchu Qing dynasty and the 2,000-year-old imperial system of government. In China, different but overlapping agendas for building a strong, modern nation-state in the face of domestic weakness and foreign incursions came from proactive Qing government officials, reformers who advocated a constitutional monarchy, and revolutionaries who supported a republican state.

The reform movement under Kang Youwei (1858–1927) initially had more support among Chinese overseas communities, which were dominated by conservative merchants, than the revolutionaries. Reformers were well-received throughout Southeast Asia and the Americas as they collected donations from the merchant elite and established branches of the Baohuanghui (Protect the Emperor Society). Revolutionary leader Sun Yat-sen (1866–1925) launched the Chinese republican movement in 1894 from Honolulu. Exiled to Tokyo in 1905, he founded the Tongmenghui (Revolutionary Alliance), an umbrella organization for Chinese student and political groups and predecessor to the Guomindang (Chinese Nationalist Party). Sun Yat-sen elucidated the concepts of nationalism (*minzu*), democracy (*min-*

quan), and people's livelihood (*minsheng*) that later were developed into his party's foundational Three Principles of the People (*sanminzhuyi*). Sun deemed the logistical and financial support of Chinese overseas important enough to describe them as "mothers of the revolution." Both Kang and Sun were natives of Guangdong and spoke local dialects, which likely helped them to gain support among Chinese overseas communities. They both sought the endorsement of Triad lodges, critical to maintaining a popular base of support.[61]

Sun Yat-sen did not personally visit Havana, but his message reached Cuba through diasporic networks and publications. Arriving in Cuba in 1902, Huang Dingzhi became an early supporter and liaison for Sun's revolutionary agenda. In Havana, Huang led a study group on the three principles, which later turned into the Cuban branch of the Guomindang. The Tokyo newspaper *Minbao* served as a basis for discussions. Huang composed essays advocating revolution in China and sent reports about activities in Cuba to the San Francisco newspaper *Shaonian Zhongguo Chenbao* (Young China Morning Post), which was launched in 1909. As Cuba's fund-raising commissioner, Huang raised over US$10,000 for Sun Yat-sen. Branches of the Three Principles of the People Association (Sanmin Tuantihui) were established in Remedios and Guantánamo. Huang viewed both the conservative merchant elite and members of the Chee Kung Tong as opposition to the revolutionary nationalist movement during this early phase.[62]

Meanwhile, the Qing government enacted a series of broad modernizing reforms in 1905. In a last-ditch effort to maintain the loyalty of Chinese overseas, the government decreed in the Nationality Law of 1909 that all Chinese abroad were subjects of the emperor based on "the principle of consanguinity." Ultimately, though, reformers increasingly joined the revolutionary movement. When a Qing naval mission stopped in the Havana harbor in July 1911, a small band of Chinese revolutionaries there launched a demonstration. How the incident was recorded by the press and remembered by later generations of Chinese nationalists is revealing of political divisions within Chinese overseas communities. Cuban newspapers, including the English-language *Havana Daily Post*, mistakenly interpreted the chaos aboard the ship as support among Qing sailors for the revolutionary cause. A 1950 community record celebrates overseas Chinese "compatriots" in Cuba delivering the revolutionary message to Qing sailors and successfully urging them to renounce their Manchu rulers. But in his 1936 memoir, Huang Dingzhi (who witnessed the event first-hand), portrays it as an instance of fortunate timing for the movement in Cuba.

The Qing court had dispatched the warship *Haiqi* as an international mission to England to congratulate King George V at his coronation ceremony. Afterward, the ship captain accepted invitations to dock in American cities with overseas Chinese communities, such as New York, Mexico, and Havana. The Casino Chung Wah and the Chinese consulate prepared to welcome the sailors with an official reception in Cuba. Sun Yat-sen's small group of supporters in Cuba saw in the event an opportunity to spread word of the revolutionary movement to Qing subjects and to raise funds.

When the ship docked on 5 August, they distributed leaflets to the sailors urging them to renounce Qing rule. Some even climbed aboard the ship to deliver speeches. The flyer questioned why Han Chinese soldiers were serving the Manchus, evoking ethnic difference: "Your nation, your home, and your family were destroyed by the Manchus." The revolutionaries also passed out leaflets during a break in a Chinese opera performance. The ship captain and a Qing official stormed out of the theater, irate at their actions. They asked the consul to arrest the Chinese revolutionaries and have the Cuban government deport them. According to Huang Dingzhi, although the situation was tense, many sailors were receptive to the speeches and invited the revolutionaries for conversation over drinks and noodles. Only three months after the incident, revolution broke out in China. When the *Haiqi* returned to Shanghai, Chinese revolutionaries there boarded the ship and mounted a new flag.[63]

The Qing government succumbed to revolutionary forces in 1911, initiating China's republican era in 1912. Sun Yat-sen was unable to generate support from more than a small percentage of the Chinese overseas until after 1911.[64] When Sun tapped into the membership and resources of the Triads, his republican movement achieved a much wider base of support in the United States and elsewhere.[65] He continued to enjoy support from Chinese in Cuba, who sent him a congratulatory message as they celebrated his provisional presidency of the new Chinese republic. Likewise, when Sun relinquished authority to Yuan Shikai, they sent him a cable urging him not to resign.[66] Because the merchant elite remained intact in Chinese overseas communities, the actual transition to a republican government under the presidency of Yuan Shikai from 1912 to 1916 brought few changes for most migrants. New organizations with new names were established, but the traditional power structure within Chinese migrant communities remained essentially unchanged.

After the death of President Yuan Shikai in 1916 and the dissolution of the short-lived republic, warlord governments emerged to control different regions of China, and international governments recognized the regime based in Beijing. The Guomindang attempted to unify the nation politically amid foreign economic intrusions and profound sociocultural transformations. As part of the New Culture movement of the 1920s, a younger generation of Chinese intellectuals embraced new forms of literature, thought, and modernity and infused these ideas into the emerging Chinese concept of national identity.[67]

It would be over a decade before the Guomindang consolidated its rule in China and its influence in Chinese overseas communities. The infant party needed to bridge class and regional differences, to eliminate warlord rule and unify the country militarily, and to construct a Chinese nation. Most Chinese migrants in the 1920s initially maintained loyalties to their families and native place rather than to a broader construction of "China." The Chinese in Cuba (and throughout the diaspora) thus had to imagine themselves as part of a broader Chinese nation in order to fully embrace the republican effort. As they made return trips, sent remittances, and invested in home village projects, Chinese overseas increasingly considered China as a focal point of transnational ties. The immigrant press and political parties were two institutions that were integral to this process.

As the nationalist movement in China gained momentum and reverberated overseas, Chinese communities throughout the Americas continued to provide funds and logistical support for political activists. Through political networks that stretched from China to San Francisco to Havana and provincial towns in Cuba, national concerns in China reached what would otherwise be remote areas of Chinese overseas communities. Cuban local histories and newspapers regularly noted the fund-raising visits of Guomindang representatives to towns such as Cienfuegos and Remedios.[68]

In 1921, Sun Yat-sen's supporters in Cuba founded a formal branch of the Guomindang, subordinate to the San Francisco unit. The Guomindang in Cuba did not initially dominate Havana's Chinatown, but competed for leadership with conservative merchant groups and the Chee Kung Tong. Chinese nationalists bemoaned their failure to disseminate Sun Yat-sen's ideas among coethnics in Cuba. That same year, the board of directors of the Cuban Guomindang solicited support from Chinese merchants to launch a newspaper. Their call for investors read: "We, in the name of the Three Principles of the People, summon patriotic comrades. It has been over ten years, yet few overseas Chinese brothers in Cuba realize them. It is not that their ideological inclination is not as noble as that of their overseas Chinese brothers of North America, Canada, and Southeast Asia. It is really because our party does not have a comprehensive organ for discussion to bring into full play these Three Principles of the People."[69] The founders raised US$20,000, and Sun Yat-sen's own calligraphy was used for the four characters of the masthead of the newspaper, the *Man Sen Yat Po* (Minsheng Ribao; People's Voice Daily). The paper reprinted articles from the nationalist weekly publication in China on republican principles and plans for governance.[70]

In what Chen Kwong Min refers to as the "Golden Age" of Guomindang history, Chinese in the Americas increasingly came into the fold of the party. From 1918 to 1922 the greatest numbers of Chinese migrants entered Cuba, elevating the Chinese population on the island to an estimated 60,000 or 70,000, among them youths and intellectuals disposed to homeland politics. After the Guomindang First All-China Representative Assembly issued a manifesto of their platform and policies, more Chinese in Cuba joined.[71]

Guomindang branches were established across Cuba. The inauguration of the Cienfuegos branch in 1923 brought together prominent Chinese from throughout Cuba, such as party president Luis Po (the wealthy merchant of the firm Weng On y Compañía who had first come to Cuba in 1886) and newspaper editor Nicolás Chancón. Also present was the mayor of Cienfuegos, who in a symbolic gesture of unity raised the Chinese flag as Luis Po raised the Cuban flag. The mayor proclaimed that China's new constitution "places the celestial Republic among the civilized nations of the world."[72] Those who delivered speeches for the occasion compared Sun Yat-sen to Cuba's national hero José Martí.

Transnational Publications

Publications on both sides of the ocean facilitated the development of transnational communities. Magazines geared toward Chinese overseas known as *qiaokan* were published in home areas and then distributed globally, thus strengthening migrants' native place ties and linking them to Chinese in other parts of the diaspora. In addition to hometown news, qiaokan contained articles on immigration restrictions, discriminatory policies, government protection of Chinese overseas, population statistics, development of communities abroad, education, unemployment and economic difficulties, and remittances and investments. They also appealed for contributions to native places, and advertising pages fostered diasporic business networks.[73]

In Cuba, four Chinese-language newspapers circulated in the early twentieth century, representing the diversity within the Chinese community in Cuba. The merchant community's *Wah Man Sion Po* (Huawen Shangbao;

Chinese Commercial Paper) began in 1914, the Chee Kung Tong's *Hoi Men Kong Po* (Kaiming Gongbao; Enlightenment Gazette) in 1920, and the Guomindang's *Man Sen Yat Po* (discussed above) in 1921. The publications engaged in debates on Cuban and Chinese politics through news translated from Spanish papers and received by cable from China. The merchant newspaper, which catered to business owners, initially published 500 to 600 copies daily, reaching a peak of 3,500 to 3,600 and dropping to 2,000 at midcentury. The Chee Kung Tong's newspaper maintained a critical stance toward the Guomindang in Cuba, dominated by upper-strata merchants.[74] In 1928, Chinese Communists in Cuba began publishing an underground newspaper with a political bent, which eventually became *Kwong Wah Po* (Guanghuabao; Bright China).

Despite their ideological differences, all of the newspapers addressed the immediate concerns of Chinese migrants and their families. For example, they regularly listed names and villages of those whose remains were sent home from the Chinese cemetery in Havana. They also bestowed social capital upon migrants within their communities by listing donors to hometown associations.[75] The newspapers' role in community formation and identity is suggested by an album of clippings from *Wah Man Sion Po*, compiled by a Chinese merchant in the sugar town of Lajas. He collected articles on what he considered to be the achievements of the Chinese community from the 1920s through the 1940s, such as the Chinese Chamber of Commerce, the Kow Kong clinic, fund-raising for the anti-Japanese war effort, and the Chinese community's glamorous candidate for "Miss Liberty" in 1943, Siu Kam Fun.[76]

Education and the Second Generation

In general, Chinese ethnic, cultural, and homeland ties diminished with the second generation, especially among children of mixed descent. However, from the nineteenth century on, members of the upper strata of Chinese Cubans made significant efforts toward promoting transnational identities among their Cuban-born children through education and cultural associations.

Chinese merchants sent their Cuban-born sons to China for education. Often, one son remained in Cuba to learn the business while another went to school in Hong Kong or Guangzhou.[77] After being immersed in Chinese language and culture for a period of time, children would return to Cuba with new skills and a connection to an ancestral homeland. Guangdong schools depended heavily on investment from Chinese abroad. Chinese in the Americas, including Cuba, constructed several buildings at the prestigious Taishan Number One Middle School in Taishan City.[78] In 1924, Chinese from Cuba funded a dormitory known as the "Cuba Hall" at Peizheng Middle School in Guangzhou.[79]

One of the most prominent schools in the Pearl River delta was the Canton Christian College, founded in 1888 by a group of American missionaries in Guangzhou.[80] The college's stated objectives were to train Chinese youth to become Christian leaders, teachers, statesmen, doctors, and businessmen who will "lead in the spiritual and moral regeneration of China."[81] Both Chinese and Americans funded the college, considered by its trustees in the United States to be the "Columbia of the Far East."[82]

Canton Christian College maintained a separate division for the children of Chinese overseas who desired "knowledge of their mother country, its language and customs."[83] At the school, Chinese Cuban children associated with huaqiao from other foreign countries. Eight boys in uniform represented Cuba and Central America on photo day in 1923.[84] That year, the president of the Overseas Chinese Students Association emphasized the importance of youth like him returning to China for education, culture, and language training in order to develop Chinese commerce and industry. In an English-language article entitled "Why Should We Come Back to China to Study," he wrote, "Of course we know why we are sent here to School. We want first to understand Chinese, our own language, without which our education will never be complete."[85]

Across the Pacific, the Chinese language schools that developed in major American cities in the early twentieth century demonstrated flexibility in approaches to reaching the second generation.[86] On 1 October 1936, the Colegio Chung Wah was established for male and female children of Chinese migrants in Cuba. By 1947, 150 students were enrolled, among them some Cubans who wanted to learn Chinese. Another language school was established in Santiago de Cuba, a major center of Chinese population on the far eastern end of the island. Catholic and Protestant missionaries and churches in Cuba also attempted to meet the educational needs of Chinese children. The Presbyterian church in the heart of Havana's Chinatown became locally known as the "Chinese church," its interior adorned with the image of the Buddhist goddess Guanyin. It held religious instruction in Cantonese and Spanish on Sunday afternoons and evening Chinese classes for children. Social engagements around church, such as baptism ceremonies and godparenthood, cemented ties between Chinese and non-Chinese. In general, however, Chinese schools were plagued by insufficient funds and facilities,

"Wakiu" (Overseas Chinese) School, Canton Christian College, 1923–24.
(Courtesy of Yale Divinity School Library, Special Collections)

and chroniclers of the Chinese Cuban community describe educational initiatives on the island as "undeveloped."[87]

Ethnic associations attempted to balance exclusivity and the preservation of Chinese culture with the need to incorporate Cuban-born children. Besides theater and schools, descendants in Cuba also participated in Chinese associations, although on a more limited basis than their parents. For example, the Cuban branch of the Guomindang formed a youth corps for Chinese boys and girls to study the principles of revolutionary leader Sun Yat-sen.[88] Promoters of Chinese culture within the community relied on the participation of second-generation youth. Associations organized bands, dance groups, and martial arts teams with both ethnic Chinese and children of mixed descent, at times geared exclusively toward their needs. Associations generally barred Cuban wives and mixed children from membership, but invited them to cultural activities, celebrations, and fund-raising events. In the few cases in which mixed descendants joined associations, they could not hold office.[89]

By the early twentieth century, Chinese in Cuba maintained transnational ties through remittances, investments, and return visits. They facilitated the migration of others from the same village by providing housing and employment in a new foreign environment. Although a few women also emigrated, most migrant families employed strategies in which wives remained in China to maintain the ancestral home and ensure continuation of the lineage.

Most of the transnational ethnic associations that formed throughout Cuba during the early twentieth century drew members based on kinship and regional ties. In addition to providing mutual aid and defense, to the extent possible, these organizations preserved Chinese ethnic identifications in Cuba. Educational and cultural institutions in Cuba also fostered the potential for an "overseas Chinese" (huaqiao) identity among some members of the second generation.

Migrant hometown ties did not preclude support for the emerging Chinese nation. Rather, community leaders tapped into preexisting networks to garner support for modernization and nation-building projects. During the first half of the twentieth century, migrants increasingly joined and donated to Cuban branches of the Guomindang, which unified China in 1927. However, even with a special bureau to handle overseas Chinese affairs, the party could not dominate the loyalties of all migrants abroad, especially after a purge of left-leaning members. It was not until China's very existence was threatened by Japanese aggression in the 1930s that the party garnered massive support for the defense of the homeland. Even then, leftist party members in Cuba continued to struggle for their own vision of a Chinese republic.

CHAPTER SEVEN

Chinese and *Cubanidad*

On 12 April 1946 Chinese minister Li Dijun and Cuban president Ramón Grau San Martín presided over the official unveiling ceremony of a monument dedicated to the Chinese who had participated in the wars for independence from Spain (1868–98). The black granite column is inscribed in Spanish and Chinese with the famous words of Cuban statesman Gonzalo de Quesada in 1892: "There was not a single Chinese Cuban deserter; there was not a single Chinese Cuban traitor."[1] Whites, blacks, mulattos, and Chinese fought side by side in the revolutionary struggles. The Chinese were subsequently valorized in Cuban national memory and historiography for their role in these wars. Beginning with the independence movement, the Chinese became part of a discourse of national identity that paved the way for their incorporation into Cuban society. The monument redeemed the nineteenth-century image of the Chinese as oppressed, racialized coolie laborers, replacing it with one of heroic mambises (freedom fighters).

Cubans, who themselves had recently achieved independence from Spain, found affinity with the Chinese Revolution of 1911 overthrowing dynastic rule and applauded migrant transnational political activity in support of the Chinese nationalists. Cuban newspapers chronicling the revolution in China noted the significance of 10 October for both young nations, marking the beginning of an independent Cuba and a modern, republican China. Commentators drew parallels between Chinese revolutionary Sun Yat-sen and Cuban independence leaders Carlos Manuel de Céspedes and José Martí, a discourse that has continued to this day.

Alongside this glorification of the Chinese freedom fighter and celebration of the republican revolution in China, however, anti-Chinese images continued to surface. As in other places in the diaspora, Chinese racial identities became "hardened" during times of political transition and social upheaval. In the 1920s and 1930s, an anti-immigrant Cuban nationalism developed alongside a politicized labor movement. Transnational Chinese in Cuba became targets of government repression, especially leftists or those outside the fold of the Guomindang, which had earned the respect of Cuban politicians and, along with the Chamber of Commerce, established itself as the voice of the Chinese colony in Cuba after 1927.

Whether as hero or villain, savior or scapegoat, patriot or spy, the Chinese became an integral component of Cuban political and social discussions. Two seemingly opposite images developed: one portraying the Chinese as an essential part of the fabric of the Cuban nation, the other portraying the Chinese as exotic and alien, and in its more aggressive form, as dangerous to the Cuban nation. Through the press, ethnic associations, and family and business alliances, Chinese merchants and diplomats came together to protest anti-Chinese sentiment in Cuba. Even as they maintained transnational ties to China, Chinese migrants defended themselves as deserving of cultural citizenship and as proper members of a Cuban nation.

Portrayals of Chinese as Unassimilable

Since the nineteenth century, Chinese workers had been used to quell strikes and temper labor movements throughout the Americas. As Barry Carr notes, planter complaints about the scarcity of laborers and the inadequacy of native Cubans in early-twentieth-century Cuban agriculture "were as much a reflection of the harsh and arbitrary conditions dominating the sugar industry as they were well-founded statements about the Cuban labor market."[2] When the immigration gates lifted for foreign contract workers during the sugar boom, thousands of Chinese flooded the Cuban market, along with even larger numbers of West Indians. As in the nineteenth century, planters separated workers of different ethnicities in part to prevent labor organizing. On the sugar mills of the Cuban-American Sugar Company (Cubanaco), for example, Spanish immigrants worked in construction, on railroads, and in boiler rooms, West Indians toiled in the fields, while Chinese were considered indispensable for the centrifugal department.[3] Many Chinese left the plantations to engage in commerce, but others stayed. The Caracas Estate in Lajas, near Cienfuegos, employed significant numbers of Chinese through the 1930s.[4]

Portrayals of Chinese immigrants as cheap labor and unfair competition lay at the heart of anti-Chinese discourse in the 1920s and 1930s. Opponents of the new immigrants included native Cuban workers whose demands for higher wages in factories and fields were not being met and Spanish shopkeepers who faced competition in the marketplace. Spanish merchants stepped up anti-Chinese campaigns through the pages of the conservative newspaper *Diario de la Marina*, chambers of commerce, and business associations. Editorials equated Cuban national identity with patriotism, morality, and Spanish culture. In contrast, they denigrated Chinese customs and lifestyle, represented by opium, gambling, and "infernal music" and fireworks on festival days. This discourse provided fuel for the worker movement, which denounced illegal importation of Chinese workers, who supposedly accepted low wages and poor work conditions.[5] In February 1924, *El Industrial* complained of the "plague of peddlers" that moved from house to house offering goods for better prices and advocated an organization devoted to protecting the Spanish against Chinese competition.[6]

An extreme view of Chinese workers as robotic strikebreakers entered the Cuban imagination through the work of one of Cuba's literary masters. In 1924, at the height of Chinese labor entry, author Alfonso Hernández Catá published the short story "Los chinos," which takes the use of Chinese strikebreakers as a central theme. In the story, a group of workers strike for better wages under the guidance of a mulatto labor agitator. Among them were Spaniards, Germans, Italians, Jamaicans, Haitians, and local blacks. In response, the estate manager brings in three wagons holding some ninety Chinese laborers. The strikers doubt that the Chinese will be able to handle the physical labor. The narrator conjures up the stereotype of Chinese as weak and effeminate, better suited for women's work than the harsh labor of the fields: "Poor yellow monkeys! . . . They were excellent at cooking in their small restaurants, or washing and ironing with skill. . . . Good for women's jobs! But to bear the sun on their backs for eight hours, and for making holes in iron, they lack manly men!" After a few days, however, the workers realize the strength and efficiency of the Chinese. A Jamaican poisons them by throwing herbs into the pot in which they boil their coffee. The Chinese die, one by one, and the police cart away those responsible. The narrator states, "I will never forget the terror of the police, or my own terror! If Chinese always instill in us an invincible sense of repugnance and distance in which there is something of fear, a dead Chinese is truly terrifying." Much to the strikers' horror, a new batch of Chinese are brought in to replace the dead. The narrator continues: "One morning, I don't know how much later, the noise of people woke me. I watched eagerly and felt the shiver of a hallucination penetrate me to the bone. From the truck had descended thirty yellow men—the same, absurdly the same, as those who I saw fall dead, as if instead of being buried they had been taken to the city to be recomposed—and with the diligence of ants, before my crazed eyes, they started working."[7]

Although the story casts the Chinese as subject to the oppression of the sugar estate, it also positions the Chinese outside of the alliance of foreign and native Cuban laborers who are striking for improved labor conditions. The nativist component of the growing Cuban nationalism opposed foreign workers. But while an exception is made for Jamaicans and Haitians, in the story it is the Chinese who are unable to cross the divide. Despite their efficiency, the Chinese are portrayed by the narrator as feminized and alien, unsuitable for a multiracial Cuban nation.

This discourse on the Chinese undercutting native wages as laborers and as merchants persisted throughout the Cuban republic. It was coupled with indictments of the Chinese character and depictions of Havana's Chinatown as vile and unsanitary. Chinatowns throughout the Americas have been portrayed in popular discourse as exotic and mysterious, filled with corruption and illegal activities. Cuban literature and mainstream press were no exception. Divisions within Chinese communities that culminated in violence enabled these negative images. China's uncertain situation during the warlord period brought homeland politics to the forefront of migrant communities. Factional violence known as "tong wars" erupted in cities in the United States, Mexico, and Cuba, provoking the intervention of the authorities and deportation of Chinese.[8]

A bloody incident in Havana's Chinatown in 1926 demonstrates how homeland politics and class divisions intersected. On 16 August, the wealthy Chinese merchant Andrés Chiu Lión and his Cuban wife were shot by a group of Chinese in front of the couple's Havana residence. Chiu was a prominent member of the Guomindang. Before dying two days later, Chiu named members of the Chee Kung Tong, including their president, as the shooters.[9] The fact that a woman was caught in the crossfire called special attention to the case, highlighting the harm interracial marriage could bring to Cuban wives. In response to the request from the Guomindang, the Cuban Ministry of the Interior proposed that the Chee Kung Tong be declared "illicit and immoral," citing its irregular procedures and "secret code" as examples of infringement of the Cuban laws on associations.[10] A spokesman for the Chee Kung Tong defended his organization in a letter of 8 September 1926, stating that "truthfully we only dedicate our activities in Cuba to the mutual protection of our members."[11] He emphasized that the organization opposed Soviet ideas, in what was certainly an effort to play to the Cuban government's fear of the burgeoning Communist movement.

The violence provided justification for an escalation of official anti-Chinese legislation across the island. In the wake of the murder, police increased vigilance in the Barrio Chino, and provincial governors were ordered to investigate branches of the Chee Kung Tong across the island. In September, the provincial governor suspended the Havana branch, considered responsible for the murder, and authorities began official inquiries in Matanzas, Santa Clara, Cienfuegos, Ciego de Ávila, Morón, Camagüey, Cueto, Santiago de Cuba, and Guantánamo. The government investigations touched the life of vegetable vendor Francisco Luis, founder and treasurer of the Cienfuegos branch. By December, his organization faced dissolution after operating for only two years. Eventually, Cuban authorities moved beyond the Chee Kung Tong and launched investigations into all Chinese associations in Cuba.[12]

The Barrio Chino murder prompted a wave of negative commentary in the Cuban press that condemned the rivalry between the Guomindang and the Chee Kung Tong and tied the latter to blackmail, gambling, opium, and immigrant trafficking. Historically, Triad lodges in the Americas possessed both the connections and infrastructure for smuggling, and the role of recreation in Chinese "bachelor" societies helped to sustain such fraternal organizations in Chinese overseas communities.[13] Amid the anti-immigrant climate of 1920s Cuba, Cuban authorities' scrutiny of the Chinese community challenged the very existence of Chinatown. Two days after the murder, the chief of the national secret police sent to the minister of sanitation a chart of the main street of the Barrio Chino, "where the Asians live in complete overcrowding and lack of hygiene," and a list of businesses in the neighborhood. Authorities launched a sanitary inspection and fined twenty-five proprietors for crowding up to ten inhabitants in a room, fostering "true nuclei of infection."[14]

Sanitation campaigns in the name of progress and modernity had targeted Chinese establishments since the beginning of the republic. Chinese laundries were depicted in fiction, newspapers, and official reports as spaces of filth, crime, and exotica. In Jorge Mañach's chronicles of the places, figures, and customs of Havana, the entry "Los chinos" depicts Chinese laundrymen as "strange beings, particularly reserved and mysterious."[15] In 1929, Jorge Le-Roy y Cassá, director of the Demographic Bureau of the Department of Sanitation, produced an influential report titled *Inmigración antisanitaria* that targeted Asian and black immigrants as detrimental to the nation's public health and criminal justice system. In his linkage of immigration and disease, he identified Chinese laundries as sources of tuberculosis and proposed suspending Chinese establishments and closing Cuba's gates to "antisanitary" immigrants.[16]

The anti-Chinese sentiment can be explained only in part by accusations of gambling, opium smoking, and disease. With the major wave of immigration in the 1920s, long-standing concerns about cheap Chinese labor and illegal entry resurfaced. In a 19 August 1926 article in *El Sol*, a high government official charged the Chinese with being a "terrible competition" to Cuban and Spanish workers. In this author's discourse, Chinese "live grouped by the hundreds" with a palate both cheap and strange: rats, lizards, dogs, and shark fins.[17] Police added this newspaper clipping to their lengthy file on the investigation of the Chinatown murder. The events in Chinatown coincided with a general Cuban government campaign against corruption, gambling, drugs, and illegal entry of migrants. Commentators conjured up an image of Chinese as harbingers of vice, and officials linked protection of Cubans with closing of the borders to Chinese. On 11 September 1926, a Cienfuegos newspaper reported that more than seventy "undesirable" Chinese in Havana "should be expelled from the national territory" for different offenses, especially drug trafficking.[18] These depictions strayed far from the image of hardworking, trustworthy Chinese in the jungle preparing a quintessential Creole meal for Cuban soldiers, and not only loyal to, but also an essential component of, the Cuban nation—an image that Antonio Chuffat would capture the following year in his history of the Chinese in Cuba.

Chinese in Labor and Political Movements

The anti-immigrant discourse portraying Chinese as cheap laborers, as weak, effeminate strikebreakers, and as corrupt, vice-ridden, and diseased aliens belied a much more complex situation on the ground. Although they were primarily recruited as laborers, by the 1920s and 1930s, most Chinese came to work as traders throughout the island. Political attachments, if any, were to China. But the use of Chinese as strikebreakers and their preponderance in small businesses did not preclude their joining Cuban organizations and adopting national concerns.

Chinese migrants have been traditionally assumed to be apolitical, and Chinese leftists in particular are underplayed in studies of the Chinese diaspora. This vacuum is not surprising, given that much of the scholarship is based on records and community histories sponsored by merchants and the Guomindang. Departing from this trend, a recent comparative study by Gregor Benton excavates detailed evidence of Chinese internationalism in locales as diverse as Cuba, Russia, and Europe.[19] A small but significant minority of Chinese migrants in Cuba did in fact bring with them revolutionary ideas and even became involved in Cuban labor and political movements.

In China, Guomindang unity had been tenuous, further threatened by a growing Communist movement. When the party reorganized in 1923, it formed a coalition with the Chinese Communist Party, which had been founded in Shanghai in 1921. The first Nationalist-Communist alliance for the purpose of national reunification in China lasted from 1923 to 1927.

Sun Yat-sen's death in 1925 exacerbated divisions within the Guomindang, both in China and in diasporic communities.[20] The Guomindang splintered ideologically. Among the ideas widely accepted by left-leaning members, headed by Wang Jingwei, were the construction of a noncapitalist Chinese economy based on state enterprise, the redistribution of rural land to farmers, and a political system democratic in nature, but not dominated by the bourgeoisie.[21]

Chiang Kai-shek, who controlled the military, assumed party leadership and formed a government based in Guangdong and Guangxi in opposition to the warlord government of Beijing in the north. From his base in the south, Chiang Kai-shek launched the Northern Expedition, with backing from the Soviet Union, to suppress warlord rule and unite China. By 1927 Chiang nominally controlled all of China, and the international community legitimized his government in Nanjing.

From this position of power, the Guomindang sought to further enlist the wealth, expertise, and loyalty of Chinese abroad, while ridding the party of opposition forces. Chiang terminated the alliance with the Communists and purged them from the party in both China and overseas, reducing the number of members. The purge resulted in the birth of new Marxist political groups among Chinese in the Americas.[22]

When the Cuban branch of the Guomindang divided along ideological lines in 1926, party activist Su Xingbo became head of the leftist faction, known as the *zhengyi* group. Su and his leftist compatriots viewed Sun Yat-sen's revolution as incomplete. They held Chiang Kai-shek and his supporters to be corrupt, antirevolutionary, and disloyal to Sun's original principles.

In particular, they advocated improved living conditions for laborers and farmers in China, in accordance with the principle of *minsheng* (people's livelihood or social welfare).[23]

Chinese nationalists in the Americas operated within a diasporic political framework. Guomindang activist Dong Fangcheng, who had served as editor of the party newspaper in Cuba, returned to China to support the Northern Expedition, but maintained close contact with the situation abroad. On 9 September 1926, Dong wrote a letter to Su Xingbo in Cuba, offering advice and inquiring about the status of party activities there. He recommended locating trustworthy comrades to deliver donations from Cuban Chinese, as the post offices and banks in China were riddled with corruption. Dong wanted to know who had replaced him as director of the party newspaper and whether or not a new left-wing magazine in Cuba called *Zhengyi Banyuekan* had been published yet. Dong also inquired about the status of the Guomindang in the rest of the Americas, including membership numbers and names of newspaper directors in the United States, Canada, and Mexico. He suggested that Su network with left-wing supporters in other cities with large communities of Chinese overseas, such as Lima and San Francisco.[24]

In the 1920s, government fear of political radicals constituted one strand of the anti-immigrant discourse in Cuba. The transnational political activities of some Chinese made them targets of the Cuban government, which grew increasingly dictatorial under the presidency of Gerardo Machado y Morales (1925–33). The leftist Guomindang activist, Su Xingbo, was arrested by Cuban officials along with nine other Chinese on charges of Communist activity. According to his memoir, collusion between local right-wing leaders of the Guomindang and Cuban officials led to his detention. Su reacted to the charges by indignantly declaring to the judge, "I am a loyal follower of Sun Yat-sen." He continued, "Chiang Kai-shek betrayed the revolution, and it is our responsibility to oppose him." The judge pressured Su to provide the names of fellow activists and their activities. In exchange for serving as informant, Su would receive US$8,000 and a beautiful Cuban woman as a reward from the Machado government. When Su did not speak, however, the judge threatened the safety of his mother in China and his wife and children in Cuba, and then threatened him with the death penalty. Back in his cell, Su was repeatedly interrogated but finally released the next day.[25]

After 1927, the Guomindang left in China embarked on a reorganization (*gaizu*) of the party, focusing on the recruitment of members from the revolutionary classes of peasants, laborers, and small businessmen. Su Xingbo continued to lead efforts to reform the Cuban Guomindang, following the lead of leftists in China. In 1928, Su Xingbo and He Xuren issued two declarations condemning the ideological shift in the Guomindang with Chiang Kai-shek's rise to leadership. They implored compatriots to uphold the three principles and reject capitalism, imperialism, and colonialism, and they condemned the right wing's "cleansing" the party of Communist ideology. Peng Zemin, head of overseas affairs for the Guomindang central office in China, supported Su's efforts, and the two published an article on reform efforts within the Guomindang.[26]

This kind of Chinese migrant involvement in homeland politics facilitated their support for democratic and anti-imperialist political movements in Cuba. The Partido Comunista de Cuba (Cuban Communist Party), founded in 1925, extended words of solidarity toward the ongoing revolutionary struggle in warlord-divided republican China. Chinese organizations in Cuba, such as the Guomindang and the Casino Chung Wah, contributed financially to the new Cuban branch of the Anti-Imperialist League.[27]

While Su Xingbo struggled for reform within the Guomindang, other left-leaning Chinese purged from the party in 1927 founded a more radical organization geared toward workers and peasants, the Alianza Revolucionaria Protectora de Obreros y Campesinos Chinos de Cuba (Guba Huaqiao Gongnong Geming Datongmeng; Chinese Cuban Revolutionary Alliance Protecting Workers and Peasants). Some Chinese migrants had connections with both groups. The Alianza established delegations in key cities of Cuba's central-eastern zone, such as Santiago de Cuba, Manzanillo, Bayamo, Guantánamo, Cienfuegos, and Jagüey Grande. Rather than an offshoot of a political organization in China, this underground, anti-imperialist group developed as a uniquely Chinese Cuban organization, with its members committed to opposing the dictatorial rule of both Chiang Kai-shek and Gerardo Machado.[28]

Its leader, José Wong (Huang Taobai), was born in Guangzhou in 1898 and had arrived in Cuba with the wave of Chinese immigrants in the early 1920s. Wong worked as a vegetable peddler and typesetter at the Havana daily *Hoi Men Kong Po*, the liberal Chinese newspaper affiliated with the Chee Kung Tong and located in the heart of the Barrio Chino. In 1929, Wong began publishing the Alianza's clandestine monthly newspaper *Gongnong Husheng* (Grito Obrero-Campesino, or Call of the Worker and Peasant).

José Wong was active in the Anti-Imperialist League, and some of his organization's principal leaders crossed ethnic lines to join the Cuban Communist Party from 1928 to 1929. Wong and other Cuban Communists were arrested on 29 May 1930 during a gathering of the party's central committee.

Although he did not hold a formal position, on that fateful day Wong went to the meeting house to retrieve propaganda materials. He was imprisoned in Castillo del Principe with Cuban political activists Fabio Grobart, José Rego López, and Filomeno Rodríguez Abascall. On 13 August 1930, the thirty-two-year-old Wong was strangled to death with a bed sheet by a bribed prison guard.[29] Communist Cubans today remember him as a martyr to their cause.

After the death of José Wong, the left branch of the Cuban Guomindang issued a declaration denouncing Chiang Kai-shek as a corrupt dictator and murderer responsible for inflation and the poor economy in China. Su Xingbo officially called for the overthrow of the Nanjing regime. The Japanese invasion of Manchuria on 18 September 1931 provided the catalyst for another alliance between left- and right-wing nationalists in China and in diasporic communities, but the struggle between the branches in Cuba continued. While supporting national unity and China's resistance against Japan in the 1930s, leftists within the Cuban Guomindang continued their efforts against Chiang. As opponents of Machado, members also supported the anti-dictatorial military coup in Cuba led by General Fulgencio Batista. In China, the left wing splintered, and by 1932 Chiang Kai-shek controlled the Guomindang.[30]

Other Chinese leftists in Cuba narrowly escaped the fate of José Wong and were deported or imprisoned for their political activities under the Machado regime. Even some upper-strata Chinese became involved in Cuban leftist political movements. The Jiujiang native Luis Li came from a prominent merchant family background. For their opposition to Machado, Luis Li and four other Chinese were scheduled for deportation to Nanjing, seat of Chiang Kai-shek's government, where their fate was sure to be dire. However, Li's wealthy uncle bribed Cuban authorities to send them to Japan instead. The Chinese Cuban lawyer and politician Manuel Capestany Abreu likely assisted the deportees, as he held influence with Machado's government. Once in Japan, the deportees escaped custody with the help of a network of Chinese revolutionaries and fled to Hong Kong. Luis Li managed to cross into Guangdong to visit his wife and daughter before returning to Cuba in late 1930.[31]

Under such intense government pressure, the Alianza disbanded and went underground in Santiago de Cuba, on the eastern part of the island. Juan Mok (Mo Youping) and Julio Su Leng (Su Zilun) took over its leadership, while living with their families and running small businesses. Mok managed a noodle factory owned by the Alianza. When members lost their jobs as a result of their political activities, they were given work in the factory.[32] Many members, however, were forced to flee the island or go into hiding. Their organization underwent several name changes during the first half of the twentieth century, but its core members remained the same.

Economic Crisis and Nationalization of Labor

The global economic crisis and related nativist movements of the 1930s formed the backdrop for the peak of anti-Asian sentiment across American societies in the twentieth century. One effect of the economic and political crises was the return of diasporic Chinese back to China.[33] Those who remained became the targets of nationalist movements that sought to exclude or limit foreign workers and businesses.[34]

In Cuba, the economic base of Chinese communities continued to be small businesses such as bodegas, fruit and vegetable stands, laundries, and restaurants. By 1932, there were 3,889 Chinese business establishments across Cuba, valued at $3,924,677. These included 1,808 grocery stores, 799 fruit and vegetable stands, 656 laundries, and 312 restaurants.[35] The 18,484 registered Chinese were divided into three categories: businessmen (8,611), workers (8,246), and miscellaneous (1,627).[36] The depression led to the loss of small businesses after 1930 and compelled many Chinese in Cuba to go back to China. On a boat to New Orleans that year, Duvon Corbitt observed over forty Chinese passengers aboard for the first leg of their return trip. Political disturbances toward the end of the Machado administration accelerated this exodus.

The rise in unemployment and resentment against foreign monopolies created a ripe atmosphere for a nativist movement. In an effort to alleviate the tensions, lawmakers enacted restrictions on foreign ethnic minorities in workplaces. From 1920 to 1940, the Cuban state transitioned from oligarchy to a nominal constitutional democracy. The period included a revolutionary social movement in 1933 and the ouster of Machado, followed by a military coup led by Fulgencio Batista. Robert Whitney traces the mass mobilization of popular classes against an elitist "oligarchic capitalism," eventually leading to a more democratic form of government. A popular rebellion against Machado's regime brought to power "a loose coalition of radical activists, students, middle-class intellectuals, and disgruntled lower-rank soldiers" to form a Provisional Revolutionary Government from September 1933 to January 1934.[37] The short-lived government envisioned a Cuba based on "social justice for all classes" and national sovereignty. The Revolution of 1933, as it is known in Cuba, broke with the past through its abrogation of the Platt

Amendment and "Cuba for the Cubans" movement. For the first time in its history, Cuba's government was not subject to the dictates of a colonial or neocolonial power.

The five-month term of left-leaning President Ramón Grau San Martín was marked by a series of reforms, including woman suffrage and an eight-hour workday. Grau's administration also passed legislation designed to promote native Cuban employment. The Cuban nativist labor movement targeted all foreigners, but in particular Jamaicans and Haitians in agriculture and Spaniards, Jews, and Chinese in retail trade.[38] The 1934 Nationalization of Labor decree mandated that 50 percent of all employees in an industrial, commercial, and agricultural enterprise be of Cuban nationality, and succeeding laws raised the requirement to 80 percent. These restrictions represented a reversal of Cuban policy since the mid-nineteenth century of seeking out foreign workers.[39] Similar laws were enacted across Latin America and the Caribbean.

The Nationalization of Labor legislation affected the Chinese in different ways. In 1938, a Chinese worker complained that his compatriots were being forced to leave the sugar company Cubanaco, despite their long-standing presence, while more recently arrived immigrants from the British West Indies were permitted to stay. The preferential treatment was likely due to a combination of British government protection of its colonial subjects and West Indians' higher levels of education and facility with the English language.[40]

Chinese businesses such as restaurants, groceries, laundries, and truck farms increasingly employed Cubans. While many Chinese returned to China, others followed the path of Spanish immigrants by applying for Cuban citizenship in order to meet the new legal requirements. The official number of foreigners in Cuba dropped significantly, from 650,353 in 1931 to 201,177 in 1943, in large part due to the massive naturalizations that took place after the 1934 law.[41]

Depending on the local situation, enforcement of the labor decree varied considerably. Chinese businesses relied on community attorneys for advice on how to circumvent the restrictions. The Cuban-born Chinese Napoleón Seuc served in this capacity in the 1940s and 1950s. Adept in both Chinese and Spanish, he helped merchants take advantage of legal loopholes in order to evade the law. One strategy was to make all employees limited partners (thereby effectively eliminating any "employees" to whom the decree applied), an arrangement sanctioned by a vestige of the commercial code from the Spanish colonial era.[42]

After a relative lull, the Nationalization of Labor law was enforced more rigorously in 1944 under the second administration of President Grau (1944–48), resulting in the unemployment of four or five hundred Chinese. In August and September 1944, members of the "Cuban Front" rioted in front of Chinese businesses. They opposed the Chinese strategy of making nonequity partners out of workers and pushed for the immediate hiring of Cubans. According to a Chinese community record, "Day after day they carried slogans in their hands and gathered at Chinese restaurants, laundries, general stores, fruit stands, etc., shouting and causing disturbances."[43] An undated poster of anti-Chinese propaganda from Cuba reads: "Don't do business with any Chinese: Don't sell to the Chinese. Don't rent to the Chinese. Don't install light or a telephone for the Chinese." Furthermore, it warned, "All who do business with Chinese will be equally considered traitors of Cuba."[44]

Defending the Community

Throughout the twentieth century, Chinese Cubans organized against anti-immigrant sentiment and policies. The same institutions that fostered transnational ties back home—shops, associations, newspapers, and consulates—served as bases from which to challenge anti-Chinese measures. Although negative commentary in the Cuban press during the 1920s specifically targeted the Chee Kung Tong and illegal immigrants, it affected the public image of Chinese of all classes, in particular the Chinese transnational merchant community. Chinese restaurants united to placate the protests outside of their establishments. With a more long-term view, the Chamber of Commerce established a federation to assist consular officials and promote the general welfare of Chinese in Cuba. The federation represented six trade organizations (Chamber of Commerce, laundry, industrial and commercial products, fruit, agriculture, and restaurant), three newspapers, and the Casino Chung Wah. It advocated "people-to-people" diplomacy and reconciliation through meetings with Cuban government officials and commercial magnates.

Native Cuban workers were not the only ones who viewed the Chinese as rivals. In the first part of the twentieth century competition between Spanish and Chinese grocery owners contributed an explicitly conservative thread to the anti-Chinese sentiment in Cuba. When the newspaper *Diario de la Marina* published a series of anti-Chinese articles from 1922 to 1923, Chinese merchants convened a meeting to improve relations with Spanish merchants.[45] But tensions between these two immigrant groups continued through the years. According to Napoleon Seuc, consumers preferred the cheaper prices and home delivery offered by Chinese shops. In 1934, Spanish merchants pressured for a presidential decree establishing a minimal distance of one hundred meters between bodegas (excluding those already in existence). Later, as legal consultant to the Chinese community, Seuc used the Cuban Constitution of 1940 as a basis for arguing against the minimal distance regulation, and the decree was eventually annulled.[46]

Above all, Chinese merchants promoted an image of the Chinese as integrated into Cuban society and as an essential component of Cuban national identity. With the retrenchment of immigration restrictions in 1926, Chinese merchants demanded a change in Cuban policies. As they had at the beginning of the century, they wanted to be treated before the law the same way that other resident foreigners were. They were especially affected by restrictions on reentering Cuba after being absent for more than eighteen months. In June, local Chinese in Cienfuegos denounced the reentry policy and the deportations of illegal Chinese residents.[47] At the national level, the Association of the Chinese Colony of Cuba and the Chinese Chamber of Commerce of Cuba protested the immigration crackdown. They portrayed the Chinese as model participants in the Cuban nation, "without violent occurrences, without intervening in the political struggles of China or this country."[48] This emphasis on passivity laid the groundwork for a "model minority" image of Chinese as nonpolitical actors in the post–World War II period.

The two organizations published a pamphlet in 1926 titled "Legitimate Aspirations of the Chinese Colony of Cuba" that invoked the history of Chinese participation in the Cuban wars for independence as a cornerstone of their claims to citizenship. The pamphlet stated: "many of our members lent their generous aid to the cause of Cuban independence, bravely fighting for the liberty of this nation, meriting what has been stated in books, pamphlets, diaries, discourses . . . from the Apostle of Independence José Martí to Gonzalo de Quesada." The authors then reminded readers that the Chinese community regularly sent delegates to the statues and tombs of Cuban heroes. They continued, "So elevated is our love for this hospitable land, that we have agreed to erect in the capital of the Republic a monument that will perpetuate the efforts and heroism of the Chinese who died for the independence of Cuba."[49]

Cuban-born Chinese who were bilingual and at ease in Cuban professional circles were key to defending the community against criticism. The

Afro-Chinese Antonio Chuffat Latour worked as an interpreter for the Guomindang and a journalist in the 1920s. In the wake of the 1926 Chinatown murder and new immigration restrictions, Chuffat published an article in a Cienfuegos newspaper defending Chinese merchants "de valor." In it, he sought to increase understanding of the Chinese immigrant community by describing differences between the various dialect groups.[50] Such articles written for Cuban newspapers further disseminated the message of Chinese integration and "legitimacy." The following year Chuffat's community history of the Chinese in Cuba was published in Spanish.

Chinese merchants also worked toward elevating their status within Cuban society through good works and alliances with the Cuban business community. They regularly donated to Cuban charities and disaster relief. On the Day of the Three Kings in 1926, for example, Chinese merchants in Cienfuegos collected a sum of $121.80 for a local asylum for elders. The campaign leaders included a prominent merchant, two association presidents, and Antonio Chuffat.[51] Common economic interests had the potential to foster cooperation between Chinese and non-Chinese merchants. In April 1934, the transnational Chinese firms Cuon Chong Long and Cong Gen Long joined non-Chinese importers in petitioning for the reestablishment of direct ship service between the port of Cienfuegos and New York.[52] In 1936, the Chinese Chamber of Commerce in Cuba became a member of two Cuban national commercial federations. Afterward, attacks in the Spanish press directed toward Chinese decreased.[53]

Although the anti-Chinese voices were prominent, they did not represent the only opinions on Chinese immigration among Cubans. A significant number of Cubans rose to the defense of the Chinese, especially in the provinces, where Chinese were generally more dispersed throughout towns. In April 1928, for example, Ludovico Soto published an article in a local Cienfuegos newspaper that praised the Chinese in Cuba. He portrayed Chinese immigrants as honorable and hardworking, reminding readers that the Chinese had initially come by force to Cuba, where they were subject to physical maltreatment and other humiliations.[54]

Just as it covered Spanish associational life, the mainstream Cuban press reported on activities and institutions in the Chinese community. On 16 June 1929, Bienvenido Rumbaut delivered a lecture at the Luisa Theater in Cienfuegos titled "The Participation of the Chinese in Our Independence." It was well attended by the public, "above all by the Chinese community in Cienfuegos."[55] The president of the professional association Ateneo, Pedro López

Dórticos, presided over the event. Ateneo's affiliation with this conference is significant, as the association regularly organized commemorations of the founding of the city in 1819 and included among its rosters celebrated men in arts and sciences.

A visit from the Chinese consul general to the provinces provided an opportunity to shine a favorable light on the Chinese communities, both to the diplomat and to other Cubans. In November 1931, the consul general and the president of the Casino Chung Wah arrived in Cienfuegos to learn about the social and economic life of the Chinese community. The president of the Guomindang in Cienfuegos, Antonio Lay, received the delegation, as well as important representatives of the Chinese community from the nearby towns of Rodas, Cumanayagua, Palmira, and Cruces. According to the Cienfuegos newspaper that reported the event, "The Consul General returned with a magnificent impression."[56]

In general, twentieth-century Cuban commentators portrayed the Chinese with broad brushstrokes, either villainous or heroic, and only recently has Cuban scholarship and literature attempted to capture some of the nuances of twentieth-century Chinese migrant life.[57] Chinese interactions in Cuban society were far less stereotypical than portrayed by Cuban writers and officials of the era. Although the Chinese practice of employing coethnics in their businesses often came under fire, businesses could serve as a space for social integration, especially after implementation of national labor policies. Chinese laundries in Havana, for example, employed young Cuban working-class women. In the 1940s, Yolanda Rodríguez La Guardia worked as an ironer in a Chinese laundry in the municipality Cerro. She nostalgically recalls the Chinese laundrymen treating the Cuban workers with respect and consideration.[58]

Fraternidad

In 1934, an association of Chinese retailers founded a new bilingual magazine *Fraternidad*, which addressed issues of immigrant incorporation and generational differences.[59] Significantly, the publication emerged amid the global economic crisis, rise in unemployment, and nativist movement in Cuba, a time when many Chinese returned home or remigrated. With sections in both Chinese and Spanish, the magazine was geared toward both Chinese and non-Chinese retailers, reflecting the desire for acceptance by the greater Cuban merchant community. The Chinese section included association business, homeland politics, and announcements relevant to the Chinese community, while the Spanish section featured stories about China and the social worlds of prominent Chinese and Cuban merchants.

Images and stories depicting the transnational Chinese community in a favorable light filled the magazine's pages. Photos of weddings to Cuban women and baptisms of second-generation children underscored Chinese migrant integration into Cuban society and national culture. Even as they maintained transnational ties to China, merchants used the press to promote an image of the Chinese as an essential component of Cuban society and national identity since the independence struggles. Furthermore, the Spanish-language articles made the magazine accessible to the generation of Cuban-born Chinese who were unable to read Chinese characters.

The name of the magazine, *Fraternidad*, or *Lianhe Yuekan* in Chinese, evoked the brotherhood forged between Chinese and Cubans during the independence struggles. The magazine also highlighted commonalities between Cuba and China as two modern, progressive, and independent nations. In March 1939, Cuban journalist Guillermo Tejeiro contributed an essay on the "exemplary" life of Sun Yat-sen for the anniversary of the leader's death.[60] The October 1939 cover featured Carlos Manuel de Céspedes and Sun Yat-sen and the date 10 October: the beginning of the Cuban independence movement in 1868 and the overthrow of the Manchu Qing dynasty in 1911. The caption states, "It is an unforgettable date for the Cuban and Chinese people that bonds them closer in the community of their sacred ideals."[61]

During the 1930s and 1940s, wealthy merchants in Cuba—among them Chinese—could unite in opposition to leftist politics on the island. Anticommunist politics became a rallying point for the upper strata of Chinese society in Cuba and Cuban elites. The Cuban Nicolás Rivero Jr. contributed an essay to *Fraternidad* on Chinese politics that positively portrayed Chiang Kai-shek as a "personal enemy of Communism."[62]

The Second World War as Watershed

The Japanese occupation of China from 1937 to 1945 and China's alignment with the United States during World War II transformed the treatment of Chinese migrants in the Americas. Despite impediments to communication and transportation, diasporic Chinese were pulled closer to their homeland through a series of broad-based, anti-Japan resistance movements. Many Chinese overseas had suffered from racial discrimination and ill-treatment, and they feared a similar fate for their compatriots under Japanese colonization.[63] Chinese politics entered the Cuban imaginary through local newspapers and magazines, fund-raisers, boycotts, and campaigns for resistance to Japan's occupation of China.

In the face of Japanese aggression, political differences among Chinese were minimized. Guomindang branches led the efforts, solidifying their position in Chinatowns across the Americas.[64] Chinese Communists in Cuba joined in the defense of homeland, and members of the leftist organization reconstituted as the more benign Alianza en Defensa de la Cultura China, which began operating in Havana in 1938.[65]

Unlike the earlier 1911 Revolution in China, anti-Japanese mobilization was marked by a high degree of interregional cooperation in the Americas. The U.S.-based umbrella organization United China Relief (Quanmei Banghua Lianhe Zonghui) channeled the efforts of a myriad of patriotic groups; the Cuban branch was established in 1941. The Cuban Overseas Chinese Association for Aiding the Resistance against Japan (Lugu Huaqiao Kangri Hou Yuan) maintained fifty-nine branches throughout the island for fund-raising. During the eight-year period of Japanese occupation, Chinese Cubans donated an impressive total of US$2,400,000 to support the resistance.[66] The success of these efforts was undoubtedly aided by an intense social pressure for Chinese donations that existed alongside this rhetoric of patriotism. At stake was a migrant's standing within the Chinese community.[67]

Public performances of patriotism toward the homeland played an important role in raising the status of Chinese migrants. The editors of *Fraternidad* published a Spanish-language pamphlet on the history of the conflict with Japan and sent it to well-established Cuban organizations such as the Centro de Veteranos.[68] They could earn the sympathy of Cuban veterans with a portrayal of a sovereign nation invaded by an imperial aggressor (Japan) and a reminder of Chinese participation in the struggles for Cuban liberation from Spain.

Advertisements in *Fraternidad* urged all consumers to boycott Japanese goods. One of these slogans proclaimed, "The Chinese who sells or buys Japanese products is a traitor to his country and must perish by divine destiny. The Cuban or foreigner who prefers Japanese to Cuban toys is opposed to the progress of the nation."[69] By promoting Cuban products, Chinese retailers could thus simultaneously demonstrate support of China and goodwill toward Cuban merchants. American author Pearl Buck's essay on the Chinese war of resistance was translated into Spanish for the June 1939 issue.[70]

Support for the Chinese resistance against the Japanese occupation movement seeped into mainstream Cuban culture. Luis Carrillo named one of his traditional *danzones* "Una taza de arroz" (a cup of rice), referencing the fund-raising movement.[71] Duvon Corbitt, who resided in Havana at the time, made the following first-hand observation: "One factor that has tended to improve the status of the Chinese in Cuba is the gallant stand made by the Chinese people against Japanese aggression. Increased knowledge of China and the Chinese, and admiration for their bravery, have gone far in erasing the feeling of superiority that was a relic of the days of the coolie trade."[72]

After the Japanese attack on the U.S. naval base at Pearl Harbor in December 1941, which precipitated the entry of both the United States and Cuba into the Second World War, wartime cooperation between allied governments led to the lifting of restrictions on Chinese entry into American ports. In the United States, men of Chinese descent enlisted with other Americans for battle in Europe, and the government repealed the long-standing Chinese Exclusion Act in 1943. Sino-Cuban diplomacy made similar progress. On 12 November 1942, Cuban and Chinese ministers José Agustín Martínez and Li Dijun signed a reciprocal treaty that eliminated immigration restrictions based on race or nationality. Under the treaty provisions, Chinese were able to enter or leave Cuban territory under the same terms as nationals of other countries. Regulations regarding travel within Cuba, residence, and work were equalized. Chinese were also guaranteed the right to establish schools, associations, publications, and burial practices in accordance with Cuban law. Cuban journalist Guillermo Tejeiro reprinted the entire text of the treaty in his work commemorating the Chinese in Cuba, calling attention to its role in erasing the injustices of the previous four decades of Cuban immigration law. He highlighted the significance of the treaty for Sino-Cuban relations and for the development of the Chinese community in Cuba.[73]

The numbers of Chinese in Cuba had declined during the economic depression of the 1930s, when the Cuban government nationalized labor and, amid antiforeign sentiment, many Chinese returned home or remigrated elsewhere. The Japanese occupation of China from 1937 to 1945, while uniting Chinese overseas, exacerbated difficulties in transnational communication and travel. The postwar shift in official policy on Chinese entry facilitated greater identification with Cuba, even as some remigrated to the United States in the 1940s. A new Cuban constitution in 1940 liberalized entry procedures for families of immigrants already in Cuba, and after World War II ended in 1945, more Chinese women came than in previous decades. Marriages between Chinese men and Cuban women also increased. Overall, relatively low numbers of Chinese women in Cuba led to a racially and ethnically mixed community of descendants by the middle of the twentieth century.

By 1943, the official Chinese population dropped to 15,822, and by 1953, to 11,834. However, the highest number of Chinese women was recorded in 1953 (484, representing 4 percent of the Chinese population).[74]

In the 1940s a new layer of Chinese professionals emerged, many of them Cuban-born. Educated in Cuba, they adeptly maneuvered between their Chinese families and Chinatown and Cuban social and professional circles. Among them were lawyers and doctors (such as Napoleón and Armando Seuc), dentists, pharmacists, journalists (such as Juan Luis Martín), accountants, and engineers. Havana boasted one of the best-known Chinatowns in the Americas. Pharmacies and shops specialized in Chinese products, such as traditional medicine, porcelains and silk, trinkets, and books and newspapers. Chinese restaurants catered to the merchant community and elite Cubans, while cafés provided cheap Cuban food for all.[75]

New merchant institutions proliferated during this period. The Association of Chinese Restaurants and Inns of Cuba (Asociación de Restaurantes y Fondas Chinas de Cuba) was established in February 1945. Its members were owners of establishments, including the opulent restaurant El Pacífico and several run by members of the Eng family. For decades, Chinese shops had provided remittance sending and banking services to Chinese in Cuba. With the increase in the number of large Chinese businesses, the Bank of China opened in October 1944. The bank was headquartered in Shanghai and maintained branches throughout China and in India, Indonesia, Australia, London, and New York.[76] New organizations in Havana explicitly linked the Chinese and Cuban communities, signaling the greater acceptance of Chinese Cubans in the postwar period. The Chinese-Cuban National Association (Asociación Nacional Chino-Cubana), for example, operated from 1943 to 1953 and promoted "better understanding and friendship between the members of the Chinese colony in Cuba and their families with Cubans" through "charitable and cultural works."[77]

Cubanidad and Mestizaje

In Cuba, the conception of racial fraternity that developed during the nineteenth-century independence wars as a basis for an inclusive national identity underwent continual reformulation during the republic. Cuban culture and national identity was a main preoccupation for noted anthropologist and ethnomusicologist Fernando Ortiz (1881–1969). Through the metaphor of the *ajiaco*, a traditional Cuban stew, he explained a dynamic national culture as consisting of multiple ingredients that, rather than melting together, contribute their distinctive characteristics.[78] Ortiz developed the concept of "transculturation," which holds that Cuban cultural identity derives primarily from indigenous, European, and African components. He grouped Asians with other less significant immigrant waves: "Indians from the mainland, Jews, Portuguese, Anglo-Saxons, French, North Americans, even yellow Mongoloids from Macao, Canton, and other regions of the sometime Celestial Kingdom."[79]

The dominant narrative of Cuban national identity becomes problematic when two foundational intellectuals of its formation—José Martí and Fernando Ortiz—either sideline Chinese immigrants or cast them as outsiders. Martí did not link his commentary on Chinese immigration to a discussion of race in Cuba, which he constrained to black, white, and mulatto. Ortiz in some of his essays relegated the Chinese to a realm completely outside of Cubanness (cubanidad). His description of the Chinese as "yellow Mongoloids" references their phenotypical difference and essential otherness. Ortiz also commented on the Chinese use of opium and practice of homosexuality. He held that among the new immigrants from China and Japan, along with merchants, fishermen, and gardeners, were spies.[80] He thus cast the Chinese as an undesirable component of cubanidad: in addition to being physically different from Europeans and Africans, they were degenerate and morally questionable, despite their heritage of a "celestial" civilization. Like Martí, Fernando Ortiz located the main generative force of Cuban culture in the mixing between Europeans and Africans because, in the context of racial tensions and violence in the republic, the black-white binary seemed to be most relevant for Cuban society.

Despite the ambivalent attitude of Ortiz and other influential Cubans toward the Chinese, members of the Chinese community were able to grasp onto the concepts of transculturation and cubanidad to assert and legitimize their contribution to the Cuban national identity and capacity for incorporation.

In the postwar period, racial categories continued to hold weight in elite Cuban circles and still determined one's social standing to a large degree. Chinese were assigned a vague color category that shifted according to context, and upper-strata Chinese in particular were acutely aware of Cuban politics of race. The Miami exile Napoleón Seuc considered postwar Cuba to be "relatively speaking, the least discriminatory of all known" societies. Of course, owing to Seuc's position as a professional and an ethnic Chinese born and educated in Cuba, he did not personally face the same challenges as new or lower-class immigrants. While Chinese merchants were able to walk in the center of the town square, people "of color" were relegated to the outer ring. The Cuban-born Armando Choy remembered a friend who was part Chinese being denied entry to a dance. Although his Chinese friend had a white mother, he was deemed "nonwhite" in this social setting.[81] Some Chinese Cubans recall being addressed as "chino" or the more derogatory "narra."[82] However, Cubans also affectionately addressed their Chinese neighbors with terms of endearment. When the Chinese used "capitán" for their customers in their laundries and fruit stands, Cubans returned the courtesy, calling the Chinese "capitán" or "paisano" (fellow countryman).[83]

As they had in the nineteenth century, Chinese men formed families with white, mulatto, and black Cuban women. The children of Chinese merchants who married women of color would be classified as mestizo. For some Chinese, mestizaje, or racial and cultural mixing, offered a conceptual pathway toward an ideology of belonging to a transcultural Cuban nation. The Chinese merchant Ramon Pin Chun Len married "la mulata Ya-Ya," a well-known fixture in her Cienfuegos neighborhood. Ya-Ya had loved and admired her Chinese husband, vigilantly safeguarding his belongings in her humble home for years after his death. For her, marrying a well-to-do Chinese merchant who became a citizen in 1928 and belonged to a Cuban lodge was considered a step up the social ladder.[84]

Discriminatory policies and racial prejudice, although mitigated during the postwar period, continued to limit the degree of integration and acceptance of the Chinese in the Cuban republic. At times, these attitudes and social divisions came from Chinese themselves. Gustavo Chui Beltrán was born in 1938 to a Chinese merchant and a black Cuban woman of lower socioeconomic status. In perhaps an extreme measure driven by the color line, Chinese business associates pressured Chui's father to eliminate his mother's name from the birth certificate. They effectively prevented her from developing a relationship with her son as he was raised by neighborhood Chinese merchants. Only years later, after the revolution, were mother and son able to reunite.[85]

Chinese merchants pursued identification with whiteness as a means for improving the social standing of their children. Some Chinese parents sought official recognition of their mixed children as white. Like Cubans categorized as black or mulatto, they preferred to elevate the social status of their children directly, through legal means if necessary, rather than counting on an inclusive ideal of nationality to protect them. In the process of distancing themselves from blackness, Chinese parents could exacerbate lines of social division.

Members of the Guomindang in Cienfuegos celebrate a Chinese wedding, October 1949. (Courtesy of Noemí Díaz de Villegas)

In 1945, José Wong Lam appealed to the lower court in Cienfuegos to have his son's birth registry changed from mestizo (mixed) to blanco (white). Although the child was the son of a Chinese man and a white woman, and his skin color was recorded as white, he had been registered as mestizo at birth. The judge in Cienfuegos denied the appeal, stating that "mestizo is no more than one born of parents of different races; and in this case the registered is the son of a yellow father and a white mother." The label "mestizo" remained. However, later that year, a reversal by the Ministry of Justice cited a 1943 census law that classified the races of inhabitants of Cuba as "blanca," "negra," "amarilla," and "mestiza" (white, black, yellow, and mixed). In the reversal, a detailed discussion of "mestizo" reveals that the category was now read as applying to children of whites and blacks, Chinese and mulattos, and Chinese and blacks, but not to children of Chinese and whites.[86]

The ambiguous label "mestizo" had appeared in Cuban censuses since 1899 and was associated with a distancing from being categorized as "black." According to Alejandro de la Fuente, the term was used by late-nineteenth-century scientists "to denote the extensiveness of miscegenation," but was opposed by some because "it designated so many racial mixtures as to become scientifically meaningless." He notes that the term's ambiguity made it popular: "In opposition to other racial labels such as *negro* or *mulato*, deemed to be more precise in Cuban racial imagery, the denomination *mestizo* had the virtue of detaching a significant portion of the Cuban population from blackness."[87]

The example of José Wong Lam indicates the pervasiveness of race and color within the concept of cubanidad. Eventually, the Chinese father prevailed in overturning his son's classification at the highest government level, though only by drawing the line more sharply between mixed children with one white and one Chinese parent, and those with one black or mulatto parent.

The Chinese in Cuban Culture

Along with European and African elements, the Chinese presence filtered into Cuban culture and everyday life through literature, music, language, and food.[88] Notwithstanding a degree of stereotyping, this effusion of Chinese influences in everyday life facilitated acceptance within Cuban society.

Until recently, scholarship has followed Fernando Ortiz's lead in focusing on the African and European elements of Cuban culture. Historically, though, the Chinese presence was impressionable enough for some of Cuba's most influential and celebrated writers to make it a central theme in their work. Ignacio López-Calvo demonstrates the presence of Chinese characters and themes in Cuban literature, beginning in the late nineteenth century, by prominent authors such as Ramón Meza y Suárez Inclán (1861–1911), Alfonso Hernández Cata (1885–1940), José Lezama Lima (1910–76), Nicolás Guillén (1902–89), Severo Sarduy (1937–93), and Miguel Barnet (b. 1940). During his long discussions with Miguel Barnet, Cuba's famous runaway slave Esteban Montejo insisted on being asked about the Chinese community in Sagua la Grande, an "unacceptable omission," as López-Calvo points out, since the Chinese had formed an indelible impression on Montejo's mind.[89]

Musicologist and novelist Alejo Carpentier y Valmont (1904–80) discusses the Chinese contribution to Cuban music and dance in his landmark *La música en Cuba* (Music in Cuba). Chinese themes in traditional Cuban *danzones* indicate their saturation in Cuban society. Titles of compositions reflect the concerns of transnational Chinese migrants during the first half of the twentieth century. Examples include: "Chinito pa' Canton" (The Chinese Goes to Canton) by Felipe Valdés and "Pa' Cantón" (To Canton) by Antonio María Romeo. At the beginning of the twentieth century, José Urfé (1879–

1957) composed the danzón "El dios chino" (The Chinese God), inspired by the Chinese deity Guan Gong.[90]

Today, Cubans consider the corneta china (also called the suona or the Chinese flute) to be a centerpiece of Cuban music. The small but shrill instrument likely originated in the nineteenth-century Chinese theaters of the Barrio Chino. At the beginning of the Cuban republic, carnival bands in Havana popularized the instrument, until they were banished between 1913 and 1937 as a threat to public order. The corneta china resurfaced in 1915 in Santiago de Cuba, where still today it is a central element of conga music.[91]

Chinese were regular participants in Cuban carnival, a quintessential Caribbean tradition. In 1930, members of the youth group Juventud Atlética de la Sociedad Chee Kung Tong first performed the Lion Dance, coiling through the Barrio Chino. Encouraged by the national tourism bureau, the Chinese community participated in Havana's carnival on a grand scale in 1941. The magazine *Fraternidad* described "a magnificent spectacular seen for the first time in Cuba." The streets of the Barrio Chino evoked "the Far and romantic Orient" with Chinese music, lanterns, dolls, flowers, and fireworks. The article reaffirmed the place of the Chinese in Cuban national culture: "The Chinese colony of Cuba thus contributes, one more time, to the greater glory and prestige of the country, as tourism is one of the principal riches of the nation."[92] By the 1950s, the lion dance, martial arts, drums, and cymbals had become a regular feature of carnival. Another fixture was Fermín Huie Ley, who became known by Cubans as "the Chinese of the carnival" as he danced congas along Havana's Paseo del Prado and Malecón.[93]

Alejo Carpentier, who frequently strolled through Havana's Barrio Chino, noted the flourishing of Cantonese opera in the 1940s. Every 10 October, Chinese opera troupes and bands performed publicly to commemorate the Chinese and Cuban national celebrations. Rather than traditional Chinese music, the Guomindang band performed Western music for Cuban national celebrations, such as the centenary commemoration of General Antonio Maceo in Santiago de Cuba. Its director was José Ramón Betancourt, a musician for the Cuban navy, and its members were ethnic Chinese youth, male and female. The band played until 1958, the year before the Cuban Revolution. Based in the building of El Pacífico restaurant, the band of the Club Cultural de Música China performed both traditional Chinese and Western music.[94]

Perhaps the most unique Chinese Cuban cultural phenomenon was the Opera Chung Wah that formed with descendants in the early 1940s. Teachers of the Club Cultural de Música China founded the new theater group

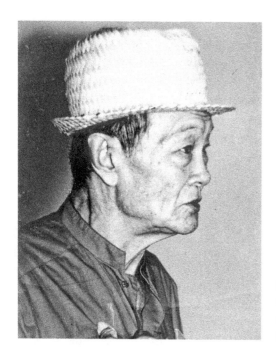

Fermín Huie Ley, "Chinese of the carnival." (Courtesy of Cátedra de Estudios sobre la Inmigración China en Cuba)

in Havana when Chinese actors departed for China and the United States with traveling troupes. They trained mixed female descendants who ranged in age from eight to twenty-eight to sing Cantonese opera. Not knowing Cantonese, the singers memorized a phonetic pronunciation written next to the Chinese characters in the libretto. By midcentury the theaters closed, facing competition from the film industry and consumer tastes for American products. More Chinese Cubans were also migrating northward during the 1940s and 1950s, especially after the repeal of the U.S. Chinese Exclusion Act in 1943. Well-known Chinese Cuban performers include Caridad Amarán, Ana Li, Yolanda Eng, and Georgina Wong. Caridad Amarán was personally trained by her father, Julián Fong (Fong Piu), an actor for the troupe Kuoc Kong. The actors were accompanied by a traditional Chinese orchestra consisting of gongs, cymbals, pentaphonic guitars, fiddles, and wooden trumpets. Some performers were not of Chinese descent, but were godchildren of Chinese in the community, attesting to both the roots Chinese planted in local communities and the effusion of Chinese cultural traditions in Cuban society.[95]

Less conspicuous but perhaps more impressionable were the imprints of the Chinese presence in Cuban vernacular speech and eating habits. Still today, Cubans use the phrase "tener un chino atrás" (to have a Chinese behind oneself) when confronted with bad luck, and "No salvarlo ni el médico chino" (Not even the Chinese doctor can salvage him/her/it) to reference a grave illness or hopeless situation. An entire vocabulary developed around the symbols of the Chinese lottery as it transformed into an unofficial Cuban game played in neighborhoods across the island.[96] Cubans fondly remember the delicious flavors of ice cream the Chinese prepared with fresh tropical fruit such as mamey, mango, banana, and guanábana, the best from the cafeteria of Havana's famous theater America. Felipe and Santiago Luis recall that the secret to its quality lay in a combination of different kinds of milk: powdered, condensed, and fresh.[97]

Chinese Cuban Identity

Cuban-born Chinese, including those of mixed descent like the opera singers, were significant in the process of incorporation into the Cuban nation. Growing up as *chinos cubanos*, they had been educated in Cuba and were Cuban citizens. Yet, their "Chineseness" remained alive through schools in China and Cuba and ethnic institutions, which helped to promote a collective "overseas Chinese" (huaqiao) identity among some second-generation youth. From the perspective of their migrant parents, ideally children would be culturally Chinese, but with a Western outlook, and trained to operate in both worlds. But it was also a distinctively Chinese Cuban identity, shaped by widespread intermarriage and patterns of settlement throughout the Cuban landscape. The children of the Chinese who had migrated to the island in the early twentieth century grew up with a Cuban national identification, which for some, translated into support of the growing popular revolutionary movement of the 1950s.

As the immigrant generation decided to remain in Cuba in the postwar period and their focus turned toward their own children, homeland ties tended to dissipate over time. Any evidence of the persistence of homeland identifications among later generations is especially significant in the case of the Chinese in Cuba, a community with a high degree of interracial unions and whose migration flow was abruptly cut off by the Cuban Revolution of 1959. By midcentury some members of the second generation maintained transnational ties to China, even while settling permanently in Cuba. In her work on contemporary Haitians in the United States, Nina Glick Schiller explains that descendants of immigrants "may continue to maintain, or may build anew, transnational relationships that reconnect them to the land of their ancestors and establish social relationships that make them participants in more than one state."⁹⁸

With Chinese men remaining "bachelors" or marrying Cuban women, Chinese cultural markers and language tended to fade among the second generation. A common assumption in Cuban scholarship is that "culture" is transmitted through mothers, with their dominant role in the upbringing and education of children. Indeed, mothers, aunts, grandmothers, godmothers, and siblings socialized children into Cuban domestic culture.⁹⁹ But this assumption is inadequate for an understanding of Chinese Cuban youth. Immigrant fathers also played an important role, particularly when they took charge of raising their children. In the absence of Chinese or Cuban mothers, neighborhood Chinese men who networked through kinship, native place, and occupation could adopt "foster" or "surrogate" parental roles.¹⁰⁰ Another common family strategy for reinforcing ethnic identifications was to encourage second-generation children to marry other ethnic Chinese or Chinese of mixed descent.¹⁰¹

Chinese men living in "bachelor" societies in the Americas maintained strong kinship networks that influenced child rearing. When the Cuban wife of vegetable vendor Francisco Luis abandoned him and their two children after a few years, he assumed full responsibility for raising their daughters Lourdes and Violeta. In addition to giving them the Chinese names Guiguí and Guipó, Francisco Luis would tell his Cuban daughters stories about his childhood in Lui Village and about the Chinese philosophers Confucius and Laozi. According to Violeta, he revered Confucius and taught them the complementary points in Catholicism. She remembers a house filled with the scent of incense and the menthol cream "that cured all ailments," her father's use of soy sauce on fish and chicken, his participation in the Chinese associations, and the performances of theater companies from Canton and Hong Kong.¹⁰²

Napoleón Seuc, the attorney for the Chinese community in Havana, was born in 1924 to a Chinese father and one of the few Chinese women in Cuba. During the Depression Seuc's father lost his fruit stand businesses, and in 1929, his mother and his three younger siblings embarked for her ancestral home in Guangdong, utilizing subsidized passages from the Chinese consulate. Due to political turmoil and the Japanese occupation in China, she was unable to return to Cuba until twenty years later. Napoleón Seuc and his older brother Armando remained in Cuba and did not see their mother until after the Chinese Communist victory in 1949. Seuc recalls growing up in his father's stores surrounded by his uncles and other neighborhood men. During the Christmas holiday, he did not know "who the Three Kings were and why they came; a lady customer and friend of my parents gave us our first toys."[103] Although Seuc grew up without his Chinese mother, he learned to speak Chinese. "I was a Cuban citizen. I was considered Cuban. I was not considered Chinese. But I think Chinese was my first language," Seuc said.[104]

In addition to neighborhood men, Cuban mothers themselves played a role in contributing to a Chinese identity. Mixed children of Cuban women and Chinese men describe their mothers learning about Chinese cuisine and customs and attending family events at the associations. Maria Isabel León, the granddaughter of a former president of the Chinese Association of Lajas (near Cienfuegos), recalled that her mother learned to cook Chinese dishes from her father. In an interview at her home in rural Lajas, she proceeded to relate the recipe for the hundred-year egg (*pidan*), a traditional delicacy.[105] Karen Isaksen Leonard demonstrates a parallel phenomenon in her examination of marriages between women of Mexican descent and men from India's Punjab province who came to work in California agriculture during the early twentieth century. Leonard finds that her original hypothesis about Punjabi male dominance and ethnicity of children is undermined by evidence that Mexican women developed a sense of individuality and kinship networks of their own.[106] Although the Punjabi immigrants' spouses were predominantly Spanish-speaking Catholic women, they "actively contributed to the construction and maintenance of a 'Hindu' identity in the United States."[107]

The life of Fernando Wong (Huang Baoshi) attests to the role of interpersonal relationships in migrant incorporation. Fernando Wong left his wife and son behind in China for the duration of his life in Cuba. Through regular correspondence he maintained a close relationship with his Chinese son. Wong's letters home went beyond updates on his business and remittances, giving his son a sense of what migrant life in Cuba was like. In this case, his son, who has never been to Cuba, has also developed a kind of Chinese Cuban identity. He safeguarded the majority of his father's letters and recently published them in a volume in China. The elder Wong's letters reveal an intimate knowledge of Cuban politics and society. Fernando Wong developed a reputation for honesty and character in the Cuban town of Sagua la Grande. He fostered close ties with the Revuelta Díaz family, becoming a "surrogate" father to one of their sons, Idalberto. The son became a regular at the Chinese shop, and he eventually came to live with Wong when his own family hit troubled economic times. The story of the Chinese migrant and his "Cuban son" is well known in Sagua today, as Idalberto Revuelta

Díaz became one of the martyrs of the Cuban Revolution. Revuelta joined the 26 of July Movement and died at age nineteen in 1958, and today a street is named after him.[108] Although Francisco Wong regularly sent home remittances and remained unattached in Cuba, his life was far from the image of a "bachelor society" migrant who works only to send the fruits of his toil to a foreign country.

Images of the Chinese in Cuba as victimized coolie or heroic freedom fighter, and descriptions by contemporary Cubans of their Chinese neighbors as "honorable" and "loyal," paper over the discrimination Chinese encountered in the twentieth century. A labor movement was repeatedly tempted toward anti-immigrant measures, and established merchants could lean the same way in an effort to reduce competition. Decades of U.S. intervention in Cuba had also shaped racial attitudes, both at official and popular levels. U.S. authorities introduced a third racial category—*amarillo* or "yellow"—into official Cuban taxonomies. By 1945, when restrictions on Asian entry into the United States had been lifted, official resistance to a son of a Chinese in Cuba being categorized as "white" still existed. Constant restrictions on Asian immigration, anti-Chinese sentiment, and qualified portrayals of Chinese as potential citizens disrupt the narrative of Cuban exceptionalism with regard to racial inclusion.

Through the first half of the twentieth century, different economic and political contexts presented "ethnic choices" to Chinese migrants in Cuba. Certain segments of Cuban society viewed the Chinese as "sojourners" who intended to reap the benefits of the Cuban economy to support families back home, while refusing to assimilate into local society. However, from the perspective of a Chinese migrant, sojourning and settling were not necessarily two distinct processes. Given the decades of transnational migration that preceded them, maintaining hometown ties was not incompatible with becoming incorporated into Cuban society. Rather, the same institutions that fostered homeland attachments could generate collective action to defend against anti-Chinese sentiment in Cuba and to improve relations with Cubans.

Publicly, Chinese merchants spearheaded two general kinds of activities, those in support of the homeland and those in support of the Chinese community in Cuba. Often, as in the case of resistance to the Japanese occupation, one movement could satisfy both needs. Chinese associations raised funds within both the Chinese and the international community to support the resistance movement. In the process, Cubans were reminded of Chinese participation in the struggles for independence from Spain and the shared ideals of the founders of the Cuban and Chinese republics.

Beginning with the birth of the Cuban republic, the Chinese became part of a discourse of national identity that paved the way for their integration into society. Official ideology expressed sympathy for the abuses they suffered as coolies and praised them for their role in the wars for independence. In Cuba, then, local reaction toward the Chinese was less pronounced than elsewhere in the Americas. Large numbers of Chinese returned home after the Depression and during the nationalization of labor campaigns. And at certain moments, Chinese became the target of campaigns in the press and outside storefronts. But the development of a transcultural Cuban national ideology and the efforts of the Chinese community ensured that these anti-Chinese reactions were mitigated. It also enabled some immigrants and most second-generation Chinese to embrace a Cuban national identity.

Anyone who had ever heard the words of Mao Tse-tung would recognize Castro for what he was. We knew he was a communist from his student days.

—"The Wing Dynasty of Miami," *Tropic*, 10 December 1967

What's the difference in the experience of Chinese in Cuba and other countries of the diaspora? The difference is that here a socialist revolution took place. The revolution eliminated discrimination based on the color of a person's skin. Above all, it eliminated the property relations that create not only economic but also social inequality between rich and poor.

—Moisés Sío Wong, *Our History Is Still Being Written* (2005)

CHAPTER EIGHT

Revolution and Remigration

Politics, warfare, and revolutions disrupt migration flows, dislocate people, and sever homeland ties, sometimes forever. Revolutions in China, 1949, and Cuba, 1959, transformed both societies and altered the fabric of transnational Chinese merchant communities. Ironically, exiles fleeing Communism in China were confronted with a similar political upheaval in Cuba just ten years later. Both longtime residents and newer Chinese migrants joined the Cuban exodus in the wake of the revolution.

The Chinese Communist Revolution of 1949 and the Chinese Diaspora

The Guomindang unified China from its seat in Nanjing in 1927, but it failed adequately to incorporate the leftist elements of its membership. In 1945, with the defeat of Japan at the end of World War II and the end of its occupation of the country, a civil war ensued between the Guomindang and the Communists, from which Mao Zedong's Red Army emerged victorious. On 1 October 1949, Mao established the People's Republic of China (PRC) on the mainland, while Chiang Kai-shek relocated the Guomindang government to Taipei. Chinese refugees fled to Taiwan, Hong Kong, and other places around the world, including Cuba. An estimated three thousand Chinese entered Cuba from 1950 to 1959, among them Catholic priests and Guomindang officials.[1]

The establishment of the People's Republic of China on the mainland in 1949 politically polarized diasporic Chinese communities. Despite the influence of the Guomindang overseas, Chinese in Cuba (and elsewhere) did not unanimously support Chiang Kai-shek. In general, he had the backing of the wealthier merchant classes. In Cuba, although the Guomindang remained influential throughout the 1950s, it lost its monopoly on the political life of the Chinese community.[2]

The Chinese leftist political organization founded decades earlier emerged as the main body of support in Cuba for the Chinese Communist Revolution. During the civil war, it supported the Communists and changed its name to Alianza Nacional de Apoyo a la Democracía China (National Alliance to Protect Chinese Democracy). In 1946, it officially registered with the Cuban government as a cultural and mutual aid association with the mission of "promoting the widest support among the Chinese community of Cuba and the Cuban people to the democratic movement of China, to progress, and to the complete liberation of that country."[3]

Mao Zedong's victory in China infused new energy into the leftist tradition within Cuba's Guomindang and the individuals and organizations that had been forced underground. After the establishment of the PRC, the Alianza demonstrated support for the new government at a public event attended by Chinese and Cuban Communists.[4] Its president, Enrique León, declared support for the PRC and advocated Cuba's recognition of the new government. But Cuba was under the political and economic influence of its North American neighbor, and a directive from Washington to support the new Chinese government never came. Nevertheless, on the tenth of October, the anniversary of the Chinese Revolution of 1911, members of the Alianza hung flags and placards on the balconies of the Guomindang building to celebrate Mao Zedong's victory. This date coincided with Cuba's commemoration of the beginning of the armed uprising against Spanish colonial rule in 1868, symbolically reinforcing the view of Alianza members that Chinese Communists and Cubans were allied in a fight against tyranny and corruption. On this occasion, confrontations erupted between Mao's supporters and the much more numerous Guomindang followers in Cuba.[5]

The Chinese Communist Revolution contributed to the Cuban government's increasingly hardline stance toward its political opponents. In 1950, the government shut down the Communist newspaper *Hoy*. When a group of Chinese protested, their own publication *Kwong Wah Po* in Santiago de Cuba became a target of government censorship and repression. The press was destroyed, and police detained thirteen Chinese for being "Communist spies," among them newspaper director Juan Mok.[6] Without the crises of the Japanese occupation or the Chinese civil war, membership and financial support for the Alianza withered somewhat, especially in an unfriendly political climate. On 4 December 1951, the Alianza in Havana declared the dissolution of the association due to lack of funds, and in 1955 its registration with the Cuban government was officially canceled.[7] But the tradition of a Chinese leftist political organization in Cuba lay dormant, ready to be mobilized during the tumultuous next decade.

Chinese Exiles and Class Stratification

Cuba continued to be a main destination for new Chinese migrants, and the spike in entries after 1949 infused the merchant community with new members and institutions and intensified class stratification. The Barrio Chino underwent significant changes in composition and types of businesses, with wealthier merchants maintaining a stronger presence. Those in the retail and grocery sectors had been able to withstand the economic tumult of the 1930s, while many unemployed laborers and small entrepreneurs were forced to leave Cuba. By 1954, there were only 130 laundries—a decrease of 163 since 1927—and 173 fruit and vegetable stands—a decrease of 362 in the same period. However, that same period of time witnessed a tremendous growth in the retail sector and rising influence of grocery owners within the Chinese community. By 1954, there were 277 Chinese groceries (an increase of 214).[8]

Several Chinese clan and regional associations constructed new buildings in the Barrio Chino during the 1950s. In 1954, the merchant community built a four-story home for the Casino Chung Wah, so opulent that it became known as "the palace" of the Chinese community. The Guomindang and the Chinese Chamber of Commerce controlled the association, and the building's first floor housed the Bank of China, attesting to the patronage among institutional leaders of the community in Havana.[9] Upper-class Chinese merchants enjoyed a mutually beneficial relationship with Cuban politicians, inviting them to inauguration ceremonies of their community institutions. The president of the Chinese Chamber of Commerce, Li Kent, who owned several shops and a home in Miramar, was decorated by President Carlos Prío Socarrás (in power 1948–52).[10] Beyond Havana, upper-class Chinese were also expanding Chinese community institutions. In August 1952, for example, Guomindang members of Cienfuegos in central Cuba celebrated the inauguration of a new building on Santa Clara Street.[11]

Chinese and the Cuban Revolution of 1959

Amid the tourist paradise of 1950s Cuba and the banquets at El Pacífico in the Barrio Chino, a growing revolutionary movement targeted government repression and corruption, dependence on the United States, and the related inflation and fluctuations of an export economy. The struggles centered on General Fulgencio Batista, who seized government power through a military coup in 1952.

For some Chinese in Cuba, ethnic identification with China, even Chinese citizenship, did not preclude national identification with Cuba and involvement in Cuban politics. Chinese migrants of all social classes joined the anti-Batista struggles. Some had survived the deportations and purges from the political struggles of the 1920s and 1930s. Others were Cuban-born children of Chinese immigrants.[12]

After Fidel Castro launched a daring but unsuccessful attack on the Moncada Army Barracks in Santiago de Cuba in 1953, several Chinese figured among those arrested. One of them, Luis Li of Jiujiang, had prominent merchant ties, as his uncle Leon Chang owned the shop Casa Asia on San Rafael Street in Havana and was a leader of the Chinese Chamber of Commerce. Although Li and four other Chinese had been deported for opposition to President Machado's dictatorial rule, he managed to return to Cuba in 1930. In the 1950s, he held clandestine meetings with other Chinese in his grocery store on Washington Street in Havana. He also joined the Popular Socialist Party (Partido Socialista Popular) in Cuba. With his name on the watch list of the Bureau of Repression of Communist Activities (Buró de Represión de Actividades Comunistas), Luis Li was arrested numerous times.

Juan Mok was also detained after the attack on Moncada Barracks, but released after a few days for lack of evidence connecting him with the incident. When repression intensified in subsequent years, Mok's family moved to Havana. He remained behind in Santiago de Cuba, working in the noodle factory and editing the newspaper *Kwong Wah Po*. After the general strike of 9 April 1958, Mok was imprisoned and his family in Havana put under house arrest.[13]

Some Cubans who became involved in the political struggles against Fulgencio Batista were of Chinese descent, children of early-twentieth-century

Chinese immigrants. Armando Choy Rodríguez, Gustavo Chui Beltrán, and Moisés Sío Wong hailed from different regional and class backgrounds. But being born on the island in the tumultuous 1930s shaped their common identity as Cubans. They became part of a generation of Cuban youth who identified with the 26 of July Movement, inspired by Castro's 1953 attack on the Moncada Army Barracks. They joined the rebels in the struggles against Batista from 1956 to 1958 and continued to serve in the Cuban army for decades after the revolution.[14]

In a recent testimonial of their experiences in the Cuban Revolution, the generals discussed their lives growing up in prerevolutionary Cuba and their motivations for joining the revolutionary movement. Moisés Sío Wong, the only one of the three with two Chinese parents, described resentment at having to work for his Chinese brother-in-law without pay while growing up. Rather than being a source of ethnic identification, memories of this common immigrant economic strategy later propelled Sío Wong to embrace socialism. Chinese youth identified with the struggles against imperialism and racial and class discrimination, more than they did with the concerns of the Chinese immigrant community. When asked if his Chinese heritage had an impact on the development of his revolutionary consciousness, Armando Choy replied, "I joined the movement as a Cuban. I thought like a Cuban, not like someone from China."[15]

The 1959 Cuban Revolution transformed the island's landscape with sweeping political, economic, and social reforms. Initially, the revolution maintained a wide base of support in Cuban society, including Chinese merchant leaders, who enjoyed a brief "honeymoon" with the new Cuban government. The January 1959 issue of the bilingual Chinese retailer magazine *Fraternidad* saluted the Cuban Revolution. In June 1960 in the Barrio Chino, the restaurant El Pacífico hosted banquets for both Fidel Castro, now the leader (officially prime minister) of Cuba, and his brother Raúl, minister of the armed forces.[16]

However, as with the rest of Cuban society, the revolution engendered profound changes in the class and institutional structure of the Chinese community. Chinese merchant relations with the new government deteriorated after the "First Declaration of Havana" on 2 September 1960, when Cuba announced its intent to establish diplomatic ties with the People's Republic of China.[17] Adding to the anxiety of Chinese merchants in Cuba, as well as officials in the United States, were reports that hundreds of technicians from Communist China were being sent to Cuba and that three long-standing Chinese newspapers in Havana would be closed. The new government in

China attempted to gain information on Chinese overseas, ultimately aiming to secure financial support. In the summer of 1960, while Castro still maintained diplomatic relations with Taiwan, the PRC sent a questionnaire to Chinese residents in Cuba requesting information about their jobs, relatives, and properties in Cuba and in China. The cover letter evoked the new ideological affinity with Cuba: "North American imperialists, aided by Batista and Chinese Nationalist reactionaries, have always sought to isolate the Chinese resident in Cuba from their country. But now the enemies of Cuba have been defeated by the revolutionary forces. And this is the hour for strengthening the ties between you and us."[18]

Other Chinese supported the Cuban revolutionary movement under the banner of a Chinese ethnic identity. The political transformation paved the way for left-leaning Chinese and their Cuban-born children to assume power within Chinese community institutions, especially after many had been imprisoned or forced underground for their activities during previous decades. Members of the main leftist Chinese political organization had maintained their building on Zanja Street in Havana's Chinatown, and after 1959, they reemerged as the Alianza Nueva Democracía China en Cuba (Chinese New Democracy Alliance of Cuba). Alianza members joined the national rally in Havana on 2 September 1960, protesting the U.S. attempt to align Latin American nations against Fidel Castro. An image of them proudly marching with a banner that proclaimed "Resident Chinese Support the Cuban Revolution and Its Leader Fidel Castro!" appeared in the popular Cuban magazine *Bohemia*.[19]

During a meeting in February 1960, second-generation Chinese Cuban Pedro Eng Herrera, Luis Li, and others announced the creation of the Milicia Popular China, Brigada José Wong (Chinese Popular Militia, José Wong Brigade) for the defense of the Cuban Revolution.[20] The name of the Chinese militia invoked the memory of the earlier Chinese Communist activist José Wong, who had been murdered by government agents in a Cuban prison in 1930. Another suggestion, reaching even further back into a Chinese revolutionary tradition, was to name the brigade after José Bu Tak, one of the Chinese captains known for his service in all three wars for independence from 1868 to 1898.

Trade unions and universities formed separate militias. Eventually, these kinds of units, including the all-Chinese brigade, became incorporated into the Milicia Nacional Revolucionaria (National Revolutionary Militia).[21] Members merged their Chinese ethnic identifications with political support of both the Chinese and Cuban revolutions. Participants opposed class structure within the Chinese immigrant community as much as within Cuban society as a whole. Of the dozens of Chinese who joined the militia, most were natives of China, but a few were mixed descendants.[22]

The Chinese militia first ascended the stage on 1 October 1960, during a public celebration of the eleventh anniversary of the People's Republic of China. Several days later, the brigade asserted control over two long-standing merchant community institutions, the Guomindang and the Casino Chung Wah. The brigade chose the transnationally significant date of 10 October for action in the heart of the Barrio Chino. With Pedro Eng at the head of about forty Chinese, the militia occupied the buildings of the Guomindang and its newspaper and for the first time raised the flag of Communist China on its balcony. In a transition relatively free of violence, a new board of directors— three of them Communists—assumed positions in the Casino Chung Wah.[23] Also in October 1960, the Havana branch of the Bank of China was nationalized, with a capital of over 1.5 million dollars.[24]

In step with Castro's revolutionary initiatives, the Chinese brigade embarked on a campaign to eliminate prostitution, gambling, and opium in Havana's Chinatown. Militarily, they fortified the Isla de Pinos (later renamed Isla de la Juventud), off the coast of Cuba, "to prevent it from becoming another Taiwan."[25] Cubans believed the island to be the site of an imminent U.S. invasion (which in April 1961 did occur at the Bay of Pigs). During the first year of the revolution, the formerly banned Chinese Communist newspaper in Santiago de Cuba transferred its operations to the Havana plant of the Communist Spanish-language daily *Hoy*. The Xinhua (New China) news agency also opened a Havana office staffed by Chinese from the mainland.[26]

While merchant elites went into exile in Miami, New York City, and Union City, New Jersey, bringing their Cuban-born children with them, most Chinese Cubans initially remained, either as supporters of the revolution or as small shopkeepers hedging their bets with the reforms of the new government. Middle- and lower-class Chinese generally did not leave Cuba until the final stage of the nationalization of private commerce in 1968 through a "revolutionary offensive" on the remaining 57,000 small businesses.[27]

The nationalization of private commerce brought profound changes in the fabric of daily life in Chinese communities across the island. Xinhui migrant Felipe Luis owned a bodega in Havana. Like many others who remained in Cuba, he was forced to become an employee of a state-owned store after the revolution. For those working in selling produce, the agrarian reforms and the depopulation of truck farms also forever altered their livelihood. Like other Cubans, Chinese who refused to work for the state depended on the black market economy.[28]

Chinese community life was also dramatically affected by new government policies intended to eradicate inequalities in Cuban society. Shortly after the revolution, leader Fidel Castro declared that the end of institutional racism had been achieved.[29] Issuing this government proclamation amid a highly charged political atmosphere effectively subsumed ethnic identities to revolutionary national ideology. The official de-emphasis on ethnic identifications, coupled with the economic reforms, led to the dissolution of most of the Chinese associations. The ethnic-based organizations lost members, dues, and building space to the needs of the revolution. One after another, the remaining Chinese associations folded. As membership in the regional and clan associations decreased during the 1960s, so did the dues required to maintain activities. Even the more prosperous clan associations suffered.[30] The Lui kinsmen from Xinhui who remained in Cuba joined the larger Zhongshan association in Havana after their own huiguan had dissolved.[31] The unauthorized occupation of the Chinese association buildings by non-Chinese also affected the viability of these cultural institutions. Lack of incoming funds led to the further deterioration of association buildings, a condition common in revolutionary Cuba.

The effect of the 1968 nationalizations on middle-class shopkeepers and their employees accelerated the exodus. Records from the Casino Chung Wah indicate that 142 members returned to China or remigrated elsewhere in 1968. Among these, only 19 were owners, while 74 were workers and 49 unemployed. Those who left for a second country were all under fifty years old.[32] With the flight of Chinese merchants, the Chinese Chamber of Commerce in Cuba dissolved in 1969.[33]

The Chinese community organizations that survived the nationalizations and emigration were profoundly altered. Keeping in step with the ideological current of the new Cuban government, the Chinese leftist organization once again changed its name to the Alianza Socialista China de Cuba (Guba Huaqiao Shehui Zhuyi Tongmeng). After the exodus of Chinese shopkeepers in 1968, the Alianza had only 138 members nationwide, the majority from Havana and Oriente, the eastern part of the island known for its tradition of rebellion against colonialism and imperialism.[34] Today, the Alianza remains the main Chinese political organization in Havana and still occupies the former Guomindang residence.

Increased participation of Cuban-born Chinese, including mixed descendants, produced the most visible change in Chinese associational life after

1959. Even before the postrevolutionary exodus of Chinese, Chinese institutions had adapted to shifting demographics. In the 1950s the Casino Chung Wah began to accept Chinese women as well as children born in Cuba to two Chinese parents, for the first time altering established patriarchal and generational standards of an immigrant organization.[35] The change reflected the higher numbers of Chinese women in Cuba during the postwar period (reaching 484 or 4 percent of the total Chinese population). By the early 1970s, association records showed an increase in membership, especially among Cuban-born Chinese.[36]

Alfonso Chao Chiu experienced these changes firsthand as he grew up in 1940s and 1950s Cuba. He learned Cantonese from his father and maintained a close relationship with Chinese institutions. After the revolution, Chao worked within the altered community structure to adapt to demographic changes while attempting to maintain Chinese cultural traditions. He persevered in the face of resistance from the native Chinese community members. In 1982 Chao (whose mother was half Chinese) became the first mixed descendant to serve as president of the Casino Chung Wah. During his term as president, the association altered regulations to accept second-generation descendants who had only one Chinese parent.[37]

Even with these efforts, most of the remaining associations fell into decline during the 1970s and 1980s. At the beginning of 1975, the traditional clan association Lun Con Cun Sol, located in the heart of the Barrio Chino, counted 179 members. Most were retired, with the exception of thirteen who worked in laundries, one in a bodega, and one for a Cuban electronics company. The sixteen members of the board of directors ranged in age from sixty-three to seventy-eight.[38] In 1977, the Casino Chung Wah in Cienfuegos still had seventy-three members, consisting of "all Chinese and their children" who complied with the regulations. Most members of the board of directors had retained Chinese nationality. Only two out of thirteen, including the president of the association, Bienvenido Li Lam, were Cuban citizens.[39] A census taken by the Casino Chung Wah in 1980 reveals the severe drop in the Chinese population in Cuba. Only 4,302 Chinese remained throughout the island, the majority from Taishan and Xinhui Counties in Guangdong Province.[40]

Chinese National Identifications in Revolutionary Cuba

During the initial years of the Cuban Revolution, the Chinese associations that managed to stay afloat witnessed a sea change among their leadership.

Those who had been persecuted by former governments and most recently fought against Batista moved into positions of leadership in the Chinese community. Their experiences during the Cuban Revolution further shaped their national identifications as Cubans. After the revolution, Luis Li became president of the Kow Kong regional association in 1960. When Li made a return trip to China, his family urged him to remain. However, before he died on 7 September 1971, "he insisted that his bones could rest just as well in Cuba as in China, since one was his original motherland and the other his adoptive motherland." Li is buried in Havana's Chinese cemetery in the section of the Alianza Socialista China de Cuba. When Juan Mok was released from jail in January 1959, he served as director of *Kwong Wah Po* until his death in 1962. Rather than being buried in the Chinese cemetery, Mok was laid to rest among the family graves of prominent Communist leader Blas Roca Calderón, attesting to the ties of solidarity across ethnic lines. Federico Chi Casio had built a life in Cuba and developed a reputation as a political coalition builder. In 1964, he was invited to China, where he died just before his scheduled return to Cuba. In a testament to his transnational life, half of his ashes were left in China, and half were brought to Cuba. When Mauro García and Pedro Eng visited his home during the course of their research on the history of the Chinese community in Cuba, they were impressed to find a shrine to José Martí.[41]

To the extent possible, the Chinese who remained in Cuba continued to send remittances home. Alberto Jo Pons, bodega owner in Cienfuegos, sent money to his family in Nanhai until his death in 1967. Amounts ranged from 100 to 150 pesos annually.[42] Francisco Luis also continued to send remittances to his Chinese daughters until his death in 1975.

Due to the altered political and economic situation in Cuba, new immigration to the island effectively ended. Tang Zhongxi represents a rare case of a Chinese woman coming to Cuba after the revolution. In 1975, the twenty-year-old Tang brought her young son to Cuba to live with her husband, the president of the Chinese association in Cienfuegos who was thirty years her senior. She experienced extreme loneliness and isolation as one of the few Chinese women admitted to Cuba during that period, living in an association building whose membership consisted mostly of older men. She has retained Chinese citizenship (as many others have done) and over a decade ago described herself as "70 percent Chinese, 30 percent Cuban," a designation as fluid as the geopolitical circumstances of a particular context.[43]

Chinese Cuban Exiles in the United States

The movement of Chinese from Cuba to the United States had historical precedent, from escaping sugar plantations in the nineteenth century to using Cuba as a springboard to northern ports during the age of exclusion or the postwar period. After 1959, however, most of the Chinese who came to the United States were political exiles. Some had fled China after 1949, only to leave an adopted homeland a decade later.

The Cuban exodus in the wake of the revolution occurred in stages, in accordance with political events on the island.[44] During the second year of the revolutionary government, Chinese merchants in Cuba joined fellow elite Cubans fleeing to Miami. Even during the first wave of exiles, however, the Chinese were not exclusively merchants. A Chinese who had years of experience on sugar estates and as a cook in Cuba placed advertisements for work over several weeks in a publication for Cuban exiles in Miami. In November 1960, the Miami weekly publication *El Avance Criollo* ran a feature on the particular experiences of Chinese Cubans. The article opens with a celebration of the Chinese historical presence and contribution to Cuba's liberation from Spain, reiterating that "the Chinese form a contingent of hardworking and law-abiding men, developing agriculture and commerce and loyally contributing to the greatness of the country." Interestingly, the article also affirms a belief in the passive nature of the Chinese: "Politics never interested them." Now, however, in the face of a common struggle, Chinese Cubans were among those eligible for recruitment into Cuban American exile politics.

One of those forced to flee was Alfonso Chiong, president of the Colonia China and director of the Chinese nationalist daily newspaper. He arrived in Miami on 27 October 1960, at the age of fifty-seven. Chiong had resided in Cuba for forty years, and he was described as being "as much Cuban or more Cuban than many." Chiong provides a different perspective on the events of 10 October 1960 that led to his exile. After being informed by government agents he must hand over the association to a new directorate, Chiong said, "I decided to not leave, renounce, or hand over. I continue to be president of the Colonia China de Cuba." He continued, "In the face of my actions, Cuban authorities—influenced by the few Chinese communists in Havana— ordered my detention." Chiong evaded arrest and fled to Santiago de Cuba, where he used his connections in the city to acquire a visa from the U.S. consulate. When the orders for his detention reached Santiago, Chiong moved on to Camagüey, where friends protected him until he safely boarded a plane to the United States.

Once in the United States, Chinese Cubans activated their own diasporic networks for support. Chiong stated: "We are poor. I arrived in Miami with five pesos, and I spent three on a taxi from the airport to the hotel; but I have family in New York that helped me immediately." Chiong took his wife and daughter to the home of his New York relatives before returning to Miami for meetings with fellow Chinese and Cubans. He considered former prime minister Manuel Antonio de Varona a close friend, recalling his inauguration of the new Chinese association building on Amistad Street and donation of a beautiful Cuban flag.[45] Chiong reiterated: "We believe that we should unite all—Chinese and Cubans—in one single front to fight for Democracy and against international Communism." He estimated that already one or two hundred Chinese had emigrated from Cuba to seek refuge in the United States. He also reported that the Guomindang government in Taiwan had formed an office in Miami to assist these compatriots and put them in contact with organized "revolutionary fronts."[46] In one case, the U.S. government granted asylum to two Chinese migrants from Cuba who had entered the country as stowaways. In the aftermath of the Cuban Revolution, Lam Ping Quan Li and Fermin Fong Hong fled to Jamaica, where they stowed away on a U.S.-bound ship. Catholic Relief Services arranged sponsors for the migrants, who were granted the same status as other Cuban refugees.[47]

Like other Cubans, Chinese families were divided over whether to remain on the island or join those fleeing for Miami, New York City, Union City (New Jersey), Toronto, and elsewhere. Representative of the ruptures of revolution are Armando and Napoleón Seuc Chiu, second-generation ethnic Chinese brothers born in Havana in the 1920s. When their mother returned to China with three younger siblings during the Depression, the two brothers were raised together by their father and neighborhood men in what Napoleón Seuc describes as "a Chinese home and environment."[48] They both entered professions, Armando as a doctor and Napoleón as an attorney, and frequently they participated in Chinese community events. Fluent in both Chinese and Spanish, Napoleón provided legal counsel for the Chinese community. By the 1950s, the Seuc family was reunited when their mother returned to Cuba. Growing up, Armando and Napoleón were influenced politically by their father, a left-leaning Chinese nationalist.

They had been inseparable growing up, so much so that people mistook them for twins. But, like thousands of other Cubans, their trajectories parted after the 1959 revolution. Napoleón, a lawyer and Guomindang member who defended the Chinese merchant community in Havana, initially supported the Cuban Revolution, as it was directed against corruption and imperialism. But, like many other Cubans, his enthusiasm waned over the course of the next two years. As active members of the Chinese community, his parents and his brother Armando accepted an invitation to an event honoring the new PRC diplomats in Cuba, but Napoleón declined. After his refusal to attend the reception and his subsequent dismissal from his position as a lawyer in the Ministry of Labor, Napoleón recalled being past the point of no return: "I felt that I had crossed the Rubicon."[49]

He joined the newly formed anticommunist Movimiento Revolucionario del Pueblo (People's Revolutionary Movement). In September 1961, he and his family boarded a Delta flight from Havana to New Orleans, becoming part of the first wave of Cuban exiles. Napoleón Seuc spent the 1960s and 1970s in San Juan (Puerto Rico), Miami, and San José (Costa Rica), engaging in anticommunist movements and criticizing the revolutionary tribunals. Eventually he settled in Miami, where in 1994, approximately three thousand Chinese Cubans accounted for less than 1 percent of the Cuban exile community.[50] After the 1970s, internal divisions in the anti-Castro movement propelled Napoleón to renounce militant action, stating, "Now I am a combatant only in the battlefield of ideas."[51] His brother Armando, by contrast, remained in Cuba, dedicating himself to the medical profession.

The secondary migration of Chinese from one diasporic location to another raises new questions about homeland politics and identity. Scholars from across disciplines have begun to examine the complex identity formations of Asian-descended people from Latin America and the Caribbean who remigrate to places like the United States and Canada. As Lok Siu notes, patterns of secondary or "serial" migration inform choices concerning marriage and family, language, cuisine, and culture.[52] In the case of the Chinese in Cuba, a few general trends can be observed.

Fleeing as exiles like other Cubans, Chinese left family and possessions behind as their businesses were nationalized. In both Florida and New York/New Jersey, Chinese settled alongside their Cuban neighbors in Little Havana, Union City, and the Upper West Side of Manhattan. The case of the Seuc family is particularly revealing of the patterns of secondary migration. While Napoleón Seuc made Miami his new home, his younger siblings who had grown up in China settled in New York's Chinatown, where they felt at home speaking Cantonese. Continuing their traditions from the Barrio Chino in Havana, Chinese Cuban exiles formed their own associations in New York and Miami.[53] After the death of his Chinese wife, Napoleón Seuc moved in Cuban social circles in Miami, and when he remarried, it was to a Cuban woman. Seuc embodied the complex, multifaceted identities of Chinese Cubans in the United States: simultaneously a Spanish-speaking Cuban exile living in Miami and a Chinese American, with relatives spread over Havana, Miami, New York, Los Angeles, and Xinhui City in Guangdong. Despite his reservations about the Cuban revolutionary government, years later Napoleón visited his brother and others in the decaying Barrio Chino in Cuba.[54]

How do their fellow Chinese Cubans across the Florida Straits situate themselves politically today? In recent years, Chinese Cubans have been reluctant to become involved in the politics of the anti-Castro Cuban exile community. The battle over the fate of the child Elián Gonzalez in Miami in 2000, for example, prompted some Chinese Cubans there to disassociate themselves from Cuban American politics.[55]

It is perhaps in the area of cuisine that Chinese Cuban culture has been most pronounced in the United States. With the influx of Chinese small-business owners fleeing Cuba after the 1968 nationalizations, Chinese Cuban restaurants sprang up around Manhattan's Upper West Side. As in Cuba, they provided inexpensive Chinese and Cuban food. In a 1968 review of the restaurant Asia Pearl, food critics for *New York* magazine noted: "Probably the only benefit that has been derived from the U.S.-Cuba estrangement is the establishment of the Cuban-Chinese restaurant as part of New York's gastronomic life . . . scattered throughout the city and most heavily along Eighth Avenue." Asia Pearl offered a Chinese and a Cuban menu, infusing dishes with tropical accents. "The fried rice dishes are good and seem to be comfortably placed between the Chinese and Cuban cooking. Pork, ham, shrimp and one called simply *special* are $1.05 each. It is the Cuban side of the menu that should be the most novel for the average New Yorker. The scope of the familiar omelet is enlarged by the addition of either banana, shrimp or Spanish sausage (from 85 to 95 cents)." The reviewers noted that mostly Spanish speakers filled the seats around the plain formica tables and at the counter.[56] Today, only a few of the original Chinese Cuban restaurants remain. La Caridad 78 Restaurant opened on Broadway in 1968 and serves "working people's Cuban and Cantonese fare." It offers classic dishes such as ropa vieja, served by older Spanish-speaking Chinese (as well as newer immigrants from China). For the clientele, the restaurants offered a touch of nostalgia in addition to a Cuban meal, contributing to a Cuban exile experience.[57]

Like their counterparts in the United States, descendants of Chinese in

Cuba have begun journeys to fill in the gaps and ruptures produced by migration. The multiple migrations and remigrations of Chinese in Cuba, especially after 1959, have produced a population of Americans of both Cuban and Chinese descent. Some of them, like photographer Maria Lau, have made their way to Havana's Barrio Chino to locate missing pieces of the puzzle of her family history and document this journey through a creative medium.[58] Writer Emily Lo's Chinese grandfather, who had married a Cuban woman, was never heard from again after he returned to China in 1949. Lo describes her motivation for a search that eventually led her to Cuba: "I just wanted to know how I fit in my family. And I wanted to know how my family fit in a larger scope of history. We had studied immigration in school, but our textbooks never considered families like mine, families that were of blended heritage before they even set foot in America. We celebrated hyphenated ethnicities all the time in our diversity-conscious curriculums, but adding one more, like Cuban *and* Chinese American, didn't fit any mold."[59]

For thirty years, from the Cuban Revolution of 1959 until the breakup of the Soviet Union, the population of ethnic Chinese in Cuba sharply declined. Despite their small numbers today, the story of the Chinese in Cuba is one that has resurfaced through a restoration project in Havana's Chinatown, helped to renew ties between Cuba and the People's Republic of China, and engaged the popular imagination. The greater Chinese Cuban community, in addition to incorporating regional, class, and generational differences extending back to the nineteenth century, includes those who embarked on secondary migrations to other countries in the wake of the Cuban Revolution.

Epilogue

In January 2012, members of the Chinese Cuban community gathered in Havana to commemorate the 125th anniversary of the founding of the Asociación Nacional Min Chih Tang (Minzhidang; formerly Chee Kung Tong). As I entered the recently renovated building, I experienced an extreme sense of disorientation. Was this the same association that over the past decade of research trips to Cuba had become an obligatory stop? Where were the newspaper clippings and mementos haphazardly stuck to the walls, the outdated selection of Chinese magazines, the elderly native Chinese sipping tea on loosely arranged chairs? Today, members and visitors are greeted with a stunning mural of the Great Wall of China spanning the entire length of the meeting room. This image, while representative of China for tourists, holds little meaning for the few remaining Cantonese migrants in Cuba. The physical changes in the association are part of a larger "revitalization" of Chinese Cuban community institutions since the early 1990s. Chinatowns throughout the world have undergone significant changes in response to demographic patterns and tourism initiatives. Today Havana's Barrio Chino—known as a "Chinatown without Chinese"—provides a unique locale for an analysis of diasporic ties, urban renewal, and ethnic identity.

The Changing Tide of Sino-Cuban Relations

Due to a complex set of ideological and national interests, the initial friendship between Cuba and China deteriorated shortly after the Cuban Revolution. The Soviet Union economically and militarily supported Cuba during the Cold War. Cuba's relationship with China was exacerbated by the Sino-Soviet dispute and the beginning of China's Cultural Revolution in 1965. Not until the end of the 1980s did relations between Cuba and China began to warm.[1]

The collapse of the Soviet Union in 1991 and the end of subsidies brought about a severe economic crisis in Cuba. The Cuban government instituted reforms resulting in a "mixed socialist economy" and the legalization of the U.S. dollar.[2] Cuba's search for new trade and investment partners coincided with China's desire to strengthen its relationship with Latin American and Caribbean nations. In 1992 General Moisés Sío Wong reactivated the Cuban-Chinese Friendship Association (Asociación de Amistad Cubano-China). In

1993 President Jiang Zemin made a landmark visit to Cuba, and the following year Fidel Castro reciprocated with a trip to China.

In recent decades China has emerged as a major diplomatic and economic power in Latin America and the Caribbean. China seeks access to natural resources such as nickel, copper, and oil, food products such as soybeans, and markets for manufactured products. In 2005 China emerged as Cuba's second largest trading partner, after Venezuela. Chinese buses and bicycles line the streets, while pressure cookers, light bulbs, refrigerators, and television sets fill Cuban homes. An additional benefit of the economic partnership for both China and Cuba is the inherent challenge to long-standing U.S. dominance in the region. Currently twelve of the twenty-three nations that recognize Taiwan are in Latin America and the Caribbean, where the Republic of China and the PRC vie for influence through local Chinese communities.[3]

Linked to the renewed China-Cuba relationship is the Chinese government's support of developments in Havana's Chinatown. In a symbolic display of friendship, China funded the construction of a traditional-style portico at the entrance of the historic district. The reach of the Chinese state into Chinese migrant communities overseas has precedents in the fund-raising activities of reformers and revolutionaries as the Qing dynasty came to an end, Guomindang agencies after 1927, and PRC organizations dedicated to attracting investment in hometowns in the reform era. However, in contemporary Cuba, with only a few hundred native Chinese who are unable to send remittances home or invest capital in China, the involvement of the Chinese government in local affairs takes on unique characteristics.[4]

Alongside diplomacy and trade, China promotes cultural and educational programs through nonprofit Confucius Institutes as a "soft power" strategy for gaining a foothold in the region.[5] At the Confucius Institute in Havana, inaugurated in 2009, Cuban students complete a three-year course of study to achieve mid-level proficiency in Mandarin, a language that would have been foreign to most of the Cantonese migrants in Cuba. The institute enrolls 180 students in fifteen weekly classes.[6] Sochi Alay, a third-generation Chinese Cuban of mixed descent, recently returned to the institute from study abroad for advanced training in teaching Chinese language. In China, Alay had studied at Zhongshan University, the historic campus of the former Lingnan University that hosted earlier generations of Chinese Cuban youth.[7] Additionally, approximately one thousand Chinese students are in Cuba learning Spanish.[8]

State policies in Cuba today are shaping identity options for later generations of Chinese. Today the broader Chinese Cuban community is composed of two major groups: *chinos naturales* (native Chinese) and *descendientes* (descendants), the children, grandchildren, and great-grandchildren of Chinese. In addition to the couple of hundred elderly native Chinese who remain, thousands of mixed descendants form contemporary Chinese Cuba. At the end of 2010, the Casino Chung Wah registered 2,392 members, and of these only 173 were native Chinese.[9]

The Revitalization of Havana's Barrio Chino

In 1993, at the festivities for the one hundredth anniversary of the founding of the Casino Chung Wah, a group of descendants discussed restoration of the Barrio Chino and solicited permission to establish a state enterprise, the Grupo Promotor del Barrio Chino (Havana Chinatown Promotion Group).[10] Its main objectives were to "recover" Chinese culture, customs, and traditions for the Cuban nation and to transform the historic Barrio Chino into a tourist zone. Initial projects included a center for Chinese arts and traditions, an evening language school with native Mandarin teachers, a martial arts club, a clinic for traditional Chinese medicine, a residence for the elderly, a pedestrian walkway with shops and restaurants, community celebrations of festivals, and maintenance of the remaining Chinese newspaper. Since 1995, descendant Roberto Vargas Lee has directed the Cuban Association of Wu Shu-Kung Fu (Asociación Cubana de Wu Shu-Kung Fu), with branches in the provinces. Cubans of all ethnic backgrounds participate in martial arts, with older practitioners drawn to *taijiquan*.[11]

The thirteen remaining Chinese clan, regional, and political associations in Havana have opened their doors to descendants, and the Min Chih Tang remains the center of social and cultural activity. The associations have also received permission to open restaurants in former meeting rooms (even the political Alianza Socialista China de Cuba runs a bustling enterprise). Since they own the buildings, the Chinese associations can profit from running restaurants, although they are burdened with heavy taxes to the Cuban state. The Chinese embassy donated materials for the restaurants, including chopsticks, porcelain spoons, fountains, teapots, tablecloths, furniture, and decorative lamps.[12] Los Tres Chinitos has become one of the most well-known restaurants, though not for Chinese cuisine. Originally a Chinese association, it is the restaurant's pizza that draws long lines of Cubans outside.

Cuba's only remaining Chinese newspaper, *Kwong Wah Po*, is temporarily closed for restoration, but is in danger of extinction. Before the revolution, it remained an important link in the maintenance of Chinese Cuban iden-

Chinese Cuban youth performing the lion dance in Havana, Cuba, May 2003.
(Photograph by author)

tity and community, with a daily circulation of 1,500. Over the past decade, circulation dropped to 600 every two weeks. In 1996, the newspaper began printing a section in Spanish for descendants who are unable to read Chinese. The century-old U.S.-made printing press is surrounded by shelves containing thousands of metal characters that must be typeset by hand. Despite support for its restoration, the intricate knowledge required for identifying traditional Chinese characters (as opposed to the simplified characters used since 1949 in Beijing) and operating the press will likely disappear with the remaining native Chinese.[13]

Chinese Cuban Ethnicity and the Role of the State

A movement that focused on a particular ethnic group after the revolution — a revolution that claims the elimination of racial distinctions as one of its pillars — is remarkable. The project is permissible precisely because of the particular role of the Cuban state in guiding its initiatives. Contradictions abound within a state project claiming to promote the Chinese Cuban community and rescue an "authentic" Chinese culture, yet spearheaded by mixed descendants and driven primarily by tourism.[14]

In 2006 the Office of the Historian of the City of Havana (Oficina del Historiador de la Ciudad de la Habana) incorporated the restoration of Chinatown into its master plan for urban renewal. This move toward centralization represents greater state control over what essentially began as a localized project by descendants of Chinese and the strengthening of official China-Cuba ties. In the process, some initiatives of the restoration project's founders have been disbanded. For example, publication of a small community magazine *Fraternidad II* ceased. Produced on a computer beginning in May 2002 and much endeared by residents, the publication contained news about the Barrio Chino, interviews with elderly Chinese accompanied by photos of them "yesterday and today," and essays on Chinese culture.[15]

Efforts from above to impose a homogenizing coherence on the Chinese Cuban "community" can be both exclusionary and artificially inclusive. The aging native Chinese in Cuba are often mere observers of the government-sponsored activities. Some of the native Chinese who lost ownership of their small businesses during the revolutionary urban reform program and watched buildings decay through disuse and neglect, for example, retain considerable skepticism about the subsequent enthusiasm of the state for revitalizing the neighborhood. Former bodega owners vividly recalled the Barrio Chino of the old days: ice cream made with fresh fruit, a plethora of Chinese food and products, Sunday cockfights after the shops had closed, and most significantly, fellow migrants.[16] For a restoration to an "authentic" Barrio Chino, a return to some form of entrepreneurial autonomy would probably accomplish more than festivals.

The Cuban-born generations, on the other hand, speak of a history of resistance to their own participation in Chinese associations, especially for those of mixed descent. The tensions embedded in the restoration project can be productive, generating possibilities for different types of claims on a Chinese identity from a range of actors, including multiracial descendants who have never been to China. Ien Ang's problematization and reconceptualization of the label "Chineseness" in the diaspora opens such possibilities for multiple interpretations of ethnicity.[17] While many descendants in Cuba have always been aware of a distant Chinese ancestry, increasingly they have begun to practice a "symbolic identification" with Chinese ethnicity.[18] Benefits may include some material gain, reconnection with a distant ancestor or homeland, and an outlet for expression within a restricted society. With the support of the state and with the participation of non-Chinese, descendants today are in the process of making a distinctive Chinese Cuban culture, which, in turn, shapes their ethnic and racial identities.[19] On the surface, essentialized markers of Chinese culture and ethnicity pervade the revitalization project. Cuban women wearing elegant *qipao* greet tourists outside of restaurants, red lanterns hang from ceilings, and youth partake in the lion dance in a practice akin to "self-Orientalization" or what Frank Scherer terms "strategic Orientalism."[20] Celebration of ancestral heritage is not limited to the Chinese in Cuba. Cubans of African, Haitian, West Indian, Jewish, and Arab descent are similarly in a constant process of negotiation with the state and an overarching Cuban national identity.[21]

Multiracial and multiethnic descendants of Chinese maintain varying notions of a Chinese identity and have begun journeys to explore an ancestral heritage and to seek answers to some of the ruptures produced by migration.[22] Julio Tang Zambrana, a third-generation mixed Chinese Cuban, approaches his own quest for ethnic identity with a skeptical eye. Although Tang's Chinese grandfather died when he was young, he grew up in Havana's Chinatown and learned about his heritage through the native Chinese hanging around in the association or neighborhood and through stories passed down by his parents. He recognizes the tenuous nature of ethnic identifications among Cubans of Chinese ancestry in post-1959 Cuba.[23]

In a discussion of Asian American identity, Lisa Lowe analyzes a short story in which two Asian American women together explore their guilt complex about not being "authentically" Chinese enough. Lowe observes that "the making of Chinese American culture—the ways in which it is imagined, practiced, and continued—is worked out as much 'horizontally' among communities as it is transmitted 'vertically' in unchanging forms from one generation to the next."[24] In a similar vein, the making of a Chinese Cuban culture is a negotiation between the state, the mixed descendants, and the native Chinese. While most can do no more than acknowledge their heritage, Julio Tang made a conscious effort to engage with Chinese culture, especially through language study in China. He enrolled in a master's program for teaching Chinese, supported by a scholarship from the Chinese government. For Chinese Cuban descendants, time spent overseas has shattered the Orientalist images of China being promoted by the revitalization project at home. Now that he has the opportunity to live in China for an extended period of time, Tang recognizes the stereotyping of a traditional Chinese culture in Cuba today: "China is more than Confucius, silk, calligraphy, ceramics."[25] He has discovered a modern China that is complex, class-stratified, and—like Cuba—in transition. While Tang has been able to learn a language critical to future Cuba-China ties and significant for his own heritage, he echoes many in his critique of proposals for Cuba's adoption of the Chinese model for capitalist economic development and consumerism under a socialist state.

Today, within the broad, supposedly inclusive category of "Chinese Cuban," subtle racialized distinctions are nonetheless maintained. Although the 1959 Cuban Revolution embraced the notion of cubanidad and declared an end to institutionalized racial discrimination, it failed to achieve a color-blind society. The editors of *Afrocuba* speak for many when they acknowledge "the advances made in Cuba since the Cuban Revolution in breaking down institutionalized racism," but argue that it is "shortsighted to think that racism has been eliminated."[26] As Cuba enters an undetermined future with the reforms of the past two decades, the unresolved question of race and cubanidad has resurfaced. Although an Afro-Cuban may be just as "Chinese" as a white Cuban, and equally attracted by the economic and cultural "pull" factors of the revitalization project, the difference is often implicitly or explicitly noted.

As contemporary Cuban society experiences a resurgence of racial discrimination toward blacks, especially in the tourist economy, the celebration of ethnic identity can reinforce racial divisions. Alejandro Campos García asserts that the recent claiming of ethnicities such as Asian "has become a tacit strategy to move from blackness as a social marker of status" in Cuba. Campos self-identifies as Afro-Cuban with some Spanish and Chinese background, and he has embarked on a quest to learn about the Asian connection. He recently discovered that his Chinese ancestor was actually female, a great-grandmother. For Campos, claiming an identity based on both his African and Chinese heritage would be a way to resist black/white binary conceptions of race and racial dynamics. An Afro-Asian identity would also "make explicit the complexity of the national ethnic-racialized background" and "challenge simplistic and almost uncontested racialized and ethnic representations."[27]

The multiracial nature of societies in Latin America and the Caribbean, coupled with the fact that the revitalization of Havana's Barrio Chino is government-sponsored, allows for an inclusive project, drawing in white, black, and mixed descendants who have made varying claims on their own Chineseness. The project brings together native Chinese and descendants, providing organization, public space, and in a restricted society, an outlet for personal expression. Alongside the state-directed initiatives percolates another phenomenon, one not marked by Chinese ornaments, chopsticks, and lion dances. A restoration is occurring *around* the touristy pedestrian walkway, and even beyond Havana in other provinces. What transpires in private interactions and among individuals is a matter often outside of the hegemonic construction of a Chinese Cuban identity. Second-, third-, and fourth-generation descendants of Chinese, by taking advantage of special economic opportunities and learning about and participating in Chinese traditions, are claiming an ethnic and cultural heritage and redefining themselves. In the process, they are ultimately forging new spaces along the margins, where the expression of identity and the satisfaction of intellectual curiosity may develop.

Rather than being restored to an approximation of what it once was, Havana's Chinatown is being remade into something new, both out of demographic and economic necessity. In this manner the Barrio Chino continues to evolve, as have other Chinatowns. In a different political and economic context, Chinese migration to Cuba would likely reflect the types of changes that have occurred elsewhere in the diaspora. Lisa Lowe points out that "rather than representing a fixed, discrete culture, 'Chinatown' is itself the very emblem of shifting demographics, languages, and populations."[28] In the 1950s, the composition of the Barrio Chino was similar to that of other "bachelor society" Chinatowns in cities such as San Francisco and New York. These Chinatowns have since been transformed due to a continual flow of migrants from mainland China (especially Fujian), Hong Kong, and Taiwan, as well as movement of original settlers to the suburbs.[29] More elderly Chinese have renewed transnational connections through a return to their Chinese village, some for the first time in fifty years, and some permanently.[30]

The degree to which any new Chinese entering Cuba will reinforce the state's urban renewal of the Barrio Chino remains an open question. As China-Cuba relations and niches for entrepreneurs grow, so does the possibility for renewed migration flows (albeit on a smaller scale). In February 2008, the Cuban National Assembly elected Raúl Castro to succeed Fidel as president of Cuba. Observers of all political leanings anxiously watch for changes, if any. Whether Cuba will follow the "China model" of transition to a market economy is unclear. But the relationship between the two nations will shape future migration trends, and the revolutionary history of the Chinese in Cuba will continue to be invoked as China plays a significant role in Cuba's present and future.

Chinese Migrants in Cuban History and National Identity

Since 1959, Cuban academics have approached scholarly research as designed to serve the greater needs of revolutionary society. In general, Cuban authors make a direct connection between the ideological aspirations of independence leader José Martí, the struggles on the ground, and their culmination in the anti-imperialist Revolution of 1959. Studies of the Chinese in Cuba have likewise been filtered through a lens of anti-imperialism, national unity, and revolutionary solidarity.[31] Cuban scholarship emphasizes the ideological link between nineteenth-century Chinese "freedom fighters" and twentieth-century immigrants who became involved in leftist politics in Cuba. Exemplary of this theme is Juan Jiménez Pastrana's 1963 book *Los chinos en las luchas por la liberación cubana (1847–1930)*, which examines Chinese participation in the struggles for Cuban liberation from slavery, from colonialism, and from U.S. imperialism.

Today, the history of the Chinese in Cuba has emerged from the sidelines of both academia and popular culture. The story of Chinese coolies and freedom fighters is being recovered and highlighted as an integral component of the story of the nation, with an emphasis on culture. Alongside the government-sponsored revival, the University of Havana has established the Cátedra de Estudios sobre la Inmigración China en Cuba (Chair of Studies on Chinese Immigration in Cuba). The prestigious Fundación Fernando Ortiz has published books and pamphlets on the Chinese, Japanese, and Korean presence for a series on the different ethnic components of a transcultural nation.[32] When Mayra Montero's novel *Como un mensajero tuyo* (translated as *The Messenger*) became available to Cubans in 2001, the fictionalized account of internationally acclaimed opera singer Enrico Caruso and his mulatto Chinese Cuban mistress, set in the Barrio Chino of 1920s Havana, generated a buzz among its residents.[33] These publications have stimulated new interest in the Chinese in Cuba, especially in the provinces. Books published in Cuba remain one of the few remaining products that are affordable for Cubans who only earn the non-convertible Cuban peso. Cuba maintains a high literacy rate, and with the lack of varied programming on state-run television and limited Internet access, many Cubans are avid readers who flood the annual book fair. At the 2012 Min Chih Tang celebration, Cubans from across the island presented local research on Chinese communities and reports on restoration efforts.[34]

Far from the state-sponsored revitalization of the Barrio Chino, militia founder and artist Pedro Eng Herrera's home in Guanabacoa, on the outskirts of Havana, is a tangible expression of his Cuban revolutionary national identity. A mural pays homage to heroes of Cuban independence and revolution, with a special emphasis on the Chinese in these battles. Born in 1935, Eng was raised primarily by his Chinese father after his Cuban mother died when he was only eighteen months old. He learned Chinese painting and language growing up, incorporating calligraphy into his artwork. Eng's work epitomizes how an overarching national ideology of cubanidad incorporates different ethnic and cultural identities. His walls are adorned with what he calls "Cuban paintings with Chinese themes," such as a hybrid portrait of Guanyin as the Virgin Mary sitting on a lotus in a Cuban landscape with a palm tree.[35] Well before the current revitalization of the Barrio Chino, Pedro Eng dutifully engaged in the work of recording Chinese Cuban history.

The natural flow of Pedro Eng's paintings evokes a history of cultural syncretism, while deemphasizing Cuban resistance to the Chinese presence. From the time Chinese first arrived in Cuba (in 1847), attitudes toward them ranged from sympathy to aversion, as they became the subject of intense debates among planters and politicians. Would docile Asian contract laborers be the answer to the impending crisis of abolition? Or, as others suggested, would they bring danger and vice to Cuban shores? Chinese were simultaneously promoted as efficient workers for progress and prosperity and criticized as harmful to the physical and moral well-being of the nation. Nineteenth-century Creole elites such as José Antonio Saco laid the foundations for the long-standing argument that inherent cultural differences made the Chinese useful as a temporary measure, but, in the long term, unassimilable into Cuban culture and society.

Thus, despite recognition of Chinese heroic and selfless acts on behalf of Cuban independence, new Chinese immigrants were not called upon to populate the nation. To the contrary, at the outset of the Cuban republic in 1902, Chinese laborers were excluded, portrayed as "aliens" to be expunged rather than incorporated into the national body. Anti-Chinese discourse and discriminatory legislation in Cuba echoed the rest of Latin America and the Caribbean with its focus on sanitation and hygiene, morality, and unfair competition.

Still, after the end of the abominable coolie trade, the Chinese who settled in Cuba encountered less discrimination than elsewhere in the Americas. During times of economic depression, Asians became a highly visible target of working-class resentment in places such as Peru, which witnessed the massacre of Chinese laborers in 1881 and the government-ordered demolition of

Pedro Eng Herrera's house in Guanabacoa, Cuba. (Photograph by author)

the Chinese quarter in Lima in 1909, and Jamaica, which became the scene of anti-Chinese riots in 1918, 1938, and 1965. Sinophobia reached even greater extremes in the Mexican context, where a growing anti-foreignism and anti-imperialism converged with the Revolution of 1910. Against a backdrop of revolutionary nationalism, a concentration of Chinese in Mexico's northern regions made them especially vulnerable to a sustained anti-Chinese campaign. The purge of the Chinese from northern Mexico in 1931 amounted to a full-blown attempt to cleanse the nation.[36]

In Cuba, Chinese were at least nominally incorporated into a conception of raceless nationhood. Chinese participation in Cuba's independence struggles and formation of interracial marriages and other alliances were key to this process. Incorporation into the Cuban citizenry began with the first Chinese who moved out of indenture in the late nineteenth century and continued with the new migrants and their children through the post–World War II era. Members of the generation of Cuban-born Chinese, encompassing those with two Chinese parents and those of mixed descent, played a significant role in local integration. Growing up as *chinos cubanos*, they had been educated in Cuba and were Cuban citizens. Yet, their Chineseness remained active through evening language classes, participation in associations, and stories told at dinnertime. Some of them, such as Antonio Chuffat through his essays and Napoleón Seuc through his legal consultations, became strong advocates for the Chinese Cuban community.

The Cuban Revolution of 1959, provoking the flight of upper- and middle-class Chinese and the end of new immigration, had an unexpected consequence for Chinese national belonging. On the one hand, Chinese ethnic identities became even more tenuous. When Cuba embarked on a socialist revolution, the declaration of the end of institutional racism held the promise of better treatment for ethnic minorities, in particular Afro-Cubans. The material and ideological needs of the revolutionary project, however, subsumed expressions of ethnicity in the name of national unity and class struggle. All supporters of the revolution were Cubans, regardless of phenotype. State revolutionary ideology and the loss of small businesses made it difficult, if not impossible, for Chinese and their descendants to actively engage in ethnic practices. On the other hand, unlike the situation in the United States, Chinese were not excluded from cultural citizenship in Cuba. The Chinese who remained on the island are simply never asked by fellow Cubans, "Where are you from?"

The collected histories in this book demonstrate nuances and layers in Chinese migration to Cuba from the middle of the nineteenth century to the present. As such, at each corner, they overturn images of Chinese migrants that have dominated historiography and literature and demonstrate the long, uneven process of becoming Cuban. The image of the Chinese migrant as an "in-between" category (between black and white, between slave and free) is undermined by coolies' testimony that they were actually treated worse than slaves. The image of the Chinese coolie as victim-turned-patriot is tempered by evidence of coolie self-interest and profiteering from the system. The image of standoffish Chinese scorning black slaves is complicated by Afro-

Asian families that developed soon after indenture. The image of a clannish bachelor Chinatown is undermined by the transnational lives that Chinese men maintained with their home villages and families. The image of Chinese merchants fleeing Castro's Cuba is countered by one of revolutionary Chinese Cuban militiamen storming the Guomindang building. Looking from the ground up, it is clear that the Chinese have been central to Cuban history from the moment of their arrival, in particular to the linked questions of race, labor, and citizenship in the postemancipation Caribbean world.

On my first trip to Cuba in March 1999, I met Mitzi Espinosa Luis, who immediately told me the story of her Chinese grandfather, Francisco Luis, and his two daughters in Xinhui, China—a story of transpacific migration, family, and separation. Although she has distant memories of her grandfather, Mitzi has always maintained a strong attachment to her Chinese heritage. In 2001, at a Chinese New Year's celebration in the Barrio Chino, Mitzi came one step closer to reconnecting with her grandfather's past when she met two elderly native Chinese, Felipe and Santiago Luis, with the same surname and from the same village. The ninety-seven-year-old Felipe, born in 1903, was about the same age as Mitzi's grandfather would have been. Through a fictive kinship for fellow villagers, Felipe and Santiago Luis came to consider Mitzi a granddaughter.

Later that year, armed with copies of old photos and letters from the Lui family in Daze, the market town nearest to Francisco Luis's village, I embarked on a journey to try to locate his descendants in China. With the assistance of the local Overseas Chinese Affairs Office, I met both of his Chinese daughters, Baoqing and Mali, as well as their children and grandchildren. When I visited their house, I was amazed to find old photos of Francisco Luis and his Cuban daughters hanging on the wall, attesting to the endurance of the family connection. Communication between the Chinese sisters and Cuban sisters resumed, with the grandchildren taking an active role in translating and sending e-mail messages.

While many Cuban youth dream of going to the United States, Mitzi Espinosa Luis had always wanted to travel to China while growing up. In May 2009, Mitzi's dream to meet her Chinese relatives became reality. At an international conference on the Chinese diaspora held in Guangzhou, Mitzi's story attracted the interest of a small group of scholars, among them Huang Zhuocai, whose own father had lived in Cuba. We hired a minivan and driver and descended upon Lui Village. Francisco Luis's two Chinese daughters had both died since my last visit, but their husbands, children, and grand-

(left) Francisco Luis's Chinese daughters, Mali and Baoqing, in Lui Village, Xinhui, China, August 2001. (Photograph by author)

(right) Francisco Luis's Cuban daughters in front of his house in Cienfuegos, Cuba, March 2002. (Photograph by author)

children gathered at the entrance gate to meet Mitzi. The relatives showered Mitzi with *hongbao* (red envelopes) and questions, filtered through Cantonese, Mandarin, and English to Spanish. We visited Francisco Luis's ancestral home, finding an old trunk with the initials "F. L." filled with Western-style clothing. At the family shrine, which includes tablets for Lui Fan's Cuban children and grandchildren, Mitzi made an offering.

Reaching even further back into Chinese Cuban history, I learned the story of indentured laborer Pastor Pelayo when I met two of his Afro-Cuban grandsons in Cienfuegos. As I strolled down the dusty streets of the former Chinese neighborhood with the Pelayo brothers, they shared their family history with me. The dilapidated skeletons of Chinese shops and associations form a stark contrast between the tourist-oriented revitalization of the Barrio Chino in Havana today and the reality of smaller provincial towns, where native Chinese are scarce. Since then, Blas Pelayo Díaz has refurbished the

Mitzi Espinosa Luis (fourth from right) meeting her Chinese relatives in
Lui Village, Xinhui, China. Huang Zhuocai (far left) is the son of a Chinese
migrant in Cuba. May 2009. (Photograph by author)

grave of his grandfather, who had come to the Spanish colony as a coolie, and
died there as a citizen of the Cuban republic, a leader of the Chinese Cuban
community in Cienfuegos, and the patriarch of a mixed Chinese and African family.

Blas composed an essay chronicling the 1993 landmark visit of China's
President Jiang Zemin to Havana. He compared this diplomatic visit with
that of Chen Lanbin, the Chinese official sent to Cuba in 1874, whose investigation into abuses in the coolie labor system helped to end it. Jiang's visit he
thought equally auspicious, representing hope for improved diplomatic and
economic ties. Blas wrote: "The moment is significantly emotional: the native at my side yells immediately in Cantonese 'Forever China!' Even though
I do not know that language, perhaps out of ethnic instinct and solidarity,
I repeat it in Spanish. In another very old native, I was surprised to see his
tired eyes filled with tears of emotion and joy."[37]

Chinese Character Glossary

The glossary includes the Chinese characters for the names of local people, places, organizations and institutions, and publications and for the terms that are significant for this study.

PEOPLE

Bu Tak, José (Hu De)	湖德
Chen Lanbin	陈蓝彬
Chi Casio, Federico (Zhu Jiazhao)	朱家兆
Dong Fangcheng	董方诚
Eng Herrera, Pedro (Wu Dizhou)	吴帝胄
Guan Gong	关公
Guanyin	观音
He Xuren	何许人
Huang Dingzhi	黄鼎之
Huang Zhuocai	黄卓才
Huie Ley, Fermín (Xu Yueren)	许悦任
Li, Luis (Li Juzhi)	李巨之
Li Kent (Li Kunyu)	李崑玉
Lin Datian	林达天
Lin Gengsheng	林更盛
Liu Chongmin	刘重民
Liu Kongjiu	刘孔就
Lü (Lui) Baoqing	吕宝庆
Lü Yuebao (Lui Guipó)	吕月保
Lü Yue'er (Lui Guiguí)	吕月儿
Lü (Lui) Yueying	吕月英
Lui Cuan Chong (Lü Qiantong)	吕钳统
Lui Fan (Lü Fanxiang/Francisco Luis)	吕番象
Mok, Juan (Mo Youping)	莫右平
Peng Zemin	彭泽民
Su Leng, Julio (Su Zilun)	苏子伦
Su Xingbo	苏星波
Tung Kun Sen (Dong Gongcheng/Pastor Pelayo)	董功城
Wong, Francisco (Huang Baoshi)	黄宝世
Wong, José (Huang Taobai)	黄淘白

253

PLACES

Dulian	独联
Enping	恩平
Jiujiang (Kow Kong)	九江
Kaiping	开平
Laishui	来水
Nanhai	南海
Panyu	番禺
Shunde	顺德
Taishan	台山
Xinhui	新会
Zhongshan	中山

ORGANIZATIONS AND INSTITUTIONS

Baohuanghui	保皇会
Chee Kung Tong (Zhigongtang)	致公堂
Guba Huaqiao Shehui Zhuyi Tongmeng	古巴华侨社会主义同盟
Guba Huaqiao Yonghu Gongnong Geming Datongmeng	古巴华侨拥护工农革命大同盟
Guomindang	国民党
Hongmen Minzhidang	洪门民治党
Jiujiang Qiaoshang Gongyiyuan	九江侨商工医院
Lingnan Daxue	领南大学
Lugu Huaqiao Kangri Houyuan	旅古华侨抗日后援
Lun Con Cun Sol (Longgang Gongsuo)	龙岗公所
On Ten Tong (Andingtang)	安定堂
Peizheng Zhongxue	培正中学
Quanmei Banghua Lianhe Zonghui	全美帮华联合总会
Sanmin Tuantihui	三民团体会
Sanminzhuyi Qingniantuan	三民主义青年团
Tongmenghui	同盟会
Tung Wah Hospital (Donghua Yiyuan)	东花医院
Zhonghua Yinyue Gongsuo	中华音乐公所
Zhonghua Zonghuiguan	中华总会馆
Zhonghua Zongshanghui	中华总商会
Zongli Yamen	总理衙门

PUBLICATIONS

Gongnong Husheng	工农呼声
Hoi Men Kong Po (Kaiming Gongbao)	开明公报
Kwong Wah Po (Guanghuabao)	光华报
Lianhe Yuekan	联合月刊
Man Sen Yat Po (Minsheng Ribao)	民生日报
Wah Man Sion Po (Huawen Shangbao)	华文商报

TERMS

gaizu	改组
Haiqi	海圻
hanjian	汉奸
huagong	华工
huamin	华民
huaqiao	华侨
huaqiao shenshang	华侨绅商
huaren	华人
huashang	华商
huayi	华裔
huiguan	会馆
kejia (Hakka)	客家
qiaojuan	侨眷
qiaokan	侨刊
qiaoxiang	侨乡
shantang	善棠
Shik Yan Kuey (Xue Ren Gui)	薛仁貴
shoushenggua	寿生寡
shuangduan yanjiu	双端研究
tongxiangren	同乡人
xiangyi weiming	相依为命
yige dai yige	一个带一个
zhengyi	正义
zhongguo renmin	中国人民
zhongxi xuetang	中西学堂

Notes

AFP   Atkins Family Papers, Massachusetts Historical Society, Boston
AHPC   Archivo Histórico Provincial de Cienfuegos
ANC   Archivo Nacional de Cuba, Havana
CCR   *The Cuba Commission Report*
exp.   expediente
ICEA   Instituto Cubano de Estabilización de Azúcar
leg.   legajo
USNA   United States National Archives, Washington, D.C.

INTRODUCTION

1. Pan, *Sons of the Yellow Emperor*, 43.

2. Okihiro, *Margins and Mainstreams*, 42. Recent perspectives from Asian American studies that examine the connections among indigenous, African, and Asian peoples in the Americas include Lowe, "Intimacies of Four Continents"; Metzger, "Ripples in the Seascape;" and Yun, *Coolie Speaks*.

3. Scholarship on indentured labor in the British Caribbean includes Tinker, *New System of Slavery*; Look Lai, *Indentured Labor*; Laurence, *Question of Labour*; and Kale, *Fragments of Empire*. For foundational work on the coolie system by Cuban historians, see Deschamps Chapeaux and Pérez de la Riva, *Contribución a la historia de la gente sin historia*; and Pérez de la Riva, *El barracón y otros ensayos*. The publication of Juan Pérez de la Riva's comprehensive *Los culíes chinos* was delayed until 2000, due to the strained nature of Sino-Cuban relations. Other major studies of slavery and indentured labor in Cuba include Knight, *Slave Society in Cuba*; Moreno Fraginals, *El ingenio*; Helly, *Idéologie et ethnicité*; Scott, *Slave Emancipation in Cuba*; Hu-DeHart, "Chinese Coolie Labour"; Dorsey, "Identity, Rebellion, and Social Justice;" Yun, *Coolie Speaks*; and Narvaez, "Chinese Coolies in Cuba and Peru."

4. See Corbitt, *Study of the Chinese*; and Herrera Jerez and Castillo Santana, *De la memoria a la vida pública* for studies of the Chinese in Cuba during the republican period. Founder of the Chinese militia Pedro Eng Herrera and former diplomat Mauro García Triana have collaborated with Gregor Benton to produce an important work on the history of the Chinese in Cuba from the coolie trade to the present, providing insights from their own experiences and from oral testimony of Chinese Cubans. See García Triana and Eng Herrera, *Chinese in Cuba*.

5. Holloway, *Immigrants on the Land*.

6. Look Lai, *Indentured Labor*, 105–6.

7. Omi and Winant, *Racial Formation in the United States*. Examples of the

potential of comparative ethnic studies include Espiritu, *Asian American Pan-ethnicity*; Foley, *White Scourge*; Molina, *Fit to Be Citizens?*; Kurashige, *Shifting Grounds of Race*; and Briones, *Jim and Jap Crow*. Vijay Prashad, *Everybody Was Kung Fu Fighting*, demonstrates cultural and political interactions between blacks and Asians over space and time. For a collection of essays that highlights cross-racial connections from an interdisciplinary and global perspective, see the special issue on "Afro-Asia" in *Afro-Hispanic Review* 27.1 (2008), guest editors Evelyn Hu-DeHart and Kathleen López.

8. See Hu-DeHart, "Multiculturalism in Latin American Studies," for a discussion of this lacuna and a review of recent studies on Asians and Middle Eastern migrants in the region.

9. Key immigration studies by Latin Americanists include Holloway, *Immigrants on the Land*; Andrews, *Blacks and Whites in São Paulo*; and Levine, *Tropical Diaspora*. Latin Americanists have recently embraced transnational and comparative approaches to their study of European immigrants. See Moya, *Cousins and Strangers*, for Spanish in Argentina; and Baily, *Immigrants in the Lands of Promise*, for Italians in Buenos Aires and New York City.

10. For studies of race, citizenship, and national identity in Cuba, see Helg, *Our Rightful Share*; Ferrer, *Insurgent Cuba*; and De la Fuente, *Nation for All*.

11. Scholarship on Asians in Latin America and the Caribbean that tackles questions of race and citizenship includes multiple articles by Evelyn Hu-DeHart, most recently "Indispensable Enemy or Convenient Scapegoat?"; Lesser, *Negotiating National Identity*; Rustomji-Kerns, *Encounters*; McKeown, *Chinese Migrant Networks and Cultural Change*; Rénique, "Race, Region, and Nation"; Wilson, *Chinese in the Caribbean*; Siu, *Memories of a Future Home*; López-Calvo, *Imaging the Chinese*; Lee-Loy, *Searching for Mr. Chin*; Lausent-Herrera, "Tusans (*tusheng*) and the Changing Chinese Community in Peru"; Look Lai and Tan Chee-Beng, *Chinese in Latin America and the Caribbean*; Romero, *Chinese in Mexico*; Schiavone Camacho, *Chinese Mexicans*; Rivas, "Negotiating Mixed Race"; and Delgado, *Making the Chinese Mexican*. See also the special issue on "Asians in the Americas: Transculturations and Power," *Amerasia Journal* 28.2 (2002), guest editors Lane Ryo Hirabayashi and Evelyn Hu-DeHart. Theresa Alfaro-Velcamp's study *So Far from Allah* examines these questions for Middle Easterners in Mexico.

12. Foundational works in U.S. immigration studies focus on the concept of "assimilation" and explanations for alienation and poverty among immigrants. See Park, "Human Migration and the Marginal Man"; and Handlin, *Uprooted*. Important works within Asian American studies on these themes include Paul Siu, *Chinese Laundryman*; Saxton, *Indispensable Enemy*; Nee and De Bary, *Longtime Californ'*; Chan, *Entry Denied*; and Yung, *Unbound Feet*. For a useful discussion of the enduring paradigm of "assimilation" into a "melting pot" and the different assumptions underlying immigration studies, see Hsu, *Dreaming of Gold*, 5–11.

13. For transnational approaches to the study of migration, see Rouse, "Mexican Migration and the Social Space of Postmodernism"; and Basch, Glick Schiller, and Szanton Blanc, *Nations Unbound*. Scholars suggest the need for more historical studies demonstrating <u>how</u> transnational networks were experienced, especially

among migrants to places other than the United States. See Foner, "What's New about Transnationalism?"; Guarnizo and Smith, "Locations of Transnationalism."

14. Skinner, *Chinese Society in Thailand*; Wickberg, *Chinese in Philippine Life*; Wang Gungwu, *China and the Chinese Overseas*.

15. Irick, *Ch'ing Policy toward the Coolie Trade*; Yen, *Coolies and Mandarins*.

16. Hsu, *Dreaming of Gold*; McKeown, *Chinese Migrant Networks*. Other recent works in Asian American and Chinese diaspora history that incorporate transnational methodologies include Yong Chen, *Chinese San Francisco*; and Azuma, *Between Two Empires*. Analyses of Japanese migration and return migration that complicate national boundaries include Hirabayashi, Kikumura-Yano, and Hirabayashi, *New Worlds, New Lives*; Tsuda, *Strangers in the Ethnic Homeland*; and Lesser, *Searching for Home Abroad*.

17. In a census after the end of the coolie trade in 1877, only 66 Chinese women were counted, compared with 40,261 Chinese men. The highest numbers appear in the 1953 census: 484 Chinese women represented 4 percent of the total Chinese population. Numerous accounts of the Chinese in Cuba mention the lack of women imported for prostitution. See, for example, Corbitt, *Study of the Chinese*, 90.

18. Chan, *Asian Americans*, 103–7.

19. Mazumdar, "'What Happened to the Women?'"

20. Chen Da, *Emigrant Communities in South China*. Major Chinese journals that include *qiaoxiang* research are *Huaqiao Huaren Yanjiu* (Overseas Chinese research) and *Huaqiao Huaren Lishi Yanjiu* (Overseas Chinese history studies).

21. Peterson, "Overseas Chinese Studies," 116; Huang Zisheng, "Lun qiaoxiang yanjiu de xianzhuang ji yiyi." Through fieldwork carried out in Wenzhou and Shenzhen, Li Minghuan links sending and receiving societies in a study of the role of Chinese immigrant associations in the Netherlands. See Li, "We Need Two Worlds."

22. Examples include Putnam, *Company They Kept*; Scott, *Degrees of Freedom*; and McGuinness, *Path of Empire*. See Erika Lee, "Orientalisms in the Americas," for a useful discussion of a hemispheric framework for the study of Asian Americans.

23. Lok Siu foregrounds the continuities and ruptures of "diasporic citizenship" among the Chinese in Panama. See Lok Siu, *Memories of a Future Home*. Adrian Burgos Jr. follows Latino baseball players as they negotiated the shifting color line in the United States, Cuba, and Puerto Rico, and Frank Guridy traces cultural encounters between Afro-Cubans and African Americans within a hemispheric frame as both groups negotiated U.S. imperialism and racial discrimination. Burgos, *Playing America's Game*; Guridy, *Forging Diaspora*.

24. Lucy Cohen, *Chinese in the Post–Civil War South*; Jung, *Coolies and Cane*.

25. For a description of this distinction, see Takaki, *Strangers from a Different Shore*, 35–36.

26. Yun, *Coolie Speaks*, 114.

27. Okihiro, *Margins and Mainstreams*, 47–48.

28. For a discussion of underdeveloped areas in Asian American studies, see

Okihiro, *Columbia Guide to Asian American History*, 219–26. For works set in rural areas, see Lucy Cohen, *Chinese in the Post–Civil War South*; Lydon, *Chinese Gold*; Chan, *This Bittersweet Soil*; and Okihiro, *Cane Fires*. Recent scholarship also focuses on the Chinese in midwestern cities. See Ling, *Chinese St. Louis* and *Chinese Chicago*.

CHAPTER 1

1. Meagher, *Coolie Trade*, 193–201.

2. Holt, *Problem of Freedom*.

3. Look Lai, *Indentured Labor*, 1–18.

4. For opposition to the indentured labor system from diverse social elements, see Look Lai, *Indentured Labor*, 154–87.

5. Shepherd, *Maharani's Misery*.

6. Meagher, *Coolie Trade*, 245–73.

7. For the nineteenth-century sugar revolution in Cuba, see Knight, *Slave Society in Cuba*, 25–46. For Cuban sugar production statistics, see Moreno Fraginals, *El ingenio*, 3:35–38; and Schmidt-Nowara, *Empire and Antislavery*, 4.

8. Knight, *Slave Society in Cuba*, 22. Population statistics are rounded to the nearest hundred.

9. Childs, *1812 Aponte Rebellion*.

10. "La Escalera" takes its name from the ladder, used as an instrument of torture during interrogation. The free mulatto and poet Gabriel de la Concepción Valdés, or Plácido, was implicated as a leader. Although later historians speculated whether or not Spain fabricated the conspiracy, Robert Paquette concludes that several distinct plots developed with an aim toward emancipation and independence. See Paquette, *Sugar Is Made with Blood*.

11. Helly, Introduction, 7.

12. Ibid., 5–8.

13. Pérez de la Riva, *Los culíes chinos*, 43.

14. Moreno Fraginals, *El ingenio*, 1:301–6.

15. Zanetti and García, *Sugar and Railroads*, 120–21; Pérez de la Riva, *Los culíes chinos*, 45–47.

16. Helly, Introduction, 9.

17. Pérez de la Riva, *Los culíes chinos*, 54–56.

18. For attempts to contract Africans, see ibid., 49–51. For arguments for the yellow trade over the black trade, see the Spanish economist Mariano Torrente's 1853 bilingual volume, *Memoria sobre la esclavitud*; and Pérez de la Riva, *Los culíes chinos*, 68–69.

19. In 1859 the governor of Yucatán asked 100 to 300 pesos for each prisoner; the following year, 160 pesos for males and 120 pesos for females age sixteen to fifty and 80 pesos for children age ten to fifteen. Pérez de la Riva, *Los culíes chinos*, 52.

20. Ibid., 51–54. The purchase price of Yucatecans ranged from 40 to 160 Mexican pesos (20 to 80 Cuban pesos) and the cost of transportation to Havana ranged from 12 to 15 pesos.

21. Pérez de la Riva, *Los culíes chinos*, 61.

22. Knight, *Slave Society in Cuba*, 116.

23. Pérez de la Riva, *Los culíes chinos*, 62.

24. For the Junta de Fomento and the first Chinese to arrive in Havana, see ibid., 60–63; and Hu-DeHart, "Chinese Coolie Labour," 69.

25. Erenchun, *Anales de la isla de Cuba*, 1329–33, reproduces a chart from the 18 September 1859 issue of *Diario de la Marina* containing statistics on colonos asiáticos: the names and origins of ships, days of navigation, and numbers embarking and disembarking from the first shipload in 1847 until 18 August 1859.

26. Pérez de la Riva, *Los culíes chinos*, 63.

27. Scholars estimate even higher numbers than the official entries recorded at ports. Pérez de la Riva suggests a total of 150,000 to Cuba, including contraband and Chinese from California. Meagher estimates 109,000 arriving in Peru. Pérez de la Riva, *Los culíes chinos*, 179; Rodríguez Pastor, *Hijos del Celeste Imperio*, 26; Meagher, *Coolie Trade*, 222.

28. Yun, *Coolie Speaks*, 17.

29. Hu-DeHart, "Chinese Coolie Labour," 69–70; Helly, Introduction, 9.

30. Pérez de la Riva, *Los culíes chinos*, 63.

31. Ibid., 66.

32. Meagher, *Coolie Trade*, 149. Statistics are from 1847 to 1 September 1873.

33. Hu-DeHart, "Chinese Coolie Labour," 75.

34. Yun, *Coolie Speaks*, 27–28.

35. *CCR*, 42–43.

36. Meagher, *Coolie Trade*, 188. For mutinies aboard coolie ships, see Pérez de la Riva, 154–58; and Meagher, *Coolie Trade*, 185–92.

37. For the link between imperialism and mass emigration from China in the mid-nineteenth century, see Kuhn, *Chinese among Others*, 107–52.

38. Chen Mengyu, "Guba huaqiao shenghuo gaikuang," 7; Glick, *Sojourners and Settlers*, 188–89; Pérez de la Riva, *Los culíes chinos*, 118; Kuhn, *Chinese among Others*, 39–40.

39. Their counterparts in Africa were also called *corredores* (runners). Hu-DeHart, "Chinese Coolie Labour," 75.

40. *CCR*, 37.

41. Meagher, *Coolie Trade*, 124.

42. Jiménez Pastrana, *Los chinos en las luchas*, 27.

43. Yun, *Coolie Speaks*, 64–71.

44. Corbitt, *Study of the Chinese*, 15–16, citing Libro 195, pp. 90–91 and Libro 196, p. 62, Junta de Fomento, ANC; Rodríguez San Pedro, *Legislación ultramarina*, 2:442. For the lack of female testimony before the 1874 commission, see Yun, *Coolie Speaks*, 63–64. She notes one case in which Chinese women signed a mass petition together.

45. Jiménez Pastrana, *Los chinos en la historia de Cuba*, 57–58.

46. Pérez de la Riva, *Los culíes chinos*, 190. Pérez de la Riva received information about the life of Carmen Montalvo from her descendants. She died in 1954 at the age of one hundred fifteen.

47. *CCR*, 48.

48. Porter, *Industrial Cuba*, 77.

49. Helly, Introduction, 9–10. For a sample contract in Spanish and Chinese, see *CCR*, Appendix.

50. Bergad, *Cuban Rural Society*, 252.

51. Pérez de la Riva, *Los culíes chinos*, 15.

52. Helly, Introduction, 22. *The Cuba Commission Report* documents ample evidence of abuse and breach of contract.

53. Cosme Baños, *Los chinos en Regla*, 25–26. Two were between fifteen and twenty; one between forty-one and fifty; one between fifty-one and sixty; one over sixty-one; and eighty-eight age unknown.

54. *CCR*, 99.

55. Levis, *Diary of a Spring Holiday*, 72–73.

56. "Planta de la Barracón, Ingenio 'San José,'" June 1875, ANC.

57. *CCR*, 56–57. During China's republican period, Xiangshan was renamed Zhongshan, after Chinese revolutionary leader Sun Zhongshan (Sun Yat-sen).

58. Levis, *Diary of a Spring Holiday*, 49.

59. McHatton-Ripley, *From Flag to Flag*, 185.

60. *CCR*, 51.

61. Ibid., 51, 57.

62. Ibid., 57–58.

63. Ibid., 57.

64. Hu-DeHart, "Chinese Coolie Labour," 86; Yun, *Coolie Speaks*, 159–62. For a comparison of racial and ethnic divisions between Chinese and others in Cuba and Peru, see Narvaez, "Chinese Coolies in Cuba and Peru," 139–43. Chinese came into conflict with Afro-Peruvian and Andean workers in Peru. See Stewart, *Chinese Bondage in Peru*, 100–101.

65. *CCR*, 98.

66. Ibid., 66.

67. McHatton-Ripley, *From Flag to Flag*, 188–89.

68. Narvaez, "Chinese Coolies in Cuba and Peru," 129–46.

69. *CCR*, 47–48.

70. Yun, *Coolie Speaks*, 154–55.

71. *CCR*, 51; Yun, *Coolie Speaks*, 152–53.

72. Howe, *Trip to Cuba*, 71–72.

73. Hazard, *Cuba with Pen and Pencil*, 267.

74. Ibid., 263.

75. Zanetti and García, *Sugar and Railroads*, 121–24.

76. For an elaboration of Chinese population in the Eastern Department according to different censuses taken before 1868, see Abdala Pupo, *Los chinos en el oriente cubano*, 39–47.

77. Hazard, *Cuba with Pen and Pencil*, 449.

78. Abdala Pupo, *Los chinos en el oriente cubano*, 57.

79. Ibid., 54–57.

80. Ibid., 59–60.

81. Pérez de la Riva, *Los culíes chinos*, 260.

82. Hazard, *Cuba with Pen and Pencil*, 149.

83. Levis, *Diary of a Spring Holiday*, 104–5.

84. Dana, *To Cuba and Back*, 63–64.

85. McHatton-Ripley, *From Flag to Flag*, 183–84.

86. Atkins, *Sixty Years*, 3.

87. Yun, *Coolie Speaks*, 61–62.

88. *CCR*, 74.

89. For discussion of the coolie contract and regulations in Cuba, see Jiménez Pastrana, *Los chinos en las luchas*, 33–50; Corbitt, *Study of the Chinese*, 66–72; Hu-DeHart, "Chinese Coolie Labour," 70–75; and Pérez de la Riva, *Los culíes chinos*, 203–25.

90. Pérez de la Riva, *Los culíes chinos*, 210–15. The royal decree of 22 March 1854, entitled "Reglamento para la Introducción y Régimen de los Colonos Españoles, Chinos o Yucatecos en la Isla de Cuba" (Regulations for the Introduction and Control of Spanish, Chinese, and Yucatecan Colonists on the Island of Cuba) is reproduced in Jiménez Pastrana, *Los chinos en la historia de Cuba*, 161–74.

91. Scott, *Slave Emancipation in Cuba*, 13–14.

92. Hu-DeHart, "Chinese Coolie Labour," 75.

93. Yun, *Coolie Speaks*, 125–27. Not until 1873 did colonial regulations stipulate that the employer must deliver contracts and *cédulas* of deceased Chinese to authorities for cancelation.

94. For examples of cédulas being withheld, see *CCR*, 82–83. A sample *cédula de vecindad*, or letter of domicile, from 1869 appears in *CCR*, Appendix.

95. Yun, *Coolie Speaks*, 111–33.

96. *CCR*, 74.

97. The 6 July 1860 regulations, entitled "Reglamento para la Introducción de Trabajadores Chinos en la Isla de Cuba" (Regulations for the Introduction of Chinese Workers to the Island of Cuba), are reproduced in Jiménez Pastrana, *Los chinos en la historia de Cuba*, 176–92. An English-language version appears in *CCR*, 130–40.

98. *CCR*, 74.

99. Porter, *Industrial Cuba*, 77–78.

100. For coolie resistance in Cuba, see Jiménez Pastrana, *Los chinos en las luchas*, 44–45; Helly, *Idéologie et ethnicité*, 211–30; Dorsey, "Identity, Rebellion, and Social Justice"; and Yun, *Coolie Speaks*. For a comparison of resistance and rebellion among Chinese coolies in Cuba and Peru, see Narvaez, "Chinese Coolies in Cuba and Peru."

101. Recorded suicides in 1862 included 173 Chinese, 130 slaves, and 43 whites out of a total population of 34,050 Chinese, 370,530 slaves, and 756,610 whites. The total population of the island was 1,396,470. Pérez de la Riva, *Los culíes chinos*, 186–9.

102. *CCR*, 50.

103. For suicide as a means of resistance among African slaves and Chinese coolies on Cuban plantations, see Pérez, *To Die in Cuba*, 25–64.

104. *CCR*, 50.

105. Levis, *Diary of a Spring Holiday*, 88.

106. Barnet, *Biography of a Runaway Slave*, 43.

107. *CCR*, 58.

108. Chuffat Latour, *Apunte histórico*, 36.

109. Pérez de la Riva, *Los culíes chinos*, 188; Abdala Pupo, *Los chinos en el oriente cubano*, 67.

110. Pérez, *To Die in Cuba*, 61, citing Saco, "La estadística criminal de Cuba en 1862," *La América* (Madrid), 12 January 1864: 5; Pérez de la Riva, *Los culíes chinos*, 188.

111. Dana, *To Cuba and Back*, 99.

112. Howe, *Trip to Cuba*, 219.

113. Levis, *Diary of a Spring Holiday*, 88–90.

114. Hu-DeHart, "Opium and Social Control," 170. In Peru, the Aspíllagas family imported opium for their plantation coolies. Their suppliers were large international British firms as well as Chinese merchants in Lima. Hu-DeHart, "Opium and Social Control," 178. See also Michael Gonzales, "Resistance among Asian Plantation Workers in Peru," 207.

115. Abdala Pupo, *Los chinos en el oriente cubano*, 61–62.

116. Levis, *Diary of a Spring Holiday*, 89–90.

117. Dorsey, "Identity, Rebellion, and Social Justice," 27.

118. Ibid., 30. For an in-depth analysis of twelve cases of Chinese coolie homicide in Cuba, see ibid.

119. *CCR*, 88. See *CCR*, 85–88 for instances of Chinese accused of crimes and the punishments they received.

120. Dorsey, "Identity, Rebellion, and Social Justice," 30, 39.

121. McHatton-Ripley, *From Flag to Flag*, 171–72.

122. Chinese coolies temporarily took control of plantations in several instances in Peru, where elites received a lesser degree of support from the nascent government and fewer African slaves were present to serve as a buffer against uprisings. Narvaez, "Chinese Coolies in Cuba and Peru," 373–74.

123. Narvaez provides examples of Chinese in Peru receiving permission to go to another plantation to purchase cheese and opium or to spend Sundays in Callao or Lima. Ibid., 163–64.

124. Sagra, *Historia física*, 149–50.

125. Hu-DeHart, "Chinese Coolie Labour," 82.

126. "Resumen por jurisdicciones del padrón general de asiáticos de la Isla, correspondiente al año de 1872," 23 September 1873, *Boletín de Colonización* 1, no. 18 (15 Oct. 1873): 5.

127. Scott, *Slave Emancipation in Cuba*, 101.

128. Abdala Pupo, *Los chinos en el oriente cubano*, 30; citing *El Redactor*, Santiago de Cuba, 9 May 1865.

129. Abdala Pupo, *Los chinos en el oriente cubano*, 30.

130. Corbitt, *Study of the Chinese*, 88, citing *Diario de la Marina*, 6 May 1865, 4 June 1868, 8 May 1869, and 16 May 1871.

131. Helly, Introduction, 25; Zhang, "Guba huagong yu zhonggu jianjiao shimo," 9.

132. Lucy Cohen, *Chinese in the Post–Civil War South*, 46–81; Tchen, *New York before Chinatown*, 227–28.

133. Look Lai, *Indentured Labor*, 193.

134. For Chinese government attitudes toward emigration and policies toward the coolie trade, see Yen, *Coolies and Mandarins*; and Irick, *Ch'ing Policy toward the Coolie Trade*.

135. Yen, *Coolies and Mandarins*, 19–22.

136. Ibid., 77.

137. Helly, Introduction, 11–12.

138. Yen, *Coolies and Mandarins*, 73–80.

139. Ibid., 122–34.

140. Jung, *Coolies and Cane*, 28–33.

141. Irick, *Ch'ing Policy toward the Coolie Trade*; Meagher, *Coolie Trade*, 289–94.

142. Chuffat Latour, *Apunte histórico*, 55–57. Helly, Introduction, 12–14. Today a plaque at the Hotel Telégrafo in Havana commemorates Chen Lanbin's visit.

143. The commission took a total of 1,176 depositions and 1,665 petitions; Yun, *Coolie Speaks*, 60. The resulting report is one of the most unusual sources for the history of indentured labor migration, as it provides detailed testimony from the coolies themselves. Although the government report was published and circulated in English, Lisa Yun offers translations and analysis of several of the petitions in their entirety.

144. *CCR*, 69.

145. Yun, *Coolie Speaks*, 76.

146. Dorsey, "Identity, Rebellion, and Social Justice," 26–27.

147. Yung Wing was well-suited for the commission, as he was from Guangdong Province and proficient in English and in Western law.

148. For the changes in official terminology for Chinese overseas, see Yen, *Studies in Modern Overseas Chinese History*, 3–30.

149. For the relevant articles of the 1877 treaty (ratified 6 December 1878) see Chuffat Latour, *Apunte histórico*, 73–79. In October 1879 the Consul General Liu Liang Yuan and Vice Consul Chung Shen Yin (to be based in Matanzas) arrived in Havana. Chuffat Latour, *Apunte histórico*, 79–85.

150. Wilson, *Ambition and Identity*, 96.

151. Hu-DeHart, "Chinese Coolie Labour," 70.

152. Knight, *Slave Society in Cuba*, 119.

153. See Hu-DeHart's overview and analysis of these debates, "Chinese Coolie Labour," 78–83.

154. For a discussion of the terminology used in coolie contracts, see ibid., 70. A sample of an 1866 contract appears in *CCR*, Appendix. The heading in Chinese is *gugong hetong* (labor contract).

155. Pérez de la Riva, *Los culíes chinos*, 12.

156. For a discussion of cases in which Chinese were referred to as property, see Narvaez, "Chinese Coolies in Cuba and Peru," 224–33.

157. Gallenga, *Pearl of the Antilles*, 88.

158. For discussions of the similarities and distinctions between slavery and Chinese indentured labor, see Scott, *Slave Emancipation in Cuba*, 29–35, 109–10; Hu-DeHart, "Chinese Coolie Labour"; Yun, *Coolie Speaks*; and Narvaez, "Chinese Coolies in Cuba and Peru."

159. Pérez de la Riva, *Los culíes chinos*, 261.

160. Meagher, *Coolie Trade*, 298–99.

161. Yun, *Coolie Speaks*, 29, 105–42.

162. Meagher, *Coolie Trade*, 298.

163. Pérez de la Riva, *Los culíes chinos*; Moreno Fraginals, *El ingenio*; Helly, *Idéologie et ethnicité*; Scott, *Slave Emancipation in Cuba*.

164. The work of scholars of slavery and sugar such as Rebecca Scott and Dale Tomich critiques the supposed contradictions between a slave labor force and modern technology. Scott demonstrates that in many ways the use of Chinese indentured laborers abetted the perpetuation of slavery in Cuba. Scott, *Slave Emancipation in Cuba*, 29–35.

165. For specific cases of Chinese using contracts to make demands, see Narvaez "Chinese Coolies in Cuba and Peru," 167–68.

166. Hu-DeHart, "Chinese Coolie Labour," 81.

167. Ibid. Recontracts in Peru similarly demonstrated shorter terms and higher pay. Narvaez, "Chinese Coolies in Cuba and Peru," 410; *CCR*, 78–80.

168. See Scott, *Slave Emancipation in Cuba*, 101–3.

169. Hu-DeHart, "Chinese Coolie Labour," 83.

170. Scott, *Slave Emancipation in Cuba*, 107.

CHAPTER 2

1. For the complex dynamics of the process of gradual emancipation, see Scott, *Slave Emancipation in Cuba*.

2. Moreno Fraginals, *El ingenio*. For a regional study of the impact of the concentration of the sugar industry on economic relations and class structure in Cienfuegos, see Iglesias García, "La concentración azucarera."

3. Bergad, *Cuban Rural Society*, 258–59.

4. Ibid., 282–86. For Spanish immigration to Cuba and its impact on the Cuban economy in the late nineteenth and early twentieth centuries, see Maluquer de Motes, *Nación e inmigración*.

5. According to Pérez de la Riva, precise numerical data are not available for the Chinese who migrated to Cuba from California in the second half of the nineteenth century, as they were registered according to the last port of exit, Mexico or New Orleans. He states that the "Californians" were particularly numerous between 1865 and 1875, reaching up to 5,000, and continued to arrive afterward. Chuffat Latour's descriptions of Chinese merchants from San Francisco and evidence from local merchant registers support the claim for an influx of Chinese who had spent time in the United States. For a discussion of the "Californians," see Pérez de la Riva, *Los culíes chinos*, 177–83, 251–52.

6. Ibid., 192.

7. U.S. War Department, *Report on the Census of Cuba 1899*, 472–75.

8. Ibid, 504–5. Although the 1899 census category of "laborer" included those employed in "agriculture, fisheries, and mining," in Santa Clara it generally referred to agricultural workers.

9. Murray to Atkins, 16 September 1884, Soledad Sugar Co. Records, AFP.

10. Atkins to Murray, 28 May 1884, Soledad Sugar Co. Records, AFP.

11. P. M. Beal to Edwin F. Atkins, 30 June 1887, Soledad Sugar Co. Records, AFP.

12. Murray to Atkins, 17 September 1885, Soledad Sugar Co. Records, AFP.

13. Murray to Atkins, 2 November 1886, Soledad Sugar Co. Records, AFP.

14. Murray to Atkins, 17 December 1885, Soledad Sugar Co. Records, AFP.

15. Atkins to Murray, 30 September 1885, Soledad Sugar Co. Records, AFP.

16. Murray to Atkins, 22 December 1885, 29 December 1885, Soledad Sugar Co. Records, AFP.

17. Murray to Atkins, 18 July 1889, Soledad Sugar Co. Records, AFP.

18. Murray to Atkins, 24 December 1885, Soledad Sugar Co. Records, AFP.

19. Murray to Atkins, 1 July 1884, Soledad Sugar Co. Records, AFP.

20. Atkins to Murray, 23 September 1885, Soledad Sugar Co. Records, AFP.

21. Murray to Atkins, 6 October 1885, Soledad Sugar Co. Records, AFP.

22. Perry, *Shanghai on Strike*. Chinese contractors in California took on a similar role as those in Guangdong; see Chan, *This Bittersweet Soil*, 346–48.

23. *CCR*, 86.

24. Hu-DeHart, "Chinese Coolie Labour," 78.

25. Yun, *Coolie Speaks*, 34.

26. For a discussion of cuadrillas during the coolie period, see Chuffat Latour, *Apunte histórico*, 36–38, 96–102; Corbitt, *Study of the Chinese*, 91; Helly, *Idéologie et ethnicité*, 231–37; and Scott, *Slave Emancipation in Cuba*, 99–101.

27. Hu-DeHart, "Chinese Coolie Labour," 77–78.

28. "Testamento," 9 November 1902, Escritura No. 142, Protocolos José Ramón Entenza, AHPC; "D. Damian Machado con Da. María de la Caridad Pérez Espinosa," No. 14, Folio 284, Tomo 2 (Moderno), Libro de Matrimonio, Registro Civil, AHPC.

29. J. S. Murray to Edwin F. Atkins, 10 April 1890, Soledad Sugar Co. Records, AFP. Further instances of Machado meeting his quotas more consistently than the colonos appear in letters of 9 June 1885, 16 June 1885, 17 April 1890, 24 April 1890, and 7 April 1892.

30. The Wilson-Gorman Tariff Act of 1894 imposed duties of 40 percent on all sugar entering the United States, leading to a decline in profits and production in Cuba and fueling Cuban discontent with Spain's mercantilist policies. Pérez, *Cuba between Empires*, 30–32.

31. Atkins, *Sixty Years*, 109.

32. Murray to Atkins, 26 October 1886, Soledad Sugar Co. Records, AFP.

33. Murray to Atkins, 28 October 1886, Soledad Sugar Co. Records, AFP.

34. Murray to Atkins, 2 November 1886, Soledad Sugar Co. Records, AFP.

35. Murray to Atkins, 16 December 1886, 4 January 1887, Soledad Sugar Co. Records, AFP.

36. J. S. Murray to E. Atkins & Co., 8 January, 11 January, 13 January, 18 January, 20 January, 27 January, 8 February, 9 February, 10 February, 12 February 1887, Soledad Sugar Co. Records, AFP. Murray reported sufficient field hands for the rest of the month, and not until "Holy Week" in April did he mention another shortage.

37. Murray to Atkins, 3 December 1885, Soledad Sugar Co. Records, AFP.

38. Murray to Atkins, 21 September, 28 September 1886, Soledad Sugar Co. Records, AFP. Murray first received news of the arrangement, in which Caledonia would keep one-third of the sugar produced, from a clerk in the Cienfuegos firm Fowler & Co. Later, a Chinese contractor named José told Murray that the amount of sugar that Caledonia would keep was 28 out of every 100 hogsheads produced.

39. Murray to Atkins, 2 December 1886, Soledad Sugar Co. Records, AFP.

40. Chuffat Latour, *Apunte histórico*, 86, 90.

41. Chan, *This Bittersweet Soil*, 345.

42. For a study of the role of food on Soledad Estate, see Pite, "Force of Food."

43. Murray to Atkins, 28 September, 30 September 1886, Soledad Sugar Co. Records, AFP.

44. Murray to Atkins, 6 October 1885, Soledad Sugar Co. Records, AFP.

45. Libro 706, February 1899, Libros del Central Soledad, ICEA, ANC.

46. Lucy Cohen, *Chinese in the Post–Civil War South*, 57.

47. Ibid., 99, 95–101.

48. Murray to Atkins, 25 August 1885, Soledad Sugar Co. Records, AFP.

49. P. M. Beal to Atkins, 18 June 1887, Soledad Sugar Co. Records, AFP.

50. Chan, *This Bittersweet Soil*, 345.

51. Murray to Atkins, 6 October 1885, Soledad Sugar Co. Records, AFP.

52. Atkins, *Sixty Years*, 116.

53. Murray to Atkins, 19 July 1888, Soledad Sugar Co. Records, AFP.

54. Murray to Atkins, 7 May 1888, Soledad Sugar Co. Records, AFP.

55. Porter, *Industrial Cuba*, 84.

56. *Boletín Oficial de la Provincia de Santa Clara*, 25 April 1883.

57. "Demanda verbal. Asiático Luciano Valle contra el id. Alejandro Acuré (conocido por Celestino) en cobro de $115.15 oro," 13 February 1883, Juzgado Municipal de Cienfuegos, AHPC.

58. Murray to Atkins, 18 May 1886, Soledad Sugar Co. Records, AFP.

59. Murray to Atkins, 20 May 1886, Soledad Sugar Co. Records, AFP.

60. Murray to Atkins, 18 April 1889, Soledad Sugar Co. Records, AFP.

61. Murray to Atkins, 12 April, 17 April, 26 April 1890, Soledad Sugar Co. Records, AFP.

62. Murray to Atkins, 1 May 1890, Soledad Sugar Co. Records, AFP.

63. Murray to Atkins, 26 May 1885, Soledad Sugar Co. Records, AFP.

64. Atkins to Murray, 14 December 1893, Edwin F. Atkins Papers, AFP.

65. Murray to Atkins, 9 July 1884 Soledad Sugar Co. Records, AFP.

66. "Fábrica Damián Machado," Libro 707, January–May 1890, ICEA, ANC.

67. Libro 706, February 1899, ICEA, ANC.

68. "Chinos en Limpa. Casa Purga," Libro 704, December 1905, ICEA, ANC.

69. Chan, *This Bittersweet Soil*, 328–31. In 1872 white workers received monthly

wages of US$30 during the winter and between $40 and $50 during the summer (with board), while Chinese workers received $22 during the winter and $30 during the summer (without board).

70. Lucy Cohen, *Chinese in the Post–Civil War South*, 86. In 1869 a recruiter believed that Chinese laborers could be hired at rates ranging from US$26 to $28 per month (paying their own transportation and rations en route).

71. Sagra, *Cuba en 1860*, 95.

72. Scott, *Slave Emancipation in Cuba*, 28–34, 98.

73. Atkins to Murray, 5 November 1884, Soledad Sugar Co. Records, AFP.

74. Murray to Atkins, 18 November 1884, Soledad Sugar Co. Records, AFP.

75. Edwin F. Atkins to General John C. Bates, 29 January 1899, Edwin F. Atkins Papers, AFP. The table of Soledad Estate's work force was drawn up for General John C. Bates, who commanded Santa Clara Province during the U.S. occupation of Cuba.

76. Murray to Atkins, 29 October 1885, Soledad Sugar Co. Records, AFP.

77. Murray to Atkins, 6 June 1888, Soledad Sugar Co. Records, AFP.

78. Murray to Atkins, 4 May 1893, Soledad Sugar Co. Records, AFP, MHS.

79. Murray to Atkins, 22 July 1884, Soledad Sugar Co. Records, AFP.

80. Murray to Atkins, 18 November 1884, Soledad Sugar Co. Records, AFP.

81. Atkins to Murray, 26 November 1884, Soledad Sugar Co. Records, AFP.

82. Edwin F. Atkins to J. N. S. Williams, 10 December 1894, Edwin F. Atkins Papers, AFP.

83. Porter, *Industrial Cuba*, 83–84.

84. Ibid.

85. The U.S. Department of War Circular Order No. 13 of 14 April 1899 applied the immigration laws of the United States to Cuba under the military occupation. Cuba, *Colección legislativa*, 47.

86. Perry, *Shanghai on Strike*.

87. Bergad, *Cuban Rural Society*, 247.

88. Corbitt, *Study of the Chinese*, 89.

89. Chuffat Latour, *Apunte histórico*, 17.

90. Chan, *This Bittersweet Soil*, 82. Sandy Lydon discusses Chinese miners and railroad laborers who introduced new labor-intensive crops to the Monterey Bay region in California in the 1860s. These crops, including tobacco and hops, mustard (transformed from weeds into "Chinese gold"), beet sugar, and strawberries, led to the diversification of agriculture. Lydon, *Chinese Gold*.

91. Cuba, Oficina del Censo, *Censo de la República de Cuba bajo la administración provisional de los Estados Unidos 1907*, 31.

92. Lim, *Hua Song*, 65, citing the *Chinese Australian Herald*, 15 June 1907.

93. Ibid., referencing Nobel Prize–winning author Henryk Sienkiewicz, 1955.

94. Residents of Paisito, interviews by author, Cienfuegos, Cuba, June 2000.

95. García Triana and Eng Herrera, *Chinese in Cuba*, 61.

96. Glick, *Sojourners and Settlers*, 69.

97. Lucy Cohen, *Chinese in the Post–Civil War South*, 83.

98. "Lista Electoral. Municipio de Cienfuegos. Provincia de Santa Clara. Censo

de Septiembre 30 de 1907," exp. 14476, leg. 261, Secretaría de Estado y Gobernación, ANC.

99. Chuffat Latour, *Apunte histórico*, 110. Machado himself borrowed money, as he took out a loan on behalf of his store for $1,247 in June 1901 (canceled in October 1902). In 1902 his shop was transferred to Cheong Chung Fat for 361 pesos gold. Folio 181, Hoja 554, Tomo 7, Libro de Comerciantes, Registro Mercantil, AHPC.

100. Five individuals were indebted to Machado when he died in 1902. In September 1893, Machado lent 300 pesos Spanish gold to Carlos Barrio; on 25 December 1896, 1,000 pesos gold, and on 25 February 1897, 1,500 pesos gold to the asiático Chan Juan Jun; on 1 March 1898, 337.10 pesos gold to the asiático Baltazar Ariza; on 14 October 1899, 79.50 pesos gold to José Comallonga; and 80 pesos silver to Antonio González Peñate (no date).

101. "Testamento," 9 November 1902, Escritura No. 142, Protocolos José Ramón Entenza, AHPC.

102. Blas and Santiago Pelayo Díaz, interviews by author, Cienfuegos and Havana, Cuba, March and December 1999, March 2002.

103. Hu-DeHart, "Chinese Coolie Labour," 81; Scott, *Slave Emancipation in Cuba*, 99.

104. Rodney, *History of the Guyanese Working People*, 43.

105. Valenzuela, "Day Laborers as Entrepreneurs?"

106. Look Lai, *Indentured Labor*, 192.

107. Given the attraction of a $50 reindenture bounty, the difficulty of purchasing land, and the Portuguese monopoly of retail trade, the Chinese in British Guiana initially experienced more obstacles to moving away from the sugar plantations. In general, though, they overcame these barriers by the end of the nineteenth century. Look Lai, *Indentured Labor*, 189–202, 301.

108. The 1899 census did not distinguish between hired hands working in the agricultural sector (classified as "agricultores" in 1907 and 1919) and those working in the manufacturing sector. See Losada Álvarez, "Cuban Labor Market."

109. The Chinese from Cuba on Bayou Lafourche worked under the supervision of a Creole who spoke Spanish. Lucy Cohen, *Chinese in the Post–Civil War South*, 46–80.

110. Wang Gungwu, *China and the Chinese Overseas*; Portes and Rumbaut, *Immigrant America*; Robin Cohen, *Global Diasporas*.

111. Wang Gungwu, *China and the Chinese Overseas*, 3–10.

CHAPTER 3

1. Martínez Fortún, *Monográficas históricas de Placetas*, 128.

2. Chuffat Latour, *Apunte histórico*. Antonio Chuffat Latour was the son of a Chinese merchant and a Cuban woman of color. In the 1920s he became a translator for the Guomindang (Chinese Nationalist Party) in Cuba and a chronicler of the Chinese Cuban community.

3. Ibid., 17.

4. Zanja Street, which today runs through Central Havana and Vedado, retraces

much of the original course of the sixteenth-century canal (Zanja Real, or Royal Canal) built to increase Havana's water supply by bringing fresh water from the Almendares River. See Scarpaci, Segre, and Coyula, *Havana*, 16–17.

5. Pérez de la Riva, *Los culíes chinos*, 249.

6. Ibid., 177–83, 251–52.

7. Cosme Baños, *Los chinos en Regla*, 19.

8. Barnet, *Biography of a Runaway Slave*, 89.

9. Scott, "Race, Labor, and Citizenship in Cuba"; Scott and Zeuske, "Property in Writing."

10. In 1887 three notary publics operated in Cienfuegos and notarized a total of 956 public documents: 506 before Don José J. Verdaguer, 250 before Don Antonio de León, and 200 before Don José Rafael de Villafuerte. Edo y Llop, *Memoria histórica de Cienfuegos*, 670.

11. "Poder para pleitos por Dn. Jose de Cuesta Castañeda y otros a los procuradores Dn. Francisco García Berrayarza y Dn. Juan Morell," 3 April 1883, Escritura No. 49, Protocolos José Rafael Villafuerte y Castellanos, AHPC.

12. Zeuske, "Hidden Markers, Open Secrets," 216–17. *Moreno* generally referred to one with dark brown skin, usually of African descent, and *pardo* to one with light brown skin, usually of mixed African and European descent.

13. "Poder para pleitos por el asiático libre Juan Galve a favor del procurador D. Mariano Alberich y González," 24 February 1880, Escritura No. 65, Protocolos Juan Hernández Castiñeyra (Verdaguer), AHPC.

14. "Confirmación de venta con pacto de retro. Asiático Antonio Rubio a los Srs. Castaño é Yntriaga," 20 October 1880, Escritura No. 284, Protocolos José J. Verdaguer, AHPC.

15. *Boletín Oficial de la Provincia de Santa Clara*, 27 April 1883.

16. From the beginning of the twentieth century, *sin otro apellido* became the most commonly used of these "hidden markers." Zeuske finds that many individuals labeled with "s.o.a." or "s.s.a." were elsewhere identified with a racial descriptor such as *moreno* or *pardo*. Zeuske, "Hidden Markers, Open Secrets," 217.

17. For example, in 1886, a sugar estate administrator was introduced as "Mr. James MacLean, without a second surname for not using one." Zeuske, "Hidden Markers, Open Secrets," 216.

18. Scott and Zeuske, "Property in Writing," 682.

19. "Testamento del asiático Marcelino Hernández," 19 September 1878, Escritura No. 374, Protocolos Emigdio Nieto y Guiote, AHPC. Marcelino Hernández's godparents were Don Joaquín Hernández and Doña María Pons.

20. "Manifestación liquidación división de adjudicación de los bienes de la herencia del asiático Marcelino Hernández sin segundo apellido," 1887, Escritura No. 52, Protocolos José J. Verdaguer, AHPC.

21. "Testamento," 9 November 1902, Escritura No. 142, Protocolos José Ramón Entenza, AHPC.

22. Machado likely recited the full names of both parents, which were then transcribed to appear to be first names.

23. *Boletín Oficial de la Provincia de Santa Clara*, 27 April 1883.

24. Ibid., 16 September 1897.

25. Ibid., 18 July 1907.

26. Helly, *Idéologie et ethnicité*, 261–82; Hu-DeHart, "Chinese Coolie Labour," 70, 82.

27. Martínez-Alier, *Marriage, Class, and Colour*, 81.

28. Yun, *Coolie Speaks*.

29. Hu-DeHart, "Race Construction and Race Relations."

30. *CCR*, 90.

31. For examples of the business of baptism of Chinese coolies, see *CCR*, 75–76.

32. Abdala Pupo, *Los chinos en el oriente cubano*, 61.

33. Scott, *Slave Emancipation in Cuba*, 89–90; Cuba, Centro de Estadística, *Noticias estadísticas . . . 1862*.

34. Edo y Llop, *Memoria histórica*, 232–33.

35. Ibid., 255–57.

36. Ibid., 256. This general positive attitude regarding the moralizing effect of raising pigs and crops changed by 1880, when pigs were often the key to self-purchase, precisely at a time when masters desired to hold on to their slaves. Scott, *Slave Emancipation in Cuba*, 141–71.

37. Edo y Llop, *Memoria histórica*, 256.

38. Dorsey, "Identity, Rebellion, and Social Justice," 42.

39. Scott, *Slave Emancipation in Cuba*, 106–7.

40. Crescencio (also known as Cencerro) took the name Cencerro Gobel, after his master Don Mariano Gobel, who "belonged to one of the most prestigious families of Cuban society" and "became an idol among the Chinese" due to his reputation for good treatment. Chuffat Latour, *Apunte histórico*, 38, 97.

41. *CCR*, 115.

42. "Expediente promovido por la asiática Teresa Sopena pidiendo rescisión de su contrata para contraer matrimonio," 1863, exp. 20277, leg. 641, Gobierno Superior Civil, ANC (located in box labeled "Correspondencia sobre colonización," exp. 20248, leg. 641, Gobierno Superior Civil, ANC).

43. Martinez-Alier, *Marriage, Class, and Colour*, 77–78.

44. The commission asked: "Have the men married? What wives? What is the condition of their wives and children, and what future have the children before them?" *CCR*, 114–15.

45. Exp. 20248, leg. 641, Gobierno Superior Civil, ANC. See discussions of this case in Corbitt, *Study of the Chinese*, 85–86; and Hu-DeHart, "Chinese Coolie Labour," 86.

46. See Guanche, *Componentes étnicos*, 84–87; and Baltar Rodríguez, *Los chinos de Cuba*, 100–105. Both Chinese and non-Chinese who I interviewed reiterated that the Chinese mostly married "con negras y mulatas" (with black and mulatto women) in Cuba. The 1874 commission also reported several Chinese men's marriages with black and mulatto women. *CCR*, 115.

47. Nicolasa's surname Hernández belonged to the man who raised her as a daughter.

48. "Expediente promovido á instancia de la parda Nicolasa Hernández para

contraer matrimonio con el asiático Ciprian Bernal," 1873, exp. 32620, leg. 931, Gobierno Superior Civil, ANC.

49. Martinez-Alier, *Marriage, Class, and Colour*, 77.

50. Nicolasa's mother lived on No. 84 Estrella Street. Nicolasa temporarily resided in the house of Don Nicolas Martínez de Valdivielso on No. 71 Aguiar Street, and Ciprian lived on 29 Bernaza Street. I thank Mitzi Espinosa Luis for familiarizing me with this neighborhood and its church on the outer border of La Habana Vieja.

51. "D. Damián Machado con Da. María de la Caridad Pérez Espinosa," 18 January 1890, No. 14, Folio 284, Tomo 2 (Moderno), Libro de Matrimonio, Registro Civil, AHPC.

52. "Testamento nuncupativo del As. Don Antonio Rubio," 7 February 1883, Escritura No. 17, Folios 67–68, Vol. 12, Protocolos José Rafael Villafuerte y Castellanos, AHPC.

53. Fouchet, *Wilfredo Lam*, 23–26. The Surrealist artist Wilfredo Lam spent much of his adult life in Spain, France (Paris), and the United States. His 1943 painting "The Jungle" is housed in the Museum of Modern Art in New York City. Lam died 11 September 1982 in Paris.

54. Zeuske, "Hidden Markers, Open Secrets," 216.

55. "D. Damián Machado con Da. María de la Caridad Pérez Espinosa," 18 January 1890, No. 14, Folio 284, Tomo 2 (Moderno), Libro de Matrimonio, Registro Civil, AHPC.

56. Damián Machado named Antonio Argüelles y Ferrer as legal guardian of his minor children. In 1910 Machado's daughter Catalina Machado Pérez married a member of the Rural Guard (an avenue for social mobility), the twenty-nine-year-old Claudio Valdés Sosa. In the couple's testament, gone from the official record are the initials s.o.a. following Damián Machado's name (although his birthplace is mentioned). Catalina is described as "native and resident of this city on Santa Cruz Street, twenty-seven years old, single, daughter of Damián Machado, native of China, and of Caridad Pérez y Espinosa, native of this city." In 1922, Catalina and Claudio had a son; his surname was derived from both father and mother (Valdés Machado), and his first name from the grandfathers on both sides (Luis Damián). Catalina's husband Claudio is described as: "Claudio Valdés Sosa, native and resident of Cienfuegos, Castillo Street, twenty-nine years old, single, Rural Guard, son of Luis Valdés Balmseda, native of Havana, and of Sixta Sosa Díaz, native of Cifuentes." "Declaratoria de Herederos de Claudio Valdés Sosa y de Catalina Machado Pérez," 1944, exp. 4629, Juzgado de Primera Instancia, AHPC. The couple's marriage is inscribed in Folio 481, Tomo 8 (Moderno), Certificado de Matrimonio, Registro Civil, AHPC, and their child's birth is inscribed in No. 1332, Folio 547, Tomo 60 (Moderno), Certificado de Nacimiento, Registro Civil, AHPC.

57. 28 May 1881, no. 698, fol. 242, Libro de Bautismos No. 15, Parroquia La Purísima Concepción S.I. Catedral de Cienfuegos.

58. "Lista Electoral. Municipio de Cienfuegos. Provincia de Santa Clara. Censo de Septiembre 30 de 1907," exp. 14476, leg. 261, Fondo Secretaría de Estado y Gobernación, ANC. After working as a seasonal farm laborer (bracero) in his

youth, Blas Pelayo worked on a boat from 1899 to 1912 and as a stevedore from 1912 to 1950, when he died.

59. Interviews, Blas and Santiago Pelayo Díaz, Cienfuegos and Havana, Cuba, March and December 1999, March 2002.

60. Cosme Baños, *Los chinos en Regla*, 33.

61. For an example of the common surname Achón among the Chinese on Soledad Estate, see table 4.

62. Cosme Baños, *Los chinos en Regla*, 33–34.

63. "Testamento del asiático Marcelino Hernández," 19 September 1878, Escritura No. 374, Protocolos Emigdio Nieto y Guiote, AHPC; "Testamento nuncupativo del As. Don Antonio Rubio," 7 February 1883, Escritura No. 17, Protocolos José Rafael Villafuerte y Castellanos, AHPC.

64. Zeuske, "Hidden Markers, Open Secrets," 219–20.

65. This practice is found throughout Roloff y Mialofsky and Forrest, *Índice alfabético*.

66. "Lista Electoral. Municipio de Cienfuegos. Provincia de Santa Clara. Censo de Septiembre 30 de 1907," exp. 14476, leg. 261, Fondo Secretaría de Estado y Gobernación, ANC.

67. "Testamento nuncupativo del As. Don Antonio Rubio," 7 February 1883, Escritura No. 17, Vol. 12, Protocolos José Rafael Villafuerte y Castellanos, AHPC. Rubio's sale of the property with a *pacto de retro* stipulated his right to repurchase it within a specified time limit and with an additional interest charge. The *pacto de retro* arrangement served as a means to raise funds. Similar to pawn shops, moneylenders historically exploited this system to take property from poor farmers and landowners.

68. "Venta de finca urbana por los Sres. D. Nicolas Castaño y Capetillo y D. Antonio Yntriago y Tocaño a favor de los menores Da. Dominica, D. Lino y Da. Luz Rubio y Garcia," 22 October 1883, Escritura No. 478, Vol. 133, Protocolos José Rafael Villafuerte y Castellanos, AHPC.

69. Data from the 1900 Merchant Register in Cienfuegos includes the name of the proprietor, the type of business and location, date of establishment, and transfers of ownership. Mitzi Espinosa Luis has begun a compilation of profiles of Chinese businesses in Cienfuegos through documents in the Archivo Histórico de la Provincia de Cienfuegos, *Indice y extractos del Registro Mercantil de Cienfuegos, 1888–1963: Los comerciantes chinos en Cienfuegos*.

70. "Juicio verbal, D. Marcelino Guerrero contra el asiático Federico Valdés en cobro de pesos 170.60," 1883, Juzgado Municipal de Cienfuegos, AHPC.

71. "Juicio verbal Ygnacio Hernández contra Lorenzo Chao," 1902, Juzgado Municipal de Cienfuegos, AHPC. La Niña Julia (products from Asia) on No. 29 San Fernando Street was registered to José Bú in 1899. In 1902 it was transferred to Justo Gonzales Regalado for $2,000 Spanish gold. Folio 153, Hoja 120, Tomo II, Libro de Comerciantes (1900), Registro Mercantil, AHPC.

72. "Testamento del asiático Marcelino Hernández," 19 September 1878, Escritura No. 374, Protocolos Emigdio Nieto y Guiote, AHPC.

73. Joff was ordered to pay the amount plus full legal costs within three days.

"Juicio verbal, D. Robustiano Álvarez, como gerente de Álvarez Castaño y Compania contra el asiático Antonio Joff en cobro de 92 pesos oro," 1883, Juzgado Municipal de Cienfuegos, AHPC.

74. The business arrangements between the three men are detailed in the following documents: "Testamento del asiático Marcelino Hernández," 19 September 1878, Escritura No. 374, Protocolos Emigdio Nieto y Guiote, AHPC; "Venta de casa y solar acusado por Don José Granda a favor de la Sociedad del Casino Asiático de las Cruces," 17 March 1880, Escritura No. 86, Protocolos José J. Verdaguer, AHPC; "Traspase de derecho por el asiático Juan de la Torre al de su clase Ramón Moya," 9 August 1880, Escritura No. 303, Protocolos de Juan Hernández Castiñeyra, AHPC; and "Manifestación liquidación división de adjudicación de los bienes de la herencia del asiático Marcelino Hernández sin segundo apellido," 1887, Escritura No. 52, Protocolos José J. Verdaguer, AHPC.

75. "Venta de casa y dominio útil de terreno por los asiáticos Ramón Moya y Juan de la Torre a favor de la morena Matilde O'Bourke," 14 August 1880, Escritura No. 300, Protocolos Juan Hernández Castiñeyra, AHPC.

76. Julia Rosa Chang Armenteros, interview by author, Lajas, Cuba, July 2002.

77. Folio 59, Hoja 293, Tomo 5, Libro de Comerciantes (1900), Registro Mercantil, AHPC; Chuffat Latour, *Apunte histórico*, 13.

78. Chuffat Latour, *Apunte histórico*, 13.

79. Although the exact year Rufino Achón migrated to Cuba is unknown, I classify him as a new migrant. Had he come to Cuba as an adolescent, he would have arrived at the earliest sometime during the 1880s, after the end of the formal coolie trade. Rufino Achón was also known as José Apon; the two names may be the result of a false identity used to enter Cuba. A non-Chinese witness for the case was Andrés Entenza y Méndez, a Cienfuegos banker involved in the sale. "Juicio verbal, Asiático Luis Achón contra el de su clase Rufino Achón," 1897, Juzgado Municipal de Cienfuegos, AHPC. Rufino Achón moved the laundry to San Carlos Street in 1914. Folio 149, Hoja 119, Tomo II, Libro de Comerciantes (1900), Registro Mercantil, AHPC.

80. One of the workers, Lázaro Tamayo, spared some of the items from the pile of debris. He related the discovery to Mitzi Espinosa Luis in 2001, when he learned of her project to recover information on Chinese merchants of Cienfuegos.

81. His name became rendered as "Chambombian" in local newspapers. In 1939 Emilio Roig de Leuchsenring (1889–1964) published an essay on "Cham Bom-bía, el médico chino" in the popular magazine *Carteles*. For detailed information on Chinese doctors and pharmacies, see García Triana and Eng Herrera, *Chinese in Cuba*, 63–71. See also Chuffat Latour, *Apunte histórico*, 42–43; and Corbitt, *Study of the Chinese*, 87–88. Chuffat Latour extols the Chinese herbal medicine for curing many Cubans, including himself.

82. Pérez de la Riva, *Los culíes chinos*, 251–52.

83. Ibid., 250–51.

84. Chuffat Latour, *Apunte histórico*, 43–44, 70.

85. Ibid., 72.

86. Ibid.

87. In 1904 it was sold to Woo Lim for 1,500 pesos gold. Folio 57, Hoja 20, Tomo I, Libro de Comerciantes (1900), Registro Mercantil, AHPC. The other branches of Weng On y Compañia in Cuba were Weng On Seng in Cárdenas (Industría and Calvo Streets), Weng On Gen in Colón (Real and San José Streets), and Weng On Chong in Sagua la Grande (Tacón Street).

88. Luis Cheng died in Havana in 1921, and his relatives in Cuba transferred his remains to China in 1926.

89. In 1922, Luis Po became president of the umbrella association Casino Chung Wah of Havana, and in 1923, president of the Cuba branch of the Guomindang. Chuffat Latour, *Apunte histórico*, 71–73, 105.

90. Ibid., 107. In 1902 Antonio Bu transferred Las Californias to Wong Weng Cong Chong Long (Benjamin Wong) for $800 Spanish gold. Folio 46, Hoja 85, Tomo 2, Libro de Comerciantes (1900), Registro Mercantil, AHPC.

91. Gobierno Provincial de Santa Clara, *Memoria explicativa*, "Relación de las sociedades de instrucción y recreo, socorros mutuos, gremios, etc. existentes en la provincia, con expresión del nombre de los presidentes de las mismas fechas de su fundación," 1 July 1904.

92. Hazard, *Cuba with Pen and Pencil*, 150.

93. *Cabildos de nación* were precursors to the later colored societies (*sociedades de color*), which played central roles in forging political communities in Cuba and diasporic linkages with African Americans. Guridy, *Forging Diaspora*, 11; Pappademos, *Black Political Activism*, 112–15.

94. Cosme Baños, *Los chinos en Regla*, 26–27.

95. For the legend of Kuang Kong de Cimarrones, see Chuffat Latour, *Apunte histórico*, 87. For discussions of San Fan Con, see Baltar Rodríguez, *Los chinos de Cuba*, 173–84; Scherer, "Sanfancón"; and Cosme Baños, *Los chinos en Regla*, 26.

96. Associations were formally registered as *sociedades de instrucción y recreo* (societies of instruction and recreation) and adhered to a standard pattern of reporting to the Spanish colonial or Cuban government the organization's name and address, regulations, directory of officers and members, monthly accounting balances and inventory, and annual election results.

97. Chuffat Latour, *Apunte histórico*, 18–19; Martín, *De donde vinieron los chinos de Cuba*; Pérez de la Riva, *Los culíes chinos*, 245.

98. Chuffat Latour, *Apunte histórico*, 49–50.

99. Pérez de la Riva, *Los culíes chinos*, 252.

100. "Sociedad Asiática de Instrucción y Recreo La Caridad," exp. 11231, leg. 369, Registro de Asociaciones, ANC.

101. "Casino Asiático Nuestra Señora de la Caridad del Cobre," exp. 678, leg. 32, Registro de Asociaciones, AHPC. See also "Sociedad Asiática de Instrucción y Recreo Nuestra Señora del Carmen," leg. 369, exp. 11232, Registro de Asociaciones, ANC; "Sociedad Asiática de Instrucción y Recreo Cristóbal Colón," leg. 428, exp. 13457, Registro de Asociaciones, ANC.

102. Chuffat Latour, *Apunte histórico*, 86–87.

103. It is likely that Francisco Gasso, described as "prestigious" and a "tireless defender of the Chinese" who understood the workings of the colonial government,

was European. In 1888 Francisco de P. Gasso is listed as secretary of Nuestra Señora del Carmen, established in 1886 on San Nicolás Street in Havana. Chuffat Latour, *Apunte histórico*, 49–50, 70; "Sociedad Asiática de Instrucción y Recreo Nuestra Señora del Carmen," exp. 11232, leg. 369, Registro de Asociaciones, ANC. Isabelle Lausent-Herrera notes that in Peru during the same period, foreigners sometimes held important positions as *apoderados*, or representatives of Chinese societies. Pedro Pa and Luis Pérez were most likely the same individuals who established the first bodega and café in the Barrio Chino and therefore had been in Cuba at least since 1858. Agustín Chuffat was a prominent merchant in Havana and relative of author Antonio Chuffat Latour.

104. Chuffat Latour, *Apunte histórico*, 57. Performances at the Lealtad Street theater were held from 6 P.M. to 10 P.M., and on Sundays from 1 P.M. to 4:30 P.M.

105. Edo y Llop, *Memoria histórica*, 454, 591–92, 659.

106. Chuffat Latour, *Apúnte histórico*, 57. I am grateful to Nancy Rao for identifying the Chinese characters for this opera. It was followed by a performance of "Shi Kong" for twelve days.

107. Edo y Llop, *Memoria histórica*, 591–92.

108. García Triana and Eng Herrera, *Chinese in Cuba*, 115.

109. Chuffat Latour, *Apunte histórico*, 110.

110. Ibid., 91–92.

111. Folio 113, 3 August 1885, Acta Capitular, AHPC; Folio 25, 21 August 1885, Acta Capitular, AHPC; Edo y Llop, *Memoria histórica*, 626–27.

112. Chuffat Latour, *Apunte histórico*, 57.

113. "Sociedad Asiática de Instrucción y Recreo Cristóbal Colón," exp. 13457, leg. 428, Registro de Asociaciones, ANC.

114. "Juicio de Faltas contra el Asiático Pastor Pelayo por herida al idem. Nicolas Aside," Juzgado Municipal de Cienfuegos, AHPC. See also "Diligencia del juicio de faltas seguido contra el asiático Felix Colón por maltrato al de su clase José Hernández conocido por Cantón," 1884, Juzgado Municipal de Cienfuegos, AHPC.

115. Perseverancia, *Los chinos y su charada*, 5.

116. Chuffat Latour, *Apúnte histórico*, 50–51. Chuffat Latour's rendering of the Chinese lottery (*chi-ffá*, or letter-flower) most likely is equivalent to *zi hua* in Mandarin.

117. Trujillo y Monangas, *Los criminales de Cuba*.

118. *Boletín Oficial de la Provincia de Santa Clara*, 20 May 1881. For similar cases from Santa Clara Province, see ibid., 10 December 1881, 6 March 1883, 14 May 1883.

119. 25 July 1898, Juzgado Municipal de Cienfuegos, AHPC [no expediente]. In 1881 Jacinto Manuel (Lion Toy) had been appointed consular agent in Cienfuegos. Chuffat Latour, *Apúnte histórico*, 90.

120. "Juicio verbal, D. Enrique Pérez de la Torre contra Celestino Sarría," 1903, Juzgado Municipal de Cienfuegos, AHPC.

121. Gobierno Provincial de Santa Clara, *Memoria explicativa*, "Relación de las sociedades de instrucción y recreo, socorros mutuos, gremios, etc. existentes en la provincia, con expresión del nombre de los presidentes de las mismas fechas de su fundación," 1 July 1904.

122. Yen, *Coolies and Mandarins*. For this process with the Chinese merchant elite community in the Philippines, see Wilson, *Ambition and Identity*.

123. Zhou, *Huaqiao huaren baike quanshu*, 151–52; Chen Kwong Min, *Meizhou huaqiao tongjian*, 641–42.

124. Hoy, *Chinese Six Companies*; Ma, *Revolutionaries, Monarchists, and China-towns*, 14–21.

125. Romero, "Transnational Chinese Immigrant Smuggling," 3.

126. Chuffat Latour, *Apunte histórico*, 82; Zhou, *Huaqiao huaren baike quanshu*, 151–52; Chen Kwong Min, *Meizhou huaqiao tongjian*, 641–42.

127. "Expediente autorizando al asiático Quong Sang para tralsadar á China los restos del asiático Jam Chung Sanz," 1886, exp. 5380, leg. 119, Gobierno General, ANC.

128. Pastor Pelayo was buried on 17 February 1913 in the following plot of Cementerio "La Reina": departamento 2, cuadro 2 derecha, fila 29, sepultura 7. For the location of other Chinese tombs, see Libro de Defunciones, 1898–1899, AHPC; and Libro de Autopsías, 1899–1922, AHPC.

129. Cosme Baños, *Los chinos en Regla*, 37.

130. Chuffat Latour, *Apunte histórico*, 82. Chen Kwong Min, *Meizhou huaqiao tongjian*, 641–42; Seuc, *La colonia china de Cuba*, 82.

131. Sonoda, "Thinking Cuban Chinese." Reports on the academies from the Chinese Ministry of Foreign Affairs are compiled in *Zhongmei guanxi shiliao*. Setsuko Sonoda's doctoral thesis (in Japanese) examines the relationship between Qing diplomatic officials and policies and Chinese communities in the United States, Canada, Peru, and Cuba, including these educational initiatives. See Setsuko Sonoda, "A Historical Study of International Migration in the Nineteenth Century: Overseas Chinese in the Americas and Their Relationships with China" (Ph.D. dissertation, University of Tokyo, 2007).

132. Chuffat Latour, *Apunte histórico*, 91, 112–13.

133. Ibid., 43.

134. Migrants worldwide relied on gathering socially or at the workplace to listen to a newspaper reader deliver the day's news. Jacobson, *Special Sorrows*, 175.

135. Chuffat Latour, *Apunte histórico*, 103–4. The hostilities in China began when the French, expanding their colonial empire, pressured China for concessions in present-day Vietnam.

136. Ibid., 97.

CHAPTER 4

1. *La Correspondencia*, 12 September 1930: 6. *Yat pak* is "one hundred" (*yi bai* in Mandarin). José Bu Tak (Hu De) became known as the mambí of "yat pa' carajo." García Triana and Eng Herrera, *Chinese in Cuba*, 7, citing oral testimony of Guillermo Eng (Wu Guoxiang), friend of General Francisco Carrillo and José Bu. Translation by Gregor Benton.

2. Ferrer, *Insurgent Cuba*, 117.

3. Quesada, *Mi primera ofrenda*; Choy, Chui, and Sío Wong, *Our History*.

4. *CCR*, 93–94.

5. Pérez de la Riva estimates the number of Chinese insurgents between 2,000 and 5,000, depending on the period and whether or not auxiliaries are included (out of a total of 7,000 to 30,000 combatants); Pérez de la Riva, *Los culíes chinos*, 265–67. Chuffat Latour estimates the number between 4,000 and 5,000; Chuffat Latour, *Apunte histórico*, 22. García Triana and Eng Herrera summarize estimates by different Cuban authors; García Triana and Eng Herrera, *Chinese in Cuba*, 9–10. For the role of the Chinese in the Ten Years' War, see Jiménez Pastrana, *Los chinos en las luchas*, 67–84; Pérez de la Riva, *Los culíes chinos*, 265–74; and García Triana and Eng Herrera, *Chinese in Cuba*, 1–13.

6. For a study of how and why some Cubans of African descent aligned themselves with Spain during the final decades of slavery and colonial rule, see Sartorius, "My Vassals."

7. Scott, *Slave Emancipation in Cuba*, 57.

8. Chuffat Latour, *Apunte histórico*, 28.

9. Scott, *Slave Emancipation in Cuba*, 58.

10. Pérez de la Riva, *Los culíes chinos*, 271.

11. Chuffat Latour, *Apunte histórico*, 29.

12. *CCR*, 93–94.

13. Ibid., 84–85.

14. Eng Herrera and García Triana, *Martí en los chinos*, 14.

15. Pérez, *Cuba between Empires*, 4–5.

16. García Martínez, "La Brigada de Cienfuegos," 172; Zeuske, "'Los negros hicimos la independencia,'" 194.

17. Jiménez Pastrana, *Los chinos en las luchas*, 86–88. Emilio Calleja was Captain General from 1886–87 and from 1893–95.

18. For disagreements among insurgent leaders and slave recruits on the boundaries of their new mobility, see Ferrer, *Insurgent Cuba*, 32–37.

19. García Triana and Eng Herrera, *Chinese in Cuba*, 69.

20. Chuffat Latour, *Apunte histórico*, 101–2. The Spanish text is: "Yo no mila gente suleto tiene arma por la mañana. No señó, pa mí no sabe, ta trabaja, quema carbon." In his rendering of this story, Antonio Chuffat portrays the Chinese "man of honor" later switching from pidgin to standard Spanish. He describes the Chinese tactic: "They were clever; when it was in their interest, they spoke Spanish, and when the matter was not in their interest, they exclaimed: 'Mi no sabe jabla español.'" Ibid., 31, 61.

21. Ibid., 102.

22. The guerrilla activities of Carlos Agüero in Matanzas Province lasted eleven months, during which he took Manguito and battled Spanish troops on the sugar mills Benemérito, Dos Hermanos, and Raíz de Jobo. Accounts of the Chinese *carboneros* appear in Chuffat Latour, *Apunte histórico*, 98–102, citing the diary of Colonel Rosendo García; and Jiménez Pastrana, *Los chinos en las luchas*, 90–93.

23. Dawdy, "*La Comida Mambisa*," 49.

24. Ibid., 51–55.

25. Ferrer, *Insurgent Cuba*, 127.

26. Nuñez, *La abuela*, 70.

27. See Scherer, "Culture of Erasure"; López-Calvo, *Imaging the Chinese*, 135–57.

28. Martí, *Obras completas*, 9:281.

29. Ibid., 9:281–82.

30. Ibid., 10:306.

31. Ibid., 4:460.

32. Ibid., 4:366.

33. Gonzalo de Quesada was a lawyer, engineer, and diplomat. An English-language translation was published as *The Chinese and Cuban Independence* while he served as the Cuban minister in Berlin. It reappeared in pamphlet form as *Los chinos y la revolución cubana* (Havana: Úcar, García y Cia., 1946) for the inauguration of a monument dedicated to the Chinese who fought for Cuban independence.

34. Quesada, *Chinese and Cuban Independence*, 15.

35. Ibid., 10–11.

36. Ferrer, *Insurgent Cuba*, 3.

37. Jiménez Pastrana, *Los chinos en las luchas*, 96, citing oral testimony of José Hernández, soldier of the Escolta del Lugarteniente General Antonio Maceo, Liberation Army, Veteran's Home, 22 February 1962, Havana.

38. Ibid., 97–98, citing oral testimony of Máximo Montes, soldier of Regiment "Castillo," Fifth Corps of the Liberation Army, Veteran's Home, 21 February 1962, Havana.

39. García Triana and Eng Herrera, *Chinese in Cuba*, 17.

40. Jiménez Pastrana, *Los chinos en las luchas*, 98–99, citing oral testimony of Federico Balsinde, soldier of Regiment "Castillo," Fifth Corps of the Liberation Army, Veteran's Home, 22 February 1962, Havana. The Spanish text is: "¿Tú quiele pollo? Mata capitán pañol."

41. García Triana and Eng Herrera speculate that from 300 to 350 participated in the War of 1895, most of them in Las Villas. García Triana and Eng Herrera, *Chinese in Cuba*, 24.

42. Atkins, *Sixty Years*, 169–70.

43. Testimony of L. F. Hughes, 20 April 1906, Claim 387, Part 1, Record Group 76, U.S./Spain Treaty Claims, USNA.

44. Folio 181, Hoja 554, Tomo 7, Libro de Comerciantes, Registro Mercantil, AHPC.

45. Published testimony from veterans are one of the main sources of information on Chinese participation in the final war of independence. See Chuffat Latour, *Apunte histórico*; Jiménez Pastrana, *Los chinos en las luchas*, 85–101; and García Triana and Eng Herrera, *Chinese in Cuba*.

46. Jiménez Pastrana, *Los chinos en las luchas*, 95, citing oral testimony of Manuel Pío Borrero, soldier of Guantánamo Brigade, First Corps of Liberation Army, and Juan E. Cedeño (nephew of Major General Jesús Rabí), soldier of the First Brigade Manzanillo Sur, Regiment Yara, Second Corps of Liberation Army, Veteran's Home, 21 February 1962, Havana.

47. Ibid., 96–97, citing oral testimony of Filomeno Alfonso, soldier of Sagua

Brigade, Fourth Corps of the Liberation Army, Veteran's Home, 22 February 1962, Havana. Serafín Sánchez was a veteran of the Ten Years' War and the Guerra Chiquita. In 1894 he published the book *Héroes humildes y poetas de la guerra* in New York.

48. Jiménez Pastrana, *Los chinos en las luchas*, 99, citing oral testimony of Manuel Moreira, soldier of the Brigade Sur, Fifth Corps of the Liberation Army, 27 February 1962, Havana.

49. Martínez Fortún, *Monografías históricas de Placetas*, 129.

50. Pan Wu was the Chinese contractor for Luis Estévez, and he owned two cane farms and two ranches. Chuffat Latour, *Apunte histórico*, 97, 116–17.

51. Chuffat Latour, *Apunte histórico*, 113.

52. Ibid.; García Triana and Eng Herrera, *Chinese in Cuba*, 22.

53. Ferrer, *Insurgent Cuba*, 150–51.

54. Roloff y Mialofsky and Forrest, *Índice alfabético*.

55. Zeuske, "'Los negros hicimos la independencia,'" 194.

56. García Martínez, "La Brigada de Cienfuegos," 172.

57. Blas and Santiago Pelayo Díaz, interviews by author, Cienfuegos and Havana, Cuba, March and December 1999, March 2002.

58. García Triana and Eng Herrera, *Chinese in Cuba*, citing oral testimony of Ramón Estrada's granddaughter Martha Velásquez Estrada, 4 November 2002.

59. Alonso Valdés, "La inmigración china," 128–30, 140. The Fondo Comisión Revisora y Liquidadora de Haberes del Ejército Libertador, containing approximately 49,000 *expedientes*, or files, is housed in the Archivo Nacional de Cuba.

60. In Santa Clara, eleven Chinese joined the Fourth Corps in 1895, four in 1896, and none in 1897. See appendix in Alonso Valdés, "La inmigración china," 141–46.

61. Ibid., 136–38, 142–43. The recorded number reflects the age of the individuals when they made their request in 1902–3. Thus, by subtracting four years, one can approximate the age of a soldier at the termination of the war in 1898.

62. Eng Herrera and García Triana, *Martí en los chinos*, 14; Jiménez Pastrana, *Los chinos en las luchas*, 95.

63. García Martínez, "La Brigada de Cienfuegos."

64. Alonso Valdés, "La inmigración china," 139–46.

65. Ferrer, *Insurgent Cuba*, 178–87.

66. For the intricacies of the process of back pay, see Zeuske, "'Los negros hicimos la independencia.'"

67. "Correspondencia enviada a Máximo Gómez por distintas personas entre los que se encuentran Aurelio García, Manuel de Cárdenas y Perfecto Gil sobre las reclamaciones a la Comisión Revisora y Liquidador de los haberes del Ejército Libertador," 2–16 January 1903, exp. 3217–3477, leg. 24, Máximo Gómez, ANC.

68. Agapito Fortún died in 1943 in Remedios at the age of 95. Martínez Fortún, *Monografías históricas de Placetas*, 128–129.

69. Jiménez Pastrana, *Los chinos en las luchas*, 97, citing oral testimony of Filomeno Alfonso, soldier of the Brigade of Sagua la Grande, Fourth Corps of the Liberation Army, Veteran's Home, 21 February 1962.

70. Ibid., 97, citing oral testimony of Filomeno Alfonso, soldier of the Brigade of Sagua la Grande, Fourth Corps of the Liberation Army, Veteran's Home, 21 February 1962.

71. D. José Bu y Alan con Da. Ana Justa Suárez, 26 June 1897, No. 282, Folio 189, Libro 7, Libro de Matrimonios de Blancos, AHPC; Da. Josefa Bú y Suárez, 29 November 1898, No. 461, Libro 25, Libro de Defunciones de Blancos, AHPC. In his marriage registration, Bu employed a standard formula in declaring himself to be the "son of José and María." The child Josefa was buried in Cienfuegos in the grave of José Pantaleon.

72. In 1901 he transferred the shop to Justo Gonzales Regalado for $2,000 Spanish gold. Folio 153, Hoja 120, Tomo 2, Registro Mercantil, AHPC.

73. Chuffat Latour, *Apunte histórico*, 29.

74. Eng Herrera and García Triana, *Martí en los chinos*, 15, citing Wu Guoxiang, "Crónica mortuoria," *Wah Man Sion Po*, 12 August 1928.

75. Scott and Zeuske, "Property in Writing," 671. For the 1899–1902 occupation, see Pérez, *Cuba between Empires*; Scott, "Race, Labor, and Citizenship in Cuba."

76. Guerra, *Myth of José Martí*, 87–88.

77. Ferrer, *Insurgent Cuba*, 128.

78. Spanish colonial law enabled slave parents to purchase the freedom of their unborn children. Gómez became president of the Directorio Central de las Sociedades de la Raza de Color (Central Directory of Societies of the Race of Color) and a general in the War for Independence.

79. Ferrer, *Insurgent Cuba*, 132–33; Fernández Robaina, *El negro en Cuba*, 24. Earlier, Morúa had followed the autonomist current, pro-Spain but in favor of reforms and civil rights for Cubans. He joined the independence movement when he returned to Cuba in 1898.

80. García Triana and Eng Herrera, *Chinese in Cuba*, 18–19. Juan Chao Sen became president of Chi Tack Tong association when it was founded in 1920. He died on 27 March 1972 and is buried in the Chi Tack Tong section of the Chinese cemetery in Havana.

81. For a critical analysis of Antonio Chuffat Latour's text *Apunte histórico de los chinos de Cuba* and his conjoining of black and Chinese social histories, see Yun, *Coolie Speaks*, 183–228.

82. Chuffat does not further specify if he was president of a specific association for people of color. His address for a reply is No. 38 Calle Real in Colón.

83. "Cartas dirigidas a Juan Gualberto Gómez por Antonio Chuffat, fechadas en la Habana a 14 y 16 diciembre 1898," exp. 921, leg. 16, Adquisiciones, ANC.

84. When Chuffat retired, he served as translator of the Cienfuegos branch of the Guomindang (Chinese Nationalist Party).

85. Rousseau and Díaz de Villegas, *Memoria descriptiva*, 270–71.

86. Iglesias Utset, *Las metáforas del cambio*, 252–53.

87. Ibid., 253. For the composition of the Partido Independiente de Color (Independent Party of Color) and the subsequent repression and slaughter, see Helg, *Our Rightful Share*.

88. Pérez, *Cuba between Empires*, 315–27.

89. Scott, *Degrees of Freedom*, 204. For an analysis of the debates and divergence regarding suffrage rights in Cuba and Louisiana, see ibid., 189–215.

90. Scott and Zeuske, "Property in Writing," 696–97.

91. "Lista Electoral. Municipio de Cienfuegos. Provincia de Santa Clara. Censo de Septiembre 30 de 1907," exp. 14476, leg. 261, Secretaría de Estado y Gobernación, ANC.

92. Guerra, *Myth of José Martí*, 190.

93. Report from Intelligence Officer Lt. Ben Lear, 23 September 1907. File 97/147, Entry 1008 (General Correspondence of the Military Intelligence Division), Army of Cuban Pacification 1906–9, Record Group 395 (Records of United States Army Overseas Operations and Commands, 1898–1942), USNA.

94. Quesada, *Mi primera ofrenda*, 136.

95. Article 65 of the Constitution of 1901; Eng Herrera and García Triana, *Martí en los chinos*, 15; Alonso Valdés, "La inmigración china," 128; Jiménez Pastrana, *Los chinos en las luchas*, 6.

CHAPTER 5

1. Pichardo Viñals, *Documentos para la historia de Cuba*, 199.

2. Saxton, *Indispensable Enemy*; Roediger, *Wages of Whiteness*; Robert Lee, *Orientals*.

3. Erika Lee, *At America's Gates*; Jung, *Coolies and Cane*, 11–13.

4. Corbitt, "Immigration in Cuba," 304–5.

5. Cuba, Oficina Nacional del Censo, *Censo de la República de Cuba 1919*, 175.

6. *Havana Daily Post*, 28 September 1913: 2.

7. Corbitt, "Chinese Immigrants in Cuba," 131. In general, census figures under-report numbers of Chinese residing in Cuba. Even within one census report, figures were contradictory. For example, the 1919 census reports 10,300 Chinese residents on one page and 16,146 on another. Corbitt, *Study of the Chinese*, 96; Cuba, Oficina Nacional del Censo, *Censo de la República de Cuba 1919*, 301–5.

8. Wright, *Cuba*, 146–47.

9. Monteagudo made this statement in a 1908 letter to Provisional Governor of Cuba Charles E. Magoon proposing the establishment of an immigration office. "Expediente, en inglés y español, referente a la inmigración de braceros," Havana, 11 July 1906–13 March 1908, exp. 82, leg. 121, Secretaría de la Presidencia, ANC.

10. McLeod, "Undesirable Aliens," 600.

11. Pérez, *Cuba: Between Reform and Revolution*, 201–5.

12. Guerra, *Myth of José Martí*, 147.

13. Ibid., 149.

14. Herrera Jerez and Castillo Santana, *De la memoria a la vida pública*, 25, citing Ramón Meza y Suárez Inclán, *La inmigración útil debe ser protegida* (Havana, 1906), 20–22. Meza delivered this paper at the Fifth National Conference on Social Services and Correction in Santiago de Cuba on 16 April 1906, in his capacity as

delegate of the Sociedad Económico de los Amigos del País and president of the conference's immigration committee.

15. For an analysis of how Chinese "coolies" in the United States became racialized as fundamentally different from the white working class, see Robert Lee, *Orientals*.

16. Guerra, *Myth of José Martí*, 147.

17. Ibid., 150.

18. Scholars have begun to explore Chinese smuggling routes across the Americas. Erika Lee, *At America's Gates*; Romero, "Transnational Chinese Immigrant Smuggling"; Delgado, *Making the Chinese Mexican*.

19. "Instancia mecanografiada del Encargado de Negocios del Imperio de China en la República de Cuba, a Carlos de Zaldo, Secretario de Estado y Justicia, en relación a la negativa del Gobierno de acceder el desembarco en la Isla, de 43 súbditos chinos," exp. 20, leg. 65, Secretaría de la Presidencia, ANC.

20. Romero, "Transnational Chinese Immigrant Smuggling."

21. "Expediente referente a la estancia en Cuba de pasajeros chinos en tránsito hacia otros países," Havana, 23 May 1908–24 March 1909, exp. 74, leg. 121, Secretaría de la Presidencia, ANC.

22. The method of bertillonage was developed in the late nineteenth century and named after Paris police clerk Alphonse Bertillon. The Department of State upheld Article 1 of Decree No. 237 of 1904 "authorizing the Commissioner of Immigration, when there is any doubt as to the identity of the person or as to his residence in the Island at the time entitling him to return to Cuba, to require these facts to be satisfactorily shown to him or to employ any other means for the ascertainment of said facts as may serve for the enforcement of the Immigration Law." "Expediente, en inglés y español, referente a la solicitud de modificaciones en la legislación vigente sobre inmigración china," Havana, 8 November 1906–24 January 1907, exp. 88, leg. 115, Secretaría de la Presidencia, ANC.

23. Hu-DeHart, "Racism and Anti-Chinese Persecution," 8–9.

24. Daniels, *Asian America*, 120–25.

25. "Expediente referente a la inmigración china," Havana, 1 September 1909–21 June 1914, exp. 83, leg. 121, Secretaría de la Presidencia, ANC.

26. Corbitt, "Immigration in Cuba," 305.

27. Herrera and Castillo Santana, *De la memoria a la vida pública*, 21, citing *El Día*, 31 October 31 1911.

28. "Chinese Entering Cuba Illegally," *Havana Daily Post*, March 14, 1913: 1.

29. Herrera Jerez and Castillo Santana, *De la memoria a la vida pública*, 22, citing *El Mundo*, 2 December 1915.

30. "Expediente referente a la inmigración china," Havana, 1 September 1909–21 June 1914, exp. 83, leg. 121, Secretaría de la Presidencia, ANC.

31. McLeod, "Undesirable Aliens," 600.

32. Corbitt, "Immigration in Cuba," 306–8.

33. Corbitt, *Study of the Chinese*, 97–98.

34. *La Correspondencia*, 21 August 1922: 1.

35. Levine, *Tropical Diaspora*, 20.

36. Letter, 23 May 1919, Box 3, Folder 309/1, Entry 135 Chinese Smuggling File, 1914–ca 1921, Segregated Chinese Records, RG 85, Records of the Immigration and Naturalization Service, USNA.

37. Letter, 17 February 1920, ibid.

38. For the smuggling of contraband alcohol, drugs, and immigrants from Cuba during the U.S. prohibition era, see Sáenz Rovner, *Cuban Connection*, 17–29. In 1924 the U.S. consul general in Havana called the city "the main base for smuggling operations." Ibid., 21.

39. Box 3, Folder 309/9, ibid.

40. Herrera Jerez and Castillo Santana, *De la memoria a la vida pública*, 33.

41. Pelayo Pérez, "El peligro amarillo y el peligro negro," 259.

42. McLeod, "Undesirable Aliens," 601, citing *La Prensa*, 22 December 1922.

43. "Contra la invasión amarilla," *El Comercio*, 27 January 1923: 2.

44. McKeown, *Melancholy Order*, 327–28.

45. Herrera Jerez and Castillo Santana, 31–32, citing *Diario de la Marina*, 29 April 1924.

46. Chuffat Latour, *Apunte histórico*, 71–72.

47. Corbitt, *Study of the Chinese*, 101–3.

48. Ibid., 104.

49. Ibid.; *Gaceta Oficial*, 4 May 1926.

50. Herrera Jerez and Castillo Santana, *De la memoria a la vida pública*, 33–35.

51. Corbitt, *Study of the Chinese*, 104.

52. Hu-DeHart, "Racism and Anti-Chinese Persecution"; Romero, *Chinese in Mexico*.

CHAPTER 6

1. Estado de Pagos, January 1921, Libro de Central Soledad, AHPC.

2. Corbitt, *Study of the Chinese*, 89. Spanish-speaking Chinese in Chinatowns of New York and San Francisco who had migrated from Cuba or elsewhere in Latin America brought with them descriptions of Havana streets.

3. Herrera Jerez and Castillo Santana, *De la memoria a la vida pública*, 151–52.

4. Chen Mengyu, "Guba huaqiao shenghuo gaikuang," provides a detailed overview of Chinese Cuban businesses and institutions.

5. For the concept "transnational social field," see Basch, Glick Schiller, and Blanc-Szanton, *Nations Unbound*.

6. Guarnizo and Smith, "The Locations of Transnationalism," 13. For a contemporary study of translocal relations between the town of Miraflores in the Dominican Republic and the Boston neighborhood of Jamaica Plain, see Levitt, *Transnational Villagers*.

7. Corbitt, *Study of the Chinese*, 115; Baltar Rodríguez, *Los chinos de Cuba*, 91–92. Zhongshan was formerly called Xiangshan, and Taishan was formerly called Xinning.

8. Lai, *Becoming Chinese American*, 92, 95.

9. Antonio Chuffat, "Los Chinos y la diversidad de dialectos," *El Comercio*, 11 September 1926: 4.

10. Chen Kwong Min, *Meizhou huaqiao tongjian*, 652–71, 679. Elsewhere in the Americas, Zhongshan Chinese concentrated in different occupations. For example, in California they became tenant farmers or nurserymen. Chan, *Asian Americans*, 64.

11. *La Correspondencia*, 21 April 1934: 1.

12. Descendants of Chinese migrants in Cuba, interview by author, Meige, Xinhui County, Guangdong Province, China, November 2001.

13. McKeown, *Chinese Migrant Networks*, 74.

14. Ibid., 74–75.

15. Lin Datian, interview by author, Dulian, Xinhui County, China, August 2001. Lin Datian is editor of *Dulian News* and the son of a Chinese migrant to Cuba, Lin Gengsheng.

16. Lim, *Hua Song*, 159.

17. Box 3, Folder 309/1, Entry 135 Chinese Smuggling File, 1914–ca. 1921, Segregated Chinese Records, RG 85, USNA.

18. Huang Zhuocai, interview by author, Guangzhou, China, May 2009.

19. "Guowai qiaobao ji guonei qiaojuan dizhi diaocha biao, jinchukou qiao you tongji biao, 1948" [Address chart of foreign overseas Chinese and their domestic dependents, chart of incoming and outgoing overseas Chinese mail, 1948], 372 juan, 2 mulu, 29 quanzong, Guangdong sheng youzheng guanliju (Guangdong Provincial Archive, Guangzhou).

20. For the role of *jinshanzhuang*, or "Gold Mountain firms" in providing Chinese overseas remittance services, see Hsu, *Dreaming of Gold*, 31–40.

21. Lin Datian, interview by author, Dulian, Xinhui County, Guangdong Province, China, August 2001.

22. Descendants of Chinese migrants in Cuba, interview by author, Meige, Xinhui County, Guangdong Province, China, November 2001.

23. Descendants of Chinese migrants in Cuba, interview by author, Meige, Xinhui County, China, November 2001; Hsu, *Dreaming of Gold*, 40–54.

24. Chan, *Asian Americans*, 103–7.

25. Nakano Glenn, "Split Household, Small Producer." This arrangement is not unique to the Chinese.

26. Liu Chongmin, *Taishan xian huaqiao zhi*, 164; Mazumdar, "What Happened to the Women?"

27. Liu Chongmin, interview by author, Guanghai, Taishan County, Guangdong Province, China, August 2001; Han Mei, "Yi ge guba huagong shi."

28. Liu Chongmin, *Taishan xian huaqiao zhi*.

29. Hsu, *Dreaming of Gold*, 91.

30. Ibid., 102–3, 106, 118–19.

31. Hom, *Songs of Gold Mountain*, 44–45.

32. Lui family, interview by author, Xinhui County, China, August 2001.

33. Okihiro, *Margins and Mainstreams*, 79; Mazumdar, "'What Happened to the Women?'"

34. McKeown, *Chinese Migrant Networks*, 71.

35. Schiavone Camacho, *Chinese Mexicans*.

36. Liu Chongmin, *Taishan xian huaqiao zhi*, 165–70. Liu Kongye was Liu Chongmin's uncle. Liu Chongmin, interview by author, Guanghai, Taishan County, Guangdong Province, China, August 2001.

37. Lui family, interview by author, Lui Village, Xinhui County, Guangdong Province, China, August 2001.

38. Herrera Jerez and Castillo Santana, *De la memoria a la vida pública*, 74.

39. A list of the major associations in Cuba appears in Chen Kwong Min, *Meizhou huaqiao tongjian*, 676–92.

40. For an interview with Felipe Luis, see Espinosa Luis, "*Si tú pleguntá.*"

41. Chan, *Asian Americans*, 64.

42. By 1950 there were 2,500 members, and plans were underway for another 100 beds to be added to the existing 140. Chen Kwong Min, *Meizhou huaqiao tongjian*, 644–45.

43. Herrera Jerez and Castillo Santana, *De la memoria a la vida pública*, 76.

44. "Jiujiang gongyiyuan zhi chengji da you keguan," *Wah Man Sion Po* (19 March 1928).

45. "Asociación Cienfueguera de Agricultores Chinos," folios 85–86, exp. 581, leg. 27, Registro de Asociaciones, AHPC.

46. Castillo Santana and Herrera Jerez, "Los lavanderos chinos," 102–4, 108; "Asociación de Lavanderos Chinos," exp. 1120, leg. 95, Registro de Asociaciones, ANC. For the laundry association in New York City, see Yu, *To Save China*.

47. García Triana and Eng Herrera, *Chinese in Cuba*, 59.

48. Ma, *Revolutionaries, Monarchists, and Chinatowns*, 21–29.

49. In 1946, the association changed its name again to Hongmen Minzhidang. Zhou, *Huaqiao huaren baike quanshu*, 150.

50. It became a political party named Zhigongdang in 1925, with Chen Jiong-ming (governor of Guangdong Province from 1920 to 1923) elected titular head. Lai, "The Kuomintang in Chinese American Communities," 179, 203–4 n. 38.

51. *La Correspondencia*, 17 July 1928: 12.

52. "Centro Republicano Asiático," folios 155–56, exp. 420, leg. 28, Registro de Asociaciones, AHPC.

53. McKeown, *Chinese Migrant Networks*, 73.

54. Lai, *Becoming Chinese American*, 115.

55. The Tung Wah Hospital, a transnational institution, served as an intermediary "hub" connecting Chinese hometowns with communities overseas. Sinn, *Power and Charity*.

56. Folio 23, Libro de Exhumaciones, 1899–1936, Cementerio de Reina, AHPC; "Lung Kuan (Gran China)," exp. 422, leg. 28, Registro de Asociaciones, AHPC. Cemetery records in Cuba indicate the name of the deceased, date of interment, location of tomb, and, if an autopsy was performed, cause of death.

57. Chen Kwong Min, *Meizhou huaqiao tongjian*, 641–42.

58. Today, cemeteries across the island starkly portray the contours of Chinese settlement and the ruptures in Cuban history. More recent tombstones display

names of deceased Chinese migrants and their Cuban wives and are adorned with Catholic symbols. In 2009, the Chinese cemetery in Sagua la Grande appeared to be in utter disrepair, a heap of overturned tombstones exposing the bones of migrants that were never shipped back to China.

59. For the inner-workings and interrelationships between Cantonese opera actors, playwrights, and audiences in Chinatown theaters, see Rao, "Public Face of Chinatown."

60. For a detailed description of different martial arts groups, see García Triana and Eng Herrera, *Chinese in Cuba*, 118–20.

61. Ma, *Revolutionaries, Monarchists, and Chinatowns*, 40–51.

62. Chen Kwong Min, *Meizhou huaqiao tongjian*, 672–73; Huang Dingzhi, "Guba de sanminyue shubaoshe," 313–15.

63. Ma, *Revolutionaries, Monarchists, and Chinatowns*, 150; Chen Kwong Min, *Meizhou huaqiao tongjian*, 672–73; Huang Dingzhi, "Guba de sanminyue shubaoshe," 319–21; *Havana Daily Post*, 10 April 1913, 10 January 1914.

64. Yen, *Studies in Modern Overseas Chinese History*; Ma, *Revolutionaries, Monarchists, and Chinatowns*; Duara, "Nationalists among Transnationals."

65. Lai, "Kuomintang in Chinese American Communities," 180.

66. Chen Kwong Min, *Meizhou huaqiao tongjian*, 672–73.

67. For the impact of the May Fourth movement on the Chinese diaspora in Singapore, see Kenley, *New Culture in a New World*.

68. Rousseau and Díaz de Villegas, *Memoria descriptiva, histórica y biográfica*, 339.

69. Chen Kwong Min, *Meizhou huaqiao tongjian*, 649–51.

70. It described, for example, the five-power constitution as outlined by Sun Yat-sen, providing that government administration shall be composed of executive, legislative, judiciary, examination, and supervisory branches.

71. Chen Kwong Min, *Meizhou huaqiao tongjian*, 673–74.

72. *El Comercio*, 16 April 1923: 1, 4.

73. For a detailed description of the contents and significance of hometown publications, see Huang and Godley, "Appendix Chapter: A Note on the Study of *Qiaoxiang* Ties," 306–42; and Hsu, *Dreaming of Gold*, 124–55.

74. Chen Kwong Min, *Meizhou huaqiao tongjian*, 649–51.

75. See, for example, *Man Sen Yat Po*, 27 March 1942: 4.

76. Album located in Museo de Lajas (uncatalogued).

77. This phenomenon paralleled the Qing society pattern of one son training for the imperial civil service exams and another learning the family business.

78. Principal of Taishan Number One Middle School, interview by author, Taishan City, Taishan County, Guangdong Province, China, August 2001.

79. He Xinquan, *Peizheng xiaoshi*, 61.

80. The nondenominational Christian college moved to the Portuguese colony of Macao in 1900 in the midst of political turmoil and returned to Canton in 1904. In 1916, it officially changed its name to Lingnan University. The college attracted students from Guandgong, Guangxi, Southern Yunnan, and Southern Guizhou, and by 1925, enrollment reached 226. Under the Chinese Communist government,

it was incorporated into Zhongshan University in 1952. Members of the board of directors and alumnae who fled mainland China founded a school in Hong Kong, which eventually became Lingnan University. Beach and Fahs, *World Missionary Atlas*; Lutz, *China and the Christian Colleges*; Dong Wang, *Managing God's Higher Learning*.

81. Beach and Fahs, *World Missionary Atlas*.

82. "Want $5,000,000 for 'Columbia in China'; Supporters of Canton Christian College Plan Great Improvements There," *New York Times*, 21 January 1914.

83. Kong Lu Cheung, "Why Should We Come Back to China to Study," *Nanda yu Huaqiao* [Lingnan University and Overseas Chinese] 1.1 (1923): 1–12. Original in English.

84. *Nanda yu Huaqiao* 1.3 (1923).

85. Kong Lu Cheung, "Why Should We Come Back."

86. Huang, "Teaching Chineseness."

87. Tejeiro, *Historia ilustrada*; Chen, *Meizhou huaqiao tongjian*, 549–50, 643–44; Seuc, *La colonia china de Cuba*, 46–52.

88. It was called the Three Principles of the People Society (Asociación Juventud China de San Min Chu I or Sanminzhuyi Qingniantuan). Tejeiro, *Historia ilustrada*.

89. Baltar Rodríguez, *Los chinos de Cuba*, 46–48, 90, 157–58.

CHAPTER 7

1. The original Spanish text is "¡No hubo un chino cubano desertor; no hubo un chino cubano traidor!" and the Chinese text is "Guba zhongguoren wuyou daogezhe, guba zhongguoren wuyou tiaowangzhe." The use of both Spanish and Chinese on this monument reinforces the claim for a hyphenated identity within Cuban society. Plans for the monument had actually begun much earlier. In March 1931 leaders of the Chinese Cuban community, Chinese diplomats, and Cuban government officials gathered in Havana to lay the foundation, with the intention to unveil the monument on 10 October. Japan's invasion of northeast China shifted the focus of the Chinese in Cuba homeward, delaying the inauguration until after the end of World War II. Chen Kwong Min, *Meizhou huaqiao tongjian*, 634–35.

2. Carr, "'Omnipotent and Omnipresent,'" 266.

3. McGillivray, *Blazing Cane*, 105.

4. "Relación de Solicitudes de Inscripción, Dirección General del Registro de Extranjeros, Secretaría de Gobernación," 1935–39, Museo de Lajas.

5. Herrera Jerez and Castillo Santana, *De la memoria a la vida pública*, 66–67.

6. Rafael Lam, "Chinos de Manila en Cuba," *Periódico Cubarte*, 25 September 2009, http://www.cubarte.cult.cu.

7. Hernández Catá, "Los chinos." See discussions of this short story in López-Calvo, *Imaging the Chinese*, 51–52; and García Triana and Eng Herrera, *Chinese in Cuba*, 94–95.

8. Baltar Rodríguez, *Los chinos de Cuba*, 68.

9. "Expediente mecanografiado y manuscrito que contiene cartas, acuses de re-

cibo, informes policiacos, decreto, reportes de periódicos, actas, etc.; en relación con la causa 1091 de 1926 seguida por el juzgado especial, por el asesinato del asiático Andres Chiu Lión y la complicidad de la sociedad China 'Chi Kong Tong' en el mismo," exp. 52, leg. 25, Secretaría de la Presidencia, ANC.

10. *El Comercio*, 2 September 1926: 4.

11. "Expediente mecanografiado y manuscrito."

12. "Centro Repúblicano Asiático," exp. 420, leg. 28, Registro de Asociaciones, AHPC.

13. Ma, *Revolutionaries, Monarchists, and Chinatowns*, 21-29.

14. "Cuadro comprensivo de la arteria principal del barrio chino, donde viven los asiáticos en completo hacinamiento y faltos de toda higien; y relacíon de las casas de comercio de tercer orden que radican en dicho barrio; enviados al parecer al Secretario de Sanidad por el Secretario de Gobernación," 28 August 1926, exp. 51, leg. 25, Secretaría de la Presidencia, ANC.

15. Castillo Santana and Herrera Jerez, "Los lavanderos chinos," 105. Jorge Mañach y Robato (1898–1961) was a Cuban writer and intellectual.

16. Amador, "'Redeeming the Tropics,'" 98–99, citing Le-Roy y Cassá, *Inmigración anti-sanitaria*. Jorge Eduardo Le Roy y Cassá (1867–1934) was known as the "Father of Sanitation Statistics in Cuba."

17. "Expediente mecanografiado y manuscrito" (see note 10).

18. *El Comercio*, 11 September 1926: 4.

19. Benton, *Chinese Migrants and Internationalism*. Karin Lee's 2005 documentary film *Comrade Dad* explores the ideological beliefs of her father, Wally Lee, and the Communist bookstore he ran in Vancouver from the mid-1960s until the early 1980s.

20. In Cuba, over 1,000 Chinese and Cubans attended a special memorial in Sun's honor. Chen Kwong Min, *Meizhou huaqiao tongjian*, 673-74.

21. So Wai-chor traces the leftist movement from its amorphous origins in 1924 to its development after the 1927 purge into a full-blown opposition force within Guomindang politics in China. So, *Kuomintang Left*.

22. Lai, "Kuomintang in Chinese American Communities," 190-91.

23. Su, "Wo luju guba jinxing geming huodong de huiyi," 41-43.

24. Ibid., 43-44. Branches of the Guomindang in the Americas originally were all under the jurisdiction of San Francisco but eventually came under the direct control of the party in China: Hawaii and Mexico in 1924, Cuba in 1925, and Peru in 1927. Lai, "Kuomintang in Chinese American Communities," 180-88.

25. Su, "Wo luju guba jinxing geming huodong de huiyi," 46-47.

26. Ibid., 51-62.

27. Benton, *Chinese Migrants and Internationalism*, 42-45; García Triana, *Los chinos de Cuba*, 233-34.

28. The organization was officially founded on 30 April 1927 on No. 62 Zanja Street. Among its members were Juan Mok (Mo Youping), Luis Li (Li Juzhi), Julio Su Leng (Su Zilun), Antonio Lejang, Jorge Lam, Julio Chang, Octavio Lan, Ángel Wong or Ledo (Huang Chengzhi), Mario Eng San (Wu Hunxing), Manuel Luis (Lu Gezi), Enrique León (Liang Zanhang), the brothers Pedro Lei (Li Yuxing) and Luis

Lei (Li Shetong), and Wenceslao Achong. Cátedra de Estudios sobre la Inmigración China en Cuba, *Las sociedades Chinas*.

29. Jiménez Pastrana, *Los chinos en las luchas*, 116–17; Baltar Rodríguez, *Los chinos de Cuba*, 70–71; Zhou, *Huaqiao huaren baike quanshu*, 151; Cátedra de Estudios sobre la Inmigración China en Cuba, *Las sociedades Chinas*.

30. Su, "Wo luju guba jinxing geming huodong de huiyi," 62–70.

31. García Triana and Eng Herrera, *Chinese in Cuba*, 31, 51. Capestany was a senator for Las Villas.

32. Benton, *Chinese Migrants and Internationalism*, 32.

33. Back in Guangdong, the provincial government facilitated the return of Chinese overseas under these dire economic circumstances. It attempted to provide temporary food and lodging, employment in factories and road building, and placement for the sick and elderly. Hsu, *Dreaming of Gold*, 202.

34. Elsewhere diasporic minorities came under suspicion for being disloyal to the host nation. In the Soviet Union, Chinese and other ethnic groups were subject to a state campaign of terror and deportation. Benton, *Chinese Migrants and Internationalism*, 27.

35. Li Kent (Li Kunyu), president of the Chinese Chamber of Commerce in Cuba, submitted a report to the Bureau of Overseas Chinese Affairs in Nanjing. Chen Kwong Min, *Meizhou huaqiao tongjian*, 643–44; Corbitt, *Study of the Chinese*, 111–12.

36. García Triana and Eng Herrera, *Chinese in Cuba*, 57.

37. Whitney, *State and Revolution*, 101.

38. Chen Kwong Min, *Meizhou huaqiao tongjian*, 645–46; Corbitt, *Study of the Chinese in Cuba*, 114; De la Fuente, *Nation for All*, 104–5. For the impact of the Nationalization of Labor decree on Jews, see Levine, *Tropical Diaspora*, 52–59.

39. Corbitt, "Immigration in Cuba," 308.

40. McGillivray, *Blazing Cane*, 113. The sharpest difference in treatment of Caribbean immigrant workers occurred between British West Indians and Haitians. See McLeod, "Undesireable Aliens"; and Carr, "Identity, Class, and Nation." For the organizational practices of British Caribbean migrants who negotiated the crossing of linguistic and political frontiers in Cuba, see Giovannetti, "Elusive Organization of 'Identity.'"

41. Cuba, *Censo de 1943*, 736; Corbitt, *Study of the Chinese*, 114.

42. Chen Kwong Min, *Meizhou huaqiao tongjian*, 645–46; Corbitt, *Study of the Chinese*, 114; Seuc, *La colonia china de Cuba*, 92–96.

43. Chen Kwong Min, *Meizhou huaqiao tongjian*, 645–46.

44. Document courtesy of Cátedra de Estudios sobre la Inmigración China en Cuba.

45. Chen Kwong Min, *Meizhou huaqiao tongjian*, 645–46.

46. Seuc, *La colonia china de Cuba*, 85–87.

47. *El Comercio*, 25 June 1926.

48. Chuffat Latour, *Apunte histórico*, 175. The text of the open letter to the president of the Republic of Cuba is reproduced in ibid., 173–76.

49. Eng Herrera and García Triana, *Martí en los chinos*, 11–12, citing Cámara de

Comercio China de Cuba y Asociación de la Colonia China de Cuba, *Legítimas aspiraciónes de la colonia china de Cuba* (Havana: Imprenta El Fígaro, 1926): 7–8.

50. Antonio Chuffat, "Los Chinos y la diversidad de dialectos, carácter de cada provincia y regiones, los imperialistas y los republicanos," *El Comercio*, 11 September 1926: 4. Juan Luis Martín also wrote articles about the Chinese community for the popular magazine *Bohemia*.

51. *El Comercio*, 11 January 1926: 3.

52. *La Correspondencia*, 16 April 1934: 2.

53. Chen Kwong Min, *Meizhou huaqiao tongjian*, 643–44.

54. *El Comercio*, 16 April 1928: 1, 3.

55. *El Comercio*, 17 June 1929.

56. *El Comercio*, 7 November 1931: 1, 8.

57. An example of a well-rounded analysis from Cuba is Herrera Jerez and Castillo Santana, *De la memoria a la vida pública*.

58. Castillo Santana and Herrera Jerez, "Los lavanderos chinos," 106.

59. The magazine was founded by the Union of Commercial Retailers of the Chinese Colony in Cuba (Unión de Detallistas del Comercio de la Colonia China en Cuba).

60. *Fraternidad*, March 1939: 4–6.

61. *Fraternidad*, October 1939.

62. "La Revolución China y el Comunismo," *Fraternidad*, May 1939: 3–10.

63. Chinese in the Philippines (another former Spanish colony under U.S. hegemony) also faced exclusionary laws and were drawn closer to China in the 1930s. Wickberg, "Anti-Sinicism and Chinese Identity Options."

64. For Nationalist Party activities in the United States during World War II, see Lai, "Kuomintang in Chinese American Communities," 194–97.

65. "Alianza en Defensa de la Cultura China," exp. 10672, leg. 355, Registro de Asociaciones, ANC.

66. Chen Kwong Min, *Meizhou huaqiao tongjian*, 647–48; Zhou, *Huaqiao huaren baike quanshu*, 244–45.

67. See Yong Chen's discussion of Chinese overseas participation in the resistance to Japanese aggression. Yong Chen, *Chinese San Francisco*, 233–37.

68. Folio 34, no. 2, caja 6, Veteranos de la Independencia, AHPC.

69. *Fraternidad*, February 1940: 6.

70. *Fraternidad*, June 1939: 4–9.

71. García Triana and Eng Herrera, *Chinese in Cuba*, 107.

72. Corbitt, "Chinese Immigrants in Cuba," 132.

73. Ibid., 130. The treaty was published in the *Gaceta Oficial de la República* on 24 December 1943 and is reproduced in Tejeiro, *La historia ilustrada*.

74. Baltar Rodríguez, *Los chinos de Cuba*, 90, 100–105.

75. García Triana and Eng Herrera, *Chinese in Cuba*, 57–58.

76. Ibid., 60–63.

77. "Asociación Nacional Chino-Cubana," exp. 9910, leg. 334, Registro de Asociaciones, ANC.

78. See Fernando Ortiz's essay "Los factores humanos de la cubanidad," *Revista Bimestre Cubana* 45 (1940): 165–69.

79. Ortiz, *Cuban Counterpoint*, 98, 103.

80. Scherer, "Culture of Erasure."

81. Seuc, *La colonia china de Cuba*, 164; Choy, Chui, and Sío Wong, *Our History*, 27–28.

82. López-Calvo, *Imaging the Chinese*, 166. Beatriz Varela suggests that the term derived from the Basque "nar" or "narra" (drag) and refers to the image of a Chinese hauling a basket or cart of fruits and vegetables. Varela, *Lo chino en el habla cubana*, 42.

83. Varela, *Lo chino en el habla cubana*, 42–43.

84. Ya Ya, interview by author, Cienfuegos, Cuba, March 2002.

85. Choy, Chui, and Sío Wong, *Our History*, 34.

86. "Rollo de apelación en expediente sobre subsanación de error en la inscripción de nacimiento de José Wong Alonso" (1945), exp. 6652, Juzgado de Primera Instancia, AHPC.

87. De la Fuente, *Nation for All*, 31–32.

88. For a detailed description of the Chinese in Cuban cultural life, see García Triana and Eng Herrera, *Chinese in Cuba*, 75–140.

89. López-Calvo, *Imaging the Chinese*, 42.

90. García Triana and Eng Herrera, *Chinese in Cuba*, 107–8.

91. Ibid., 111–13; Pérez Fernández and Rodríguez González, "La corneta china (suona) en Cuba."

92. *Fraternidad*, March 1941: 7.

93. García Triana and Eng Herrera, *Chinese in Cuba*, 111–13.

94. Chen Kwong Min, *Meizhou huaqiao tongjian*, 649–50; García Triana and Eng Herrera, *Chinese in Cuba*, 110; Baltar Rodríguez, *Los chinos de Cuba*, 162–64. Alejo Carpentier published an essay on Chinese theater in *Información*, 17 May 1944.

95. For Chinese Cuban opera troupes, see Chen Kwong Min, *Meizhou huaqiao tongjian*, 649–50; Baltar Rodríguez, *Los chinos de Cuba*, 156–66; and García Triana and Eng Herrera, *Chinese in Cuba*, 114–18. Internal disagreements led some of the teachers to split from the Opera Chung Wah and form three new theater companies.

96. Varela, *Lo chino en el habla cubana*, 31–54; Valdés Bernal, *Lengua nacional e identidad cultural del cubano*, 111–33.

97. Espinosa, "'Si tú pleguntá,'" 135–36.

98. Glick Schiller, "Transmigrants and Nation-States," 96. Georges Fouron and Nina Glick Schiller define second-generation transnational youth as those whose lives and identities have been shaped by a transnational social field, whether born in the United States or in Haiti, whether they return or not. Fouron and Glick Schiller, "Generation of Identity." For case studies of second-generation transnational life, see Levitt and Waters, *Changing Face of Home*.

99. Baltar Rodríguez, *Los chinos de Cuba*, 105–7, 174; Rodríguez Ruiz, "Rela-

ciones inter-étnicas e interraciales en el Barrio Chino," 115. Rodríguez cites the case of a Chinese father and white, Catholic mother whose son speaks, reads, and writes Chinese, took first communion, and professes the "cult of the ancestors."

100. For a comparative case of Barbadian foster or surrogate parents, see Chamberlain, *Family Love in the Diaspora*.

101. Álvarez Rios, *La inmigración china*, 65.

102. Violeta and Lourdes Luis Quintana, interview by author, Cienfuegos, Cuba, March 2002.

103. Seuc, *La colonia china de Cuba*, 3. Seuc's mother, along with his younger brother and two sisters, became "refugees of war" in their Cantonese town during the Japanese occupation.

104. Napoleón Seuc, interview by author, Miami, September 2000.

105. Maria Isabel León, interview by author, Lajas, Cuba, July 2002.

106. Leonard, *Making Ethnic Choices*, 7–8.

107. Ibid., 215.

108. Through much legwork and perseverance, Mitzi Espinosa Luis has uncovered these additional details of Huang Baoshi's life in Sagua la Grande.

CHAPTER 8

1. García Triana, *Los chinos de Cuba*, 17.

2. Herrera Jerez and Castillo Santana, *De la memoria a la vida pública*, 147.

3. "Alianza en Defensa de la Cultura China," exp. 10672, leg. 355, Registro de Asociaciones, ANC.

4. Among those in attendance was Aníbal Escalante, who was later denounced by Fidel Castro. García Triana and Eng Herrera, *Chinese in Cuba*, 30.

5. Álvarez Ríos, *La inmigración china en la Cuba colonial*, 78–83.

6. Eng Herrera and García Triana, *Martí en los chinos*, 31–35.

7. Alianza en Defensa de la Cultura China," exp. 10672, leg. 355, Registro de Asociaciones, ANC.

8. Herrera Jerez and Castillo Santana, *De la memoria a la vida pública*, 151–52.

9. Chang, "La inmigración china en Cuba," 133.

10. García Triana and Eng Herrera, *Chinese in Cuba*, 60, 62.

11. *El Comercio*, 13 August 1952: 5.

12. Through oral histories, García Triana and Eng Herrera have uncovered details of several Cubans of Chinese descent who participated in the revolutionary struggles of 1952 to 1958. García Triana and Eng Herrera, *Chinese in Cuba*, 33–45.

13. Ibid., 31–32.

14. Choy (b. 1934) is president of the State Working Group for the Cleanup, Preservation, and Development of Havana Bay, and Chui (b. 1938) is president of the Casino Chung Wah. Sío Wong (b. 1938) returned to active service in 2006 and became president of the Cuban-Chinese Friendship Association. When he died on 12 February 2010, his ashes were placed in the pantheon of the Revolutionary Armed Forces in Colón Cemetery.

15. Choy, Chui, and Sío Wong, *Our History*, 33.

16. Herrera Jerez and Castillo Santana, *De la memoria a la vida pública*, 157.

17. García Triana, *Los chinos de Cuba*, 49.

18. The questionnaire from the Association of Chinese Returnees to the Motherland requested the following information for each Chinese overseas and spouse: full name, address, place and date of birth, place of employment and salary or income, property in Cuba and abroad; names, addresses, and ages of children; and names and addresses of relatives in China. "Peiping Surveys Chinese in Cuba," *New York Times*, 5 July 1960: 18.

19. Choy, Chui, and Sío Wong, *Our History*, 24.

20. Pedro Eng Herrera, interview by author, Havana, Cuba, March 2002.

21. García Triana and Eng Herrera, *Chinese in Cuba*, 52.

22. Pedro Eng Herrera, interview by author, Havana, Cuba, March 2002.

23. Herrera and Castillo Santana, *De la memoria a la vida pública*, 160.

24. García Triana and Eng Herrera, *Chinese in Cuba*, 63.

25. Pedro Eng Herrera, interview by author, Havana, Cuba, March 2002.

26. R. Hart Philips, "Chinese in Cuba Plan Red Paper," *New York Times*, 10 July 1959: 8.

27. Pérez, *Cuba: Between Reform and Revolution*, 341; Herrera Jerez and Castillo Santana, *De la memoria a la vida pública*, 168.

28. Felipe Luis, interview by author, Havana, Cuba, March 2002.

29. For an insightful analysis of racial ideologies and policies intended to eliminate inequalities, see Sawyer, *Racial Politics in Post-Revolutionary Cuba*.

30. Zhou, *Huaqiao huaren baike quanshu*, 150–52.

31. Felipe Luis, interview by author, March 2002, Havana, Cuba.

32. Herrera Jerez and Castillo Santana, *De la memoria a la vida pública*, 168.

33. García Triana and Eng Herrera, *Chinese in Cuba*, 60.

34. Herrera Jerez and Castillo Santana, *De la memoria a la vida pública*, 165.

35. Alfonso Chao Chiu, interview by author, Havana, Cuba, June 2003.

36. Baltar Rodríguez, *Los chinos de Cuba*, 90; Herrera Jerez and Castillo Santana, *De la memoria a la vida pública*, 168.

37. Alfonso Chao Chiu, interview by author, Havana, Cuba, June 2003. Chao died on 28 December 2004.

38. "Lung Con Cun Sol," exp. 26371, leg. 1270, Registro de Asociaciones, ANC.

39. "Casino Chung Wah," exp. 1577, leg. 122, Registro de Asociaciones, ANC.

40. Baltar Rodríguez, *Los chinos de Cuba*, 92; García Triana and Eng Herrera, *Chinese in Cuba*, 32.

41. García Triana and Eng Herrera, *Chinese in Cuba*, 31–32, 78.

42. María Silvia Jo Sardiñas, interview by author, Cienfuegos, Cuba, March 2002.

43. Tang Zhongxi, interview by author, Cienfuegos, Cuba, July 2002.

44. Pedraza, *Political Disaffection*.

45. Manuel Antonio de Varona founded the Student Revolutionary Directorate in 1930 and was imprisoned and exiled for his participation in anti-Machado and anti-Batista campaigns. He served as prime minister of Cuba from 1948 to 1950. He died in Miami in 1992 at the age of eighty-three.

46. "Odian al Comunismo, Chinos de Cuba. Colaboran con la Revolución, Chinos de Cuba que se Exilan," *El Avance Criollo*, 18 November 1960: 5, 26–27.

47. "2 Chinese Who Fled Cuba Win Right to Stay in U.S.," *New York Times*, 7 August 1963: 9.

48. Seuc, *La colonia china de Cuba*, 3.

49. Ibid., 149.

50. Alfonso Chardy, "Chinese Cubans Seek to Build Unity in Exile," *Miami Herald*, 5 March 1994: 1B. The statistic is for Dade County, Florida.

51. Seuc, *La colonia china de Cuba*, 158–59.

52. Lok Siu, *Memories of a Future Home*. Steven Masami Ropp examines Asian Latinos in Los Angeles, and Edith Chen contrasts Chinese Dominicans in the Dominican Republic and in the United States, while Robert Chao Romero suggests the need for a new intellectual space within which to theorize these kinds of social formations within the fields of Latin American, Latino, and Chicano studies. See Ropp, "Secondary Migration and the Politics of Identity"; Chen, "'You Are Like Us,'"; and Romero, *Chinese in Mexico*.

53. Zhou, *Huaqiao huaren baike quanshu*, 150–52.

54. Napoleón Seuc, interview by author, Miami, September 2000.

55. After washing up on Miami's shore in December 1999, Elián González prompted an international tug-of-war when his Cuban relatives in Miami waged a court battle to keep him in the United States. He was returned to his father in Cuba six months later, after the Supreme Court turned down a last-minute appeal.

56. Jerome Snyder and Milton Glaser, "Asia Pearl," *New York*, 18 November 1968.

57. The restaurant's website is www.lacaridad78.com. Lok Siu, "Chino Latino Restaurants."

58. Lau, "'71' Series Photo Essay."

59. Lo, "Cuban-Chinese Familia," 217.

EPILOGUE

1. García Triana, *Los chinos de Cuba*, 83.

2. In November 2004, U.S. dollars in circulation were replaced with "convertible pesos," and a 10 percent fee was imposed on conversion of dollars to the new currency.

3. Recently published books on China's engagement with Latin America and the Caribbean include Ellis, *China in Latin America*; Gallagher and Porzecanski, *The Dragon in the Room*; Hearn and León-Manríquez, *China Engages Latin America*. See also the special issue "From the Great Wall to the New World: China and Latin America in the 21st Century," *The China Quarterly* 209 (2012).

4. For a comparative view of Chinese investment in local Chinese communities in Mexico and Cuba, see Hearn, "Harnessing the Dragon."

5. As of June 2009, 282 Confucius Institutes (and 272 Confucius Classrooms) had been established in 83 countries and regions. The Americas are home to 87 institutes and 205 classrooms. The organizations are spread across the United States,

Canada, Mexico, Peru, Columbia, Cuba, Chile, Brazil, Bahamas, Argentina, Costa Rica, and Jamaica. Confucius Institute Online (www.chinese.cn).

6. Chen Weihua, "Confucius Institute helps to bridge cultural, language gap," *China Daily*, 7 June 2011: 11.

7. Sochi Alay, interview by author, Havana, Cuba, July 2010.

8. Chinese students used their newly acquired Spanish to serve as liaisons and interpreters for foreign delegates at events such as the 2008 Summer Olympic Games in Beijing.

9. Casino Chung Wah, Census, 31 December 2010. The organization has been re-named Federación Casino Chung Wah.

10. For an account of the project's inception by one of its founders, see Eng Menéndez, "Revitalización de las tradiciones chinas en Cuba."

11. For Chinese educational and cultural initiatives, see Montes de Oca Choy and Vargas Lee, "Levando a la práctica la cultura china."

12. Álvarez Ríos, *La inmigración china en la Cuba colonial*, 53–54.

13. Abel Fung, interview by author, Havana, Cuba, June 2003.

14. For a more in-depth analysis of these dynamics, see López, "Revitalization of Havana's Chinatown."

15. The original magazine *Fraternidad* was founded in 1934 as the official publication of the Union of Commercial Retailers of the Chinese Community in Cuba. See Chapter 7 for a discussion of its significance for the Chinese Cuban community.

16. Espinosa, "Si tú pleguntá."

17. Ang, *On Not Speaking Chinese*.

18. Gans, "Symbolic Ethnicity." Gans addresses this concept in relation to later-generation white ethnics in the United States. For the dynamic process of ethnic construction, see Waters, *Ethnic Options*.

19. For case studies of Asian American youth in the United States who embody this "social construction" perspective on ethnicity, see Min, *Second Generation*.

20. Scherer, "Sanfancón"; López-Calvo, *Imaging the Chinese*, 80–89.

21. For examples, see Chailloux Laffita, *De dónde son los cubanos*.

22. For the experiences of Chinese Americans exploring their ancestral heritage in China, see Louie, *Chineseness across Borders*.

23. Julio Tang interview with Dmitri Prieto-Samsonov, "A Chinese in Cuba, a Cuban in China (Part I)," *Havana Times*, 16 June 2011 (www.havanatimes.org).

24. Lowe, *Immigrant Acts*, 64.

25. Julio Tang interview with Dmitri Prieto-Samsonov, "A Chinese in Cuba, a Cuban in China (Part II)," *Havana Times*, 20 June 2011 (www.havanatimes.org).

26. Pérez Sarduy and Stubbs, *Afrocuba*, 7.

27. Yun, "Signifying 'Asian' and Afro-Cultural Poetics," 216.

28. Lowe, *Immigrant Acts*, 65.

29. Kwong, *Chinatown, N.Y.*; Fong, *First Suburban Chinatown*.

30. Visits to the Chinese cemetery in Havana also reveal several exhumations for return passage of bones to China.

31. Pérez, "In the Service of the Revolution." An example is Ibarra, *Ideología mambisa*.

32. See, for example, Grupo Promotor del Barrio Chino, "Presencia china en Cuba."

33. Other recent fictional portrayals of Chinese Cuban experiences include Cristina García's novel *Monkey Hunting* (2003) and Zoé Valdés's *La eternidad del instante* (2004). For a detailed analysis of images of the Chinese in Cuban literature, see López-Calvo, *Imaging the Chinese*.

34. Valdés Millán's *Una cultura milenaria en el siglo XX guantanamero* is a recent publication on the Chinese in Guantánamo.

35. The title of this painting is "Aparición de la Guanyin en los campos de Cuba" (Apparition of Guanyin the countryside of Cuba). Pedro Eng Herrera, interview by author, Havana, Cuba, March 2002.

36. For further reading on these incidents, see Rodríguez Pastor, *Herederos del Dragón*; Johnson, "The Anti-Chinese Riots of 1918 in Jamaica"; and Romero, *Chinese in Mexico*. A useful comparison can also be made with the racialization of Chinese in white settler colonies, such as Australia and South Africa. See Fitzgerald, *Big White Lie*; and Yoon Jung Park, *A Matter of Honour*.

37. Blas Pelayo, "Short Chronicle of the Visit of the President of the People's Republic of China, Jiang Zemin, to Havana, from November 21, 1993 to November 22, 1993." My translation.

Bibliography

ARCHIVAL AND DOCUMENTARY SOURCES

People's Republic of China

Guangdong Provincial Archive (Guangdong Sheng Dang'anguan), Guangzhou
  Guangdong Province Bureau of Overseas Chinese Affairs (Guangdong Sheng Qiaowuchu)
  Guangdong Province Postal Service Management Bureau (Guangdong Sheng Youzheng Guanliju)
National Library of China (Guojia Tushuguan), Beijing
  Foreign Newspaper Collection
Zhongshan Document Center (Sun Zhongshan Wenxianguan), Guangzhou
Zhongshan University Library (Zhongshan Daxue Tushuguan), Guangzhou
Zhongshan University Institute of Southeast Asian Studies (Zhongshan Daxue Dongnanya Lishi Yanjiusuo), Guangzhou
Taishan City Archive (Taishanshi Dang'anguan)
Taishan City Overseas Chinese Affairs Office (Taishanshi Renmin Zhengfu Qiaowu Bangongshi)
Xinhui Jingtang Library (Xinhui Jingtang Tushuguan), Xinhui City
Xinhui City Archive (Xinhuishi Dang'anguan)
Xinhui Overseas Chinese Affairs Office (Xinhuishi Renminzhengfu Qiaowu Bangongshi), Xinhui City

Cuba

Archivo Nacional de Cuba, Havana
  Adquisiciones
  Donativos y Remisiones
  Gobierno General
  Gobierno Superior Civil
  Instituto Cubano de Estabilización de Azúcar
  Máximo Gómez
  Miscelanea de Expedientes
  Registro de Asociaciones
  Secretaría de la Presidencia
Archivo Histórico Provincial de Cienfuegos
  Actas Capitulares
  Cementerio de Reina, Libro de Exhumaciones
  Juzgado Municipal de Cuba
  Juzgado de Primera Instancia
  Protocolos Notariales
  Registro de Asociaciones

Registro Civil
Registro Mercantil
Archivo Parroquial de la Ciudad de Cienfuegos
Biblioteca Nacional José Martí, Havana
    Colección Cubana
    Colección Julio Lobo
Biblioteca Municipal de Cienfuegos
Museo "Benny Moré" de Lajas

United States

Massachusetts Historical Society, Boston
    Atkins Family Papers
New York Public Library
United States National Archives, Washington, D.C.
    Record Group 76, Spanish Treaty Claims Commission
    Record Group 85, Records of the Immigration and Naturalization Service
    Record Group 395, Records of United States Army Overseas Operations and
        Commands, 1898–1942

NEWSPAPERS AND PERIODICALS

El Avance Criollo (Miami)
Boletín de Colonización (Havana)
Boletín Oficial de la Provincia de Santa Clara (Santa Clara)
Diario de la Marina (Havana)
El Comercio (Cienfuegos)
El Republicano (Cienfuegos)
Fraternidad (Lianhe yuekan) (Havana)
Fraternidad II
Havana Daily Post
Hoi Men Kong Po (Havana)
Huaqiao Banyuekan (Nanjing)
Kwong Wah Po (Havana)
La Correspondencia (Cienfuegos)
Miami Herald
Man Sen Yat Po (Havana)
Nanda yu Huaqiao (Guangzhou)
New York Times
Wah Man Sion Po (Havana)

BOOKS, ARTICLES, AND DISSERTATIONS

Abdala Pupo, Oscar Luis. *Los chinos en el oriente cubano: Apuntes sobre la presencia china en el siglo XIX*. Santiago de Cuba: Ediciones Santiago, 2003.

Alfaro-Velcamp, Theresa. *So Far from Allah, So Close to Mexico: Middle Eastern Immigrants in Modern Mexico*. Austin: University of Texas Press, 2007.

Alonso Valdés, Coralia. "La inmigración china: Su presencia en el Ejército Libertador de Cuba (1895–1898)." *Catauro* 2.2 (2000): 127–46.

Álvarez Ríos, Baldomero. *La inmigración china en la Cuba colonial: El Barrio Chino de La Habana*. Havana: Publicigraf, 1995.

Amador, José G. "'Redeeming the Tropics': Public Health and National Identity in Cuba, Puerto Rico, and Brazil, 1890–1940." Ph.D. diss., University of Michigan, 2008.

Andrews, George Reid. *Blacks and Whites in São Paulo, Brazil, 1888–1988*. Madison: University of Wisconsin Press, 1991.

Ang, Ien. *On Not Speaking Chinese: Living between Asia and the West*. New York: Routledge, 2001.

"Asians in the Americas: Transculturations and Power." *Amerasia Journal* 28.2 (2002), a special issue with guest editors Lane Ryo Hirabayashi and Evelyn Hu-DeHart.

Atkins, Edwin F. *Sixty Years in Cuba: Reminiscences of Edwin F. Atkins*. Cambridge, Mass.: Riverside Press, 1926. Reprint, New York: Arno Press, 1980.

Azuma, Eiichiro. *Between Two Empires: Race, History, and Transnationalism in Japanese America*. New York: Oxford University Press, 2005.

Baily, Samuel L. *Immigrants in the Lands of Promise: Italians in Buenos Aires and New York City, 1870–1914*. Ithaca: Cornell University Press, 1999.

Baltar Rodríguez, José. *Los chinos de Cuba: Apuntes etnográficos*. Havana: Fundación Fernando Ortiz, 1997.

Barnet, Miguel. *Biography of a Runaway Slave*. Translated by W. Nick Hill. Willimantic, Conn.: Curbstone Press, 1994.

Basch, Linda, Nina Glick Schiller, and Cristina Szanton Blanc. *Nations Unbound: Transnational Projects, Postcolonial Predicaments, and Deterritorialized Nation-States*. New York: Routledge, 1994.

Beach, Harlan P., and Charles H. Fahs, eds. *World Missionary Atlas*. New York: Institute of Social and Religious Research, 1925.

Benton, Gregor. *Chinese Migrants and Internationalism: Forgotten Histories, 1917–1945*. London and New York: Routledge, 2007.

Bergad, Laird W. *Cuban Rural Society in the Nineteenth Century: The Social and Economic History of Monoculture in Matanzas*. Princeton: Princeton University Press, 1990.

Bettinger-López, Caroline. *Cuban-Jewish Journeys: Searching for Identity, Home, and History in Miami*. Knoxville: University of Tennessee Press, 2000.

Briones, Matthew M. *Jim and Jap Crow: A Cultural History of 1940s Interracial America*. Princeton: Princeton University Press, 2012.

Burgos, Adrian, Jr. *Playing America's Game: Baseball, Latinos, and the Color Line*. Berkeley: University of California Press, 2007.

Carr, Barry. "'Omnipotent and Omnipresent'? Labor Shortages, Worker Mobility, and Employer Control in the Cuban Sugar Industry, 1910–1934." In *Identity and Struggle at the Margins of the Nation-State: The Laboring Peoples of Cen-*

tral America and the Hispanic Caribbean, edited by Aviva Chomsky and Aldo Lauria-Santiago, 260–91. Durham: Duke University Press, 1998.

Castillo Santana, Mario G., and Miriam Herrera Jerez. "Los lavanderos chinos en La Habana del siglo xx: Paisajes urbanos, sociabilidades y memoria colectiva." Catauro 9.17 (2008): 99–109.

Cátedra de Estudios sobre la Inmigración China en Cuba, Casa de Altos Estudios Don Fernando Ortiz. Las sociedades chinas: Pasado y presente. Havana: 2007. [CD]

Chailloux Laffita, Graciela, ed. De dónde son los cubanos. Havana: Editorial de Ciencias Sociales, 2005.

Chamberlain, Mary. Family Love in the Diaspora: Migration and the Anglo-Caribbean Experience. New Brunswick, N.J.: Transaction, 2006.

Chan, Sucheng. Asian Americans: An Interpretive History. Boston: Twayne, 1991.

———. This Bittersweet Soil: The Chinese in California Agriculture, 1860–1910. Berkeley: University of California Press, 1986.

Chang, Federico. "La inmigración china en Cuba: Asociaciones y tradiciones." In De dónde son los cubanos, edited by Graciela Chailloux Laffita, 117–64. Havana: Editorial de Ciencias Sociales, 2005.

Chen, Edith Wen-Chu. "'You Are Like Us, You Eat Plátanos': Chinese Dominicans, Race, Ethnicity, and Identity." Afro-Hispanic Review 27.1 (2008): 23–40.

Chen, Yong. Chinese San Francisco, 1850–1943: A Trans-Pacific Community. Stanford: Stanford University Press, 2000.

Chen Da (Ch'en Ta). Emigrant Communities in South China: A Study of Overseas Migration and Its Influence on Standards of Living and Social Change. New York: Institute of Pacific Relations, 1940.

Chen Hansheng, ed. Huagong chuguo shiliao huibian [Collected historical materials on the emigration of Chinese labor]. Beijing: Zhonghua shuju, 1984.

Chen Kwong Min. Meizhou huaqiao tongjian (The Chinese in the Americas). New York: Overseas Chinese Culture Publishing Co., 1950.

Chen Mengyu. "Guba huaqiao shenghuo gaikuang" [The general situation of Cuban overseas Chinese]. Part I. Huaqiao Banyuekan 29 (August 15, 1933): 7–11.

Cheung Kong Lu. "Why Should We Come Back to China to Study." Nanda yu Huaqiao 1.1 (1923): 1–12.

Childs, Matt D. The 1812 Aponte Rebellion in Cuba and the Struggle against Atlantic Slavery. Chapel Hill: University of North Carolina Press, 2006.

China, Zongli geguo shiwu yamen. Chinese Emigration: Report of the Commission sent by China to Ascertain the Condition of Chinese Coolies in Cuba, 1874. Shanghai: Imperial Maritime Customs Press, 1876. Reprint, Taipei: Ch'eng Wen, 1970.

———. Zhongmei guanxi shiliao [Historical materials on Chinese American relations]. Taipei: Zhongyang yanjiuyuan jindaishi yanjiusuo [Academia Sinica: Institute of Modern History], 1968.

Choy, Armando, Gustavo Chui, and Moisés Sío Wong. Our History Is Still Being Written: The Story of Three Chinese-Cuban Generals in the Cuban Revolution. New York: Pathfinder Press, 2005.

Chuffat Latour, Antonio. *Apunte histórico de los chinos en Cuba*. Havana: Molina y Cia., 1927.

Cohen, Lucy M. *Chinese in the Post-Civil War South: A People without a History*. Baton Rouge: Louisiana State University Press, 1984.

Cohen, Robin. *Global Diasporas: An Introduction*. Seattle: University of Washington Press, 1997.

Corbitt, Duvon Clough. "Immigration in Cuba." *Hispanic American Historical Review* 22.2 (1942): 280–308.

———. *A Study of the Chinese in Cuba, 1847–1947*. Wilmore, Ky.: Asbury College, 1971.

Cosme Baños, Pedro. *Los Chinos en Regla 1847–1997: Documentos y comentarios*. Santiago de Cuba: Editorial Oriente, 1998.

Cuba. *Colección legislativa de la isla de Cuba, 1899*. Havana, 1900.

———, Centro de Estadística. *Noticias estadísticas de la Isla de Cuba, en 1862*. Havana: Imprenta del Gobierno, 1864.

———, Oficina del Censo. *Censo de la República de Cuba bajo la administración provisional de los Estados Unidos 1907*. Washington: Office of the Census of the United States, 1908.

Dana, Richard Henry, Jr. *To Cuba and Back: A Vacation Voyage*. Boston: Ticknor and Fields, 1859.

Daniels, Roger. *Asian America: Chinese and Japanese in the United States since 1850*. Seattle: University of Washington Press, 1988.

Dawdy, Shannon Lee. "*La Comida Mambisa*: Food, Farming, and Cuban Identity, 1839–1999." *New West Indian Guide/Nieuwe West-Indische Gids* 76.1–2 (2002): 47–80.

De la Fuente, Alejandro. *A Nation for All: Race, Inequality, and Politics in Twentieth-Century Cuba*. Chapel Hill: University of North Carolina Press, 2001.

Delgado, Grace Peña. *Making the Chinese Mexican: Global Migration, Localism, and Exclusion in the U.S.-Mexico Borderlands*. Stanford: Stanford University Press, 2012.

Deschamps Chapeaux, Pedro, and Juan Pérez de la Riva. *Contribución a la historia de la gente sin historia*. Havana: Editorial de Ciencias Sociales, 1974.

Dorsey, Joseph C. "Identity, Rebellion, and Social Justice among Chinese Contract Workers in Nineteenth-Century Cuba." *Latin American Perspectives* 31.3 (2004): 18–47.

Duara, Prasenjit. "Nationalists among Transnationals: Overseas Chinese and the Idea of China, 1900–1911." In *Ungrounded Empires: The Cultural Politics of Modern Chinese Transnationalism*, edited by Aihwa Ong and Donald M. Nonini, 39–60. New York: Routledge, 1997.

Edo y Llop, Enrique. *Memoria histórica de Cienfuegos y su jurisdicción*. 3rd ed. Havana: Úcar, García y Cía., 1943.

Ellis, R. Evan. *China in Latin America: The Whats and Wherefores*. Boulder, Colo.: Lynne Rienner, 2009.

Eng Herrera, Pedro J., and Mauro G. García Triana. *Martí en los chinos, los chinos en Martí*. Havana: Grupo Promotor del Barrio Chino de La Habana, 2003.

Eng Menéndez, Yrmina G. "Revitalización de las tradiciones chinas en Cuba: El proyecto integral de reanimación del Barrio Chino de La Habana." In *Cultura, tradición y comunidad: Perspectivas sobre la participación y el desarrollo en Cuba*, edited by Adrian H. Hearn, 200-243. Havana: Imagen Contemporánea, 2007.

Erenchun, Félix. *Anales de la isla de Cuba: Diccionario administrativo, económico, estadístico y legislativo*. Havana: Imprenta La Habanera, 1858.

Espinosa Luis, Mitzi. "*Si tú pleguntá, a mi gusta hacé cuento*. 'If you ask, I'll be happy to tell you': Felipe Luis Narrates His Story." Translated by Kathleen López. In *The Chinese in the Caribbean*, edited by Andrew R. Wilson, 129-42. Princeton: Markus Wiener, 2004.

Espiritu, Yen Le. *Asian American Panethnicity: Bridging Institutions and Identities*. Philadelphia: Temple University Press, 1992.

Fernández Robaina, Tomás. *El negro en Cuba 1902-1958: Apuntes para la historia de la lucha contra la discriminación racial*. Havana: Editorial de Ciencias Sociales, 1994.

Ferrer, Ada. *Insurgent Cuba: Race, Nation, and Revolution, 1868-1898*. Chapel Hill: University of North Carolina Press, 1999.

Fitzgerald, John. *Big White Lie: Chinese Australians in White Australia*. Sydney: University of New South Wales Press, 2007.

Foley, Neil. *The White Scourge: Mexicans, Blacks, and Poor Whites in Texas Cotton Culture*. Berkeley: University of California Press, 1997.

Foner, Nancy. "What's New about Transnationalism? New York Immigrants Today and at the Turn of the Century." *Diaspora* 6.3 (1997): 355-75.

Fong, Timothy. *The First Suburban Chinatown: The Remaking of Monterey Park, California*. Philadelphia: Temple University Press, 1994.

Fouchet, Max-Pol. *Wilfredo Lam*. Barcelona: Ediciones Poligrafa, S.A., 1976.

Fouron, Georges E., and Nina Glick Schiller. "The Generation of Identity: Redefining the Second Generation within a Transnational Social Field." In *Migration, Transnationalization, and Race in a Changing New York*, edited by Héctor R. Cordero-Guzmán, Robert C. Smith, and Ramón Grosfoguel, 58-86. Philadelphia: Temple University Press, 2001.

"From the Great Wall to the New World: China and Latin America in the 21st Century." *China Quarterly* 209 (2012), a special issue.

Gallagher, Kevin P., and Roberto Porzecanski. *The Dragon in the Room: China and the Future of Latin American Industrialization*. Stanford: Stanford University Press, 2009.

Gallenga, Antonio Carlo Napoleone. *The Pearl of the Antilles*. London: Chapman and Hall, 1873.

Gans, Herbert J. "Symbolic Ethnicity: The Future of Ethnic Groups and Cultures in America." *Ethnic and Racial Studies* 2.1 (1979): 1-20.

García Martínez, Orlando F. "La Brigada de Cienfuegos: Un análisis social de su formación." In *Espacios, silencios y los sentidos de la libertad: Cuba entre 1878 y 1912*, edited by Fernando Martínez Heredia, Rebecca J. Scott, and Orlando F. García Martínez, 163-92. Havana: Ediciones Unión, 2001.

García Triana, Mauro G. *Los chinos de Cuba y los nexos entre las dos naciones*.

2 vols. Havana: Sociedad Cubana de Estudios e Investigaciones Filosóficas, 2003.

García Triana, Mauro, and Pedro Eng Herrera. *The Chinese in Cuba, 1847–Now.* Edited and translated by Gregor Benton. Lanham, Md.: Lexington Books, 2009.

Giovannetti, Jorge L. "The Elusive Organization of 'Identity': Race, Religion, and Empire among Caribbean Migrants in Cuba." *Small Axe* 10.1 (2006): 1–27.

Glick, Clarence E. *Sojourners and Settlers: Chinese Migrants in Hawaii.* Honolulu: University Press of Hawaii, 1980.

Glick Schiller, Nina. "Transmigrants and Nation-States: Something Old and Something New in the U.S. Immigrant Experience." In *The Handbook of International Migration: The American Experience*, edited by Charles Hirschman, Philip Kasinitz, and Josh DeWind, 94–119. New York: Russell Sage Foundation, 1999.

Gobierno Provincial de Santa Clara. *Memoria explicativa del Estado y desenvolvimiento de la Hacienda Provincial, y de los trabajos realizados por el Gobierno y Consejo de la Provincia durante el año fiscal de 1903 á 1904, redactada en cumplimiento del precepto contenido en el artículo 27 de la Ley Orgánica Provincial de 10 de Marzo de 1903.* Havana: Imprenta de Rambla y Bouza, 1904.

Gonzales, Michael J. "Resistance among Asian Plantation Workers in Peru 1870–1920." In *From Chattel Slaves to Wage Slaves: The Dynamics of Labor Bargaining in the Americas*, edited by Mary Turner, 201–23. Bloomington: Indiana University Press, 1995.

Grupo Promotor del Barrio Chino. "Presencia china en Cuba." Havana: Fundación Fernando Ortiz, Ediciones GEO, 1999.

Guanche, Jesús. *Componentes étnicos de la nación cubana.* Havana: Fundación Fernando Ortiz, 1996.

Guarnizo, Luis Eduardo, and Michael Peter Smith. "The Locations of Transnationalism." In *Transnationalism from Below*, edited by Michael Peter Smith and Luis Eduardo Guarnizo, 3–34. New Brunswick, N.J.: Transaction, 1998.

Guerra, Lillian. *The Myth of José Martí: Conflicting Nationalisms in Early Twentieth-Century Cuba.* Chapel Hill: University of North Carolina Press, 2005.

Guridy, Frank Andre. *Forging Diaspora: Afro-Cubans and African Americans in a World of Empire and Jim Crow.* Chapel Hill: University of North Carolina Press, 2010.

Handlin, Oscar. *The Uprooted: The Epic Story of the Great Migrations That Made the American People.* Boston: Little, Brown, 1951.

Han Mei [Liu Chongmin]. "Yi ye guba huagong shi" [A page in the history of a Chinese laborer in Cuba]. *Wuyi Qiaoshi* 7 (1989): 32–33.

Hazard, Samuel. *Cuba with Pen and Pencil.* Hartford, Conn.: Hartford Publishing Company, 1871.

Hearn, Adrian H. "Harnessing the Dragon: Overseas Chinese Entrepreneurs in Mexico and Cuba." *China Quarterly* 209 (2012): 111–33.

Hearn, Adrian H., and José Luis León-Manríquez, eds. *China Engages Latin America: Tracing the Trajectory.* Boulder, Colo.: Lynne Rienner, 2011.

Helg, Aline. *Our Rightful Share: The Afro-Cuban Struggle for Equality, 1886–1912.* Chapel Hill: University of North Carolina Press, 1995.

Helly, Denise. *Idéologie et ethnicité: Les Chinois Macao à Cuba: 1847–1886*. Montreal: Les Presses de l'Université de Montréal, 1979.

———. Introduction. *The Cuba Commission Report: A Hidden History of the Chinese in Cuba*. Baltimore: Johns Hopkins University Press, 1993.

Hernández Catá, Alfonso. "Los chinos." In *Piedras preciosas*, 111–21. Madrid: Editorial Mundo Latino, 1927.

Herrera Jerez, Miriam, and Mario Castillo Santana. *De la memoria a la vida pública: Identidades, espacios y jerarquías de los chinos en La Habana republicana (1902–1968)*. Havana: Centro de Investigación y Desarrollo de la Cultura Cubana Juan Marinello, 2003.

He Xinquan, ed. *Peizheng xiaoshi 1889–1994* [History of Peizheng School]. Guangzhou: Peizheng zhongxue, 1994.

Hirabayashi, Lane Ryo, Akemi Kikumura-Yano, and James A. Hirabayashi, eds. *New Worlds, New Lives: Globalization and People of Japanese Descent in the Americas and from Latin America in Japan*. Stanford: Stanford University Press, 2002.

Holloway, Thomas H. *Immigrants on the Land: Coffee and Society in São Paulo, 1886–1934*. Chapel Hill: University of North Carolina Press, 1980.

Holt, Thomas C. *The Problem of Freedom: Race, Labor, and Politics in Jamaica and Britain, 1832–1938*. Baltimore: Johns Hopkins University Press, 1992.

Hom, Marlon K. *Songs of Gold Mountain: Cantonese Rhymes from San Francisco Chinatown*. Berkeley: University of California Press, 1987.

Howe, Julia Ward. *A Trip to Cuba*. Boston: Ticknor and Fields, 1860.

Hoy, William. *The Chinese Six Companies*. San Francisco: Chinese Consolidated Benevolent Association, 1942.

Hsu, Madeline Y. *Dreaming of Gold, Dreaming of Home: Transnationalism and Migration between the United States and South China, 1882–1943*. Stanford: Stanford University Press, 2000.

Huang, Belinda. "Teaching Chineseness in the Trans-Pacific Society: Overseas Chinese Education in Canada and the United States, 1900–1919." Ph.D. diss., Princeton University, 2009.

Huang, Cen, and Michael R. Godley. "Appendix Chapter: A Note on the Study of Qiaoxiang Ties." In *Qiaoxiang Ties: Interdisciplinary Approaches to 'Cultural Capitalism' in South China*, edited by Leo Douw, Cen Huang, and Michael R. Godley, 306–42. London: Kegan Paul International, 1999.

Huang Dingzhi. "Guba de sanminyue shubaoshe" [The *Sanmin* Study Society of Cuba]. In *Huaqiao yu xinhai geming* [Overseas Chinese and the 1911 Revolution], edited by Zhongguo shehui kexueyuan jindaishi yanjiusuo, 312–30. Beijing: Zhongguo shehui kexue chubanshe, 1981.

Huang Zhuocai. *Guba huaqiao jiashu gushi* [Family letters and stories of a Chinese in Cuba]. Guangzhou: Jinan daxue chubanshe, 2006.

Huang Zisheng. "Lun qiaoxiang yanjiu de xianzhuang ji yiyi" [On the present state and significance of *qiaoxiang* research]. *Huaqiao Huaren Lishi Yanjiu* 28.4 (1994): 1–3.

Huaqiao shi lunwen ziliao suoyin [Index of articles and materials on overseas Chinese history]. Guangzhou: Zhongshan daxue dongnanya lishi yanjiusuo and Zhongshan daxue tushuguan, 1981.

Huaqiao yu qiaowu shiliao xuanbian [Selected materials on overseas Chinese and overseas Chinese affairs]. 2 vols. Guangzhou: Guangdong renmin chubanshe, 1991.

Hu-DeHart, Evelyn. "Chinese Coolie Labour in Cuba in the Nineteenth Century: Free Labour or Neo-slavery?" *Slavery and Abolition* 14.1 (1993): 67–86.

———. "Indispensable Enemy or Convenient Scapegoat? A Critical Examination of Sinophobia in Latin America and the Caribbean, 1870s to 1930s." *Journal of Chinese Overseas* 5.1 (2009): 55–90.

———. "Multiculturalism in Latin American Studies: Locating the 'Asian' Immigrant; or, Where Are the *Chinos* and *Turcos*?" *Latin American Research Review* 44.2 (2009): 235–42.

———. "Opium and Social Control: Coolies on the Plantations of Peru and Cuba." *Journal of Chinese Overseas* 1.2 (2005): 169–83.

———. "Race Construction and Race Relations: Chinese and Blacks in Nineteenth-Century Cuba." In *Encounters: People of Asian Descent in the Americas*, edited by Roshni Rustomji-Kerns, 108–11. Lanham, Md.: Rowman and Littlefield, 1999.

———. "Racism and Anti-Chinese Persecution in Sonora, Mexico, 1876–1932." *Amerasia* 9.2 (1982): 1–28.

Ibarra, Jorge. *Ideología mambisa*. Havana: Instituto Cubano del Libro, 1967.

Iglesias García, Fe. "La concentración azucarera y la comarca de Cienfuegos." In *Espacios, silencios y los sentidos de la libertad, Cuba 1879–1912*, edited by Fernando Martínez Heredia, Rebecca J. Scott, and Orlando García Martínez, 85–107. Havana: Ediciones Unión, 2001.

Iglesias Utset, Marial. *Las metáforas del cambio en la vida cotidiana: Cuba 1898–1902*. Havana: Ediciones Unión, 2003.

Irick, Robert L. *Ch'ing Policy toward the Coolie Trade, 1847–1878*. Taipei: Chinese Materials Center, 1982.

Jacobson, Matthew Frye. *Special Sorrows: The Diasporic Imagination of Irish, Polish, and Jewish Immigrants in the United States*. Cambridge, Mass.: Harvard University Press, 1995.

Jiménez Pastrana, Juan. *Los chinos en la historia de Cuba: 1847–1930*. Havana: Editorial de Ciencias Sociales, 1983.

———. *Los chinos en las luchas por la liberación cubana (1847–1930)*. Havana: Instituto de Historia, 1963.

Johnson, Howard. "The Anti-Chinese Riots of 1918 in Jamaica." *Caribbean Quarterly* 28.3 (1982): 19–32.

Jung, Moon-Ho. *Coolies and Cane: Race, Labor, and Sugar in the Age of Emancipation*. Baltimore: Johns Hopkins University Press, 2006.

Kale, Madhavi. *Fragments of Empire: Capital, Slavery, and Indian Indentured Labor in the British Caribbean*. Philadelphia: University of Philadelphia Press, 1998.

Kenley, David L. *New Culture in a New World: The May Fourth Movement and the Chinese Diaspora in Singapore, 1919–1932*. New York: Routledge, 2003.

Khan, Aisha. *Callaloo Nation: Metaphors of Race and Religious Identity among South Asians in Trinidad.* Durham: Duke University Press, 2004.

Knight, Franklin W. *Slave Society in Cuba during the Nineteenth Century.* Madison: University of Wisconsin Press, 1970.

Kuhn, Philip A. *Chinese among Others: Emigration in Modern Times.* New York: Rowman and Littlefield, 2008.

Kurashige, Scott. *The Shifting Grounds of Race: Black and Japanese Americans in the Making of Multiethnic Los Angeles.* Princeton: Princeton University Press, 2007.

Kwong, Peter. *Chinatown, N.Y.: Labor and Politics, 1930–1950.* New York: Monthly Review Press, 1979.

Lai, Him Mark. *Becoming Chinese American: A History of Communities and Institutions.* Walnut Creek, Calif.: AltaMira Press, 2004.

———. "The Kuomintang in Chinese American Communities before World War II." In *Entry Denied: Exclusion and the Chinese Community in America, 1882–1943,* edited by Sucheng Chan, 170–212. Philadelphia: Temple University Press, 1991.

Lau, Maria. "'71' Series Photo Essay." *Afro-Hispanic Review* 27.1 (2008): 247–50.

Laurence, K. O. *A Question of Labour: Indentured Immigration into Trinidad and British Guiana, 1875–1917.* New York: St. Martin's Press, 1994.

Lausent-Herrera, Isabelle. "Tusans (*tusheng*) and the Changing Chinese Community in Peru." *Journal of Chinese Overseas* 5.1 (2009): 115–52.

Lee, Erika. *At America's Gates: Chinese Immigration during the Exclusion Era, 1882–1943.* Chapel Hill: University of North Carolina Press, 2003.

———. "Orientalisms in the Americas: A Hemispheric Approach to Asian American History." *Journal of Asian American Studies* 8.3 (2005): 235–56.

Lee, Robert G. *Orientals: Asian Americans in Popular Culture.* Philadelphia: Temple University Press, 1999.

Lee-Loy, Anne-Marie. *Searching for Mr. Chin: Constructions of Nation and the Chinese in West Indian Literature.* Philadelphia: Temple University Press, 2010.

Lee Sung, Betty. *Mountain of Gold: The Story of the Chinese in America.* New York: Macmillan, 1967.

Leonard, Karen Isaksen. *Making Ethnic Choices: California's Punjabi Mexican Americans.* Philadelphia: Temple University Press, 1992.

Le-Roy y Cassá, Jorge. *Inmigración anti-sanitaria.* Havana: Dorrbecker, 1929.

Lesser, Jeffrey. *A Discontented Diaspora: Japanese Brazilians and the Meanings of Ethnic Militancy, 1960–1980.* Durham: Duke University Press, 2007.

———. *Negotiating National Identity: Immigrants, Minorities, and the Struggle for Ethnicity in Brazil.* Durham and London: Duke University Press, 1999.

———, ed. *Searching for Home Abroad: Japanese Brazilians and Transnationalism.* Durham: Duke University Press, 2003.

Levine, Robert. *Tropical Diaspora: The Jewish Experience in Cuba.* Gainesville: University Press of Florida, 1993.

Levis, Richard J. *Diary of a Spring Holiday in Cuba.* Philadelphia: Porter and Coates, 1872.

Levitt, Peggy. *The Transnational Villagers*. Berkeley: University of California Press, 2001.

Levitt, Peggy, and Mary C. Waters, eds. *The Changing Face of Home: The Transnational Lives of the Second Generation*. New York: Russell Sage Foundation, 2002.

Lim, Christine Suchen. *Hua Song: Stories of the Chinese Diaspora*. San Francisco: Long River Press, 2005.

Li Minghuan. *"We Need Two Worlds": Chinese Immigrant Associations in a Western Society*. Amsterdam: Amsterdam University Press, 1999.

Ling, Huping. *Chinese Chicago: Race, Transnational Migration, and Community since 1870*. Stanford: Stanford University Press, 2012.

———. *Chinese St. Louis: From Enclave to Cultural Community*. Philadelphia: Temple University Press, 2004.

Liu Chongmin, ed. *Taishan xian huaqiao zhi* [Taishan County overseas Chinese gazette]. Taishan: Taishan xian qiaowu bangongshi, 1992.

Lo, Emily. "A Cuban-Chinese *Familia.*" In *Cuba: Idea of a Nation Displaced*, edited by Andrea O'Reilly Herrera, 215–22. Albany: State University of New York Press, 2007.

Look Lai, Walton. *Indentured Labor, Caribbean Sugar: Chinese and Indian Migrants to the British West Indies, 1838–1918*. Baltimore: Johns Hopkins University Press, 1993.

Look Lai, Walton, and Tan Chee-Beng. *The Chinese in Latin America and the Caribbean*. Leiden: Brill, 2010.

López, Kathleen. "The Revitalization of Havana's Chinatown: Invoking Chinese Cuban History." *Journal of Chinese Overseas* 5.1 (2009): 177–200.

López-Calvo, Ignacio. *Imaging the Chinese in Cuban Literature and Culture*. Gainesville: University Press of Florida, 2008.

Losada Álvarez, Abel F. "The Cuban Labor Market and Immigration from Spain, 1900–1930." *Cuban Studies* 25: 147–64.

Louie, Andrea. *Chineseness across Borders: Negotiating Chinese Identities in China and the United States*. Durham: Duke University Press, 2004.

Lowe, Lisa. *Immigrant Acts: On Asian American Cultural Politics*. Durham: Duke University Press, 1996.

———. "The Intimacies of Four Continents." In *Haunted by Empire: Geographies of Intimacy in North American History*, edited by Ann Laura Stoler, 191–212. Durham: Duke University Press, 2006.

Lutz, Jessie Gregory. *China and the Christian Colleges, 1850–1950*. Ithaca: Cornell University Press, 1971.

Lydon, Sandy. *Chinese Gold: The Chinese in the Monterey Bay Region*. Capitola, Calif.: Capitola Book Company, 1985.

Ma, L. Eve Armentrout. *Revolutionaries, Monarchists, and Chinatowns: Chinese Politics in the Americas and the 1911 Revolution*. Honolulu: University of Hawaii Press, 1990.

Maluquer de Motes, Jordi. *Nación e inmigración: Los españoles en Cuba (ss. XIX y XX)*. Gijón: Ediciones Jucar, 1992.

Martí, José. *Obras completas*. 26 vols. Havana: Editorial de Ciencias Sociales, 1975.

Martín, Juan Luis. *De donde vinieron los chinos de Cuba: Los jaca, los joló, los puntí y los amoyanos, en la vida cubana*. Havana: Editorial Atalaya, 1939.

Martinez-Alier, Verena. *Marriage, Class, and Colour in Nineteenth-Century Cuba: A Study of Racial Attitudes and Sexual Values in a Slave Society*. Cambridge: Cambridge University Press, 1974.

Martínez Fortún, J. A. *Monografías históricas de Placetas*. Remedios, 1944.

Mazumdar, Sucheta. "'What Happened to the Women?' Chinese and Indian Male Migration to the United States in Global Perspective." In *Asian/Pacific Islander American Women: A Historical Anthology*, edited by Shirley Hune and Gail M. Nomura, 54–78. New York: New York University Press, 2003.

McGillivray, Gillian. *Blazing Cane: Sugar Communities, Class, and State Formation in Cuba, 1868–1959*. Durham: Duke University Press, 2009.

McGuinness, Aims. *Path of Empire: Panama and the California Gold Rush*. Ithaca: Cornell University Press, 2007.

McHatton-Ripley, Eliza. *From Flag to Flag: A Woman's Adventures and Experiences in the South during the War, in Mexico, and in Cuba*. New York: D. Appleton, 1889.

McKeown, Adam. *Chinese Migrant Networks and Cultural Change: Peru, Chicago, Hawaii, 1900–1936*. Chicago: University of Chicago Press, 2001.

———. *Melancholy Order: Asian Migration and the Globalization of Borders*. New York: Columbia University Press, 2008.

McLeod, Marc C. "Undesirable Aliens: Race, Ethnicity, and Nationalism in the Comparison of Haitian and British West Indian Immigrant Workers in Cuba, 1912–1939." *Journal of Social History* 31.3 (1998): 599–623.

Meagher, Arnold J. *The Coolie Trade: The Traffic in Chinese Laborers to Latin America, 1847–1874*. Bloomington, Ind.: Xlibris, 2008.

Metzger, Sean. "Ripples in the Seascape: The *Cuba Commission Report* and the Idea of Freedom." *Afro-Hispanic Review* 27.1 (2008): 105–21.

Min, Pyong Gap, ed. *Second Generation: Ethnic Identity among Asian Americans*. Walnut Creek, Calif.: AltaMira Press, 2002.

Molina, Natalia. *Fit to Be Citizens?: Public Health and Race in Los Angeles, 1879–1939*. Berkeley: University of California Press, 2006.

Montes de Oca Choy, María Teresa, and Roberto Vargas Lee. "Levando a la práctica la cultura china: La Cátedra de Estudios Chinos y la Escuela Cubana de Wushu." In *Cultura, tradición y comunidad: Perspectivas sobre la participación y el desarrollo en Cuba*, edited by Adrian H. Hearn, 162–99. Havana: Imagen Contemporanea, 2007.

Moreno Fraginals, Manuel. *El ingenio: Complejo económico social cubano del azúcar*. 3 vols. Havana: Editorial de Ciencias Sociales, 1978.

Moya, José C. *Cousins and Strangers: Spanish Immigrants in Buenos Aires, 1850–1930*. Berkeley: University of California Press, 1998.

Munasinghe, Viranjini. *Callaloo or Tossed Salad? East Indians and the Cultural Politics of Identity in Trinidad*. Ithaca: Cornell University Press, 2001.

Murray, David R. *Odious Commerce: Britain, Spain, and the Abolition of the Cuban Slave Trade*. Cambridge: Cambridge University Press, 1980.

Nakano Glenn, Evelyn. "Split Household, Small Producer and Dual Wage Earner: An Analysis of Chinese-American Family Strategies." *Journal of Marriage and the Family* 45.1 (1983): 35–48.

Narvaez, Benjamin Nicolas. "Chinese Coolies in Cuba and Peru: Race, Labor, and Immigration, 1839–1886." Ph.D. diss., University of Texas at Austin, 2010.

Nee, Victor G., and Brett de Bary. *Longtime Californ': A Documentary Study of an American Chinatown.* New York: Pantheon Books, 1972.

Nuñez Jiménez, Antonio. *La abuela.* Havana: Ediciones Letras Cubanas, 1998.

Okihiro, Gary Y. *Cane Fires: The Anti-Japanese Movement in Hawaii, 1865–1945.* Philadelphia: Temple University Press, 1991.

———. *The Columbia Guide to Asian American History.* New York: Columbia University Press, 2001.

———. *Margins and Mainstreams: Asians in American History and Culture.* Seattle: University of Washington Press, 1994.

Omi, Michael, and Howard Winant. *Racial Formation in the United States: From the 1960s to the 1980s.* New York: Routledge and Kegan Paul, 1986.

Ortiz, Fernando. *Cuban Counterpoint: Tobacco and Sugar.* Translated by Harriet de Onis. New York: Alfred Knopf, 1947. Reprint, Durham: Duke University Press, 1995.

Pan, Lynn. *Sons of the Yellow Emperor: A History of the Chinese Diaspora.* New York: Kodansha International, 1990.

Pappademos, Melina. *Black Political Activism and the Cuban Republic.* Chapel Hill: University of North Carolina Press, 2011.

Paquette, Robert L. *Sugar Is Made with Blood: The Conspiracy of La Escalera and the Conflict between Empires over Slavery in Cuba.* Middletown, Conn.: Wesleyan University Press, 1988.

Park, Robert E. "Human Migration and the Marginal Man." *American Journal of Sociology* 33.6 (1928): 881–93.

Park, Yoon Jung. *A Matter of Honour: Being Chinese in South Africa.* Johannesburg: Jacana Media (Pty) Ltd., 2008.

Pedraza, Silvia. *Political Disaffection in Cuba's Revolution and Exodus.* New York and London: Cambridge University Press, 2007.

Pérez, Louis A., Jr. *Cuba: Between Reform and Revolution.* 4th ed. New York: Oxford University Press, 2011.

———. *Cuba between Empires, 1878–1902.* Pittsburgh: University of Pittsburgh Press, 1983.

———. "In the Service of the Revolution: Two Decades of Cuban Historiography, 1959–1979." *Hispanic American Historical Review* 60.1 (1980): 79–89.

———. *To Die in Cuba: Suicide and Society.* Chapel Hill: University of North Carolina Press, 2005.

Pérez, Pelayo. "El peligro amarillo y el peligro negro." *Cuba Contemporánea* 9 (1915): 251–60.

Pérez de la Riva, Juan. *El barracón y otros ensayos.* Havana: Editorial de Ciencias Sociales, 1975.

———. *Los culíes chinos en Cuba (1847–1880): Contribución al estudio de la inmigración contratada en el Caribe.* Havana: Editorial de Ciencias Sociales, 2000.

Pérez Fernández, Rolando, and Santiago Rodríguez González. "La corneta china (suona) en Cuba: Una contribución cultural asiática trascendente." *Afro-Hispanic Review* 27.1 (2008): 139–60.

Pérez Sarduy, Pedro, and Jean Stubbs, eds. *Afrocuba: An Anthology of Cuban Writing on Race, Politics and Culture.* Melbourne and New York: Ocean Press, 1993.

Perry, Elizabeth J. *Shanghai on Strike: The Politics of Chinese Labor.* Stanford: Stanford University Press, 1993.

Perseverancia, Ramón de. *Los chinos y su charada: Folleto de actualidad.* Havana: Imprenta La Primera de Belascoaín, 1894.

Peterson, Glen. "Overseas Chinese Studies in the People's Republic of China." *Provincial China* 7.1 (2002): 103–21.

Pichardo Viñals, Hortensia. *Documentos para la historia de Cuba.* Havana: Editorial de Ciencias Sociales, 1976.

Pite, Rebekah E. "The Force of Food: Life on the Atkins Family Sugar Plantation in Cienfuegos, Cuba, 1884–1900." *Massachusetts Historical Review* 5 (2003): 59–93.

Porter, Robert P. *Industrial Cuba: Being a Study of Present Commercial and Industrial Conditions, with Suggestions as to the Opportunities Presented in the Island for American Capital, Enterprise, and Labour.* New York: G. P. Putnam's Sons, 1899.

Portes, Alejandro, and Rubén G. Rumbaut. *Immigrant America: A Portrait.* 2nd ed. Berkeley: University of California Press, 1996.

Prashad, Vijay. *Everybody Was Kung Fu Fighting: Afro-Asian Connections and the Myth of Cultural Purity.* Boston: Beacon, 2001.

Putnam, Lara. *The Company They Kept: Migrants and the Politics of Gender in Caribbean Costa Rica, 1870–1960.* Chapel Hill: University of North Carolina Press, 2002.

Quesada, Gonzalo de. *Mi primera ofrenda.* New York: Imprenta de El Porvenir, 1892.

———. *The Chinese and Cuban Independence.* Leipzig: Breitkopf and Härtel, 1912.

Ramos Hernández, Reinaldo, Arturo A. Pedroso Alés, and Flor Inés Cassola Triana. "Luchas por el control del Barrio Chino de la Habana (1926)." *Catauro* 2.2 (2000): 34–49.

Rao, Nancy Yunhwa. "The Public Face of Chinatown: Actresses, Actors, Playwrights, and Audiences of Chinatown Theaters in San Francisco during the 1920s." *Journal of the Society for American Music* 5.2 (2011): 235–70.

Rénique, Gerardo. "Race, Region, and Nation: Sonora's Anti-Chinese Racism and Mexico's Postrevolutionary Nationalism, 1920s–1930s." *Race and Nation in Modern Latin America*, edited by Nancy P. Appelbaum, Anne S. Macpherson, and Karin Alejandra Rosemblatt, 211–36. Chapel Hill: University of North Carolina Press, 2003.

Rivas, Zelideth María. "Negotiating Mixed Race: Projection, Nostalgia, and the Rejection of Japanese-Brazilian Biracial Children." *Journal of Asian American Studies* 14.3 (2011): 361–88.

Rodney, Walter. *A History of the Guyanese Working People, 1881–1905*. Baltimore: Johns Hopkins University Press, 1981.

Rodríguez Pastor, Humberto. *Herederos del dragón: Historia de la comunidad china en el Perú*. Lima: Fondo Editorial del Congreso del Perú, 2000.

———. *Hijos del Celeste Imperio en el Perú*. Lima: Instituto de Apoyo Agrario, 1989.

Rodríguez Ruiz, Pablo. "Relaciones inter-étnicas e interraciales en el Barrio Chino de La Habana (Un estudio desde los chinos y sus descendientes)." *Catauro* 2.2 (2000): 103–26.

Rodríguez San Pedro, Joaquín. *Legislación ultramarina*. 13 vols. Madrid: Imprenta de los Señores Viota, Cubas y Vicente, 1865–68.

Roediger, David. *The Wages of Whiteness: Race and the Making of the American Working Class*. London and New York: Verso, 1991.

Roloff y Mialofsky, Carlos, and Gerardo Forrest, comps. *Índice alfabético y defunciones del Ejército Libertador de Cuba Guerra de Independencia iniciada el 24 de Febrero de 1895 y terminada oficialmente el 24 de Agosto de 1898*. Havana: Imprenta de Rambla y Bouza, 1901.

Romero, Robert Chao. *The Chinese in Mexico, 1882–1940*. Tucson: University of Arizona Press, 2010.

———. "Transnational Chinese Immigrant Smuggling to the United States via Mexico and Cuba, 1882–1916." *Amerasia Journal* 30.3 (2004/2005): 1–16.

Ropp, Steven Masami. "Secondary Migration and the Politics of Identity for Asian Latinos in Los Angeles." *Journal of Asian American Studies* 3.2 (2000): 219–29.

Rouse, Roger. "Mexican Migration and the Social Space of Postmodernism." *Diaspora* 1.1 (1991): 8–23.

Rousseau, Pablo L., and Pablo Díaz de Villegas. *Memoria descriptiva, histórica y biográfica de Cienfuegos y las fiestas del primer centenario de la fundación de esta ciudad*. Havana, 1920.

Rustomji-Kerns, Roshni, ed. *Encounters: People of Asian Descent in the Americas*. Lanham, Md.: Rowman and Littlefield, 1999.

Saco, José Antonio. *Colección póstuma de papeles científicos, históricos, políticos y de otros ramos sobre la isla de Cuba*. Havana: Miguel de Villa, 1881.

Sáenz Rovner, Eduardo. *The Cuban Connection: Drug Trafficking, Smuggling, and Gambling in Cuba from the 1920s to the Revolution*. Translated by Russ Davidson. Chapel Hill: University of North Carolina Press, 2008.

Sagra, Ramón de la. *Cuba en 1860, o sea cuadro de sus adelantos en la población, la agricultura, el comercio y las rentas públicas*. Paris: L. Hachette y ca., 1863.

———. *Historia física, económico-política, intelectual y moral de la Isla de Cuba*. Paris: L. Hachette y ca., 1861.

Sartorius, David. "My Vassals: Free-Colored Militias in Cuba and the Ends of Spanish Empire." *Journal of Colonialism and Colonial History* 5.2 (2004).

Sawyer, Mark Q. *Racial Politics in Post-Revolutionary Cuba*. New York: Cambridge University Press, 2006.

Saxton, Alexander. *The Indispensable Enemy: Labor and the Anti-Chinese Movement in California*. Berkeley: University of California Press, 1971.

Scarpaci, Joseph L., Roberto Segre, and Mario Coyula. *Havana: Two Faces of the Antillean Metropolis*. Rev. ed. Chapel Hill: University of North Carolina Press, 2002.

Scherer, Frank F. "A Culture of Erasure: Orientalism and Chineseness in Cuba, 1847–1997." Master's thesis. York University, 2000.

———. "Sanfancón: Orientalism, Self-Orientalism, and 'Chinese Religion' in Cuba." In *Nation Dance: Religion, Identity, and Cultural Difference in the Caribbean*, edited by Patrick Taylor, 153–70. Bloomington: Indiana University Press, 2001.

Schiavone Camacho, Julia María. *Chinese Mexicans: Transpacific Migration and the Search for a Homeland, 1910–1960*. Chapel Hill: University of North Carolina Press, 2012.

Schmidt-Nowara, Christopher. *Empire and Antislavery: Spain, Cuba, and Puerto Rico, 1833–1874*. Pittsburgh: University of Pittsburgh Press, 1999.

Scott, Rebecca J. *Degrees of Freedom: Louisiana and Cuba after Slavery*. Cambridge, Mass.: Harvard University Press, 2005.

———. "Race, Labor, and Citizenship in Cuba: A View from the Sugar District of Cienfuegos, 1886–1909." *Hispanic American Historical Review* 78.4 (1998): 687–728.

———. *Slave Emancipation in Cuba: The Transition to Free Labor, 1860–1899*. Princeton: Princeton University Press, 1985.

Scott, Rebecca J., and Michael Zeuske. "Property in Writing, Property on the Ground: Pigs, Horses, Land, and Citizenship in the Aftermath of Slavery, Cuba, 1880–1909." *Comparative Studies in Society and History* 44.4 (2002): 669–99.

Seuc, Napoleón. *La colonia china de Cuba (1930–1960): Antecedentes, memorias y vivencias*. Miami: Ahora Printing, 1998.

Shepherd, Verene A. *Maharani's Misery: Narratives of a Passage from India to the Caribbean*. Kingston: University of the West Indies Press, 2002.

Sinn, Elizabeth. *Power and Charity: The Early History of the Tung Wah Hospital, Hong Kong*. Hong Kong: Oxford University Press, 1989.

Siu, Lok. "Chino Latino Restaurants: Converging Communities, Identities, and Cultures." *Afro-Hispanic Review* 27.1 (2008): 161–71.

———. *Memories of a Future Home: Diasporic Citizenship of Chinese in Panama*. Stanford: Stanford University Press, 2005.

Siu, Paul C. P. *The Chinese Laundryman: A Study of Social Isolation*, edited by John Kuo Wei Tchen. New York: New York University Press, 1987.

Skinner, G. William. *Chinese Society in Thailand: An Analytical History*. Ithaca: Cornell University Press, 1957.

Sonoda, Setsuko. "Thinking Cuban Chinese from the Qing Government's Domestic Policy (1880s–1890s)." Paper presented at the VI Festival de Chinos de Ultramar, Conferencia Teórica Internacional, Emigración China en la Modernidad, Havana, 31 May–2 June 2003.

So Wai-chor. *The Kuomintang Left in the National Revolution, 1924–1931: The Leftist Alternative in Republican China*. Hong Kong: Oxford University Press, 1991.

Stewart, Watt. *Chinese Bondage in Peru: A History of the Chinese Coolie in Peru, 1849–1874*. Durham: Duke University Press, 1951.

Sung, Betty Lee. *Mountain of Gold: The Story of the Chinese in America*. New York: Macmillan, 1967.

Su Xingbo. "Wo luju guba jinxing geming huodong de huiyi [Memoir of my revolutionary activity in Cuba]." *Xinhui wenshi ziliao xuanji* [Selection of cultural and historical materials of Xinhui] 9 (1983): 37–70.

Takaki, Ronald. *Strangers from a Different Shore: A History of Asian Americans*. Boston: Little, Brown, 1989.

Tchen, John Kuo Wei. *New York before Chinatown: Orientalism and the Shaping of American Culture, 1776–1882*. Baltimore: Johns Hopkins University Press, 1999.

Tejeiro, Guillermo. *Historia ilustrada de la Colonia China en Cuba*. Havana, 1947.

Tinker, Hugh. *A New System of Slavery: The Export of Indian Labour Overseas, 1830–1920*. London: Oxford University Press, 1974.

Torrente, Mariano. *Memoria sobre la esclavitud en la isla de Cuba, con observaciones sobre los asertos de la prensa inglesa relativos al trafico de esclavos*. London: C. Wood, 1853.

Trujillo y Monagas, José. *Los criminales de Cuba*. Barcelona, 1882.

Tsuda, Takeyuki. *Strangers in the Ethnic Homeland: Japanese Brazilian Return Migration in Transnational Perspective*. New York: Columbia University Press, 2003.

U.S. War Department. *Report on the Census of Cuba 1899*. Washington: Government Printing Office, 1900.

Valdés Bernal, Sergio. *Lengua nacional e identidad cultural del cubano*. Havana: Editorial de Ciencias Sociales, 1998.

Valdés Millán, Ana. *Una cultura milenaria en el siglo XX guantanamero*. Guantánamo: Editorial El Mar y la Montaña, 2005.

Valenzuela, Abel, Jr. "Day Laborers as Entrepreneurs?" *Journal of Ethnic and Migration Studies* 27.2 (2001): 335–52.

Varela, Beatriz. *Lo chino en el habla cubana*. Miami: Ediciones Universal, 1980.

Wang, Dong. *Managing God's Higher Learning: U.S.–China Cultural Encounter and Canton Christian College (Lingnan University), 1888–1952*. Lanham, Md.: Lexington Books, 2007.

Wang Gungwu. *China and the Chinese Overseas*. Singapore: Times Academic Press, 1991.

Waters, Mary C. *Ethnic Options: Choosing Identities in America*. Berkeley: University of California Press, 1990.

Whitney, Robert. *State and Revolution in Cuba: Mass Mobilization and Political Change, 1920–1940*. Chapel Hill: University of North Carolina Press, 2001.

Wickberg, Edgar. "Anti-Sinicism and Chinese Identity Options in the Philippines." In *Essential Outsiders: Chinese and Jews in the Modern Transformation of Southeast Asia and Central Europe*, edited by Daniel Chirot and Anthony Reid, 153–83. Seattle: University of Washington Press, 1997.

———. *The Chinese in Philippine Life, 1850–1898*. New Haven: Yale University Press, 1965.

Williams-León, Teresa, and Cynthia L. Nakashima, eds. *The Sum of Our Parts: Mixed Heritage Asian Americans*. Philadelphia: Temple University Press, 2001.

Wilson, Andrew R. *Ambition and Identity: Chinese Merchant Elites in Colonial Manila, 1880–1916*. Honolulu: University of Hawaii Press, 2004.

———, ed. *The Chinese in the Caribbean*. Princeton: Markus Wiener Publishers, 2004.

Wright, Irene Aloha. *Cuba*. New York: Macmillan, 1910.

Yen Ching-hwang. *Coolies and Mandarins: China's Protection of Overseas Chinese during the Late Ch'ing Period (1851–1911)*. Singapore: Singapore University Press, 1985.

———. *Studies in Modern Overseas Chinese History*. Singapore: Times Academic Press, 1995.

Yu, Renqiu. *To Save China, To Save Ourselves: The Chinese Hand Laundry Alliance of New York*. Philadelphia: Temple University Press, 1992.

Yuan Ding and Chen Liyuan. "1946–49 nian Guangdong qiaohui taobi wenti" [Evasion of overseas Chinese remittances in Guangdong, 1946–1949]. *Huaqiao Huaren Lishi Yanjiu* 3 (2001): 9–20.

Yun, Lisa. *The Coolie Speaks: Chinese Indentured Laborers and African Slaves in Cuba*. Philadelphia: Temple University Press, 2008.

———. "Signifying 'Asian' and Afro-Cultural Poetics: A Conversation with William Luis, Albert Chong, Karen Tei Yamashita, and Alejandro Campos García." *Afro-Hispanic Review* 27.1 (2008): 183–211.

Yung, Judy. *Unbound Feet: A Social History of Chinese Women in San Francisco*. Berkeley: University of California Press, 1995.

Zanetti, Oscar, and Alejandro García. *Sugar and Railroads: A Cuban History, 1837–1959*. Translated by Franklin W. Knight and Mary Todd. Chapel Hill: The University of North Carolina Press, 1998.

Zeuske, Michael. "Hidden Markers, Open Secrets: On Naming, Race-Marking, and Race-Making in Cuba." *New West Indian Guide/Nieuwe West-Indische Gids* 76, nos. 3 & 4 (2002): 211–41.

———. "'Los negros hicimos la independencia': Aspectos de la movilización afrocubana en un hinterland cubano. Cienfuegos entre colonia y República." In *Espacios, silencios y los sentidos de la libertad: Cuba entre 1878 y 1912*, edited by Fernando Martínez Heredia, Rebecca J. Scott, and Orlando F. García Martínez, 193–234. Havana: Ediciones Unión, 2001.

Zhang Kai. "Guba huagong yu zhonggu jianjiao shimo" [Chinese laborers in Cuba and the establishment of Sino-Cuban diplomatic relations]. *Huaqiao Huaren Lishi Yanjiu* 4 (1988): 3–11.

Zhou Nanjing, ed. *Huaqiao huaren baike quanshu* [Encyclopedia of overseas Chinese]. Beijing: Zhongguo huaqiao chubanshe, 1998.

Acknowledgments

My journey tracing the history of the Chinese in Cuba began with my own migration from the field of East Asian to Latin American and Caribbean studies. Along the way, the generosity of scholars, archivists, and librarians and the willingness of Chinese Cubans to share their memories, letters, and photographs with me made this work possible.

In Cuba, the Archivo Histórico Provincial de Cienfuegos is a repository of documentation on the rich, layered history of Chinese settlement. I am grateful to the staff and to former director Orlando García Martínez, who warmly welcomed me and taught me much about local history. Long days in the Cienfuegos archive interspersed with forays into former Chinese neighborhoods and cemeteries were made more productive and enjoyable with Mitzi Espinosa Luis's friendship and keen eye for detail. Now as the cultural liaison for the Asociación Nacional Min Chih Tang, she continues to help researchers, filmmakers, photographers, and individuals tracing family histories. In Havana, I thank the staffs of the Archivo Nacional de Cuba and the Biblioteca Nacional José Martí. Through the Casa de Altos Estudios Don Fernando Ortiz de la Universidad de La Habana, led by Eduardo Torres Cuevas, my exchanges with Federico Chang, Jesús Guanche Pérez, María Teresa Montes de Oca Choy, and Sergio Valdés Bernal on the Chinese in Cuban history and identity have been invaluable. Mario Castillo Santana, Pedro Cosme Baños, Mercedes Crespo, Yrmina Eng Menéndez, Tomás Fernández Robaina, Miriam Herrera Jerez, Fe Iglesias García, Yanet Jiménez Rojas, Fernando Martínez Heredia, and Julio Tang Zambrana also welcomed me and shared insights and resources. A host of Chinese Cuban community leaders and members helped me along the way, among them Jorge Alay Jo, Alfonso Chao Chiu, Jorge Chao Chui, Armando Choy Rodríguez, Gustavo Chui Beltrán, Carmen Eng Acuay, Abel Fung, María Lam Lee, Felipe Luis, Santiago Luis, Neil Paneque, Mirta Sam Echavarría, and Moisés Sío Wong. I am indebted to Violeta and Lourdes Luis Quintana and Blas and Santiago Pelayo Díaz for our exchanges over the course of a decade. Pedro Eng Herrera generously shared material from his personal collection, and he and his wife Belkis have welcomed me and other foreign scholars into their home, a living museum.

Documentary material on the Chinese overseas is scattered throughout China, reflecting the paths of migrants and the traces they left behind. I am grateful to the staffs of the many archives and libraries I visited. I thank Gao Weinong, Huang Kunzhang, Li Anshan, Liu Quan, Wan Xiaohong, Yuan Ding, Zhang Yinglong, and Zhou Yu'e for orienting me to research in China. Zheng Liren was instrumental in connecting me with the Institute of Overseas Chinese Studies at Jinan University in Guangzhou, which served as a home base for my research. Chen Liyuan accompanied me for much of my fieldwork in Guangdong and welcomed me into her home in Xinhui, where I took part in traditional festivals and learned first-hand about the central role of the ancestral village for Chinese families. I also benefited from the expertise of Wuyi University retired professor Mei Weiqian and local historian of Taishan Liu Chongmin during visits to emigrant hometowns and conversations over dim sum. The overseas Chinese affairs offices of Taishan City and of Shadui and Daze in Xinhui County and the Returned Overseas Chinese Federation of Xinhui City provided assistance with locating descendants of emigrants to Cuba. I am especially grateful for the efforts of Huang Zhuocai, Evelyn Hu-DeHart, Keng We Koh, Isabelle Lausent-Herrera, Rebecca Scott, Dale Wilson, and Xu Yun toward Mitzi Espinosa Luis's reunion with her Chinese relatives in May 2009.

In the United States, I thank the staffs of the New York Public Library, Library of Congress, and National Archives, as well as Peter Drummey of the Massachusetts Historical Society for his assistance with accessing the Atkins Family Papers.

I am indebted to Rebecca Scott for the profound influence she had on the formative stages of my research. Her work on slave emancipation, labor, and citizenship has informed my own questions about Chinese migration to Caribbean colonies. Throughout graduate school and beyond, she has remained a model of intellectual generosity and scholarly rigor. While providing me with a solid grounding in Chinese history, Ernie Young encouraged my pursuit of a project that ultimately moved me outside the field. I am also grateful to Ruth Behar, Sueann Caulfield, Chun-shu Chang, Fernando Coronil, Erik Mueggler, Silvia Pedraza, Leslie Pincus, and Julie Skurski for their contributions to my training as a scholar and teacher.

Since I began work on this topic, I have enjoyed exchanges with scholars who offer different disciplinary and theoretical approaches to the study of the Chinese diaspora in Latin America and the Caribbean. I have learned much from the work and example set by Evelyn Hu-DeHart, who has truly pioneered research in this area and has connected with an entire generation of scholars. She offered detailed, thoughtful recommendations for improving this book. I have also greatly benefited from the scholarship and encouragement of Walton Look Lai, Isabelle Lausent-Herrera, and Lisa Yun. Ricardo Laremont and Lisa Yun have taken time out, each time I see them, to share scholarly insights and practical advice. My work is informed by and in dialogue with the exciting work on Asians in Latin America and the Caribbean from Jason Chang, Clara Chu, Grace Delgado Peña, Fredy González, Adrian Hearn, Erika Lee, Anne-Marie Lee Loy, Jeffrey Lesser, Ignacio López-Calvo, William Luis, Adam McKeown, Ben Narvaez, Gonzalo Paz, Gerardo Rénique, Zeli Rivas, Robert Chao Romero, Julia Schiavone Camacho, Lok Siu, and Elliot Young. My experiences in the archives and at conferences have been enhanced by their companionship over Chinese Cuban meals in Havana, banquets in Hong Kong, or roti and "liming" in Trinidad.

A visiting faculty position at Hamilton College through the Consortium for Faculty Diversity in Liberal Arts Colleges program enabled me to write a detailed prospectus for the book and teach specialized classes amidst a supportive intellectual community. I am grateful to members of the Department of History, especially Kevin Grant, Shoshana Keller, Robert Paquette, Lisa Trivedi, and Tom Wilson. I also benefited immensely from feedback on my work during my first tenure-track position at the City University of New York. I thank colleagues in the Department of Latin American and Puerto Rican Studies (LAPRS) at Lehman College: David Badillo,

Laird Bergad, Forrest Colburn, Licia Fiol-Matta, Alyshia Gálvez, Teresita Levy, Milagros Ricourt, and Xavier Totti, as well as Tim Alborn, Mario González-Corzo, José Luis Rénique, and the Bildner Center for Western Hemisphere Studies, directed by Mauricio Font. My cohort of the CUNY Faculty Fellowship Publications Program in Spring 2008, led by Virginia Sánchez-Korrol, provided invaluable feedback on individual chapters, and I thank Cindy Lobel, Vicky Núñez, Jodie Roure, Paula Saunders, Loti Silber, and Peter Vellon.

Several intellectual communities at my home institution, Rutgers University, have welcomed me and supported me in countless ways. I especially thank colleagues in the Department of Latino and Hispanic Caribbean Studies: Ulla Berg, Yarimar Bonilla, Carlos Decena, Zaire Dinzey-Flores, Tatiana Flores, Aldo Lauria-Santiago, Tania López-Marrero, Nelson Maldonado-Torres, Yolanda Martínez-San Miguel, Michelle Stephens, and Camilla Stevens. In the Department of History, I thank my fellow historians of Latin America, Kim Butler, Temma Kaplan, Camilla Townsend, Gail Triner, and Mark Wasserman, for welcoming me into their fold. Aldo Lauria-Santiago read the entire manuscript (twice) and provided encouragement, insightful critiques, endless sources, and friendly nudging as I moved it into its final stages. Paul Clemens kindly offered suggestions for improvement on the entire manuscript and has been a continuous source of support. I am also grateful for the support and advice of Mia Bay, Carolyn Brown, Kayo Denda, Ann Fabian, Carlos Fernández, Marisa Fuentes, Daniel Goldstein, Doug Greenberg, Peter Guarnaccia, Allan Punzalan Isaac, Jennifer Jones, Nancy Hewitt, Rick Lee, Rocio Magaña, Jim Masschaele, Robert Montemayor, Donna Murch, Anjali Nerlekar, Bob Ramos, Nancy Rao, Joanna Regulska, Laura Schneider, Tom Stephens, Andy Urban, and Virginia Yans. I have benefited immensely from involvement with the Collective for Asian American Studies Scholarship, Critical Caribbean Studies (especially through a working group led by Michelle Stephens in Spring 2012), the Center for Ethnicity and Race, and the Women of Color Scholars' Initiative, which provided a subvention grant.

I presented portions of this research at various conferences and workshops. A lecture and workshop series for Ford postdoctoral fellows titled "Cross-National Intimacies between the United States and Latin America" at Brown University in Spring 2009, organized by Rhacel Salazar Parreñas, helped me to revise individual chapters. I am also grateful to Greg Benton and Terence Gómez for initiating the March 2011 workshop "From Ethnic to National Identification among Chinese Migrants' Descendants: A Comparative Study," at the University of Malaya, which sharpened my thinking on the Cuban-born generation of Chinese.

Numerous colleagues, friends, and mentors dispersed among institutions have provided feedback on this work as well as advice on research, teaching, and navigating academia. I thank José Amador, Adrian Burgos, Kornel Chang, Edith Chen, Matt Childs, Sherman Cochran, Alejandro de la Fuente, Anne Eller, Sujatha Fernandes, Carolina Gonzalez, Frank Guridy, Jesse Hoffnung-Garskof, Aisha Khan, Franklin Knight, Madeleine López, Adrian López-Denis, April Mayes, Gillian McGillivray, Tom McGrath, Marc McLeod, Yoon Jung Park, Rebekah Pite, Tom Pohrt, Ana Y. Ramos-Zayas, Gerardo Rénique, Robyn Rodríguez, Mario Ruiz, David Sartorius, Bill Seraile, Ned Sublette, Bill Van Norman, Chad Williams, and Michael Zeuske. Much of the writing of this book took place in New York City, full of stimulation, but lacking in tranquility. Fellow visiting researchers from the Center for the Study of Ethnicity and Race at Columbia University have become lifelong friends. I will always treasure my conversations at the Hungarian, and now, via e-mail, with Matt Briones, Suzie Pak, Alia Pan, and Amy Cabrera Rasmussen, and I thank Gary Okihiro for his continued support of the kind of work we do. I am also grateful to Jack Tchen and the Asian/Pacific/American Institute at New York University for their interest in this project and institutional affiliation.

This book was made possible by major fellowship support from the USIA-IIE Fulbright Program for research in the People's Republic of China and from the Ford Foundation. I am grateful for funding from the Department of History, the Rackham Graduate School, and the Center for Chinese Studies at the University of Michigan; the City University of New York's PSC-CUNY Research Award and Lehman College's George N. Shuster Fellowship and Scholar Incentive Award; and Rutgers University's Office of the Vice President for Research and Economic Development.

Evan Taparata and John Ting, both Rutgers alumni, provided dependable research assistance. As the manuscript began to look more like a book, Dean Grodzins provided key suggestions for polishing the prose.

I am fortunate to publish my first book with the University of North Carolina Press. Elaine Maisner offered important editorial advice as well as unending enthusiasm and patience throughout the process. Dino Battista, Caitlin Bell-Butterfield, Paul Betz, Kim Bryant, and the rest of the staff make a wonderful team, and manuscript editor John K. Wilson's attention to detail is much appreciated. I also thank Lou Pérez for his generosity throughout the years with all of us who work in Cuban history and his astute questions and suggestions for this book.

My family and friends have supported me and my work in countless ways. The Lópezes, the Baileys, and the Bettingers have always encouraged me, and I owe a special thanks to Eileen McSweeney for her help and humor, and to Belinda Ortalan for her warmth and reliability. A circle of friends from childhood to college, among them Barbara Bratter, Kahti Daly, Amie Hughes, Jaime Lynch, and Renu Mago, have been my cheerleaders. The staff and regulars of Las Américas in West Harlem offered a daily dose of café con leche and good wishes. Tiki, Sampson, and Brick provided quiet comfort and shared my nocturnal habits. I thank my life partner, Jim Bailey, and my son Bobby, for their love and laughter.

This book is dedicated to the memories of Pastor Pelayo and Francisco Luis and to their families in Cuba and China today.

Index

NOTE: "Chinese diaspora" refers to the general flow of Chinese from China; "Chinese migrants" refers to particular groups. The entries for Chinese in general actually refer to Chinese in Cuba: e.g., Chinese free laborers; Chinese immigrants, twentieth century; Chinese merchants; Chinese indentured laborers; and Chinese labor contractors, except when specified within the category. "Chinese Cubans" in this index refers to Chinese in Cuba today.

immigrants, twentieth century; Chinese indentured laborers; Immigrant workers in Caribbean and Latin America

Aside, Nicolás, 109

Asociación Cienfueguera de Agricultores Chinos, 178

Asociación de Lavanderos Chinos, 179

Assimilation, 8, 98, 124, 152, 248

Association of Chinese Restaurants and Inns of Cuba, 209

Ateneo, 204–5

Atkins, Edwin F., 36, 54, 58, 60, 61, 64, 65, 68, 69, 70, 71, 73, 75

Atkins, Grace, 69

"August Revolution," 141

Australia, 77, 173

Bahía Honda, 141

Banderas, Quintín, 141

Bank of China, 209, 223, 227

Baohuanghui, 181

Baptisms, 1, 38, 88–89, 91, 92, 93, 96, 97

Barnet, Miguel, 213

Barracoons, 27, 29–30, 46

Barrio Chino (Chinatown), 11, 157, 235, 245, 285 (n. 2); Chinese actors and musicians and, 181, 214; Chinese associations and, 178, 179, 223; Chinese businesses and, 83, 99, 166, 167, 209, 223, 224; Chinese newspapers and, 198; Cuban Revolution and, 225, 226, 227, 229; establishment of, 83; sanitation/hygiene and, 194; today, 237, 238, 239, 241, 243–44, 250; violence in, 193, 194

Batista, Fulgencio, 199, 200, 224, 226, 230

Battle of Las Guásimas, 119

Battle of Nuevas de Jobosí, 121

Beal, P. M., 60, 68, 129

Benton, Gregor, 196

Bergad, Laird, 55

Bernal, Ciprian, 93–94, 273 (n. 50)

Bertillonage, 151, 284 (n. 22)

Betancourt, José Ramón, 214

Black Cubans. See Afro-Cubans

Bohemia, 226, 292 (n. 50)

Boletín de Colonización, 62

Bone repatriation, 3, 111, 180–81, 230, 297 (n. 30)

Bosch, Joaquín, 130

Brazil, 5, 6–7, 16, 21, 148

British Guiana, 16, 80, 270 (n. 107)

Bruzón, José, 133

Bu, Antonio, 104, 276 (n. 90)

Buck, Pearl, 207

Bu Fan Son. See Bu, Antonio

Bureau of Repression of Communist Activities, 224

Burial of Chinese in Cuba, 111–12, 180–81, 230, 282 (nn. 71, 80), 287 (n. 56), 287–88 (n. 58), 294 (n. 14). See also Bone repatriation

Bu Tak, José, 117, 121, 122, 133, 135–36, 140, 142, 226, 278 (n. 1), 282 (nn. 71–72)

Bú y Suárez, Josefa, 135, 282 (n. 71)

California: anti-Chinese repression and, 10, 56, 146; Chinese actors, musicians and acrobats from, 107, 181; Chinese labor contractors and, 66, 267 (n. 22); Chinese laborers in, 11, 68, 71, 152, 269 (n. 90); Chinese merchants to Cuba from, 4, 10, 83–84, 102–4, 105–6, 109, 114, 165, 266 (n. 5); Chinese migrants of, 12, 56, 111; Sanyi vs. Siyi Chinese from Pearl River Delta and, 168–69, 286 (n. 10); truck gardening by Chinese laborers and, 77, 269 (n. 90). See also United States

"Californians," 102–4, 105–6, 109, 114, 165, 266 (n. 5)

Camagüey Province, 28, 29, 102, 119, 120, 121, 172, 194, 231, 232

Caminos de Hierro de la Habana, 33

Campo, Facundo, 108

Campos, Saturino, 86

Campos García, Alejandro, 243

Canary Islanders, 20, 55, 61, 75, 76, 147, 149

Canton (Guangzhou), 25, 47, 62, 168, 186, 187, 198

Canton Christian College, 187, 188, 288–89 (n. 80)

Capestany Abreu, Manuel, 199, 291 (n. 31)

Caridad Pérez y Espinosa, María de la, 94, 95

Carnival, 214

Carpentier y Valmont, Alejo, 213, 214, 293 (n. 94)

Carr, Barry, 191

Carrillo, Francisco, 121, 122, 130

Carrillo, Luis, 207–8

Cartaya Chung, Carlos, 131

Caruso, Enrico, 245

Casino Asiático de Cruces, 100

Casino Asiático de Placetas, 106

Casino Asiático Nuestra Señora de la Caridad del Cobre, 106

Casino Chung Wah, 111, 177, 180, 183, 198, 202, 205; in 1950s and 60s, 223, 227, 228; 1980s to present, 229, 239, 294 (n. 14), 297 (n. 9)

Casinos asiáticos. See Chinese associations

Castillo, Adolfo, 128

Castillo, Mario, 179

Castro, Fidel, 224, 225, 226, 228, 238, 244, 294 (n. 4)

Castro, Raúl, 225, 244

Catholicism, 38, 97, 105; burial of Chinese and, 111, 112, 180; Chinese associations and, 106, 108; education for Chinese and, 187. See also Baptisms

Cédulas, 38, 40, 62, 85–86, 91, 121, 263 (n. 93)

Centrales, 55

Céspedes, Carlos Manuel de, 119, 191, 206

Chan, Sucheng, 66, 68, 71, 77

Chan Bom Bia, 102, 275 (n. 81)

Chancón, Nicolás, 185

Chang, Leon, 224

Chang Nan Ko (José Asan), 101, 130–31

Chao Chiu, Alfonso, 229, 295 (n. 37)

Chao Sen, Juan, 137, 282 (n. 80)

Chee Kung Tong, 3, 179–80, 182, 186, 193–94, 198, 202, 214, 237, 239

Chen Chi Weng Kueng, 108

Chen Kwong Min, 185

Chen Lanbin, 48, 251

Chen Mingyuan, 39–40

Chiang Kai-shek, 196, 197, 198, 199, 206, 221, 222

Chi Casio, Federico, 230

China

—geography: Amoy (Xiamen), 22, 25, 46; Canton (Guangzhou), 25, 47, 62, 168, 186, 187, 188, 198, 288–89 (n. 80); emigration, from southeastern provinces, 24–25; Fujian Province, 4, 22, 24–25, 26, 46, 170; Jiujiang, 169, 172, 199, 224; qiaoxiang (overseas Chinese home area), 9–10, 170, 172–74, 175, 176; transnational migration and, 166, 168–71, 173, 177, 219; women left behind in, 9, 170, 173–77; Zhongshan, 137, 168, 169, 228, 286 (n. 10). See also Chinese diaspora; Chinese immigrants, twentieth century; Chinese indentured laborers; Chinese merchants; Chinese migrants; Four counties; Guangdong Province; Pearl River Delta region; Taishan; Three counties

—history: Chinese Communist Revolution, 217, 221–23; Chinese Revolution, 183, 190–91, 207, 222; coolie trade from, 1, 4, 21–27, 46–47; Cuban Revolution and, 237; Cultural Revolution, 237; current reach into the Americas, 238, 296–97 (n. 5); current relations with Cuba, 237–38, 297 (n. 8); dissolution of republic in 1916, 183–84; Japanese occupation of, 177, 181, 189, 199, 206–8, 219, 221, 289 (n. 1), 294 (n. 103); leftist movement in, from 1924, 196, 290 (n. 21); Nationality Law (1909), 182; Sino-French War, 113, 278 (n. 135); Sun Yat-sen movement, 95, 103–4, 130, 181–82; Taiping Rebellion, 120. *See also* People's Republic of China; Qing dynasty

Chinatowns, 99, 125, 153, 207, 209, 237, 244, 285 (n. 2)

Chinese associations, 104, 105–6, 110, 111, 135, 276 (n. 96); in Cienfuegos, 1, 107, 108, 110, 178–79, 180, 204–5, 229; Cuban Revolution and, 223–24, 228–30, 231; festivals and holidays and, 108, 109, 177–78; mixed descendants in, 229; today, 237, 238, 239; in twentieth century, 177–81, 188, 189

Chinese Chamber of Commerce, 111, 154, 169, 186, 223, 224, 228; campaigns against Chinese exclusion, 202, 204

Chinese Communist Party, 196

Chinese Communist Revolution (1949), 217, 221–23

Chinese Consolidated Benevolent Association (CCBA), 111

Chinese-Cuban cuisine, 209, 216, 234

Chinese-Cuban National Association, 209

Chinese Cuban opera, 214–15, 293 (n. 95)

Chinese Cubans: identifying with Chinese ethnicity, 241–42, 297 (n. 18); movement to promote cultural identity of, 240–44, 248; racial category and, 243; in United States, 231–35
—local-born: anti-Batista struggles and, 224–25; Chinese associations and, 188, 228–29; Chinese Cuban identity of, 216–18; Cuban culture and, 214–15; Cuban Revolution and, 226–27, 248; defending Chinese community during nativist movement, 203–4, 292 (n. 50); education and, 112–13, 186–88; in independence movement,

132, 140; mixed descendants, 87, 188, 208–9, 211, 217, 218, 227, 229, 238–39, 293–94 (n. 99); post–World War II discrimination, 210–13, 219; professionals, 209; religion and, 187; today, 238–39, 248; transmission of Chinese culture and, 217–18, 293–94 (n. 99); transnational youth of, 216–17, 293 (n. 98)

Chinese diaspora: in the Americas, 4, 221, 246–47; Cantonese opera and, 181; in Caribbean, 45, 80, 270 (n. 107); Chinese newspapers and, 113, 278 (n. 134); after Chinese Revolution, 222; Chinese-Western academies and, 112; Communism and, 196, 290 (n. 19); patterns of migration, 81; returning to China, 200, 249–51, 291 (n. 34); scholarship on, 8, 82, 298 (n. 36); secondary migrations and, 233–35, 296 (n. 52); truck gardening and vegetable growing and, 77, 78

Chinese doctors, 101–2, 123, 275 (n. 81)

Chinese Exclusion Acts (1882), 86, 125, 144, 146, 149, 152, 161; repeal of, 208, 215

Chinese freedom fighters (*mambises*), 114, 154, 226, 248, 278 (n. 1); Chinese indentured laborers becoming, 44, 117, 119–20; Cuban regard for, 117, 118, 125–27, 128, 133, 134–36, 142, 190, 191, 203, 246, 280 (n. 33), 289 (n. 1); documentation of, 131–33; extent of, 1870s, 119, 127–28, 129, 279 (n. 5); in noncombatant roles, 101, 118, 122–23, 129, 130–31, 279 (nn. 20, 22); post-independence lives, 134, 138–39; reasons for becoming, 119–20, 126; second-generation Cuban-born Chinese as, 132, 140; securing social position in Cuba, 118, 127, 134–36, 137; stereotyping of, 125–27; Ten Years' War (1868–78), 44, 117, 119–20, 121, 122–23, 126, 129; as veterans, 132, 133, 134, 137, 207, 280 (n. 45); voting rights for all men after independence and, 140–41; War for Independence (1895) and, 128–31, 132–33, 280 (n. 41), 281 (nn. 60–61, 68); wars for independence (1868–98), 4–5, 82, 101, 127, 154, 190, 203, 289 (n. 1)

Chinese free laborers, 5, 6, 7; businesses and, 83, 84, 86–87, 99–100, 114; cédulas and, 62, 85–86, 91; charcoal workers and, 123, 124; Chinese associations and, 82, 83; Chinese labor contractors and, 1, 62, 63–64, 66–71, 78, 80; cuadrillas and, 1, 56, 62–64, 66, 68, 69, 79–80, 114, 129; to Cuba from United States, 56, 266 (n. 5); as day laborers, 62, 80, 84, 146; food provided for, 66–68, 71; housing for, 68; leisure time and, 68–69, 80; marriage and, 90, 92–94, 95–96, 114; notaries and, 84–85; Panama Canal and, 60; peddling and, 2, 77, 78; racial issues and, 73–76; refusing to work in some conditions, 69–70, 75; religion and, 96, 97, 104; skilled labor and, 62, 76; as strikebreakers, 191, 192–93, 195; sugar production industry and, 56, 58–76; vs. transnational Chinese merchants, 103, 104, 114; truck gardening and, 77–78, 81, 269 (n. 90); types of work done, post-indenture, 56–58, 78–79, 267 (n. 8), 270 (n. 108); universal male suffrage and, 97–98; wages in Cuba, 71, 72–73, 79; wages in United States, 71, 268–69 (n. 69), 269 (n. 70); white concerns about free settlers, 89; women workers, 57, 91; work on sugar plantations, 89, 114. *See also* Chinese labor contractors; Chinese merchants

Chinese General Cemeteries, 112, 135

Chinese immigrants, twentieth century: actors and musicians, 181; anti-Batista struggles and, 224, 230, 294 (n. 12); bone repatriation to China and, 3, 111, 180–81, 230, 297 (n. 30);

burial in Cuba, 111–12, 180–81, 230, 282 (nn. 71, 80), 287–88 (n. 58), 294 (n. 14); businesses and, 166, 167, 178–79, 200; Chinese nationalism and, 113, 181–85, 219–20; to Cuba, post-independence, 142–43, 146, 154, 170–72, 191–92, 283 (n. 7); to Cuba, World War I and after, 1–2, 4, 155–56, 158–60, 161, 165–66, 185; Cuban citizenship and, 191, 201, 224, 229, 248; Cuban culture affected by, 213–16; in Cuban labor and political movements, 195–200; from Cuba to United States, 231–34; Cuba used to circumvent U.S. exclusion of, 4, 144, 150, 156, 165; deportation and, 158, 199, 203, 224; exclusion by law from Cuba, 10, 76, 143, 146, 148, 149–55, 158–59, 160, 161, 269 (n. 85); fictionalized accounts of history of, 245, 298 (n. 33); Japanese occupation of China and, 177, 181, 189, 199, 206–8, 219, 294 (n. 103); laundries, 179, 194–95, 200, 205, 223; letter-writing, 171–72, 174; maintaining ties to China, 165, 166, 168, 169, 171, 172–73, 180–81, 218, 219; medical help for, 178, 287 (n. 42); Nationalization of Labor decree and, 201–2, 220; nationalization of private commerce and, 227–28; 1940s to 2000s, 208–9, 221–22, 223, 230; religion and, 3, 180; restaurants and, 102, 114, 131, 181, 200, 202, 209, 214, 224, 225; returning to China, 2, 169–70, 199, 200, 201, 220, 244; sanitation/hygiene, as reason to bar, 153, 154, 158, 193, 194–95; smuggled to United States from Cuba, 144, 149, 150, 156–57, 158, 285 (n. 38); Spanish immigrants and, 202–3; summary of, in Cuba, 246–49; Sun Yat-sen movement and, 182, 183, 184–85, 188, 196, 206, 288 (n. 70), 290 (n. 20); transnational organizations and associations, 177–81; transpacific families, 3,

173–77; in United States, 145–46, 152, 171–72; vegetable growing, 178–79; voting rights and, 78, 96, 97, 138, 140–41; women Chinese migrants, after World War II, 208–9, 229, 230. *See also* Anti-Chinese repression; Chinese merchants

Chinese indentured laborers: alongside African slaves, 28, 29, 30, 31–32, 37, 42, 113; baptisms and, 1, 88–89; becoming freedom fighters, 44, 117, 119–20; cédulas and, 38, 40, 85–86, 121, 263 (n. 93); commission examining, 6, 39, 42, 47–50, 89–90, 91, 119, 153, 265 (nn. 143, 147), 272 (n. 44); contract regulations and, 6, 15, 28, 36–39, 50–51, 52, 263 (n. 93); in Cuba and Peru, 4, 17, 28, 31–32, 39, 41, 262 (n. 64), 264 (nn. 114, 122–23), 266 (n. 167); escaping contracts, 62; forced recruitment to independence movement, 120; forming families, 90–95, 249; freedom from contracts and, 44–45, 52–53, 54; housing for, 29–30, 35; jail and, 42–43, 92; marriage and, 6, 37, 88, 91–92, 272 (n. 44); mines and other work, 28, 33–35, 36, 41–42, 45; mortality rate, 28–29, 262 (n. 53); naming of, 1, 28, 63, 96–97; numbers of, to Cuba, 22–24, 261 (n. 27); opium use and, 41–42, 264 (n. 114); poor treatment of, 28, 30–31, 32, 34–35, 36–37, 39, 40, 41, 48, 50; Qing dynasty position on Chinese subjects abroad and, 8–9, 45–46, 48, 49–50; rebellions of, 6, 31–32, 39, 42–44, 264 (n. 122); recontracting, 1, 36, 37–39, 40, 44, 51, 52, 105, 120, 266 (n. 167); referring to, in restricting Chinese immigrants, 148, 152–53; religion and, 38, 88; returning to China and, 1, 39, 40, 45; runaways, 43–44, 51, 62, 118; scholarship on, 5, 82; ships carrying, 15–16, 22, 23, 24, 27–28, 261 (n. 25); slavery compared

to, 22, 37, 41, 50–53, 88, 248–49, 266 (n. 164); sugar plantations and, 1, 6, 22, 42–44; sugar production industry and, 28, 29–33, 39–40, 50; suicide and, 39–41, 89, 263 (n. 101); in United States, 81, 270 (n. 109); women, 27, 90–91, 259 (n. 17), 261 (nn. 44, 46). *See also* Chinese free laborers; Coolie trade

Chinese labor contractors: in California, 66, 267 (n. 22); Chinese free laborers and, 1, 62, 63–64, 66–71, 78, 80; food provided for laborers and, 66–68; social mobility and, 78–79, 95–96, 270 (nn. 99–100); sugar production industry and, 65, 69–70; War for Independence (1895) and, 129. *See also* Machado, Damián

Chinese lottery, 109, 216, 277 (n. 116)

Chinese merchants: anti-Chinese violence against, 193–94; beginning as indentured, 86–87; burial and, 111–12; businesses and, 99–100, 101–2, 169, 223–24, 274 (nn. 69, 71), 274–75 (n. 73); from California to Cuba, 4, 10, 83–84, 102–4, 105–6, 109, 114, 165, 266 (n. 5); campaigns against exclusion, 146, 149–50, 154–55, 161, 202–3; Chinese associations and, 104, 111; Chinese free laborers and, 103, 104, 114; Chinese nationalism and, 219–20; of Cienfuegos, 204–5; in Cuba and Peru, 112; Cuban Revolution and, 219, 221, 225–26, 233; education and, 112–13, 131, 186–88, 278 (n. 131), 288 (n. 77); exiles to United States, 227, 228, 231–32; after independence, 137–39; maintaining ties to China, 110–13, 131, 186–88; marriage and, 93, 94–95, 131; newspapers of, 102, 182, 185–86, 205–6, 292 (n. 59); political movements and, 199; post–World War II discrimination, 210–11; pursuing "whiteness," 211–12; Qing dynasty fall and, 183; trafficking of

Chinese migrants to Cuba, 159, 160; transnational businesses and, 103, 104, 114, 149–51, 155, 161, 168–69, 191, 204–5; War for Independence (1895) and, 130–31

Chinese migrants: in the Americas, 168, 206, 207, 208; to California, 12, 56, 111; Cuban Revolution and, 216, 219, 221; first, to Caribbean, 15–16; gender imbalance toward men, 9, 16, 27, 175, 259 (n. 17); microhistorical approach to studying, 11–12; from Pearl River Delta region, 25–26, 166, 168, 169, 173, 187; Qing dynasty and, 8–9, 45–46, 47, 49–50, 110–11, 112, 114, 182; stereotyping of, 125–26, 196. *See also* Anti-Chinese repression; Chinese diaspora; Chinese immigrants, twentieth century; Chinese indentured laborers

Chinese newspapers, 197, 198, 278 (n. 134); bilingual, 205–6, 207, 292 (n. 59), 297 (n. 15); Chinese merchants and, 102, 182, 185–86, 205–6, 292 (n. 59); Chinese nationalism and, 113, 182, 288 (n. 70); Cuban Revolution and, 227; today, 239–40

Chinese New Year, 107, 112, 177–78

Chinese postindenture experiences: black and Asian cooperation and, 99–101, 113–14; burial and, 111–12; businesses and, 83–84, 99–100, 101–2, 114, 274 (nn. 69, 71), 274–75 (n. 73); Chinese associations and, 105–6, 108; Chinese patriotism and, 113; culture and community, 104–10; festivals and holidays, 107–8; gambling and, 109–10; interracial marriage of Chinese men and black women, 92–94, 98, 114, 272 (n. 46); naming legitimate parents, 97, 274 (n. 65); opera and theater, 106–7, 108–9, 276–77 (n. 103), 277 (nn. 104, 106); property ownership and, 98–99, 274 (n. 67); religion and, 97, 104–5, 106;

social legitimacy and, 96–98, 114, 274 (n. 65); sugar plantations and, 82–83; surnames and, 96–98; types of work done, 56–58, 78–79, 267 (n. 8), 270 (n. 108). *See also* Chinese free laborers

Chinese refugees, 221–22, 231

Chinese restaurants, 102, 114, 131, 181, 200, 202, 209; Chinese-Cuban exile restaurants, 234, 239; El Pacífico restaurant, 214, 224, 225

Chinese Revolution (1911), 183, 190–91, 207, 222

Chinese Six Companies (San Francisco), 111

Chinese transnational businesses, 102–4, 114, 149–51, 155, 161, 168–69, 191, 204–5

Chinese women migrants, 9, 57; as coolies, 27, 90–91, 259 (n. 17), 261 (nn. 44, 46); twentieth century, 208–9, 229, 230

Chiong, Alfonso, 231–32

Chiong, Andrés, 123

Chiu Lión, Andrés, 193

Choy Rodríguez, Armando, 211, 225, 294 (n. 14)

Chuffat, Agustín, 107, 108, 276–77 (n. 103)

Chuffat Latour, Antonio, 90, 114, 131, 248, 277 (n. 116); as Chinese labor contractor, 62; in Cienfuegos, 137–38, 140–41, 142; after Cuban independence, 137–38, 282 (n. 82); early life, 103, 113; in Havana, 108, 109, 135, 169, 276–77 (n. 103); history of Chinese in Cuba written by, 82, 123–24, 195, 204, 270 (n. 2)

Chui Beltrán, Gustavo, 211, 225, 294 (n. 14)

Chung Leng. *See* Pérez, Luis

Chung Si, 105

Cienfuegos, 96, 250–51, 277 (n. 119); anti-Chinese sentiment and, 158, 194, 195; Chinese associations and, 1, 107,

Soviet Union and, 237, 296 (n. 2); establishment of republic, 1, 12, 71, 84, 97, 117, 133–36, 140, 144–45, 190–91; immigration of Chinese relaxed, World War I, 1–2, 4, 155–56; independence movement, 117–20, 122, 124–28, 132–34, 140, 181; nationalist cuisine, 123–24; Nationalization of Labor decree, 201–2; nationalization of private commerce, 227–28; nativist movement, 1930s, 191, 200–202; People's Republic of China and, 225–26, 227, 295 (n. 18); Spain and, 1, 4, 18, 104, 106, 114, 119–20, 121, 129, 133–34; Spanish reconcentration policy and, 129, 131; U.S. influence on, for anti-Chinese immigration, 10, 76, 143, 145, 146, 153, 154, 158–59, 161, 269 (n. 85); U.S. intervention, 133, 139–40, 141, 143, 145, 158, 219; voting rights for all men, 1, 78, 96, 97, 138, 140–41; "whitening" immigration, 19–20, 145, 147–49; women Chinese migrants, 9, 27, 208–9, 229, 230, 259 (n. 17), 261 (nn. 44, 46); women's suffrage, 201; Yucatecans in, 21, 88, 148, 260 (nn. 19–20)

— geography: Abreus, 59, 84, 94, 98–99, 101, 107; Cruces, 59, 84, 100, 106, 107; El Cobre, 33–34, 35, 41–42, 45; Escambray Mountains, 122; Guantánamo, 29, 141, 182, 194; Isla de Pinos, 29, 227; Lajas, 59, 84, 101, 107, 186, 192, 218; maps, 29, 59; Oriente Province, 28, 29, 120, 132, 228; Regla, 27, 28, 32, 83–84, 96–97, 104–5, 111–12; Remedios, 110, 122, 131, 135, 172, 182, 281 (n. 68); Rodas, 59, 79, 84, 107, 110, 205. *See also* Camagüey Province; Cienfuegos; Havana; Matanzas Province; Sagua la Grande; Santa Clara Province; Santiago de Cuba

— immigration policies: from 1900s, 146–49, 154, 155, 156, 159–60, 161, 191–92, 283 (n. 9), 284 (n. 22); after

1926, 160, 201, 203; World War II and after, 208–9

— U.S. occupation of: 1899–1902, 110, 134, 136, 138–39, 140, 146, 269 (n. 85); 1906–1909, 141–42, 150, 151, 153–54

Cuba-China relations, 237–38, 297 (n. 8)

Cuba Contemporánea, 158

Cuban-American Sugar Company (Cubanacao), 191

Cuban Association of Wu Shu-Kung Fu, 239

Cuban-Chinese Friendship Association, 237

Cuban Communist Party, 198–99

Cuban Constitution (1940), 203, 208

Cuban exile communities, 231–34, 295 (n. 45); cuisine and, 234, 296 (n. 57); in Miami, 233–34, 296 (n. 55); in New York, 233, 234

Cubanidad, 210, 213, 243

Cuban literature, 213

Cuban music and dance, 213–14

Cuban newspapers, 113, 204

Cuban Overseas Chinese Association for Aiding the Resistance against Japan, 207

Cuban Revolution (1959), 4, 135–36; burial of Chinese and, 230; China and, 237; Chinese associations and, 223–24, 228–30, 231; Chinese Cuban identity after, 221, 226–27, 248; Chinese exiles to United States after, 231–34; Chinese immigrants and, 216, 219, 221; Chinese merchants and, 219, 221, 225–26, 233; de-emphasis on racial categories after, 243; scholarship on Chinese in Cuba after, 245, 298 (n. 34)

Cuon Chong Long, 204

Dana, Richard Henry, Jr., 15, 36, 40

Dawdy, Shannon, 124

Decree No. 570, 160

Decree No. 603, 154–55

De la Fuente, Alejandro, 212

Pa, Pedro, 107, 276–77 (n. 103)
Pact of Zanjón, 121
Panama Canal, 60
Pan Wu, 130, 281 (n. 50)
Panyu, 168
Partido Comunista de Cuba, 198
Partido Republicano Chee Kung Tong, 179, 287 (n. 50)
Pascual, Pedro, 69
Patronato system, 54, 58, 61, 79
Pearl River Delta region, 24–27, 166, 168, 169, 173, 187. *See also* Four counties; Three counties
Peddling, 2, 77, 78, 192
Pelayo, Blas, 1, 96, 132, 140, 273–74 (n. 58)
Pelayo, Pastor (Tung Kun Sen), 110; as coolie, 1, 4, 26, 250–51; as free laborer, 54, 79, 82; grave of, 111, 250–51, 278 (n. 128); life of, 1, 95–96, 108, 109, 114, 132; naming of, 88–89; voting rights and, 97–98, 140
Pelayo, Ramón, 1
Pelayo, Santiago, 96
Pelayo Díaz, Blas, 96, 250–51
Peng Zemin, 198
People's Republic of China (PRC), 221–22, 238; Cuba and, 225–26, 227, 295 (n. 18). *See also* China—history
Pérez, Luis, 83, 107, 276–77 (n. 103)
Pérez, Periquito, 130
Pérez de la Riva, Juan, 21, 37, 51, 102, 106
Pérez y César, Juan, 98
Permanent Treaty, 141
Perseverancia, Ramón de, 109
Peru, 177, 180, 246–47; coolie trade and, 4, 6, 49; indentured Chinese migrants in, 39, 41
Philippines, 21, 50, 127, 292 (n. 63)
Pin Chun Len, Ramon, 211
Planter's Banner, 67
Platt Amendment, 139–40, 141, 145, 153, 161, 200–201
Po, Luis, 159, 185
Pons, Alberto Jo, 230

Pons, Alfonso, 180–81
Popular Socialist Party, 224
Porter, Robert, 39, 69, 75
Portugal, 16, 22, 24, 47, 48
Prío Socarrás, Carlos, 223
Prohibition era, 144, 157, 285 (n. 38)
Prohibition of Coolie Trade Act, U.S. (1862), 10, 47
Protestant church in Cuba, 187
"Protest of Baraguá," 121–22
Puentes Grandes, 33
Puerto Príncipe, 20, 33, 94, 102
Puerto Rico, 17, 43

Qiaojuan (overseas Chinese dependents), 173–74
Qiaokan (Chinese magazines), 185
Qiaoxiang (overseas Chinese home area), 9–10, 11, 170, 172–74, 175, 176
Qing dynasty: Chinese immigrants advocating overthrow of, 179, 180; Chinese migrants abroad and, 8–9, 45–46, 47, 49–50, 110–11, 112, 114, 182; coolie trade and, 24, 26, 45–47, 48, 49–50; outlawing emigration, 25, 46, 50; overthrow of, 12, 104, 154, 181–85, 190–91; queues (Chinese men's long braids) and, 24, 27, 32, 128; Sino-French War, 113
Qing Ming festival, 178
Quesada y Arosteguí, Gonzalo de, 117, 126, 127, 142, 190, 203, 280 (n. 33)
Queues (Chinese men's long braids), 24, 27, 32, 128
Quinta Benéfica de Kow Kong, 178, 287 (n. 42)
Quong Sang, 111

Rabí, Jesús, 130
Race: Cuban independence movement and, 124, 125, 126, 132; immigration policies, 1900s on and, 147–49; after independence, 136
Racial classification: for Chinese, 85, 87, 88, 94; color terms, 86, 88, 271 (n. 12);

Envisioning Cuba

Kathleen López, *Chinese Cubans: A Transnational History* (2013).

Lillian Guerra, *Visions of Power in Cuba: Revolution, Redemption, and Resistance, 1959–1971* (2012).

Carrie Hamilton, *Sexual Revolutions in Cuba: Passion, Politics, and Memory* (2012).

Sherry Johnson, *Climate and Catastrophe in Cuba and the Atlantic World during the Age of Revolution* (2011).

Melina Pappademos, *Black Political Activism and the Cuban Republic* (2011).

Frank Andre Guridy, *Forging Diaspora: Afro-Cubans and African Americans in a World of Empire and Jim Crow* (2010).

Ann Marie Stock, *On Location in Cuba: Street Filmmaking during Times of Transition* (2009).

Alejandro de la Fuente, *Havana and the Atlantic in the Sixteenth Century* (2008).

Reinaldo Funes Monzote, *From Rainforest to Cane Field in Cuba: An Environmental History since 1492* (2008).

Matt D. Childs, *The 1812 Aponte Rebellion in Cuba and the Struggle against Atlantic Slavery* (2006).

Eduardo González, *Cuba and the Tempest: Literature and Cinema in the Time of Diaspora* (2006).

John Lawrence Tone, *War and Genocide in Cuba, 1895–1898* (2006).

Samuel Farber, *The Origins of the Cuban Revolution Reconsidered* (2006).

Lillian Guerra, *The Myth of José Martí: Conflicting Nationalisms in Early Twentieth-Century Cuba* (2005).

Rodrigo Lazo, *Writing to Cuba: Filibustering and Cuban Exiles in the United States* (2005).

Alejandra Bronfman, *Measures of Equality: Social Science, Citizenship, and Race in Cuba, 1902–1940* (2004).

Edna M. Rodríguez-Mangual, *Lydia Cabrera and the Construction of an Afro-Cuban Cultural Identity* (2004).

Gabino La Rosa Corzo, *Runaway Slave Settlements in Cuba: Resistance and Repression* (2003).

Piero Gleijeses, *Conflicting Missions: Havana, Washington, and Africa, 1959–1976* (2002).

Robert Whitney, *State and Revolution in Cuba: Mass Mobilization and Political Change, 1920–1940* (2001).

Alejandro de la Fuente, *A Nation for All: Race, Inequality, and Politics in Twentieth-Century Cuba* (2001).

CPSIA information can be obtained
at www.ICGtesting.com
Printed in the USA
BVHW032218260819
556900BV00002B/89/P

9 781469 607139